LANGUAGE, COGNITION
AND DEAFNESS

COMMUNICATION

A series of volumes edited by:
Dolf Zillmann and Jennings Bryant

LANGUAGE, COGNITION
AND DEAFNESS

MICHAEL RODDA
CARL GROVE
University of Alberta, Edmonton

 LAWRENCE ERLBAUM ASSOCIATES, PUBLISHERS
1987   Hillsdale, New Jersey   London

Lawrence Erlbaum Associates, Inc., Publishers
365 Broadway
Hillsdale, New Jersey 07642

Library of Congress Cataloging-in-Publication Data

Rodda, Michael.
  Language, cognition, and deafness.

  Bibliography: p.
  1. Deaf—Means of communication.   2. Children,
Deaf—Language.   3. Sign language.   I. Grove, Carl.
II. Time.
HV2471.R64   1987   305'.9'08162   86-32865
ISBN 0-89859-877-X

Printed in the United States of America
10   9   8   7   6   5   4   3   2   1

Credits

Graphic Materials

Quotations as indicated in the text

A.G. Bell Association, W.J. Watts, Deaf children and some emotional aspects of learning, *Volta Review*.

Allen and Unwin, S. Gregory, *The deaf child in the family*.

American Annals of the Deaf, M.T. Greenberg, Hearing families with deaf children: Stress and functioning as related to communication method, *American Annals of the Deaf*.

American Psychiatric Association, R.L. Sharoff, Enforced restriction on communication: Its implications for the emotional and intellectual development of the deaf child, *American Journal of Psychiatry*.

Century Hutchinson, Ltd., S. Toulmin & J. Goodfield, *The discovery of time*.

Chas. C. Thomas, J.A. Pahz & C.S. Pahz, *Total communication*.

Croom Helm, L. Lawson, The role of sign in the structure of the deaf community; M. Vogt-Svendsen, Effects of oral preschool compared to early manual communication education and communication in deaf children. In *Perspectives on British Sign Language and deafness*.

Eastman, Gilbert C., Washington, DC. *First International Symposium on Sign Language Research*, Swedish Association of the Deaf.

Evans, Lionel, Newcastle, England, *Psychological factors related to the lip-reading achievement of deaf children*.

Excepta Medicine, U. Bellugi & E.S. Klima, Language: Perspective from another modality, *Brain and Mind*.

Gallaudet College and Richard M. Meisegeier, N. Groce, Beyond institutions: The history of some American deaf; An example from Martha's Vineyard. *Deaf Community and the Deaf Population*.

Gallaudet College and Nancy E. Kensicki, G. Gustason, Does Signing Exact English work? *Teaching English to the deaf*.

Gallaudet College and D.S. Martin, H. Hamilton, Linguistic encoding in short-term memory, *International Symposium on Cognition, Education and Deafness*.

Gower Publishing Company, M. Blaxter, *The meaning of disability*.

Harris, George, *Broken ears, wounded hearts*.

Hodder & Stoughton, Ltd. and Murray Pollinger, L. Watson, *Lifetide*.

Journal of British Association of Teachers of the Deaf, G.P. Ivimey, *The perception of speech;* G.W. Nix, *How total is total communication? Teacher of the Deaf; Journal of British Association of Teachers of the Deaf*.

Lexington Books, J.E. Nash & A. Nash, *Deafness in Society*.

Linstock Press, P. Ladd & V. Edwards, British Sign Language and West Indian Creole. *Sign Language Studies*.

Linstock Press, C. Erting, Language policy and deaf ethnicity in the United States, *Sign Language Studies*.

Los Angeles Neurological Societies, J.E. Bogen, The other side of the brain, *Bulletin of the Los Angeles Neurological Societies*.

MIT Press, N. Chomsky & E. Walker, *Explorations in the biology of language*.

National Association of the Deaf, J.D. Schein, *A rose for tomorrow;* C. Baker & R. Battison, *Sign language in the deaf community: Essays in honor of William C. Stokoe*.

Pro-Ed, Austin, TX, R.B. Wilbur, *Sign language and sign systems*.

Rainbird, R. Leakey, *The making of mankind.*
Routledge and Kegan Paul, D.E. Pritchard, *Education and the handicapped.*
Royal National Institute for the Deaf, *Methods of communication used in the education of deaf children.*
Swets Publishing Service, A. van Uden, *Diagnostic testing of deaf children.*
Tavistock Publications, E.J. Miller & G.V. Gwynne, *A life apart.*

Contents

Preface

This book is intended as an introduction to the field of communication and deafness, with particular reference to cognition and the various forms of language used by hearing impaired people. It is aimed at an audience comprising teachers and student teachers of the deaf, speech pathologists and students of speech pathology, social workers and students of social work, psychologists and students of psychology and, to some extent, the parents of deaf children and deaf people themselves. It attempts to provide a concise summary of the topic and, indeed, as well as being for the audience just described, it will be useful to anyone with an interest in the psychological, sociological, and linguistic ramifications of hearing loss.

The book is broken down into eight chapters that can be read out of sequence without too much damage to their comprehensibility. Chapter 1 deals with the basic facts about deafness, and may be omitted by the reader with specialist knowledge. Chapter 2 deals with the cultural background and the history of education of the deaf. Chapter 3 summarizes the recent studies of American Sign Language, which have been instrumental in stimulating much of the current interest in manual communication systems, particularly the work of Ursula Bellugi and her associates. Most books covering this topic tend to assume that the reader has a working knowledge of psycholinguistics. We think this is a little unrealistic and, therefore, also have included in this chapter a brief but fairly comprehensive review of different approaches to the study of language. Chapter 4 deals with the cognitive basis of communication. It is probably more abstract than the other chapters and may be of less interest to the non-technical reader. Chapter 5 covers the role of communication in the development of the deaf child, including the controversial question of educational method. In chapter 6 we deal with some of the fascinating implications of sign language research for studies of the physiology and evolution of human communication systems in hearing as well as in deaf people. Finally, in chapters 7 and 8, we review some of the educational and psychological implications and current trends in sign language and deafness research.

At the end of each chapter, we make some suggestions for further reading. These are books that we have found to be particularly informative, entertaining, and readable.

The topic of the book is a growth area in both psychology and the study of deafness, and we cannot hope to provide a comprehensive survey of all its aspects. We do hope that the research described proves sufficiently interesting to the reader to encourage further exploration of the field. We apologize to those researchers whose work we had to neglect, but it was impossible to include everything, even though the citations total over 700. We hope that we communicate to the reader our own sense of excitement and enthusiasm for the topic. If we do not, then we have failed—deafness is a fascinating human condition, and deaf people are a delightful group of people to know and to work with. We count ourselves privileged to have had the opportunity to see in action the language, social systems, political activism, and many other attributes of deaf culture. We are humbled by the achievements of our deaf colleagues, friends, and students. If in some way we have communicated these achievements to the hearing world, we will be more than satisfied.

ACKNOWLEDGMENTS

In writing the book, we have been assisted by a large number of individuals, and we would like to give our thanks to them all. First, we should thank Lawrence Erlbaum, our publisher, and Jack Burton and Sondra Guideman, members of his staff. They provided the stimulus for us to do something we had often talked about but had never been motivated to finish. Our colleagues in the Department of Educational Psychology and the Faculty of Education at the University of Alberta provide a stimulating atmosphere and an appreciation of academic endeavors—without that reinforcement we might not have been motivated to complete our task. In particular, we should name Dr. R.S. Patterson, Dr. W.H. Worth, Dr. E. Miklos, Dr. Harvey Zingle, Dr. Ken Gough, Ms. Mary Ann Bibby, Mr. Roger Carver, and Mrs. Emma Collins. Their help made it possible for us to finish the book. Three libraries—the Royal National Institute for the Deaf in London, England, the University of Alberta Library system in Edmonton, and the Alberta School for the Deaf Library in Edmonton, also provided valuable assistance without which the book could not have been completed. Our thanks go to them and their patient and resourceful staff.

Many individual colleagues and students helped us over the months it took to complete the book, but one in particular, Ceinwen Cumming, has a unique specialist knowledge of language and deafness. She gave freely of this knowledge, and our thanks are due her as a colleague and friend, as they are to all the students and faculty in the deafness programs of the University of Alberta. John Denmark is one of the pioneers in the field of behavior and deafness, and it has been our privilege to work with him for most of our careers. Chapter 7 owes much to his influence—we frequently quote the major study we worked on together and which generated the data base we use in the factor analysis reported in that chapter. We are grateful to John for his unselfish willingness to share his ideas and experience, and for his advice over the years.

We would also like to thank our families for putting up with us, our files, our paper, and our ability to occupy every available unoccupied space in our homes, and then still to complain that we did not have enough room in which to work. Again, without their patient support, the book would not have been finished.

A special thank you goes to our administrative colleagues at the University of Alberta: President, Vice-Presidents and Deans; they have resisted the temptation to reduce administration to only recording student enrollments and class size, and still have an appreciation of the mission and purpose of the University. Many of their colleagues in other universities could do well to emulate them. If they did, they might be surprised to find that faculty and adminstrators can serve a common purpose.

We also wish to express our appreciation to the many publishers and authors who gave us permission to quote from their books, monographs, or journals. Shared knowledge is the essence of any academic endeavor—we thank not only those listed in the credits, but all who influenced our thinking and our ideas.

Finally, we have to thank Patti Hill, Heather Tulk, and Marlene Spencer, research assistants in the Department of Educational Psychology, University of Alberta, and Arlene Unger and Kathy Jensen, two staff members of the Publication Services Unit, Faculty of Education, University of Alberta. Their painstaking attention to detail saved us many hours of work, and their willingness to maintain an enthusiastic interest in our task kept us going when we were tempted to be discouraged. A special thank you is due to Naomi Stinson who produced the final manuscript. Without her help, it is possible that the book might have been lost to posterity.

Michael Rodda
Edmonton, Alberta, Canada

Carl Grove
Pinner, Middlesex, England

Dedicated to:
Jerome D. Schein
and
Wladyslaw Sluckin

Friends, advocates, teachers, and scholars

LANGUAGE, COGNITION
AND DEAFNESS

1

PSYCHOLOGY, AUDIOLOGY, AND DEAFNESS

In this chapter, we set the scene for subsequent discussion. We begin by describing the nature of hearing impairment and its complex (and often misused) terminology. Then we discuss what to most people is the major effect of deafness—the poor speech and lipreading skills of hearing-impaired people and their associated difficulties with spoken language. Finally, we introduce the concept of deafness as a social, rather than psycholinguistic, phenomenon.

The general term *hearing impairment* can be defined as loss of hearing that is severe enough to produce disorders of communication requiring remedial or educational treatment. The disability is, like most, a continuum, but it can be for practical purposes divided into two distinct groups—those children, adolescents, or adults who are *deaf* and those who are *hard of hearing*. In childhood, deaf children or students with impaired hearing require education by methods suitable for pupils with little or no naturally acquired speech or oral language. Hard of hearing children or students are those with impaired hearing whose development of speech and oral language follows the same pattern as their hearing peers, although not necessarily at the same rate. Such students require special educational provision, but not necessarily the same educational methods as are used for deaf students.

The classification of deafness into the categories of deaf and hard of hearing is useful in schools and elsewhere, but it does mask one important variable, the age of onset of deafness. Specifically, depending on whether deafness occurs congenitally, before or after the development of language, or on whether deafness occurs in childhood or in adult life, the effects on the individual vary both qualitatively

1

and quantitatively. Therefore, the terms *deafness* and *hard of hearing* should invariably be qualified by one of two adjectives—*prelingual* or *adventitious*—which specify the age of onset, or they should be replaced by the term *deafened* when adventitious hearing loss occurs in adult life.

Obviously the definitions just described represent rough classifications rather than definitive statements. One consequence of this has been a failure on occasion to identify and consider a separate group of children and adults who present unique problems—the prelingual profoundly deaf. As the name implies, these individuals have no residual hearing for practical purposes and their handicap precedes the development of speech and language because it occurs in approximately the first 2 years of life. Many such deaf adults and students are, in practice, congenitally deaf and have etiologies of genetic origin. In all cases, they have been subject to severe sensory, oral-aural language and emotional deprivation. They present unique problems, and although audiologically and linguistically speaking it may be proper to regard deaf, hard of hearing, and hearing individuals as forming a continuum, psychologically they do not. Indeed, considerable harm can result and has resulted from a failure to appreciate the special problems facing deaf children in infancy and in later stages of development. Throughout the remainder of this text we refer to and, indeed, are mainly concentrating on *deafness*, and we usually apply this term to that group of individuals who have severe or profound hearing losses predating the acquisition of spoken language. The term *hard of hearing* refers to those with lesser but significant degrees of handicap, and the term *hearing-impaired* refers usually to deaf and hard of hearing people collectively.

Unfortunately, the literature on deafness and on hard of hearing students and adults frequently fails to make the distinctions described in the previous paragraph. The terms also have sociological as well as audiological or psychological ramifications. Therefore, we are not always able to maintain the distinctions with complete clarity, particularly because in a number of major studies of hearing-impaired people, it is difficult to know exactly which group formed the focus of the research. What we do is try to avoid making statements about deaf people that more correctly refer to hard of hearing people, and vice versa; a common and unfortunate failing in the literature. It is this failure that allows us to believe in the fiction that deaf people are able to function psychologically, educationally, and socially in the same way as hearing people. They cannot, which does not mean that deaf people are in some ways inferior, but rather that they interact with their environment in a different way.

Prevalence of Hearing Impairment

The preeminent demographer of deafness is Jerome D. Schein of New York University. Written with Marcus Delk, his study of *The Deaf Population of the United States* (Schein & Delk, 1974) provides a wealth of data on the status of the American adult deaf population. For the younger age range, the population of students in schools, programs, and classes for the hearing-impaired in the United States is surveyed annually by the Center for Assessment and Demographic Studies at Gallaudet College, and the College publishes informative and interesting data on the characteristics of these students. However, the survey itself does not establish prevalence rates, because it surveys students who are already in programs for the hearing-impaired, rather than the population at large. In practice, an unknown number of hearing-impaired children are either misdiagnosed or never even identified; many others are diagnosed later in life than is either technically necessary or educationally desirable (e.g., Lyon & Lyon, 1981-82; Rodda & Carver, 1983).

At the time of writing, another major prevalence survey is being undertaken in the United Kingdom by the Medical Research Council's Institute of Hearing Research, but the final data have yet to be published. Preliminary reports by Davis (in Lutman & Haggard, 1983), and by Haggard, Gatehouse, and Davis (1981) indicate an overall prevalence rate of 4.5% for significant hearing impairment in the population of the United Kingdom (roughly a Better Ear Average Hearing Level, BEA of 45dB, see p. 7). This rate is somewhat lower than that found by Schein and Delk (1974), but the definition of significant hearing impairment is probably a little more conservative.

Table 1.1 is based on the data of Schein and Delk (Tables II.10 and II.11, pp. 28/29). It is surprising to the uninitiated because it shows hearing impairment to be a problem of some magnitude. Even prelingual profound deafness is not the small problem it is often assumed to be. In fact for *prevocational deafness*, the prevalence rate is about twice (2/1,000 population) the rate that we have characteristically used for planning purposes in the past (1/1,000). The difference explains why it was possible for Rodda (1970) to locate samples of deaf students in the United Kingdom that were more than 100% of the estimated total population, and also explains a number of other similar discrepancies in the demography of deafness. As Schein and Delk (1974) clearly established, hearing impairment is a major educational problem, and it probably explains far more academic retardation and developmental delay than we are aware of. In the United States alone there are an estimated 13.5

TABLE 1.1

Prevalence Rates for Deafness and Hearing Impairment in Civilian,
Noninstitutionalized Population of the USA in 1971

	Rate/100,000—All Ages	
	Deafness Age at Onset <19 years	Bilateral Impairment All Ages at Onset
Males	205	3938
Females	201	2583
Males and Females	203	3237

Source—J.D. Schein and M. Delk, 1974, *The Deaf Population of the United States*, tables II.10/II.11, published by the National Association of the Deaf.

million adults (6.6% of the population) who have some degree of hearing impairment, of whom about 400,000 became deaf before the age of 19 years and 200,000 before the age of 3 years.

The Cause, Measurement, and Remediation of Hearing Loss

It is not the purpose of the text to provide basic information on the ear, hearing, and audiology (the science of hearing assessment and aural remediation). Nevertheless, it is important to provide some information in order for the reader to understand what causes hearing loss and what the terms deafness and hearing impairment mean in a concrete sense.

An Audiogram

Figure 1.1a shows a schematic diagram of the ear and Fig. 1.1b a pure tone *audiogram*. The two axes of the audiogram record the degree of hearing loss in *decibels* (dB), and frequency of the pure-tone sound used in testing in *hertz* (Hz). The line marked zero is the theoretical level of hearing of average unimpaired young adults. In practice, the average young adult probably hears a little better because the zero line reflects a statistical average, and it includes some

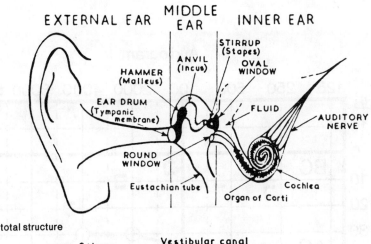

(a) The total structure

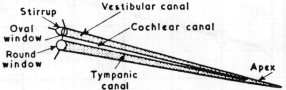

(b) An elongated version of the organ of Corti

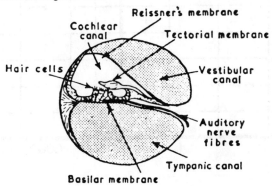

(c) A cross-section of the organ of Corti

FIG. 1.1a.   A schematic diagram of the ear.

Source—M. Rodda (1967), *Noise and Society*, Edinburgh: Oliver & Boyd.

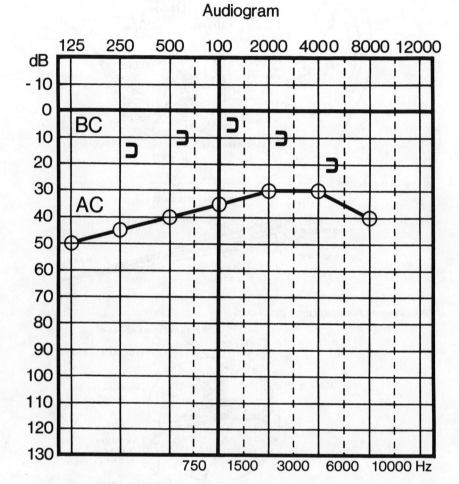

FIG. 1.1b.   Shows a pure-tone audiogram. AC is testing when sound is presented through the external ear. BC is testing when the sound is presented through a vibrator.

older and some mildly impaired ears. For this reason and because we are dealing with averages, hearing losses on the audiogram can range from -10dB to +110dB. Scores outside these ranges are not usually possible because they reflect the range of conventional audiometric equipment. However, the audiologist, particularly at the upper limit, will sometimes note a "No response" (NR)—meaning that the hearing may be worse than the maximum possible hearing loss shown on the audiogram.

The BEA loss refers to the average hearing loss in dB in the best ear for the most important frequencies for the reception of speech, generally regarded as 500, 1,000 and 2,000 Hz but sometimes including 4,000. However, hearing losses can and do vary with frequency. For example, sometimes losses are greater in the higher frequencies than in the lower ones, and the shape of the audiogram assists the audiologist in diagnosis and remediation, as do many other tests of speech, sound, and hearing reflexes.

In Fig. 1.1b, the curve marked 'AC' shows a right ear *air conduction* audiogram, in which the sound is presented through earphones in the normal way. Curve 'BC' shows the *bone conduction* audiogram for the same ear, and in this case the sound is presented through a tactile vibrator, usually placed behind the ear. In bone conduction the sound is conducted in three ways. Inertial lag results in movement of the stapes (see Fig. 1.1a) resulting in movement of the oval window, and the *organ of Corti*, the main receptor of hearing, is also stimulated directly. In addition, the vibration of the skull causes the air in the outer ear to vibrate, and some sound is conducted through the normal air conduction route. These three sources of sound are called *inertial*, *distortional*, and *osseotympanic* bone conduction respectively. Hearing losses affecting the mechanical parts of the ear are called *conductive*; those affecting the organ of Corti and auditory pathways are called *sensori-neural*. Air conduction measures both conductive and sensori-neural losses and does not distinguish them. Bone conduction separates conductive from sensori-neural losses, and so provides important diagnostic information.

Causes and Types of Hearing Loss

Sensori-neural hearing losses can be subdivided into those resulting from damage to the organ of Corti in the ear itself, and those (sometimes called *central losses*) occurring in the neurological processes that transmit the sound signals up to and including the cortical areas of the brain. The adjectival descriptions we apply to different degrees of hearing loss are:

	BEA Pure Tone Loss
Normal	−10 to 25dB
Mild	26 to 40dB
Moderate	41 to 55dB
Moderately Severe	56 to 70dB
Severe	71 to 90dB
Profound	>91dB

A motor mower approximates to a sound intensity of 90dB, and people with profound hearing losses will not be able to hear this sound or a normal telephone bell even when they are close to them. They might get a slight sense of vibration. Conductive losses are in- variably less than 60dB and, therefore, any loss above this level must include a sensori-neural component.

Deaf people usually have hearing losses in the severe or profound category, but because deafness implies membership of an ethnic group (pp. 42 to 43) some deaf people may have quite mild impair- ments and may on rare occasions even be hearing.[1] Hearing children of deaf parents are also sometimes bicultural—members of both the hearing and the deaf communities. Definitions are arbitrary, and we refer to these special situations only so the reader clearly understands that the audiological definition of deafness is only one way of look- ing at the problem.

The causes of deafness are many and they are constantly chang- ing. Figure 1.2, reproduced from Boothroyd (1982, p. 50), is a use- ful synopsis, and it also shows the type of hearing loss associated with each cause, the time it can affect hearing and whether the loss is always the same (stable), whether it becomes progressively worse (progressive) or whether it varies in severity (fluctuating). Impacted wax is probably the most frequent cause of a mild hearing loss, and it is easily and completely treatable. A number of other conductive losses often can be alleviated by medical treatment, and those that are not responsive to treatment can be helped considerably by a properly fitted hearing aid. Sensory and neural losses cannot be cured medically, and a cochlear implant is still only a crude aid to hearing (perhaps more correctly described as an aid to lipreading). Rubella epidemics still occur, although their effects are less severe because rubella vaccination has protected at least part of the population at risk, pregnant women. Unfortunately, there are still many females of

---

[1]In at least one interesting case, an aphasic individual with normal hearing has chosen to identify with the deaf community. His auditory processing difficulties mean that he lacks speech, and sign language opens up new avenues of communi- cation and social interaction. Because of schooling and other influences the indi- vidual has identified closely with deaf people all his life. Audiologically, this person is not deaf; sociologically he is clearly a member of the deaf ethnic group.

CAUSE		TYPE			TIME ACQUIRED			HEARING LOSS					STABILITY			ADDITIONAL IMPAIRMENTS
General Cause:	Specific Example:	Conductive	Sensory	Neural	Before birth	Around birth	After birth	Mild	Moderate	Severe	Profound	Total	Stable	Progressive	Fluctuating	
GENETIC	Dominant	○	●		●	●	●	●	●	●	●	●	●	○		
	Recessive	○	●		●	●	●	●	●	●	●	●	●	○		
DISEASE	Rubella	○	●	●	●			●	●	●	●		●			●
	Rh factor		●	●	●			●	●	●	●		●			●
	Meningitis		●	○			●			●	●	●	●	○	○	○
	Mumps		●				●			●	●	●	●			
	Otitis media	●					●	●	●						●	
DRUGS	Teratogens	●	●	●	●			●	●	●	●		●			●
	Ototoxins		●				●			●	●	●	●			
TRAUMA	In utero	●	●	●	●			●	●	●	●		●			●
	Prematurity		●	●		●		●	●	●	●		●			●
	At birth		●	●		●		●	●	●	●		●			●
	Anoxia		●	●		●	○	●	●	●	●		●			●
	Noise		●				●	●	●	●			●			
	Head blow	●	●				●	●	●	●	●	●	●			○
	Impacted wax	●					●	●	●						●	

● = Probable ○ = Possible

FIG. 1.2. Causes and characteristics of hearing impairment.
Reproduced from A. Boothroyd (1982), *Hearing impairments in young children*, p. 50. Copyright 1982, reprinted by permission of Prentice-Hall, Englewood Cliffs, NJ.

childbearing age who have not been vaccinated, and still others who do not realize that a periodic booster vaccination is necessary.

The pattern of hearing losses, their causes, and the ability to remediate losses through hearing aids and other prosthetic aids, and through educational treatment, have changed drastically in the last 50 years or so. Nevertheless, as the data of Schein and Delk (1974) show, hearing losses are still a major scourge, and we have not had in recent years, and are not likely to have in the near future, any major changes in the prevalence rates for prelingual profound deafness of genetic origin. It is to be hoped the day will arrive when the science of medicine will be such that children will not be born with or develop hearing impairments in any significant numbers, but at the present state of our knowledge this has to be regarded as a pious hope rather than a practical proposition. We no longer medically diagnose hearing impairment as resulting from "mother marked" (St. John Roosa, 1885), but the largest diagnostic category for hearing impairments is still "cause unknown."

The Hearing Aid

The hearing aid consists basically of a microphone, an amplifier and an output into a tube connecting with an ear mold that must be properly placed in the ear (see Fig. 1.3). Figure 1.4 shows how a hearing aid can modify the audiogram of a hard of hearing person. Hearing aids come in many different shapes and sizes—radio frequency transmission systems used in classrooms with hearing-impaired students are about the size of a pack of cigarettes and "in-the-ear" aids are small enough to be placed in the concha of the outer ear. Today, the most commonly used aids are "behind-the-ear" models, but the radio transmission models found in many classes for deaf children are important in these settings.

A hearing aid only amplifies sound, and it cannot restore hearing in the way spectacles help sight because it lacks three characteristics of the human ear. First, it does not have its sensitivity—it amplifies over only a very limited range of frequencies (see Fig. 1.4). Second, it lacks its directionality—it cannot locate and orient sounds in space. Third, it lacks its selectivity—it amplifies only selected sounds in a fixed pattern, whereas the human ear is able to respond selectively and differently to sound.

Hearing aids also can be adapted to assist in telephone communication. If a person does not use an aid, or if the aid is unsuitable for telephone communication, an amplified telephone headset can be provided as an alternative. Attachments also are available for assisting a hard of hearing person to "listen" to radio or television.

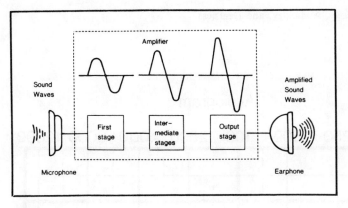

(a) Basic stages

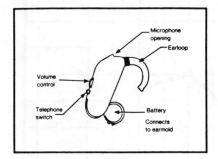

(b) Components of a behind-the-ear aid

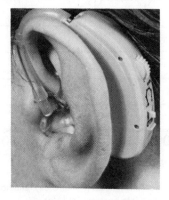

(c) Photograph of a hearing aid in place

FIG. 1.3. A schematic figure of a hearing aid.

Reproduced by courtesy of Thibodeau's Hearing Aid Centre and Thibodeau's Special Instruments, Edmonton, Alberta.

Based on the *Hearing Aid Handbook* by Wayne J. Staab, published by Tab Books, Blue Ridge Summit, PA. Reproduced with permission of the author.

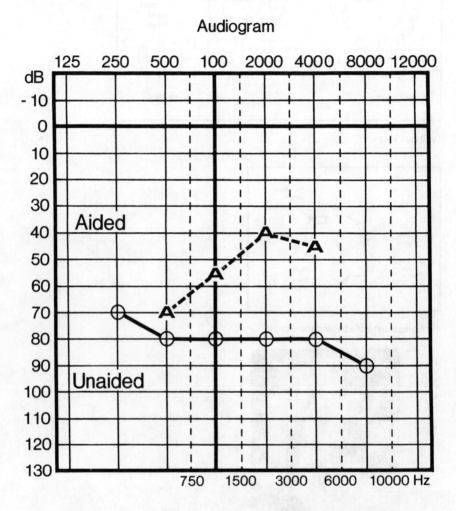

FIG. 1.4.   Shows the right ear, pure-tone audiogram when unaided (the circles), and how fitting a hearing aid improves hearing but does not return it to normal (the 'A's).

However, it should be emphasized that all of these aids only can help people with marginal hearing ability to make better use of their residual hearing. If residual hearing is inadequate, the aids will be of limited value.

Other Aids for Hearing-Impaired People

There are other aids available for hearing-impaired people that enable them to make use of other senses, particularly sight. If the hearing loss is too great to allow for the use of amplified sound, a deaf person may use a *Telephone Device for the Deaf* (TDD). A typed message is translated into a digital code and sent through the telephone to another TDD user. A receiver decodes the message and presents it in written form, usually as a visual display. The transmitter and receiver are the same unit, and provided they are not used to transmit simultaneously, one TDD user can interactively communicate with another. Closed captioned television sets are available to deaf people who have a converter that attaches to or is part of their TV set. A signal transmitted with the main TV signal is converted into a written paraphrasing of the spoken words. The captions are displayed at the bottom of the screen, but are not visible to people who are not using a caption decoder. Open captions, which do not need a decoder, are available occasionally on broadcast TV and more frequently on videotapes or films. They are visible to all. There also are some interesting experiments taking place on simultaneous captioning, that is, captioning live broadcasts as they take place—the primary delay in developing this system is a lack of suitable software to program the computers that are necessary to keep pace with the spoken word.

It is interesting that the development of aids for deaf people that depend on the use of reading are now making this activity a more meaningful experience for deaf students, and are assisting them to integrate by giving them the same experiences as their hearing peers. We may or may not approve of the time children, adolescents, and adults spend watching TV and talking on the telephone; nevertheless, we cannot deny their significance in modern life. Recent developments mean that for the first time deaf people are now able to watch TV and talk on the telephone. Time will tell if this is good or bad; however, we think it is likely these changes will increase the motivation of deaf students to learn to read and, therefore, their overall reading achievements. If so, then they can only be regarded as beneficial.

Other aids available for deaf people include visual warning devices such as door "bells" or baby alarms. Most of these work on the

PLATE 1.1.   Shows a TDD (Telephone Device for the Deaf).
Source—Instructional Technology Centre, University of Alberta.

PLATE 1.2.   Shows a captioned TV with a blow-up of the captions.
Source—Instructional Technology Centre, University of Alberta.

principle of picking up a sound and then using it to switch on (or on and off, repetitively) a visual display, usually an ordinary household lamp. In fact, there is no reason why any auditory warning cannot be displayed visually. Sometimes, as in alarm clocks or fire alarms, it is very important that we modify the hearing environment for deaf people. In other cases, such as when using a car horn, it is either not very practical or not very useful to do so. Deaf people cope very well as drivers and pedestrians (despite some myths to the contrary), and visual modifications are not necessary. In still other situations, for example, public address announcements at airports, modifications would be desirable, but we have failed to appreciate their importance for both hearing-impaired and hearing people. Finally, it is worth mentioning that "hearing ear" dogs can be a help for some deaf people. Apart from the cost of training, the biggest problem is that in mixed hearing and deaf households it is hard for the dogs to maintain their skills. Hearing people, for example, answer the doorbell when the dog is trained to do so. If this happens often enough, the dog forgets.

Speech Development

An important prerequisite to the development of speech is the development of internalized language. Failure to develop these structures reduces speech to a mechanical skill, having no significance for the child as a means of communication. Hence, speech training that is not coupled with an analysis of the child's language skills results merely in parrot-like repetition of sounds. Unfortunately, in many cases this type of speech is exactly what is produced by deaf children. They are taught speech mechanically rather than to develop it as a communicative and interactive process based on language. Therefore, it is hardly surprising that they then frequently reject not only speech, but hearing aids as well. If they are also in an educational program that does not use sign language, they are eventually deprived of all language input. Too often, under these conditions, teachers and other professionals adopt the attitude that the child *must* learn speech because it is good for him or her. In extreme cases, the question, "Can the child learn speech?" is never asked; nor is the question, "What can we do to make speech an enjoyable and motivating experience?"

The beginnings of speech lie in the natural gestures of the body, and all verbal communication retains at least some vestiges of this form of symbolization. Even when reading the written word, we will tend to reinforce the meaning of the sentences by the visual memory of reinforcing signs, particularly those used during the first year of life when the primary means of communication is through these gestures and through emotive sounds such as crying. Ultimately, such gestures develop into a skill that enables the child to communicate very specific meanings, such as in pointing to an object or differentiating between a request and an order only on the basis of body stance and position. Interestingly, in the deaf child the gesture of pointing develops into a highly sophisticated communication system that is part of the syntax of sign language (see pp. 148 and 260), whereas a hearing child develops speech sounds to fulfill a similar role, and so retains pointing only as a relatively unrefined part of the communication system.

At approximately 1 year of age, hearing children say their first distinguishable, although hardly intelligible, word. It does not appear with startling suddenness. Reception precedes expression, and children have been exposed to a considerable amount of verbal language through hearing during their first year of life. It is the assimilation, coding, and classifying of this input that enables them to relate a word to an object and, in later life, an object to an idea. Like walking, once the first step is taken progress is extremely rapid—by 15 months, hearing children have an average vocabulary of about 20 words, by 24 months, about 270 words, by 36 months, about 1,225 words, and by 6 years, about 2,600 words. Even more critical is the development of knowledge of the rules of language, and by 5 years, average hearing children have the ability to use all the basic grammatical rules of their spoken language. Such achievements and the rapidity of the growth of speech and language during these early years of life are impressive. But mislearning may occur, and the origins of certain speech problems are sometimes found in responses that were learned inappropriately. For example, it has been suggested that, in some cases, stuttering results from early attempts by children to match the rhythm, and fluency of adult speech with an inadequate vocabulary. Furthermore, knowledge of language and the use of language should not be confused, and the level of language and speech should not be confused with the emotional and cognitive development of the child. For example, many educable mentally retarded children, in later life, have seemingly fluent speech. As a result, unrealistic informal evaluations are made of their cognitive and emotional development, and these, in turn, generate unrealistic expectations.

A good example of the interaction between language and emotional and cognitive development is found in the concept of self as embodied in speech. It is not usually until about the age of 4 years that the pronoun "I" becomes a significant part of the child's vocabulary. Prior to this age, most children fail to differentiate themselves as a person from their environment. The two are the same, and so they will use expressions like "Me go bye-bye" or will use their name to refer to themselves. Only when a sense of self as distinctly different from the world at large is developed will the "I" pronoun come into significant use and, indeed, it alters its form as children go through a period of evaluating their self-identity and their place in the environment. It is for this reason that much of children's communication is aimed at locating and identifying self and exploring emotions and feelings, rather than in merely transmitting and receiving information. During this period, the question, "Where did I come from?" is an attempt by the child to establish his or her self-identity, and the question is much better interpreted as saying, "Who, what, why, and how am I distinctly different from my environment?" Unfortunately, deaf children often cannot ask these questions or, if they can, nobody is available who can communicate answers in a language they can understand. Not surprisingly, self-identity and self-esteem, that is, respect for oneself as a person, suffer (see chapter 2).

Classification of Communication Disorders

Classic texts (for example, Skinner & Shelton, 1979) usually identify four major classes of communication disorders. They are disorders of: articulation, rhythm,, voice, and language symbolization. Table 1.2, based on Dearman and Plisko (1981), gives some data on the relative prevalence rates of different speech disorders in public schools in the United States.

The speech problems of deaf children are only broadly related to disorders of communication as classically described in speech pathology, but it is useful to identify these disorders in order to place the special problems of the deaf speaker in their correct context. However, in identifying them, and even at the risk of being simplistic, it must be emphasized that they are problems of articulatory speech and of language that develop in hearing children. Their focus is on remediation, whereas for deaf children the focus of speech teaching should be on generating and reinforcing natural speech and language skills.

The difference between speech remediation and speech development is important, and it is one of the reasons why learning sign language improves the speech of deaf children (see Montgomery, 1966, for a classic study that shows that good signers are also better speakers). Conversely, the emphasis placed on articulatory processes

TABLE 1.2
Estimated Prevalence of Speech and Language Disorders
in the United States

Problem	Expected Prevalence (by Percent)	Expected Number of Children
Functional articulation	3.0%	1,245,000
Stuttering	.7	290,500
Voice disorders	.2	83,000
Cleft palate	.1	41,500
Cerebral palsy	.2	83,000
Retarded speech development	.3	124,500
Impaired hearing	.5	287,500
Language delay	1.0	415,000
Total	6.0%	2,570,000

Source—N. Dearman and V. Plisko *The condition of education*, published Washington, DC: National Center for Education Statistics, 1981.

and mechanical oral language skills in much remedial work with deaf children is self-defeating. We will help deaf children to develop speech by emphasizing natural speech development (see Ling & Ling, 1978, for an excellent exposition of the principles involved), rather than focusing on remediation. Only later, if speech has become a meaningful method of communication, should we try to correct specific articulatory defects; the first objective has to be to develop the communicative competence and interest without which speech has no meaning.

The disorders of *articulation* referred to in the previous paragraph consist of oral inaccuracies such as substitutions (e.g., wock for rock), omissions (e.g., low for blow), additions (e.g., buhlue for blue) and distortions (e.g., scweam for scream). Specific distortions often are identified as special problems and the main ones are: (a) *baby talk*—in which the child makes substitutions that are similar to those made by children very early in speech development; (b) *lulling*—a phenomenon associated with defective r, l, t, d, or s sounds; (c) *lisping*—the characteristic disorder of the sibilants, especially s and z; and (d) *delayed speech*—in which the child uses only a narrow range of consonants and as a result the speech is unintelligible or of low intelligibility.

In addition to disorders of articulation, speech *rhythm,* can be distorted so as to result in speech that is conspicuous or unpleasant or, sometimes, unintelligible. Characteristically, the distortions are produced by any one or any combination of over prolongation of the speech sounds, unnecessary repetitions of the speech sounds, fixations on a particular speech sound, and oscillations of rhythm, or pitch. The best known example of disorders of rhythm is stuttering. Although stuttering may have emotional components in its etiology, primary stuttering usually is regarded as an organic condition in which repetition and prolongation of speech sounds is the major factor. In children, the primary stutterer may even be unaware of his or her condition, whereas secondary stuttering, resulting from emotional causes, results in intense fear of communicating, and may be associated with facial contortions as the child attempts to produce normal speech.

Voice disorders are sometimes called *dysphonias,* and the first dimension in which such disorders can occur is that of pitch. The approximate pitch of male voices is 125 Hz, female, 200 Hz, and children's, 325 Hz (see Ling, 1976, p. 189 for more information). Based against such standards, hearing-impaired children and adults may have voices that are too high or too low in pitch. Additionally, they may have voices that show too little pitch variation, the extreme of which would be the monotone. Finally, voices may be stereotyped in inflections such as the "sing-song" type of voice or voices may have pitch breaks such as occur normally during male adolescence or anger. As well as pitch, voice can vary in intensity, resulting in voices that are too loud, too weak, tremulous, stereotyped in loudness patterns, or having no voice at all (*aphonia*). Finally, voices differ in more subjective ways in respect of quality (*timbre*). Timbre means that even though people are speaking at the same pitch and intensity and in the same dialect, they still sound different. It is mainly a product of individual differences in the resonating characteristics of the oral and nasal passages, but it also is determined, in part, by the nature of sound produced by the vocal folds. It is variation in these vibratory characteristics produced by variation in the air flow through the glottis (the narrow opening at the top of the larynx) that produces different voices in the same speaker, even though the fundamental frequency of the voice has not changed. Voices also can differ in their nasality and in whether resonance is based more in the throat (female) or in the chest (male).

Disorders of symbolization involve failures in the normal processes of symbol formulation. Older texts (e.g., McGinnis, 1963) differentiated receptive from expressive communication, and this distinction is still found widely in the literature. In our view, it originates largely in the study of adult aphasics and has little relevance to younger children, except in one or two special situations. In children, we are dealing with a developmental process, and impairment of receptive communication is invariably associated with impairment of expressive communication. Rather than referring to aphasia or language disorders as receptive or expressive, a better way of describing these disorders is to refer to them as specific language disorders (Rodda 1976; Taylor, 1964). Such disorders are conceptually distinct from speech; language disorders deal with the raw material of speech without which speech cannot develop normally.

Some Specific Speech Problems

Approximately three-quarters of children with *cerebral palsy* have speech problems. The primary cause is damage to those parts of the brain controlling the muscles involved in speech production, and in severe cases the damage may be so great that it prevents any voluntary movement of the speech organs, leaving active only certain basic reflexes. Consequently, attempts by the child to speak result in severe spasms and "overflow" that preclude the development of a normal speech pattern. In addition, there are two secondary factors that complicate and, without remediation, retard speech development in cerebral palsied children. They are a lack of motivation resulting from a history of failure in the use of speech, and a lack of language stimulation because of a failure by parents and others to ensure that the cerebral palsied child is exposed to linguistically stimulating experiences. Finally, as if this were not enough, cerebral palsied children are more likely to have secondary handicaps that themselves impair language development; indeed, many cerebral palsied children have additional hearing impairment or hearing-processing difficulties.[2]

The largest single specific problem of speech that will face the speech therapist, psychologist, or the special education teacher is *stuttering*. Around 40% of speech problems fall into this classification. Approximately 7 people in 1,000 are stutterers, although it must be emphasized that for some of them the disability will be quite minor. Permanent stuttering is rare, and for most children afflicted in this way, stuttering is an intermittent occurrence dependent both on the words being used and on the emotional tone of the environment.

Cleft palate is another speech disorder that the speech therapist and special education teacher will face, although surgical techniques now prevent the extreme speech problems caused by this condition. The disorder can be hereditary or it can be caused by external causes, such as malnutrition, and certain drugs, such as cortisone. Clefts vary in severity, and as we have already stated, much of the damage resulting from clefts can be remediated by surgery or by the use of a prosthesis. Even so, disorders of speech will remain and, of course, so will the accompanying psychological problems. The effect of a cleft palate on speech is to increase nasality, produce defective articulation, distort the flows of air through the oral orifices, and distort the general respiratory control of speech. Clefts often lead to abnormality in the muscular tensions and contractions in the speech or speech-associated muscles. Like stutterers, more specific maladaptive responses may be learned and lead to even greater impairment of communication. Thus, children with a cleft palate or who stutter may learn to avoid eye contact, develop unusual head postures, bite the lips, or cover the mouth. In the extreme, they will make no attempt to engage in vocal communication.

One of the major causes of speech and language difficulties in children operates indirectly through central cognitive and motor processing activities, rather than through direct impairment of speech. In extreme cases *retarded children* may have no speech at all; in less extreme cases speech is of late onset and receptive and expressive abilities are below average. The delay can be severe; for example, some 5-year-old retarded children have speech only at an equivalent level to a 12- to 18-month-old nonretarded child. With older retarded children, the development of speech appears to be correlated with

[2]The book *Joey* (Deacon, 1976) is a moving account of how communication difficulties can "cut off" a handicapped individual from the world at large. Joey, suffering from cerebral palsy, was eventually able to write his story because another handicapped friend learned how to understand him. Together, and with the help of others, they put his story into print.

mental age, but in practice the development of motor skills has an equally significant impact on the development of speech in these children. *Down's Syndrome* children, in particular, show very wide variation in their speech and language skills, greater than is implied from their differences in measured intelligence.

As well as specific speech problems resulting from, say, an enlarged tongue in Down's Syndrome children, some retarded children suffer from some simple practical problems that might be best described as problems of communicative intent. Such problems involve low speech intensity, disfluencies in speech, sentence length and sentence form, difficulties in the use of comparatives and superlatives, and difficulties in the correct labeling of pictures and objects. Another frequent problem is that some retarded children just do not appreciate that sounds, speech, and language enable them to manipulate their environment and to obtain appropriate satisfactions. It is for this reason that speech difficulties in such children may respond well to appropriate operant techniques of behavior modification rather than specific teaching of speech and language, as do more simple receptive communication skills in more severely retarded children.

Another interesting approach to the remediation of language and speech problems in retarded children is found in the use of sign language as a method of communication. In Great Britain, Margaret Walker has developed the Makaton vocabulary for this purpose (Walker & Buckfield, 1983), and this vocabulary is also used in Canada. It is based on basic signs taken from British Sign Language and uses a simple vocabulary to produce a relatively sophisticated communication system. The use of sign language in this way has proven to be beneficial in facilitating not only the development of language, but general social development as well, and, interestingly, many retarded children or adults who learn to use sign language then go on to develop the speech skills that they previously lacked. Techniques of parental support such as those described by Sobsey and Bienick (1983) can also be of vital significance, because they allow parents and children to develop methods of communicating through sign language. For many, such techniques allow easy and satisfying interactive communication about basic physical needs and other aspects of daily living, and remove some of the tensions that exist when parents and children are unable to communicate about those needs through speech.

There are many other organic causes of defective speech, and almost any malformation of the structures involved in speech can cause articulation defects. Certainly the special education teacher, the psychologist, the linguist, and many other professionals need to be aware of these possibilities and to ensure that children with defective speech receive a full clinical examination. However, the organic cause often is only the precipitating event, and the emotional problem may eventually become a more important component. The speech processes have a remarkable ability for adaptation, and most speech sounds can be made in a variety of ways. Thus, overconcern on the part of either teacher or parent may aggravate the problem by drawing the child's attention to it. Most minor speech problems are best dealt with by warm, nondemanding natural correction, which enables children to correct their own errors by comparing their speech with that of a normal speaker. It is this feedback that is either missing or distorted for the deaf or hard of hearing child, and it is why remediation of the speech of such children presents special and different problems for the speech pathologist and the teacher of the hearing-impaired.

Speech and the Deaf Child

One difficulty for deaf children and their parents is the confusion that frequently arises in arriving at a diagnosis of deafness. The problems described in the previous section are sometimes mistaken for hearing impairment, and conversely, deaf children, adolescents, and adults are prone to be misdiagnosed as mentally retarded or behaviorally disturbed (see Denmark & Eldridge, 1969 for important, original studies of this problem). The speech difficulties and "gestural" communication of profoundly deaf students and adults confuse the uninitiated, and even if correctly diagnosed, their problems still may be viewed as speech problems resulting from impairment of hearing, rather than oral language problems resulting from the inadequacies of the visual and kinesthetic stimuli they are required to process to understand speech through lipreading. We return to these complex issues in later chapters. We raise them now so that the reader will have some sensitivity to them in the subsequent discussion.

In fact, the inability to hear in early childhood results usually in speech that is "arrhythmic, monotonal, lacking in rhythm and pitch, and containing poor phrasing. It can be intelligible to small audiences and can be functional. It is seldom pleasing" (French, 1971, p. 217). There are a number of textbooks describing specific techniques for remediating deaf speech; in recent years the better ones range from Connor (1971) to Ling and Ling (1978). Unfortunately, teaching speech to deaf children is still as much an art as a science, and the only real way to learn these skills is through an apprenticeship with a master teacher. Textbooks help, but they do not provide the practical skill that can come only through experience.

Despite the need for specific training, there are a number of points that can be made to help teachers, parents, and others. Therefore, however briefly, we refer to speech and the deaf child with no apology—our personal philosophy, and one shared by many deaf people, is that if deaf students can learn speech, they should, and all deaf students should be given some opportunities to try to learn speech. The problem is not in learning speech, but in imposing it on deaf children. If we teach speech to deaf children in a way that destroys their self-esteem and self-identity, and in a way that attacks the role models provided by successful deaf people, we will deprive deaf children of experiences that are vital to their overall educational development.

Lip (Speech) Reading

Lipreading[3] is not speaking, but it is an essential ingredient of the learning process when the deaf child is learning to speak. The following practical suggestions will increase the ability of hearing-impaired students or adults to understand speech in situations where they are using lipreading and, therefore, their ability to generate meaningful speech.

One of the most obvious suggestions concerns the visibility of the speaker. Uniform lighting with little glare will facilitate lipreading, and conversely, it is almost impossible to lip-read during daylight a person who is standing in front of a window—the face is in too much shadow. Another common habit that makes it difficult to lip-read is pacing and talking simultaneously and, of course, many teachers face the chalkboard or other aids and talk with their back to the class. Contextual cueing also is vital in lipreading because, as we discuss in the next paragraph and in more detail in chapter 4, success depends on the ability to do a great deal of intelligent guessing. As a result, anything that aids context, for example, paraphrasing by teacher or student and the use of overhead projectors, will greatly facilitate understanding.

It is possible to refine lipreading skills through practice and exposure to appropriate materials, but many factors affect the development of these skills. In one of the few experimental investigations of

---

[3]Usage varies with "speech reading" being the more preferred form in North America, and "lipreading" in Europe. We prefer "lipreading" and will usually use this form in preference to "speech reading." We do so, not because of our United Kingdom background, but because to us it is a more accurate description of the processes involved (see pp. 212 to 218).

this problem, Evans (1964) concluded:

> Children with substantial residual hearing, good intelligence and high
> visual recognition scores were good all-round lip-readers. Conversely, the
> more profoundly deaf children of below normal intelligence and with low
> visual recognition scores were poor lip-readers. In children with similar se-
> verity of hearing loss, a combination of good intelligence and high visual
> recognition ability was the condition conducive to successful lipreading.
> (p. 131)

Later research (to be reviewed in chapter 4) has rendered these
claims equivocal. In particular, the alleged relationship between hearing loss and pure lipreading skill has not been confirmed. As we shall
also see, another vital factor is the ability of the deaf child to retain
acoustic information in short-term memory. To these we might add
some as yet unexplored personality variables. By definition, lip-readers are gamblers. On the basis of an incomplete and fragmented perception, they use their knowledge of context, semantics, and syntax
to guess at the intended meaning of a message. Therefore, if they are
reserved or cautious by temperament, they may be less willing to
adopt the guessing strategies used by a good lip-reader. In such situations, the student or adult may benefit from the use of cued speech
developed by Cornett (1967). Cued speech reduces much of the
guesswork involved by providing supplementary hand cues that help
distingish the elements of speech that can be confused in the lip-read
pattern. As the student becomes more proficient, the cues can be
phased out.

Speech

If deaf students are to develop good speech (or even speech of some
limited practical usefulness), they will do so only if good teaching is
combined with an environment reinforcing and supporting its use.
Such an environment assumes speech can only develop from language, and so it will also emphasize the use of sign language to fos-
ter communication and develop language competencies that can be
used as a springboard for speech development. It will make every
possible use of residual hearing through appropriate amplification
aids and techniques, provided these are not stressful for the student
(late fitting of a hearing aid invariably generates some initial stress
that should not be confused with a continuing rejection of the aid).
Finally, the overall environment should be one in which speech is regarded as normal, but not one in which it intrudes into other activities and thereby results in a child or student being deprived of
normal learning experiences. If these conditions are met, then it is

appropriate for some effort to be made to facilitate the development of deaf children's speech, following some basic principles.

Speech and Hearing. The distinctive features of speech vary for hearing people, let alone deaf students. Therefore, any assessment of speech objectives should clearly relate features such as the frequency composition or degree of nasality to the audiogram of the child. For example, a child with severe high frequency deafness will be unable to hear the plural marker -s sound. In such situations, the teacher should either deal with other sounds or ensure that visual cueing is available to help the student distinguish this characteristic of speech. Similarly, the acoustic characteristics of speech can aid speech discrimination or make it more difficult. Voiced consonants are of higher intensity than unvoiced ones, accented syllables than unaccented, and stressed vowels than unstressed ones. The skilled speech teacher uses this information to decide the best material to use with the child, and the best order in which to work with different problems. Ling's (1976) five-sound test is an excellent diagnostic tool with which to facilitate these decisions.

Articulation. As we have already discussed, most skilled teachers of speech to deaf students do not advocate early remedial work on articulation. They advocate concentrating on the flow of language—rhythm, intonation, and stress. Later, articulatory goals can be established, but such goals are less important in the beginning than the development of coordinated and fluent speech.

Competence Varies With Position. The ability of deaf children to use a specific phoneme (a basic unit of sound, see chapter 3) in one context does not mean they can use it in others, and they will need to practice consonants in initial, medial, and final positions. It also is important to note that in developing competencies in speech, it is as necessary, as in any learning, to structure the process so that the more difficult elements follow the easier ones (e.g., learning some phonetic elements such as the "th" sound should occur before learning others such as the "t" sound because the first is easier to produce and learn). Perry (1978) has a useful tabulation of the different types of material that can be used in teaching lipreading, and these can, in turn, be related to the most effective order of teaching speech material (see, for example, Ling, 1976).

Syntax and Morphology. Children learn the syntactical rules of language before they learn the morphological rules,[4] and they do so in a specific order. For example, third person singular forms are learned before plurals. There is every reason to believe, and no good

---

[4]Morphology refers to the smallest meaningful units of language. They may be free-form (e.g., girl) or bound as the "ish" in girlish. See chapter 3.

reason not to believe, that it is better for deaf children to learn the components of speech in a similar order, and tests such as the Teacher Assessment of Grammatical Structures (TAGS, Moog & Kozak, 1982) are an invaluable aid in establishing language competence, a vital prerequisite to establishing speech goals.

Vorce (1971), in a survey of schools and programs for hearing-impaired students, established that there was a wide diversity of opinion in the practices of American schools in teaching speech in both oral and total communication programs. Distressingly, 6 out of 21 schools did not have a written speech curriculum, and much of the focus of the others seemed to be on individual remedial programming. It cannot be emphasized too strongly that speech is an integral part of the school program. Speech should not dominate the curriculum, but the place for teaching speech is in the natural settings of the classroom, and elsewhere. Individual therapy is important for some students and, perhaps, all students at some time. By itself, it will achieve very little.

The order of importance of remediating different speech characteristics also was rated by the schools in the Vorce Survey (see Table 1.3). Some interesting points can be made. First, the emphasis on individual therapy probably resulted in the focus on articulation. It can be contrasted with an early but important study by John and Howarth (1965) that gave a research base to what good teachers of speech to deaf children have usually advocated: Aspects of breath, stress and accent, and syllabic interaction are of much greater significance than articulation. Articulation should not be ignored, but we cannot emphasize too strongly that the improvement in speech quality and intelligibility resulting from work on the rhythmic and intonational aspects of deaf children's, students', and adults' speech is much greater than improvements from work on specific articulatory skills. In fact, working on articulation will achieve little as long as the problems of rhythm and intonation remain uncorrected.

Language Assessment

One of the first scientific records of language development in a child was made almost 200 years ago by Tiedman in 1787 (Grove & O'Sullivan, 1976). A hundred years later, Darwin thought the area worthy of study (Darwin, 1877) and, ever since, the descriptive tradition has continued unabated—through Jean Piaget to Noam Chomsky, Eric Lenneberg, and Aleksandr Luria and, more recently, an entire field of child language researchers, including Roger Brown, Lois Bloom, and Paula Menyuk. Alongside the development of the

TABLE 1.3
Rated Importance of Remediating Speech Characteristics in Schools
and Programs for the Hearing Impaired

Aspect of Speech	Rank (Median)	Range
Development of pleasant voice quality	3	1-8
Articulation of consonant sounds	3	1-7
Articulation of vowel sounds	3	1-6
Orthographic system	4	1-13
Appropriate pronunciation	4	1-10
Monitoring of voice	6	1-13
Development of suitable rhythm	6	1-13
Conventional intonation patterns	6	1-12
Improvement of breath control	6	1-11
Appropriate stress and accent	7	1-10
Suitable variety in pitch levels	8/9	1-13
Improve rate of speaking	9	3-13
Practice for speech motor skills	11/12	1-13

Source—E. Vorce, 1971, Speech curriculum. In L.E. Connor (Ed), *Speech for the deaf child: Knowledge and use*, published and reproduced by permission of the Alexander Graham Bell Association for the Deaf, Washington, DC.

descriptive tradition, we have parallel developments in the structured assessments of psychological attributes—mental testing. The father of the mental testing movement was, of course, Sir Frances Galton, but it was Alfred Binet who brought it to the prominence it holds in modern contemporary society. Unfortunately, both Galton and Binet favored a model that focused on testing using normative scores and a series of associated statistics. Such a focus delayed the development of adequate methods of assessing language and communication, whether in deaf or hearing students. Therefore, knowledge of developmental processes was not applied, and this in turn delayed better understanding of these processes.

Tests for Language and Communication

A comprehensive list of tests or techniques that may be used to assess English language and communication skills in deaf students is given in Table 1.4. The table selects from available tests those that are thought to be of most practical value. It includes both published and unpublished tests, but only unpublished tests that are reasonably available to researchers and clinicians. It is not a comprehensive list of all language tests, and it includes no academic achievement tests.

In addition to the tests described in Table 1.4, there are at least five methods of assessing language samples that are of value in evaluating performance and developing prescriptive programs. These are the language analyses described by Lee (1974), Bloom and Lahey (1978), Crystal, Fletcher, and Garman (1976), Kretschmer and Kretschmer (1978), and Tyack and Gottsleben (1974). The procedures developed by these authors provide interpretative assessment of recorded samples of language. Each method takes slightly different perspectives, but all provide developmental sequences of language skills against which the performance of individual students can be compared. They are not "tests" in the traditional psychometric sense, and therefore any validity they possess is limited to face validity. In all probability, they do assess language in a meaningful way, but they require considerable training and experience before they can be used reliably, and the average classroom teacher does not find them easy. Nevertheless, when properly used by trained clinicians, they add to our understanding of the language of deaf students, and to the focus needed for developing individual remedial programs. They are important additions to our methods of assessment, and should not be discarded because they are time consuming and difficult.[5]

Four other language specialists have approached language assessment in a different way. Streng (Streng, Kretschmer, & Kretschmer, 1978), Ling (1976), van Uden (1977), and Blackwell, Engen, Fischgrund, & Zaracadoolas (1978) have all developed practical manuals of instruction in speech or language. Two, Ling and van Uden, have concentrated on oral English language and speech; the other two have concentrated on language itself. Ling and van Uden are practically based—using their own experience to develop highly structured instructional regimes. Streng and Blackwell both use

---

[5]See chapter 4, p. 169 to p. 172 for an example of a language sample analysis using the Kretschmer technique.

TABLE 1.4

A Description of Some Tests of Language and Communication Skills
of Use in Working With Deaf Populations

NAME OF TEST	RESPONDENTS	DESCRIPTION	REFERENCE
Assessment of Children's Language Comprehension (ACLC)	Hearing 2-6 years	Receptive language skills are assessed as Vocabulary, 2 word, 3 word, and 4 word phrases.	Foster, C.R., Giddan, J.J., & Stark, J. *Assessment of children's language comprehension.* Palo Alto: Consulting Psychologists' Press.
Comprehension in the Profoundly Deaf	Deaf, 13-14 years; hearing, 9 years	An experimental test of verbal comprehension. Ss read six passages of 300 words, answering eight questions on each. A 1/4 multichoice paradigm. Deaf found inferior to hearing Ss 4-5 years younger.	Conrad, R. (1971). The effect of vocalizing on comprehension in the profoundly deaf. *British Journal of Psychology, 62,* 147-150.
Direction Tests	Deaf, Test I: 5 years. Test II: 7-8 years	Test of Ss' ability to respond to spoken directions. Test I: 10 items, relating to a set of toys, scored 0, 1, or 2. Test II: 12 items. Ss to draw marking on a sheet of geometrical figures. Scored 0, 2, or 3 (max. 30). Deaf Ss appear to gain approximately 50% scores of hearing.	Solly, G. (1975). *Direction tests.* Worcester: Service for Hearing Impaired Children.

Table 1.4 cont.

NAME OF TEST	RESPONDENTS	DESCRIPTION	REFERENCE
Expressive One-word Picture Vocabulary Test	Hearing, 2-11 years	Measures expressive vocabulary and gives a brief assessment of intelligence, but used cautiously as a test of expressive vocabulary.	Gardiner, M.F. (1979). *Expressive one-word picture vocabulary test.* Novato, CA: Academic Therapy Publications.
Grammatical Analysis of Elicited Language (GAEL)	Hearing and deaf, 5-9 years	Uses toys and other articles to elicit spontaneous and imitated language. A number of expressive language scales are developed from the structured stimuli.	Published by Central Institute for the Deaf, St. Louis.
Picture Story Language Test (PSLT)	Hearing and deaf, 7-17 years	Ss to write short essay about pictorial stimulus. Essays analysed in terms of length, number of sentences, syntactic structure, abstraction.	Myklebust, H.R. (1965). *Developmental disorders of written language. Vol. I: Picture story language test.* New York: Grune & Stratton.
Hobsbaum-Mittler Sentence Comprehension Test (SCT)	Normal and SSN, preschool and school age	Receptive pictorial multichoice format, one target and 2-3 distractors per item. Fifteen psycholinguistic subtests, four sentences for each. Subtest profiles used for SSN/normal comparisons, experimental studies.	Mittler, P., Jeffree, D., Wheldall, K., & Berry, P. (1974, March). *Assessment and remediation of language comprehension and production in severely subnormal children: Final report to SSRC.* Hester Adrian Research Centre, University of Manchester.

Table 1.4 cont.

NAME OF TEST	RESPONDENTS	DESCRIPTION	REFERENCE
Illinois Test of Psycholinguistic Abilities (ITPA)	Normal and handicapped, 2-10 years	Twelve subtests said to measure basic skills (typically 20-40 items per subtest). Dimensions employed: auditory and visual reception, association, expression, closure, sequential memory.	Kirt, S.A., McCarthy, J.J., & Kirk, W.D. (1968). *Illinois test of psycholinguistic abilities*. Urbana, IL: University of Illinois Press.
Imitation, Comprehension Production Test (ICP)	Younger students with developmental preschool language levels. Four-year-olds score almost perfectly	Receptive pictorial multichoice format with 2 choices each for 10 grammatical contrasts Assessments of Imitation, Comprehension, or Production allow comparison to be made.	Fraser, C., Bellugi, U., & Brown, R. (1963). Control of grammar in imitation, comprehension, and production. *Journal of Learning and Verbal Behavior, 2*, 121-135.
Language Assessment Battery	Hearing impaired children, 6-16 years in a developmental sequence	A screening test of 36 items, and more intensive subtests of vocabulary and phrase structures. Vocabulary level controlled and final version standardized on 134 students in auditory/oral, visible English, or total communication programs.	Reich, C., Keeton, A., & Lindsay, P. (1981). The language assessment battery. *The ACEHI Journal, 7*, 155-163.

Table 1.4 cont.

NAME OF TEST	RESPONDENTS	DESCRIPTION	REFERENCE
Language Modalities Test for Aphasia (LMTA)	Adult aphasics	Auditory and visual stimuli of pictures, numbers, and other materials provide a schematic breakdown developed by the authors. Allows stimulus to be held constant while performance on a variety of tests is assessed. An experimental test for assessing factors in communication.	Wepman, J.M., & Jones, L.B. (1961). *Language modalities test for aphasia.* Chicago: University of Chicago.
Learning of Factual Information	Deaf, 11-19 years	Sixteen passages from school readers presented by expert communicators. Four passages to each of four methods of communication. Ss to answer 36 questions about the material. A 1/3 multichoice.	White, A.H., & Stevenson, V.M. (1975). The effects of total communication, manual communication, oral communication, and reading on the learning of factual information in residential school deaf children. *American Annals of the Deaf, 120,* 48-57.
Minnesota Test for Differential Diagnosis of Aphasia	Adult aphasics	Forty-seven subtests of audition, visual perception and reading, speech and language, visual motor perception and writing. Numerical relations and arithmetic processes. Pictorial and verbal material.	Schuell, H. (1965). *Minnesota test for differential diagnosis of aphasia.* University of Minnesota Press.

Table 1.4 cont.

NAME OF TEST	RESPONDENTS	DESCRIPTION	REFERENCE
Northwestern Syntax Screening Test (NSST)	Normal and handicapped, 3-8 years	Receptive and expressive subtests, each of 20 items. Pictorial multichoice, two confusible targets and two distractors per item. Both subtests involve linguistic features such as subject, object, pronouns, prepositions, voice, negation, tense, and so forth. Total scores derived.	Lee, L.L. (1970). A screening test for syntax development. *Journal of Speech and Hearing Disorders, 35,* 103-112.
Peabody Picture Vocabulary Test (PPVT)	Hearing, 2-18 years	Verbal test of vocabulary also used as a brief assessment of intelligence. Pictorial multichoice, consisting of two forms. Anglicized version exists.	Dunn, L.M. (1970). *Peabody picture vocabulary test.* Circle Pines, MN: American Guidance Services.
Pre-school Language Scale (PLS)	Hearing, 2-6 years	Pictorial-verbal test assessing two areas— auditory comprehension and verbal activities. In addition has a section on articulation. Has a number of subtests such as Differentiation of Self, Temporal Ordering, and Size Conservation.	Zimmerman, I.L., Steiner, V.G., & Evatt, R.L. (1969). *Pre-school language scale.* New York: Chas. E. Merrill.

Table 1.4 cont.

NAME OF TEST	RESPONDENTS	DESCRIPTION	REFERENCE
Porch Index of Communicative Ability (PICA)	Aphasic patients	Eighteen test tasks relating to 10 common objects (pen, key, etc.), involving verbal, gestural, and graphic responses. Quality of each response assessed using a 16-point scoring scale (16 = complex response, down to 1 = no response).	Porch, B.E. (1967). *Porch index of communicative ability*. Palo Alto,CA: Consulting Psychologists' Press.
Reynell Developmental Language Scales (RDLS)	Normal and handicapped, 6 months-6 years	Comprises a verbal comprehension scale (nine sections of increasing complexity) and an expressive language scale (three sections). Includes modification to enable highly handicapped Ss to respond by eye movement.	Reynell, J. (1969). *Reynell developmental language scales*. Windsor: NFER.
Sentence Comprehension Tests	Deaf, Test 1: 5 years, Test 2: 7-8 years	Oral sentence comprehension tests, containing selections of material from Gates-McGinitie. Development discontinued owing to high guessing rate (personal communication, 1975).	Solly, G. (1975). Test of comprehension and spoken language for use with hearing impaired children. *The Teacher of the Deaf, 73*, 74-85.

Table 1.4 cont.

NAME OF TEST	RESPONDENTS	DESCRIPTION	REFERENCE
Teacher Assessment of Grammatical Structure (TAGS)	Hearing or language impaired, preschool to 8 years and older	A teacher assessment devised in a developmental sequence. Three levels (Pre, Simple, and Complex Sentence) assessed for Comprehension, Imitated Production, or Prompted Production.	Moog, J.S., & Kozak, V.J. (1982). *Teacher assessment of grammatical structures.* St. Louis, MO: Central Institute for the Deaf.
Test of Auditory Comprehension of Language (TACL)	Hearing, 3-7 years	Tests vocabulary and verbal syntactical structures using pictorial multichoice format.	Published by Teaching Resources Corporation, Boston.
Test of Communication Skill	Deaf, 16-21 years	Experimental multichoice test of receptive communication skills. Broken into 20 "message classes" and with high and low novelty items.	Grove, C., O'Sullivan, F.D., & Rodda, M. (1979). Communication and language in severely deaf adolescents. *British Journal of Psychology, 70,* 531-540.
Test of Expressive Language Ability (TEXLA))	Deaf/Hearing, 6-12 years in developmental sequence	Short and long forms with controlled Grade 1 vocabulary. Assesses 12 grammatical principles. Normed on 65 hearing impaired and 17 hearing students.	Bunch, G.O. (1981). *Test of expressive language ability.* Toronto: G.B. Services
Test of Language Development (TOLD)	Hearing, 4-9 years	Pictorial and verbal test of expressive and receptive language, auditory discrimination, and articulation.	Published by Empiric Press, Austin, Texas.

Table 1.4 cont.

NAME OF TEST	RESPONDENTS	DESCRIPTION	REFERENCE
Test of Receptive Ability (TERLA)	Deaf/Hearing, 6-12 years in developmental sequence	Short and long forms with controlled Grade 1 vocabulary. Assesses 12 grammatical principles. Normed on 92 hearing impaired and 27 hearing students.	Bunch, G.O. (1981). *Test of receptive language ability*. Toronto: G.B. Services.
Test of Syntactic Ability (TSA)	Deaf, 10-19 years	A battery of tests using multichoice format. Six major aspects of syntax, derived from Chomskian theory: verb usage, conjunction, negation, question formation, relativisation, and pronominalization. Designed to detect typically deaf language errors. Standardized.	Quigley, S.P., Steinkamp, M.W., Power, D.J., & Jones, B.W. (1978). *Test of syntactic abilities*. Beaverton, OR: Dormac.
Three-minute Reasoning Test	Normal adults	Ss to make true/false decisions about AB letter pairs, given a short sentence describing their relationship. To attempt as many as possible in three minutes. Total score out of 64 sentences correlates .59 with IQ. Used to measure human performance in stress and drug studies.	Baddeley, A.D. (1968). A three-minute reasoning test based on grammatical transformation. *Psychonomic Science, 10*, 341-342.

Table 1.4 cont.

NAME OF TEST	RESPONDENTS	DESCRIPTION	REFERENCE
Utah Test of Language Development (UTLD)	Normal and handicapped, 0:9 years-16:0 years	Fifty-one test items adopted from standardized tests, scored right or wrong, increasing in difficulty; total score used to derive language age (LA).	Meecham, M.J., Jex, J.L., & Jones, J.D. (1967). *Utah test of language development*. Salt Lake City: Communication Research Associates.
Verbal Language Development Scale	Hearing, Birth-15 years	Development of the Vineland Social Maturity Scale, using a check list completed by interview. Gives a developmental language level.	Meecham, M.J. (1959). *Verbal language development scale*. Circle Pines, MN: American Guidance Service.

developmental psycholinguistics as a base but, like Ling and van Uden, Streng favors a relatively structured approach focusing on speech, whereas Blackwell uses English in a highly structured form based on the theories of transformational grammar developed by Chomsky (see pp. 119 to 127). Evaluation in all these programs is part of an ongoing process; as the children progress through the curriculum, appropriate assessments determine whether they have achieved mastery of the earlier developmental phases.

In fact, in most clinical practice, the focus tends to be on practical performance in language rather than on linguistic competence. As O'Sullivan (1977) points out, when we are considering skills such as reading comprehension and vocabulary, spelling and grammatical use, they are derived from, but are not identical to, competence in language. Therefore, studies of competence in deaf children have, with some notable exceptions, lagged behind similar studies with hearing children. An investigation by Tervoort and Verberk (1967) was one of the first exceptions. Their study used psycholinguistic techniques of analysis and showed deaf students to be competent in language, even though their performance in English often was severely delayed. Klima and Bellugi (1979), Siple (1978), and Wilbur (1979) have continued to extend and develop studies of this type, alongside more practically based studies such as those of West and Weber (1974), Ivimey (1976), and Hoffmeister (1982). We explore this topic in more detail in chapter 5.

The differences in the approach of the authors described in the previous paragraphs have as much to do with structure in teaching as with oral speech or sign language or with different theoretical bases. Teachers of deaf students have long vacillated between those who favor structured and those who favor unstructured approaches, particularly in the teaching of speech and English. More recently, the tangential question of whether English *should be taught as a second language* also has surfaced, although, of course, different methodological approaches also are favored in second language teaching. There are probably no definitive answers to these questions—which approach is right will depend on the individual student, the grouping of students within different schools and programs, the early language experiences of the student, and the preference of the parents for oral or manual communication. The right approach also probably has a great deal to do with our emerging understanding of perceptual, cognitive, and linguistic processing in the hearing-impaired population, a topic we explore throughout the rest of this text.

Perceptual Processing and Language

Ivimey (1981) reviews experimental studies that show how perception and cognition interact (e.g., Bever, 1973). When we listen to sentences in a noisy environment, those that are probable are perceived more frequently, while those that are improbable are perceived less frequently. Similarly, individual words in a sentence may be inaudible, but when placed in meaningful sentences they become audible. Ivimey goes on to describe some of his own research showing that the ability to produce different verb tenses is closely related to the ability of deaf students to interpret correctly the time references of written English sentences.

One problem in discussing a linguistic concept such as tense is that different languages employ different tense forms, or may not (as in Chinese) even have a tense system such as English users would understand it.[6] In fact, sign languages such as American Sign Language (ASL) do not oblige their users to place tense on every main verb. A second problem is that signed and spoken languages employ radically different ways of expressing grammatical processes; where spoken languages use *temporal* mechanisms, sign languages use *spatial* processes (chapter 3). The contrast between a temporal and a spatial processing system is an important one, and has implications for neurological organization in deaf and hearing people. In hearing people, language is generally localized in the left cerebral hemisphere and is organized temporally. Is it localized in the right hemisphere in deaf people, as one would predict on the basis of the use of visual/spatial cognitive representation in sign language? Lenneberg (1967) concluded it was not, but his data were limited, his conclusion was premature, and there are some studies suggesting that the cognitive representation of sign language is right-hemisphere dominant. We review these studies (e.g., Phippard, 1974) at length in chapter 6, and conclude, with other researchers such as Hardyck, Tzeng, and Wang (1978), that as yet the evidence in support of major differences in brain function between hearing and deaf respondents is confused and insubstantial.

Despite our present uncertainty about neurological processing in deaf students, there can be little doubt that systematic evaluation should give some consideration to these factors. At present it rarely does, even in the more obvious situation of the assessment of multi-handicapped deaf students who have a high probability of having minimal brain damage with associated perceptual dysfunction or

---

[6]Possibly some of the difficulty noted by Ivimey's subjects may relate to confusion between sign and oral language rule systems.

specific language disorder. We have a range of clinical tests, such as the Frostig Test of Visual-Motor Coordination (Frostig, Lefever, & Whittlesey, 1964) and those of Feuerstein (1979), and experimental techniques, such as those described by Dodd and White (1980). We are beginning to apply these techniques in the study of reading and other language skills in hearing students, but we still persist, when discussing deaf students or adults, in regarding speech, ASL, English, thinking, and auditory or visual perception as separate systems. Rather, we should focus on the integrative and underlying cognitive processes and, in the long term, their neurological representations.

Cognitive psychology and psycholinguistics have rediscovered semantics during the 1970s and, although not rejecting traditional psycholinguistic theory and transformational grammar, they have moved to incorporate semantic structures and meaning within a more broadly formulated theory. In general, the psychology of deafness has yet to discover semantics and, in consequence, our assessments of deaf students do not include all that is necessary to obtain a total picture of the interaction between perceptual processing, cognitive and linguistic skills. Proving and accepting that ASL is a language (chapter 3) is only a first step; the next step is to explore the particular cognitive maps, syntactical rules and morphological processes that are characteristic of those students whose language develops without the benefit of auditory coding processes, and to apply this knowledge in the clinic and the classroom.

Deafness as an Ethnic Concept

So far in this chapter, we have mainly focused on deafness as an audiological concept, or a speech and language problem, although we did point out at the beginning that such a definition only has limited application. In sociocultural settings, which includes schools as well as society at large, deafness is much more properly defined as membership of an ethnic group composed of those who are deaf. To be a member of such a group implies an element of choice: The individual must wish to belong; and an element of acceptance: The group must accept the individual as a member. The importance of the terms *hard of hearing* and *deaf* is not just audiological; it reflects the fact that there are two distinctly separate ethnic groups with different conceptions of the world at large (Spradley & Spradley, 1978). Hearing people may have difficulty recognizing this fact, but hearing-impaired people do not. They clearly know if they are deaf, hard of hearing, hearing or in a state of *anomie* (belonging to none of these groups and existing in a kind of "nether world").

Of all of the basic information presented in this chapter, the concept of ethnicity of deafness is preeminent. It pervades all that follows. If it is not accepted, then most of what follows in the later chapters of the book is indefensible. In fact, the ethnic nature of deafness is well established (see Nash & Nash, 1981; Stokoe & Battison, 1981), and Nash and Nash (pp. 8-9) assert that using American Sign Language is only one of the factors needed to classify a person as ethnically deaf. They describe and explore social institutions, social class structure, social attitudes and values, and socialization processes in deafness. Using the techniques of anthropology, they clearly establish the existence of a deaf community. We are not members of this community, and we will be satisfied if we are ascribed the sociological status of the "wise" (Goffman, 1963) which, we hasten to add, is not to be confused with the possession of wisdom. We do hope in subsequent chapters to explore many of these issues in more detail, and to establish the importance of American Sign Language (or its equivalent in other cultures) and the ethnicity of deafness, as part of the educational process for deaf children.

Summary

Defining hearing loss is a fairly simple matter of audiological assessment, although the interpretation of the simple pure-tone audiogram is more difficult. Defining deafness is exceedingly complex; it is as much, if not more, a sociological phenomenon as an audiological definition. A hearing aid can only help some people with hearing losses; it cannot help all, particularly those with a sensori-neural loss, and it cannot restore normal hearing. In this chapter we have discussed some of these concepts, and some of the many conditions other than deafness which can also cause speech defects and language difficulties. Even if other handicaps are not present, hearing losses mean that many deaf students are seriously delayed in the development of English language, and we describe a number of techniques for assessing their competencies in this and other languages. Finally, we raise in capsule form a number of the topics which provide the main focus of the text. They are explored in more detail in subsequent chapters.

Further Reading

The classic audiological text on deafness is by Dick Calvert and Richard Silverman (1975) *Speech and Deafness*. In *The Speech of Hearing Impaired Children*, Andreas Markides (1983) both gives a concise historical perspective and provides a great deal of up-to-date information on speech teaching. Other excellent books are by Arthur Boothroyd (1982), *Hearing Impairments in Young Children*, Frederick Martin (1986), *Introduction to Audiology*, and Mark Ross (1982), *Hard of Hearing Children in Regular Schools*. Hilde Schlesinger and Kathryn Meadow's (1972) *Sound and Sign: Childhood Deafness and Mental Health*, is a little specialized for this chapter, but it is a classic text for those interested in the problems of deafness. Leo Jacobs (1982) expresses a deaf person's point of view in *A Deaf Adult Speaks Out*, as does Arden Neisser (1983) in *The Other Side of Silence*. Kathryn Meadow (1980) gives a psychological perspective in *Deafness and Child Development*.

2

THE CULTURAL CONTEXT

We established in chapter 1 that hearing impairment is not merely a physical problem. It has a wide range of psychological and social consequences, and its effects on individuals critically depend on the values and attitudes of the culture into which they are born. Our predominantly Western culture does not, as the Spartans did, resort to killing handicapped babies at birth, but its response to hearing impairment—and to other handicaps—often is emotional and insensitive. In this chapter we chart some of the social history of deafness: how hearing society has reacted to deaf people; the growth of manual methods of communication; the appearance of oralism; and the evolution of deaf culture. At the same time we set the scene for more detailed discussions of some of the issues appearing in later chapters.

Manual Methods of Communication

As Jean Hough (1983) has observed, manual communication systems have a long history; indeed signed language may well have predated the spoken form. Therefore, although the main focus of this book is on the communication methods employed by deaf people, it is worth noting that there are many other examples of visual-gestural systems:

1. Until quite recently, American Indians and other cultures developed and used various sign languages (Hough, 1983; Tweney & Hoemann, 1973), and some researchers have regarded these systems as the residue of a phase of evolution in which signing

may have played a vital survival role (see chapter 6). An anonymous writer in the *American Annals of the Deaf and Dumb* (1852) gives detailed descriptions of many Amerindian signs and compares them with American Sign Language.

2. Although not strictly necessary for survival, it also is interesting to note that to overcome the limitations imposed by their vow of silence, certain monastic orders have evolved sign languages of varying degrees of complexity. These systems may have influenced theatrical convention in Elizabethan England to employ a series of formal hand shapes that communicated different emotions (Burns, 1964). Doubt, repulsion, and similar feelings, were all expressed by standardized gestures (Fig. 2.1), and traces of this system remained in popular dramatic art forms until silent movies were replaced by the "talkies." Similar gestures are, of course, still retained in many traditional theaters throughout the world.

3. Similar to the art forms just described, there are many examples of the use of formalized gestures in religious or civil rituals. Sometimes the manual actions can be traced back to unexpected sources: The Roman Catholic act of crossing oneself is of Hermetic origin; the complex hand and arm configurations of traditional Hindu dancing may stem from the martial arts techniques of Southern India. Watson (1976) has given fascinating descriptions of traditional Indonesian dancing—largely comprising formal manual movements—and its extraordinary expressive power.

4. Sign language systems also have served more nefarious purposes, and a variety of hand signals and gestures have been employed by people who need to communicate covertly: spies and members of secret societies. The Thugs, for example, specialized in ritual murder and had a series of formal signs such as ALL CLEAR and—obviously very useful—KILL (see Fig. 2.2) (Daraul, 1961).

5. Finally, gesture is an important attribute in all nonverbal communication. The use of such gesture often is unconscious, and the topic is badly underresearched. In fact, if it were researched more intensively, it could provide valuable insights into the relationship between signed and spoken languages (Brannigan & Humphries, 1969; Kimura, 1973; Schever & Ellman, 1982; see also chapter 6), even though gestural systems range from the loosely informal to the highly structured, and few could be regarded as language in any strict sense (see chapter 3). Nevertheless, the existence of such systems emphasizes the fact

FIG. 2.1.   Standard "signs" used in Elizabethan theater.

Source—T. Burns, 1964, Non-verbal communication, *Discovery*, *XXV*(10), p. 35.

FIG. 2.2.   Manual signs employed by the Thugs.

Source—A. Daraul (1961), *Secret societies*, London: Frederick Muller.

that manual communication is not grossly unnatural; it is a normal attribute of human behavior whether used by deaf or by hearing people.

The symbol systems referred to in the previous paragraph are methods of signaling. They were not developed as languages in their own right, although they can be used to provide a visual code for a spoken language. In contrast, there is evidence that the formalized sign language of deaf people dates back as a language to at least 386 B.C. Pahz and Pahz (1978) quote Socrates as saying: "If we had neither voice nor tongue, and yet wished to manifest things to one another, should we not, like those which are at present mute, endeavor to signify our meaning by the hands, head, and other parts of the body?" (p. 5). Unfortunately, another influential Greek philosopher, Aristotle, asserted that deaf people were always "dumb," speaking incoherently and stuttering (see Bender, 1970; Hodgson, 1984), and as Bender points out, Aristotle's position was subsequently taken to imply that deaf people were incapable of reason (i.e., stupid). As a result, for many years deaf children were denied any kind of education (as were the large bulk of the population), although Augustine also makes reference to the use of sign language by deaf people, and as early as 1557 Girolamo Cardano (1501-1576) was actively advocating the education of deaf students using a form of visual communication (Scouten, 1984).

For reasons we explore later, systematic studies of the signing systems of deaf people were not conducted until the late 1950s, even though informal studies of Amerindian sign languages were first made in the 19th century and continue to this day. In the late 1950s, William Stokoe (1960), a classicist and anthropologist, developed a way of analyzing and coding in writing the signs of American Sign Language (ASL). We describe Stokoe's classification of sign parameters in more detail in chapter 3. For the moment, it is enough to say that any sign can be defined as a combination of three fundamental features: the shape adopted by the signer's hand(s); the location of the sign relative to the signer's body; and the movements involved in the production of the sign.

It should be emphasized that although some of the hand shapes of ASL are superficially similar to the finger spelled letters of the American one-handed sign alphabet, sign language and finger spelling constitute separate systems of communication. Sometimes signs of recent origin incorporate the hand shape of a letter from the finger spelled alphabet, and an ASL user may occasionally resort to spelling out an English word when no suitable sign is available. However, in general the two systems function independently (Wilbur, 1982).[1] Even so, recording sign language discourse is complicated, and the methods are still being developed. As a rule, capital letters are used to signify signs, and subscripts may be added to give supplementary (and usually essential) syntactical information (Klima & Bellugi, 1979; Wilbur, 1979). In this volume, we do not provide a detailed summary of the notation system; instead we will employ the symbols in contexts where their meaning is self-evident.

Figure 2.3 illustrates the nature of sign language and the major aspects of transcribing and analysis. Plate 2.1 reproduces a series of "still" figures that have some approximation to the continuous flow of signs representing the ASL statement: "Remember on Tuesday, the two of us are going to a picnic. If it rains it will be cancelled." The figure also shows (a) the English "glosses" that represent the signs, and (b) the description of the sentence with comments on movement and expression.

Besides illustrating the complexity of the signing system, Fig. 2.3 shows why it was possible for many years for sign language to be perceived as a form of pantomime—an *iconic* method of communication, as it is usually termed. Wilbur (1979) describes some of the problems involved in the translation of ASL:

> The lack of a traditional orthography for sign language has also contributed, because it has led to the use of inadequate glosses (names of signs). Glosses do not indicate crucial information about the way a sign is made; for example, in the sentences "John hit Bill" and "Bill hit John," the verb would be glossed ... as HIT for both sentences, even though in each sentence the verb would start and end at different points. Thus, the gloss obscures information about the formation of the sign that is critical to the understanding of the nature of sign language. The use of glosses allowed only crude analyses of the language, and indeed many people did little more than compare a glossed sentence to an English sentence. This resulted in conclusions that ASL consisted of unordered, mimetic gestures and was incomplete, inferior, situation-bound, and concrete. (p. 3)

This view of sign language as an inherently inadequate communication system has persisted until very recently, although based on little more than prejudice and superficial observation. In chapter 3 we consider the linguistic standing of ASL at greater length. For now, in

---

[1]Hough (1983) points out that finger spelling was developed as a means of secret communication, rather than as an aid for deaf people. For a remarkable instance, see Robert Graves' (1961) reconstruction of Druidic finger spelling and its close relationship with Ogham, the pre-Roman British alphabet. It seems that the Druids kept both finger spelling and orthography secret from the lay population as part of an elaborate cipher and sign language system lacking any modern parallel.

Remember on Tuesday the two of us are going to a picnic. If it rains, it will be cancelled.

PLATE 2.1.   The "still" sections of the verbal message analyzed in Fig. 2.3.

English Translation

Remember on Tuesday the two of us are going to a picnic. If it rains, it will be cancelled.

American Sign Language

REMEMBER   Right "A" hand shape moves to left base thumb. Includes "head movement" forward. Slight questioning expression

REMEMBER (continued)

No sign   on   Next sign (Tuesday) is made in future "time line" to distinguish present or past Tuesdays.

FIG. 2.3   Illustrates sign language using a series of still figures and the various aspects of transcribing sign language.

Source—Debra L. Russell and Instructional Technology Centre, University of Alberta.

TUESDAY   Initialized "T" made in a circular, clockwise motion.

Brief pause   "comma"

(the) TWO   Classifier indicating 2 people

(of us)   moved in direction of the signer and the addressee, thereby indicating the two of us rather than the two of them or one of us and another person.

PICNIC   Local base sign for sandwich varied to give picnic. Eyes wider because this is the focal point of the communication.

Fig. 2.3 (cont.)

merges into

GO

Open '5' classifier hand begins near to upper body.

GO

(continued)

merges into a closed hand
(almost a '0') in neutral space (i.e., space not assigned to the "two of us"); arm fully extended.

Brief pause

"Stop"

Body shifts backwards, slight head tilt to the right

IF

Conditional. Standardized ASL sign for "if." Made near the eye, touching the cheekbone, slight back-and-forth movement, eyebrows raised, quizzical expression.

Fig. 2.3 (cont.)

(it) RAINS Open 5 claw hand modulated to show rain. Movement from the wrist. Maintains quizzical expression as part of pivot.

CANCEL Left base hand, right is a "1" classifier. The sign begins with right hand raised moving toward

CANCEL (continued) and touches the base with one "X" motion across the base.

Pictures are of Debra L. Russell, B.Ed.,
CSC Sign Language Interpreter, University of Alberta

Fig. 2.3 (cont.)

order to understand why manual methods should have remained for so long "in the wilderness" and why things have now dramatically changed, we need to consider the issue from a wider perspective.

A Brief History of Sign Language and Oral Education

Brennan and Hayhurst were not talking about sign language when they said "That our language is called barbarous is but a fantasy, for so is, as every learned man knoweth, every strange language to any other" (Brennan & Hayhurst, 1978, p. 234). They were quoting Sir Thomas More (1477-1535) on the controversy of translating the Bible from Latin into English! The epithets are familiar—"barbarous," "vulgar," "rude," "without logic," and "crude." English was inadequate and inelegant. The problem was that English was a bastardized language developed from Norman French and Anglo Saxon, a vernacular language used by an uneducated, uncultured, and illiterate populace. Therefore, it had no place in "polite" society and its use in Science or the Arts was inconceivable. Until the early 1970s, the prevailing view of the sign languages used by deaf people was similar to that which existed toward English at the time of Sir Thomas More.[2] For example, despite accepting the importance of sign language, Myklebust (1964) could write:

> While the sign language has advantages for some deaf people, it cannot be considered comparable to a verbal symbol system.... Therefore, although speechreading has limitations as compared to auditory language, we must assume it is the most suitable receptive language system when deafness is present. (p. 235)

In contrast, approximately 20 years later, Boothroyd (1982), an audiologist and the product of a rigidly oral regime, declared:

> Sign languages achieve a speed and an efficiency similar to those of spoken language, and since the movements of sign language are fully accessible through vision, totally deaf children should have no difficulty acquiring competence and skills with signs—always assuming they have lots of meaningful interaction with people who use sign language naturally and fluently. (p. 127)

There were two reasons for the shift in position reflected in these two quotations. The first was that sign languages (in particular American Sign Language) were studied and their identity and

---

[2]See Table 2.1 (p. 59) for some of the historical highlights in deaf education and in the social/political development of deaf people.

structure as languages became irrefutable. Second, the sociocultural aspects of the deaf community became better known, better understood, and more widely accepted in the community at large. But why was signing regarded as inferior to lipreading and speech in the first place?

The Origins of American Sign Language

Hough (1983) remarks that, prior to the work of Cardano (and, perhaps, the Spanish monk Ponce de Leon—1520-1584), not only finger spelling but signing was regarded chiefly as a mnemonic device or as a device for secret communication. In 1620, another Spaniard, Juan Pablo Bonet (1570-1629), published a book describing for the first time the modern one-handed finger spelling system. Bonet's system was taken to France in the 18th century by Jacob Pereria (1715-1790), and it was here that Abbé Charles Michel de l'Epée (1712-1789) and Abbé Roch-Ambroise Cucurron Sicard (1742-1822) played a vital role in formalizing the use of sign language in classroom teaching. Abbé de l'Epée combined the existing French Sign Language with an added set of methodical signs (*Les signes methodiques*) to represent grammatical structures that were not used in French Sign Language (see Baker & Cokely, 1980). Interestingly, he predated contemporary arguments about *Manually Coded English* (MCE) by about 200 years. After de l'Epée's death, Sicard continued his work that had been published earlier as a manual of signs and teaching methods (de l'Epée, 1784).

Thomas Hopkins Gallaudet's (1787-1851) work in teaching Alice Cogswell and how Alice's father raised funds for Gallaudet to visit Europe to learn techniques of educating deaf students are also widely reported in the literature of deafness (one of the most succinct accounts is in Baker & Cokely, 1980). Briefly, Gallaudet's approaches to the schools founded by Thomas Braidwood (1715-1806) in Britain were rejected, unless he indentured himself for 3 years. Instead, he proceeded to France, where Sicard allowed him access to his school and the teaching methods he used in instruction. After 3 months he returned to America with Laurent Clerc (1786-1869), a deaf teacher, and in 1817 opened the first public school for the deaf in the United States, The School for Deaf Mutes at Hartford, Connecticut. It used a sign language based on that of de l'Epée, but very quickly it incorporated into this language some of the American signs used prior to 1817.[3] Modern American Sign Language developed from these two

---

[3]The main evidence for concluding that modern American Sign Language is a derivative of two distinct languages rather than just Old French Sign Language is

primary sources.

The Growth of Oralism

During the 19th century, oral techniques using lipreading and speech and any residual hearing became increasingly popular in the education of deaf students, although as a method they dated back to the 14th century or even earlier (see Savage, Evans, & Savage, 1981, for a brief but informative history; and Pritchard, 1963, for a highly detailed account). Despite early experiments, the origins of the present day oral methods are found most clearly in 16th century Spain. The reasons were more economic than altruistic. "Deaf *and dumb*" persons could not legally inherit, so there was considerable motivation for wealthy Spanish families to find teachers who could teach their deaf children to speak. It would seem Pedro de Ponce de Leon is the first recorded oral teacher of such students, and Bender (1981) quotes *Antiquités d'Espagne*'s:

> Peter of Ponce taught deaf mutes to speak with extraordinary perfection. He is the inventor of the art. He has already instructed in this manner, two brothers and a sister of the constable, and is now actually occupied with teaching the son of the Governor of Aragon, deaf-mute from birth like the preceding ones. The most surprising thing in his art is that all his pupils all reason very well. I am keeping one of them don Pedro de Velasco, brother of the constable, a writing in which he tells me that it is to father Ponce that he is indebted for knowing how to talk. (p. 309)

Juan Pablo Bonet was another important Spanish educator—and his book describing his methods, based on those of Ramirez de Carrion, influenced others in the field. Oral teachers also were found in the succeeding generations in Switzerland (Johann Konrad Amman, 1669-1724), England (Henry Baker, 1698-1806, and Thomas Braidwood, 1715-1806), France (Jacob Rodriguez Pereria, 1715-1790), and Germany (Samuel Heinicke, 1729-1804 and Friedrich Moritz Hill, 1805-1874). During this same period the mantle of oral teaching passed from Spain to Germany, and in fact the oral method also was known as the German method. It had two phases in Germany. Heinicke first developed the method, but when asked to resolve the manual/oral controversy, the University of Leipzig and the Zurich Academy pronounced in favor of de l'Epée's manual

---

[3](cont'd) found in the study of cognates, signs in two languages that have a historical affinity. According to Baker and Cokely, only about 60% of ASL signs are related to French Sign Language. Therefore, there must have been other input, a suggestion confirmed by Clerc's own concern that other signs were being incorporated into the language imported from France.

TABLE 2.1

Highlights in the History of Education of Hearing-Impaired
Students

1528	Roelof Huysman (1443-1485) (Germany)
	• Better known as Rudolphus Agricola, a transplanted Dutch educator
	• in a posthumous publication, reports a case of a congenitally deaf man being able to read and write (in *De Inventione Dialectica*)
c. 1530-1576	Girolamo Cardano (1501-1576) (Italy)
	• physician and mathematician discovers Agricola's report and expands on it, advocating the use of visual symbols in education of the deaf in his books, *Paralipomenon* and *Die Vita Propa Liber*
c. 1550	Pedro Ponce de Leon (1520-1584) (Spain)
	• begins teaching a group of deaf children from noble families
	• establishes a school for the deaf at the monastery of San Salvador
1620	Juan Pablo Bonet (1579-1620) (Spain)
	• publishes the first known book on education of the deaf in Madrid titled *Reducción de las Letras y Arte para Enseñar a Hablar los Mudos* (Simplification of the Letters and Method of Teaching Deaf-Mutes to Speak)
1644	Sir Kenelme Digby (England)
	• reports his personal observations of Bonet's methods in Spain and of their success in his book, *Treatise on the Nature of Bodies*, influencing similar developments in England
1648	John Bulwer (1614-1648) (England)
	• influenced by Digby's reports to take interest in the education of the deaf, publishes his famous *Philocophus, or The Deafe and Dumbe Man's Friend*, which describes how deaf people could be taught to speak through lipreading.

1659-1669   William Holder (1616-1698) and John Wallis (1616-1703)
                 (England)

                 • both claim to be the first successful teacher of the deaf
                   in England (Holder begins in 1659 but presents results in
                   1666, whereas Wallis presents in 1660 and 1662
                   respectively)

                 • bitter rivals, carry on a long-running feud that helps to
                   focus attention on the education of the deaf in Britain

1680   George Dalgarno (1628-1687) (England)

                 • Scots educator in Oxford publishes *Didascalopcophus*, or
                   The Deaf and Dumb Man's Tutor

                 • advocates the use of a two-handed manual alphabet in
                   teaching language to deaf children, a forerunner of the
                   British manual alphabet and precursor of Bell's "lettered
                   glove"

1692   Johann Konrad Amman (1669-1724) (Netherlands)

                 • transplanted Swiss physician develops and publishes
                   methods for teaching speech and lipreading to the deaf
                   child in his *Surdus Loquens* (The Speaking Deaf) in
                   Amsterdam

                 • father of pure oralism

1720   Henry Baker (1698-1774) (England)

                 • said to operate the first educational program for the deaf
                   in England, teaching speech and lipreading to deaf
                   children selected on basis of ability to benefit from his
                   teaching

1734-1780   Jacobo Rodriguez Pereria (1715-1780) (France)

                 • "The First Teacher of the Deaf and Dumb in France,"
                   according to his biographer

                 • uses a one-handed manual alphabet that represented
                   phonic qualities

1754   Samuel Heinicke (1727-1790) (Germany)

      •   father of German oralism

      •   gains an international reputation for the development of
         the oral method of teaching deaf children

      •   establishes first known oral school for the deaf in the
         world in Saxony (Leipzig, 1778)

      •   aims to help the deaf participate in the social and
         professional life of the whole community

      •   demands equal schooling for deaf pupils

1760   Charles Michel Abbé de l'Epée (1712-1789) (France)

      •   establishes world's first public school for the deaf
         (Institution Nationale des Sourds-Muets) in Paris

      •   first to be open with teaching methods and to train
         teachers of the deaf without any conditions

      •   advocates the manual method as the primary language of
         instruction, showing that education was possible without
         speech

1760   Thomas Braidwood (1715-1806) (Scotland)

      •   begins first school for the deaf in Great Britain in his
         mathematics school in Edinburgh, gradually replacing it

      •   establishes a dynasty in oral education with schools in
         Edinburgh, London, and Birmingham

1779   Abbé Stork (Austria)

      •   opens a state school for the deaf in Vienna at Emperor
         Joseph's request

      •   a student of the Abbé de l'Epée

1783   Francis Green (1742-1809) (United States)

      •   an American father of a deaf son enrolled in the
         Braidwood school in London, publishes *Vox Oculis*
         Subjecta (The Voice Made Subject to the Eyes) in
         London, the first detailed account of the Braidwood
         methods

      •   the first to actively advocate the establishment of a
         school for the deaf in the United States

1790   Roch Ambroise Abbé Sicard (1742-1822) (France)

                        • succeeds Abbé de l'Epée

                        • is rescued from death at the hands of a crazed mob
                          during the French Revolution on the strength of his
                          reputation as an educator of the deaf

                        • publishes *Théorie des Signes*, a comprehensive dictionary
                          of signs used by the deaf (1818)

1810   John Stanford (United States)

                        • first to begin instruction of deaf children in the United
                          States (New York)

                        • eventually establishes the New York Institution for the
                          Instruction of the Deaf and Dumb (1818)

1812-1817   John Braidwood (?-1819) (United States)

                        • grandson of Thomas Braidwood and former headmaster
                          of the Edinburgh School, migrates to the United States
                          and opens a private school for deaf children at request
                          of Thomas Bolling in Virginia

                        • unsuccessful due to his abrasive personality

1815-1816   Thomas Hopkins Gallaudet (1787-1851) (United States)

                        • with the support of a group of parents of deaf children,
                          travels to Europe to train as a teacher of deaf

                        • the Braidwoods refuse to divulge their methods

                        • goes to Paris where he is welcomed by Abbé Sicard who
                          impresses upon him the superiority of sign language and
                          trains him in the educational methods used in the Paris
                          school

1816   Laurent Clerc (1786-1869) (United States)

                        • former deaf student of the Abbé Sicard and teacher at
                          the Paris school, arrives in the United States with
                          Gallaudet to begin teaching the deaf

1817   The first permanent school for the deaf in the United States,
                        the American Asylum for the Deaf and Dumb (now the
                        American School for the Deaf), opens its doors in Hartford,
                        Connecticut on April 15 with Thomas Gallaudet as its
                        headmaster and Laurent Clerc as the teacher

1821	Johann Baptist Graser (1766-1841) (Germany)

- opens an experimental school in Bayreuth which became the forerunner of modern mainstreaming methods for deaf students (it proved to be a failure)

- revives the oral tradition begun by Heinicke in Germany

1830	Friedrich Moritz Hill (1805-1874) (Germany)

- most influential European educator of the deaf in 19th century throughout Europe, begins his career as a disciple of Graser

- trains many teachers of the deaf in the pure oral tradition

1831	Ronald McDonald (Canada)

- a lawyer sent from Lower Canada to Hartford to be trained by Laurent Clerc opens the first school for the deaf in Canada on June 15 in Champlain, Quebec

- school closes after only 5 years due to lack of funds

1843	Horace Mann (1796-1859) and Samuel Gridley Howe (1801-1876) (United States)

- visit European schools for the deaf and return to the United States enthusiastically advocating the use of the oral method in American schools

1847	*The American Annals of the Deaf and Dumb* (now *American Annals of the Deaf*) commences publication in the United States under the auspices of the Convention of American Instructors of the Deaf and Conference of Executives of American Schools for the Deaf

1848	The first permanent school for the deaf in Canada, L'Institution Catholique des Sourds-Muets, opens in Montreal at the direction of the Bishop of Montreal, Msgr. I. Bourget, and is operated by an order of priests, the Community of Clerics of St. Viator

1856	Education of the deaf begins in English Canada with the founding of the Halifax Institution, Nova Scotia by William Gray, a deaf graduate of the Braidwood school in Edinburgh

1857   Edward Miner Gallaudet (1837-1917) (United States)

- is appointed superintendent of the Columbia Institute for
  the Deaf, Dumb, and Blind founded by Amos Kendal in
  Washington, DC

- son of Thomas Hopkins Gallaudet

- begins life's work in education of the deaf at the
  Columbia Institute

- strong advocate of development of oral skills in deaf
  students

1864   Abraham Lincoln signs into law an act empowering the
                        Columbia Institute to confer college degrees, becoming
                        world's first (and for many years only) college for the deaf—
                        later renamed as Gallaudet College

1864   Gardiner Greene Hubbard (1822-1897) (United States)

- father of Mabel Hubbard, a deaf girl who later marries
  Alexander Graham Bell

- begins agitating with the State of Massachusetts for the
  establishment of an oral school for the deaf

- successful after 3 years of lobbying

1867   The Massachusetts State Legislature passes an act enabling the
                        establishment of the Clarke School for the Deaf in
                        Northampton, Massachusetts, after John Clarke, a wealthy
                        Northampton philanthropist provides a $50,000 gift to help
                        establish it

1869   The first oral day school for the deaf, the Boston School for
                        Deaf-Mutes (later renamed the Horace Mann School), opens
                        in Boston, Massachusetts

1872   Alexander Graham Bell (1847-1922) (United States)

- opens an oral training school for teachers of the deaf in
  Boston

- uses the Visible Speech Symbols developed by his father,
  Alexander Melville Bell, in 1864, consisting of
  alphabetical symbols representing the position of vocal
  organs for each speech sound

1880   A national gathering of deaf adults organizes the National
                        Association of the Deaf (NAD) in Cincinnati, Ohio with
                        education of the deaf as its chief concern

1880   The International Convention of Educators of the Deaf,
                meeting in Milan, Italy, passes a resolution recommending the
                abolition of the manual method in favor of the oral method,
                triggering a world-wide conversion to oralism

1880   The French Government awards the Volta Prize, a prestigious
                French scientific award, to Alexander Graham Bell in
                recognition of his gift to mankind—the telephone (this
                award, named after Alessandro Volta, the Italian physicist, is
                awarded infrequently only after an extraordinary invention or
                discovery)

1887   Using his private funds, Bell founds the Volta Bureau in
                Washington, DC for the increase and diffusion of knowledge
                in the area of deafness

1890   Bell endows the American Association to Promote the
                Teaching of Speech to the Deaf (later renamed the
                Alexander Graham Bell Association for the Deaf) with its
                headquarters at the Volta Bureau

1891   Edward Miner Gallaudet establishes a teacher training
                program with an emphasis on the combined method
                (articulation with signing) at Galaudet College, despite Bell's
                strenuous opposition which was to pave the way to an
                irreconcilable schism between the oral and manual factions in
                North America

1902   Martha Brun establishes a school in Massachusetts to teach
                lipreading using the Muller-Walle method developed in
                Germany

1903   Edward B. Nitchie teaches deaf children in New York City,
                later shifting his focus to teaching lipreading to adults and
                creates the New York League for the Hard of Hearing

1929   Cora and Rose Kinzie publish in the United States the first
                of a series of books which provide material for teaching
                lipreading to adults and children

1940   The Canadian Association of the Deaf (C.A.D.) is founded
                by David Peikoff who then raises a $50,000 fund,
                administered by C.A.D. to enable deaf Canadian students to
                obtain higher education

1942   Marie K. Mason explores the use of film in teaching
                lipreading and writes an extensive treatise. *A
                Cinematographic Technique for Testing More Objectively the
                Visual Speech Comprehension of Young Deaf and Hard of
                Hearing Children* as a doctoral dissertation at Ohio State
                University

1944	Anna M. Bugner publishes in Illinois *Speech-Reading—Jena Method* that advocates use of kinesthetic as well as visual cues
1962	David Anthony introduces in the United States "Seeing Essential English," a manually coded English sign system
1965	The "Babbidge Report," a study of education of the deaf in the United States commissioned by the federal government, is released, exposing the "unsatisfactory state of education of the deaf" in the United States and making far-reaching recommendations to improve the situation
1967	Dr. Orrin Cornett introduces Cued Speech, a visible phonetic form of speech based on lip movements supplemented by hand movements, at Gallaudet College
1967	A deaf teacher at the Indiana School for the Deaf, Roy K. Holcomb, introduces concept of "Total Communication," a communication philosophy incorporating aural-oral methods with manual communication in a single package
1975	The United States Congress passes Public Law 94-142, "The Education of All Handicapped Children" Act, giving a great impetus to the mainstreaming of hearing impaired children into regular schools

methods rather than those of Heinicke. Hill later resurrected oral teaching but moved toward the less structured *Mother Method* favored by Pestalozzi. The Mother Method focused on language development through use rather than the teaching of grammar. Hill enjoyed more continuing success than Heinicke, and Germany became a major influence in the development of oral teaching methods in other countries. In particular, German educators were very influential at the Milan Congress (p. 68).

A less frequently reported aspect of the American history of deaf education concerns Francis Green (died 1809) and John Braidwood (died 1819). Green, with his son Charles, visited Thomas Braidwood in Edinburgh. His son was admitted to the school and Green spent some time there. As a result, Green became as lyrical in his praises of the school as Samuel Johnson, who had much to do with popularizing Braidwood as a teacher. On his return to the United States, Green tried to persuade the authorities to establish a school using Braidwood's oral methods, which he regarded as superior to the sign language of de l'Epée. He even conducted the first survey of deaf people in the United States (see Deland, 1931, cited by Moores, 1982), and shortly after Green's death in 1809, John Braidwood, one of the grandsons of Thomas, tried to establish a school in Baltimore. As a result of the political climate during the Anglo-American War of 1812, and because of John Braidwood's abrasive personality, the school soon closed (Pritchard, 1963).

The oral method again crossed the Atlantic to North America in 1843. Horace Mann (1796-1859) and Samuel Gridley Howe (1801-1876) visited European Schools. They were as impressed as a compatriot, John Clarke (1789-1869), had been by the German schools using oral teaching techniques. When they returned to the United States, their early attempts to found a public oral school in Massachusetts were defeated, but the success of Harriet Rogers in instructing deaf students orally and a gift from Clarke eventually led to two bills in the state legislature. The first established the Clarke Institution for Deaf Mutes at Northampton, Massachusetts; the second provided public funds for the education of deaf students aged 5 to 10 years, with some possibility for extending this period (Waite, 1967, p. 121). In this same period, the Institution for the Improved Instruction of Deaf Mutes (now the Lexington School for the Deaf) opened in New York City and the Horace Mann School, the first oral day school for deaf students, opened in Boston. In the 1930s, Mildred Groht, who was associated with the Lexington School, published her book, *Natural Language for Deaf Children*, and this book has had a particular influence on oral approaches in North America into the 1960s and even the 1970s. It advocated the same principles as those put forward by Hill in Germany 100 years earlier, and subsequently the mantle for this approach has fallen on van Uden in Holland with his advocacy of the Maternal Reflective Method.

Possibly the most instrumental figure in the oral education of deaf students is Alexander Graham Bell (1847-1922). He began lecturing on speech at Boston University shortly after his arrival in Canada from London, England, and in 1872 he opened his School for Vocal Physiology in Boston. He used the Visible Speech Symbols developed by his father, whereby alphabetical characters showed the position of the vocal organs for each speech sound. In 1877 he married Mabel Hubbard,[4] his young deaf student. Later, Mabel's father and George Sanders helped to finance Bell's experiments on

---

[4]It is evident that Bell's intense commitment to the oral method reflected his emotional involvement with this one deaf person who seemed to demonstrate its success. As we shall see, some deaf students do make impressive progress in oral regimes—unfortunately, the majority do not. Had Mabel been more typical in this respect, Bell's attitude, and the subsequent history of deaf education in the United States, might have been strikingly different.

the harmonic telegraph, a forerunner of the telephone. In 1880 the French Government awarded the inventor the Volta Prize of 50,000 francs in recognition of his scientific marvel, the telephone, and Bell used the money to establish the Volta Laboratory in Washington, DC, where scientific experiments could be undertaken.

In 1887, following the sale of his patent on the flat phonograph record, he founded the Volta Bureau "for the increase and diffusion of knowledge related to the deaf." Three years later Bell and other teachers of the deaf founded the Alexander Graham Bell Association for the Deaf, an organization dedicated to the oral method. The purpose of the organization was "to promote the teaching of speech and lipreading to the deaf" (A.G. Bell Association, 1970, pp. 148-149). The headquarters for the Volta Bureau and the A.G. Bell Association is in Washington, DC, and over the years it has grown in stature and importance. The International Parents' Organization was founded in 1958 as an offspring of the A.G. Bell Association. Its aim is to advocate better educational and vocational opportunities for deaf children. The Oral Deaf Adults' Section of the Association was formed in 1964 by its oral deaf members. Their aim was to help deaf young people and their families. The last member of this constellation was the American Organization of the Hearing Impaired, founded in 1968. Scholarships and numerous publications are also sponsored by the Alexander Graham Bell Association.

In Europe, the debate between the proponents of oral education and those of manual methods was seemingly resolved at the International Congress on the Deaf and Dumb held at Milan in Italy in 1880. The Congress was at the time and subsequently described as "international." In fact, the problems of distance were such that North American educators, particularly those using manual methods of communication, were poorly represented. European advocates of oral education dominated the proceedings and therefore, not surprisingly, the Conference resolved:

> This Congress considering the incontestable superiority of speech over signs in restoring the deaf-mute to society, and in giving him a more perfect knowledge of the language, declares that the oral method ought to be preferred to that of signs for the education and instruction of the deaf and dumb ... and considering that the simultaneous use of speech and signs has the disadvantage of injuring speech, lipreading, and precision of ideas, declares that the pure oral method ought to be preferred ... and considering that a great number of the deaf and dumb are not receiving the benefit of instruction recommends that Governments should take the necessary steps that all the deaf and dumb may be educated. (Pritchard, 1963, p. 92)

It ended with the cry "Vive la parole," and the dominance of oralism in the education of deaf children in Europe and her colonies was established for almost a century.

In North America the conflict between the oral approaches to educating deaf students and those advocating the use of manual communication continued unabated after the Milan Conference. The conflict was reflected in the dual achievements of Alexander Graham Bell and Edward Miner Gallaudet (1837-1917), although, in fact, Bell was awarded an honorary degree by Gallaudet College in 1880 (see Boatner, 1959). That he accepted the degree is somewhat surprising, given his antagonism toward the formation of what we would now call "a deaf subculture." Nevertheless, whatever Bell's views and despite his firm opposition, the development of American Sign Language as a modern language owes much to the existence of Gallaudet College, founded in 1864 as a liberal arts institution for deaf students, named in honor of Thomas Hopkins Gallaudet and with his son, Edward Miner Gallaudet, as its first president.

The survival after the Milan Conference of formal sign language in the United States can be contrasted with the situation in Great Britain and elsewhere. In America could be found schools using the combined method, deaf people continued to teach deaf children, and a flourishing deaf culture evolved outside the paternalistic and religiously dominated welfare system that existed in Great Britain and Europe.[5] Indeed, in Great Britain it was not until the early 1960s that social work and rehabilitation studies developed as a separate profession from missionary work in the field of deafness. Prior to that time, the large majority of social services had their origins in the desire to "convert" the deaf or, at least, make it possible for them to have access to religious teachings. In a sense, Bell was more honest than many of his contemporaries—he, at least, had no qualms about identifying "a deaf variety of the human race"!

Bell's persuasive influence, his financial support for oralism, and his bitter opposition to Gallaudet permeated education of the deaf for a hundred years or more, and undoubtedly delayed for several decades some of the significant changes that were to take place in more recent years. A similar role was played in Britain by the late

---

[5]It is hard to judge if the Institutes or Missions for the Deaf in Great Britain helped or hindered deaf people. They certainly provided support and vehicles for social interaction, but their paternalistic approaches also undoubtedly hindered the development of a flourishing independent and indigenous deaf culture. However, it is unlikely that in their absence a British institution similar to Gallaudet would have developed. Therefore, they did provide a mechanism for the retention of some kind of formal sign language (see p. 71).

Sir Alexander Ewing, who with Irene Goldsack, later his wife, established at the University of Manchester in 1919, the first and for many years the only, university-based, full-time program for training teachers of deaf students in Great Britain. The rigidly oral approach of this institution continues and despite the existence of more recently established training programs in other universities, the use of sign language in the education of deaf students in England and Wales is very much a minority movement.[6] Scotland and Ireland are somewhat different and are rather more pragmatic in their educational approaches.

British Sign Language

After the Milan Conference, there was vigorous opposition to the use of any sign language in schools for deaf students in Great Britain. Nevertheless, and despite the influence of the Ewings, British Sign Language (BSL) continued to evolve, but mainly outside the classroom. The tradition was an old one, and in fact the first schools for deaf students in Britain were oral schools founded by members of the Braidwood dynasty. Interestingly, the only short break with the oral tradition first came in one of Braidwood's own schools. Another grandson of Braidwood, also called Thomas, was the principal of the General Institution for the Instruction of Deaf and Dumb in Birmingham (Pritchard, 1963, p. 27). On his death in 1825, the new principal, Louis du Paget, introduced de l'Epée's methods, and for the next 50 years manual methods of instruction dominated. It was during this time that the four schools were founded that retained some commitment to the use of sign language in the English educational system—Manchester, Liverpool, Exeter, and Doncaster. Doncaster, in particular, stood out against limiting the education of deaf students to oral only methods, until policy changes in the 1970s vindicated its position and led to some slight shifts in attitudes. However, as Ladd and Edwards (1982) point out, the system of signs in use in these schools was a form of Pidgin Sign English, a trend continued by the more recent development of Signed Systematic English and the Paget-Gorman Sign System, systems that are now advocated for use with some deaf students in Great Britain.

---

[6]In describing the overall situation, the influence of schools such as Doncaster and, more recently, Newcastle should not be forgotten. As we see later, they have continuously advocated the use of some form of manual coding system to supplement or replace visual coding systems based on lipreading.

Any retention of British Sign Language as a formal language was mainly achieved by the Missions for the Adult Deaf, and, at least at the time they were founded in the 19th century, British Sign Language had probably enough "similarity between the different dialects ... for them to achieve mutual intelligibility" (Ladd & Edwards, 1982, p. 111). Unfortunately, documentation and research into the historical antecedents of sign languages in Britain is less readily available than it is in the United States, so what happened to the language over the years is less clear. Nevertheless, even today there is a recognized, mutually intelligible, adult sign language, British Sign Language. It is equivalent to American Sign Language, and recent research into its grammar is summarized in chapter 8. However, the oral dominance of the British schools denies most British deaf students the opportunity to learn this language until late adolescence or adult life. Table 2.2 (reproduced from Ladd & Edwards, 1982, p. 112) shows the present continuum of sign languages in Britain, and what is referred to as "broad BSL" is used and retained only in clubs for deaf people. The lack of a Gallaudet College to act as a model and to develop BSL has had an obvious impact on its level of development and semantic and syntactical complexity. But perhaps of even greater significance is the attitude that English is a superior language, an attitude that has affected both the British and the American deaf communities.

The Great Controversy

From the previous discussion, it should already be obvious that the education of deaf children has always generated controversy. Until very recently, professionals involved in teaching, counseling, and social work were polarized between two irreconcilable and mutually hostile philosophies. Supporters of what we now term *total communication* contended that deaf children must have access to any and all channels of communication, including manual and oral methods. The oralists argued that only residual hearing and/or lipreading and speech should be employed in communicating with deaf children and adults (although some accepted the use of various finger spelling systems). In the main, present day supporters of oralism, the neo-oralists, draw their support from some teachers of the deaf and some of the major training establishments for these teachers. Social workers, linguists, psychologists, some teachers, and deaf people themselves (when anyone bothers to consult them) tend to favor total communication methods. Over the years, the debate

TABLE 2.2

The Continuum of British Sign Languages

| "Broad" BSL used in deaf clubs. | → | BSL with some fingerspelling used by older deaf people and those educated in schools in Scotland and NE England where attitudes toward signing have been more favorable. | → | PSE with some BSL syntax used by educated or professional people to each other. Also used by some conference interpreters and social workers. | → | PSE with increasing reliance on lip patterns used by deaf teenagers from oralist day schools to each other and up the scale, and by most conference interpreters. |

Source—P. Ladd and V.K. Edwards, 1982, British Sign Language and West Indian Creole, *Sign language studies, 35*, p. 112. Reproduced with permission.

has taken on the character, almost, of a religious schism.[7]

We can only speculate as to why oralism emerged in the 19th century and so rapidly came to dominate the thinking of educationalists. One factor is the tendency for Western culture, after the Renaissance, to become increasingly verbal. In the past, a largely illiterate population was more willing than we are today to accept and employ symbolic methods of communication—*semiotic systems* in today's terminology—as exemplified by heraldry (Rothery, 1985), Gothic architecture (Bazin, 1962; Fulcanelli, 1971; Houvet, 1968), and imported Eastern concepts of mime and dance such as the Harlequin, the Morris Men, and the Jesters. It is probably no accident that the vigorous growth of the oral method in the last century coincided with the first serious attempts by the developed countries to institute public systems of education and eradicate illiteracy. Anyone promoting alternative methods of communication was no doubt perceived to be working against this initiative. Even proponents of Braille—a cipher based on spoken language—had to struggle to gain acceptance for their system. It is easy to see that signed languages would attract an even more hostile reception.

Oralism also seems to embody many of the characteristics of iconoclastic movements throughout history—dogmatism; authoritarian tendencies; support for verbal materials and strong opposition to the use of images and symbols; the desire to suppress alternative viewpoints; and the use of propaganda in place of rational discussion. There is, indeed, a quasi-religious facet to oralism that is prone to surface occasionally; see, for example, an extraordinary article by Edward Nitchie, then Principal of the New York School for the Hard-of-Hearing, entitled "The spiritual side of lip-reading" (Nitchie, 1910).

Whatever their reasons, proponents of oralism often have gone to astonishing lengths to impose their views on deaf children and their parents. In their publications, the oral method is usually presented as the only acceptable way of educating deaf students; indeed, even the very existence of sign language is frequently ignored. As Mindel and Vernon (1971) remark, "the literature is of little help in understanding why oralism's adherents defend it so evangelically. It often reads more like propaganda and patent-medicine testimonials

---

[7]A survey of 52 deaf persons conducted on behalf of the Lewis Committee in the U.K. found that of 31 orally educated respondents, 10 approved and 21 disapproved of their method of instruction; of 21 educated using combined methods, 19 approved and only 2 disapproved (because they had not used finger spelling). Despite an obviously clear expression of opinion, the report comments: "we stress the need to interpret the results with caution" (Lewis, 1968, p. 82).

than scientific writing" (p. 70). As a result, in Massachusetts for example, the Legislature—like those of other American States—passed a law *forbidding deaf children to use sign language in school*.[8] In England, Sir Alexander Ewing declared before a Government Committee that he would regard the use of manual methods strictly as a last resort for students failing to achieve *any score* in tests of English (Lewis, 1968, para. 181, italics added).

In such a climate, it is scarcely surprising that the educational attainments of hearing-impaired children have suffered (see chapters 4 and 5), and doubts have begun to arise about the effectiveness of the oral method. (See, e.g., Kohl, 1966; Sharoff, 1959/60; and the powerful critique by Brennan, 1975.) As a result, in the early 1970s an increasing number of American schools for the deaf and schools for the deaf in other countries began to adopt total communication as the primary method of instruction. In England, the Lewis committee also cautiously supported experimental investigations of the use of manual methods of communication in such schools, and, at the same time, evidence began to accumulate that the early use of sign language by deaf children contributes to improved linguistic, social, and even oral skills. Even if it does not, it certainly does not seem to detract from the development of these skills (chapter 5). Finally, researchers have begun to study the structure of ASL and, in America at least, manual methods of communication generally have ceased to be regarded as unnatural or undesirable.

The history of deafness is one of denial—denial that the experiences of deaf children, students, and adults are uniquely different from those of hearing people. Such denial led to the extremes of oral education advocated by Alexander Graham Bell and his successors. Strangely, in an attempt to destroy deaf culture, the denial of the special nature of deafness probably strengthened it. Because deaf people were discriminated against socially, like the Scots they clung all the more tenaciously to their institutions, language, and culture. Finally, in the 1970s, for reasons we have already discussed, the most obvious aspect of deaf culture, its language, became not only visible, but in some senses desirable. Exposure to sign language in classrooms, on television, in society at large, and even at presidential inaugurations, led to greater appreciation of its beauty and effectiveness as a vehicle of communication and as an art form.

---

[8]It is interesting to speculate how such a law would be enforced, because deaf children left to their own devices will always develop a form of sign language. Were they to be punished by law for doing so?

Unfortunately, despite some changes for the better, the oral versus total communication controversy still rages, with a continuing advocacy by some groups of only oral teaching methods in schools for deaf students and elsewhere. This advocacy is unfortunate, because it owes much to a dedicated and sincere desire to help deaf children. Expressed in a more realistic and pragmatic manner, it would win the support of deaf people and the deaf community. It is not the need for some oral communication that is in dispute: it is the espousal of this method of communication to the exclusion of all others, particularly American Sign Language. When the advocates of oralism attack the use of sign language, they attack not only a communication method, but the whole social and cultural fabric of deafness. Not surprisingly, deaf people object and in turn advocate their right to support and maintain their own institutions.

Another unfortunate consequence of the controversy should be emphasized. In devoting so much time and effort to the war of words with their rivals, the advocates of oral and total methods of communication have had few opportunities and little inclination to do basic research. Often, in this book, we comment on the need for further studies, frequently in areas where specialists in the field of deafness would have had no difficulty in resolving the fundamental issues had they not been distracted by the "political" debate. For example, in focusing on communication method, educationalists have failed to identify other aspects of the teaching situation that may play just as great a part in promoting cognitive and social development. Seventy years ago, in a short but highly perceptive paper, Hill (1911) suggested that it would be best to drop the oral-manual controversy and seek instead "to find and apply the best methods that can be devised" whatever the medium. Yet, today we have scarcely begun to follow up on Hill's proposal, even though there are strong indications that factors other than mode of communication make a significant impact on the educational progress of deaf children (see, e.g., Breslaw, Griffiths, Wood, & Howarth, 1981; Howarth, Wood, Griffiths, & Howarth, 1981; Ivimey, 1977c; Reynolds, 1976; Thompson, 1927; Wood, 1980).

Some Aspects of the Deaf Culture

A culture has basically four subsystems (Williams, 1972): social relations, language, technology, and ideology. The culture of deafness is technically defined as a subculture. It does not, for example, have its own government or clothing. Nevertheless, it does have distinct organizations, attitudes, values, and social structures. It is beyond the scope of this book to describe all aspects of this culture and Nash and Nash (1981) have already started to do so. Nevertheless, it is worthwhile focusing briefly on two areas—art forms and language—so that we can illustrate its diversity and richness.[9]

The development of deaf artists and of a deaf art forms are quite distinct, and should not be confused. Two of the more famous early deaf artists are John Brewster, Jr. (1766-1854), the Maine painter, and Donald Tilden (1860-1935), the Californian sculptor. These artists are an important aspect of the deaf culture—they are two of its folk heroes. Nevertheless, their art form is not a deaf art form—it is stylistically similar to that of other artists of their time. Brewster is "primitive"—lacking in form and perspective (see Plate 2.2); Tilden is representational but lacking in imaginative stimulus. Along with people such as the deaf chess players described by Font and Ladner (1979), they are important because they provide appropriate role models for deaf students. Deaf students can aspire to emulate them and their ability to mainstream, but their art form often still reflects the desire to conform and belong to hearing society.

The relatively recent public emergence of a truly deaf art form in language, theater, and poetry is of greater significance in understanding the experience of deaf people than deaf artists painting or sculpting works that reflect experience that both hearing and deaf people can understand. With some notable exceptions, such as the National Theater of the Deaf in the United States, much of the art is of poor quality, but its importance is in its existence. Creativity often generates junk, but in this case it also generates a public record of the deaf experience. Out of this experience grows a sense of belonging and of being—the sense of deaf pride that we referred to earlier. A good example is the play "Sign Me Alice" by Gil Eastman (1974, see p. 321)—on the surface it is a take-off of "Pygmalion." However, the two share a deeper underlying structure. What is common are the similar experiences—those of Shaw's

---

[9]Interestingly, when we first started work in the area of deafness, we thought and wrote of the "deaf subculture" as if it was subservient to a hearing culture. We now feel to do so is wrong and patronizing. The culture of deafness is far too rich to be thought of in this way. It has language, literature, poetry, and art forms as rich as those found in most hearing cultures. It is definitely not subservient to the hearing culture. Rather it is a separate culture with equal right to stand alongside those of the hearing majority, but sharing some aspects in common. As is so often the case in social science our jargon reflects our intrinsic value judgments and prejudices. Is the hearing culture a subculture of deafness when studied by the deaf sociologist? Indeed, is there such a thing as the hearing culture?

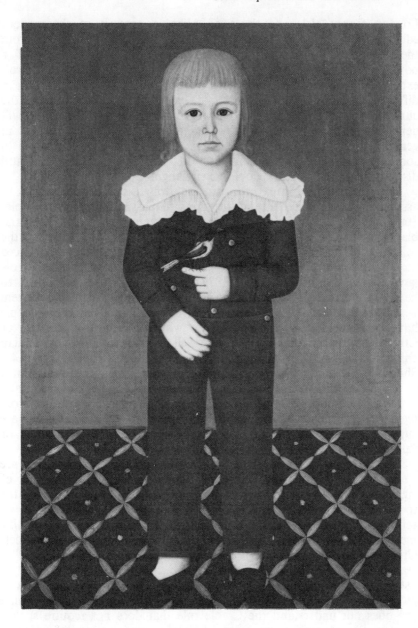

PLATE 2.2.   Boy with a Finch by John Brewster, Jr. (1766-1854).

Reproduced by kind permission of Abbey Aldrich Rockefeller Folk Art Center, Williamsburg, Virginia, USA.

London flower girl, and those of Alice, a product of the modern educational system for deaf students. Both become alienated from their language and cultural origins because of the influence of a powerful teacher. Both subsequently rediscover themselves. Alice's experience will become different not because she is placed in a different school, but because of meaningful changes in the curriculum and the educational process. These changes, in turn, will depend on changes in our attitudes toward handicapped people in general, and deaf people in particular; attitudes that have changed in some major ways over the last 20 years, but that also still discriminate against deaf people, their language, and their culture.

An interesting comparison can be drawn between attempts to assimilate deaf students and attempts to assimilate black people. Starting with Victorian missionaries who covered both piano legs and black bodies, Western society has constantly felt threatened by the existence of different cultures. This feeling is most clearly evidenced in the attempt to destroy language. Writing of West Indian Creole language in Britain, Edwards (1979) says: "It is rare for Creole to be looked on as a perfectly logical and adequate linguistic system which is the vehicle of a very lively culture. And very few people have considered the harmful effect which constant correcting of Creole features might have on the self-confidence of West Indian children and on their motivation to learn standard English" (p. 14). She also points out that generations of teachers have tried and failed to eliminate the semantics and syntax of the Creole language, and explores the subtle ways in which prejudices are handed down from teacher to teacher, so reinforcing the very behavior they are supposed to prevent (see pp. 265 to 266 for a fuller discussion of this problem).

The parallels between educating West Indian and deaf students are clear, and have much to do with the acceptance and knowledge of sign languages as languages, and the concept of raising deaf children to be bilingual (Kannapell, 1974, 1979, and chapter 5). Again we refer to Edwards' discussion of Creole. She cites ad hoc teaching methods in which the teacher arbitrarily and inconsistently corrects Creole from an English framework. She gives an example of a teacher correcting "smell" to "smells," but not correcting "stand" to "stands," or, indeed, a later "smell" to "smells." The teacher fails to enunciate the English rule requiring an -s marker, probably because she does not understand the Creole rule that does not require such a marker. She also gives examples where the hypercorrected form of a word has become the norm (e.g., *teeth, peas, shoes*—which no longer exist in Creole in the singular). She concludes that "explanations should be postponed until the child's literacy is firmly founded on his own speech patterns" (p. 68).

Whatever the arguments about the place of sign language in the education of deaf children, the issues in the education of West Indian children are fairly clear. Therefore, following similar arguments, we can state that at a very minimum teachers of deaf children must understand and be expressively fluent in both sign language and the syntax of spoken English. If they are not, then they will not be able to build the bridge between the two languages. Teachers of French to English speaking students are generally thought to be more proficient if they are fluent in both languages. However, we do not make the same requirement of teachers of deaf students.

In fact, it seems to us that more should be demanded of hearing and deaf teachers of deaf students than mere proficiency in two languages. A knowledge of the culture of deafness is vital so deaf students can know and understand that culture and so they can be provided with appropriate role models to facilitate the development of an adequate self-image. To identify these needs merely states that teachers should be literate and culturally sensitive individuals—a requirement that we fully accept for teachers of hearing individuals, but deny for teachers of deaf students in respect of deafness. That we do so perhaps reflects more on cultural influences in hearing society than in deaf society, and we look at this problem in more detail in the next sections of this chapter and in chapter 5.

The Middle-Class Influence

There is general agreement among educational theorists that mainstream education is dominated by middle-class values, and has as a primary objective the acculturation of the student to these values. As a result, a large number of minority groups, and indeed a large number of students, have been "born to fail" (see Wedge & Prosser, 1973). In the study bearing that title, one in 16 of the school population of Great Britain were found to be seriously educationally disadvantaged, but there are widespread regional disparities. Such disparities frequently reflect the presence or otherwise of minority subcultures. The data for the United States and Canada are similar (see Coleman et al., 1966), and one of the important areas in which these disadvantaged groups differ is language: language experience and language use.

In looking at this problem, Basil Bernstein (1972), a British sociologist, suggested a fundamental distinction between formal, precise language use (*elaborated code*) and informal, situation-bound speech (*restricted code*). Bernstein's argument was that whereas middle-class people have access to both codes and can choose which to use, many working-class children and adults are unable to employ elaborated codes. His position was unfortunate, for it was interpreted as meaning that working-class language was inferior to middle-class language. Subsequent attempts to eradicate this belief from professional practice have been largely unsuccessful, despite soundly based research and carefully argued countertheories, such as that of Labov (1976). Yussen and Santrock (1978) succinctly summarize the problem in the context of black English:

> There are also lively debates about whether black English is simply different from standard English or whether it is deficient in some respects (Engelmann, 1970; Williams, 1970). A complicating factor is that all children actually have different language codes and can switch from one to another (e.g., Gay & Tweney, 1976). Many teachers accept the point of view that the speech is deficient, because black ghetto children do poorly on standardized tests of language comprehension and reading. One obvious reason for poor performance is that the tests are presented in standard English. However, there is another reason of equal importance. Children's language performance often is evaluated in the context of unnatural questioning and probing by teachers; teachers unknowingly set up barriers to good performance by the manner in which they ask questions. This is true both in language instruction and in formal testing for language achievement. (p. 284)

Labov (e.g., 1970, 1976), in particular, has explored the significance of the distinction between working-class and middle-class language. He argues that middle-class values are supportive of the elaborated code, which also is seen to be closely associated with success in employment or in other social settings. In contrast, working-class communication favors direct speech with a focus on clarity of communication. Nash and Nash (1981) have developed this thesis in the context of deafness in two ways. First, they have looked at deaf sign language, and second, they have looked at what they regard as the middle-class dominance of oral approaches to teaching deaf students.

Sign Language and Social Class

When discussing sign language, Nash and Nash (1981) assert that "the middle class acts on the presumption that there is a standard form of English" (p. 33). They also relate this to the elaborated and restricted codes of Bernstein and to the facility with which code switching is possible for sophisticated, verbally proficient, middle-class speakers. Restricted codes operate through a referential system, and such codes and systems are characteristic of some of the closely knit communities that are relatively isolated from the mainstream. Nash and Nash correctly identify American Sign Language as a "non-standard linguistic form within the American speech community." It is nonstandard because it is an alien language form, and because it is a Creole. It is important to note that it is not non-standard because it is a visual language, any more than printed English is nonstandard because it uses a visual symbol system.

The position taken by Nash and Nash is rather different from that of many other linguists, particularly Stokoe, Woodward, and Bellugi, who have considered one end of the continuum of American Sign Language as a distinctly separate language, analogous to the languages of the Francophone communities in Canada. Moores (1974, 1982) has argued that their position reflects the fact that they study adult language forms and do not take account of the constraints imposed on the language by the use of visual rather than auditory modalities. Whatever the place of sign language on a theoretical continuum of different languages, there can be no doubt that it is a *working language* (a term that might be preferable to that of working-class language). This gives it certain characteristics that emphasize ease and directness of communication, and that reduce the importance of what we might describe as verbal frills. Unfortunately, these verbal frills have achieved an importance in identifying social class and social status that are out of all proportion to their linguistic significance.

Oral Approaches

The value of speech and lipreading as a method of communication is widely accepted by deaf people. Therefore, it is important in this section and elsewhere to differentiate between oral approaches to deaf education as a philosophy and the use of such approaches to the exclusion of the effective use of sign language systems in classrooms and elsewhere. Conrad (1979) discusses the threat that sign language can present to some hearing people. He refers, for example, to the "signing alternative, which is then usually suggested as a last resort, [and] is also regarded as dangerous, almost hostile; teachers feel superstitiously threatened by its use" (p. 310). He gives a number of quotes that support this hypothesis, a particularly revealing one being from van Uden (1970)—"building up a primitive own world view, different from ours." These fears have not only influenced the education of deaf students, but also other areas of special education. For example, discussing the case of Nadia, a young autistic girl whose extraordinary artistic skills were destroyed by intensive language training, Lyall Watson (1979) remarks:

> Our entire educational effort seems to be dedicated to making others over in our image, turning out carbon copy people who faithfully reproduce all our mistakes. "Better," we seem to be saying, "a poor imitation of ourselves, than something different, something threatening." An eminent child psychologist sums up Nadia's case by concluding that, if the loss of her gift is "the price that must be paid for language ... we must, I think, be prepared to pay that price on Nadia's behalf" ... Must we? I am far from convinced. (pp. 374-375)

Unfortunately, such feelings can easily be exploited by persons with an axe to grind to justify their position or reinforce an alleged need. A disturbing example is a scientifically unacceptable discussion of the work of Conrad in the *Volta Review*, a journal circulated to and read by many parents of hearing-impaired children. In a section titled "Forum," an article by Arnold (1983) is headlined "Does Oralism Cause Atrophy of the Hearing Impaired Child's Brain?" The title of the article is an oversimplification of a complex scientific issue formulated as a tentative hypothesis. However, the important point is not the scientific question, but its editorial presentation in a manner and form which, in our opinion, is intended to play on the understandable fears of parents about the consequences of deafness for their child. The famous "Vive la parole" of the Milan Conference continues with little more scientific basis than it had 100 years ago.

Nash and Nash (1981) bring a note of sense and reality to this discussion by analyzing the motivation of ardent adherents of oral only education (and, indeed, of social intercourse): "Oralism as a formal system emerged to account for the presence of a deaf child in a hearing family in a way that would allow the parents to continue their understanding of parenthood virtually unchanged" (p. 24). At birth or shortly thereafter, a contract is entered into that is supportive of middle class values. "Work hard, your child will become verbally fluent (in speech) and therefore occupationally and socially successful." The contract has an additional advantage for the professional—it shifts ultimate accountability to the parent. If the student is not orally successful, the home environment is the reason. Again Nash and Nash (1981) express it eloquently:

> Thus a circle is established that continually attributes blame for lack of success to the parents, who, regardless of how hard they work, fail to produce a "speaking" person like themselves. In fact, it can even be suggested that the more work done by the parents, the more guilty they feel. Within oralism, of course, the process just described dovetails with some parents' ideas about what might have caused deafness in the first

place; for example, "We did something to cause this condition," or "We must have sinned and are being punished." (pp. 24-25)

The argument comes full circle as is clearly shown in the study of Bernstein and Henderson (1969). When uninformed hearing people were questioned about the consequences of deafness, middle-class respondents focused on verbal deficiency and working-class respondents on thinking processes. It is interesting to speculate that the class backgrounds of professionals in the field of deafness might reveal more about the nature of the debate about oral methods of education than arguments about speech processes or the linguistics of sign language.

The motivation to reinforce sociocultural values that emphasize the importance of speech, verbal fluency, and occupations that are highly dependent on these attributes can be contrasted with the much greater need for parents and families to reorient the dynamics of the family to permit acceptance and integration of the deaf child. Harris (1982) has summarized this process as including: (a) the parents' ability to deal with grief and reach mature acceptance of deafness; (b) the availability of family crisis intervention support; (c) the availability of a supportive social network; and (d) providing the opportunity to make informed choices about communication methods and language development. A focus on speech development alone frequently prevents families from dealing with these more expressive aspects of their relationships with a deaf child. When this happens, the long-term consequences are often tragic.

As we noted earlier, in fact the belief that speech and "humanness" are synonymous is probably as old as philosphical and scientific thinking. It was the Justinian code of Roman law that originally established that the lack of speech, not deafness, deprived a citizen of all legal rights and responsibilities, and prior to that handicapped children in Sparta were simply thrown into a deep cavern called Apothetae (see Pahz & Pahz, 1978). So it is not surprising that hearing parents have cultural values and attitudes that reinforce the desire to restore normal hearing to their deaf child. The resolution of these problems is to be found in dealing with the emotional responses to the deaf child, and not with the obvious symptoms; but exactly how this is done will vary from family to family, depending on the particular family constellation and the individual attributes of the child rather than on a preconceived stereotype. As Roger Carver (1984, p. 20), himself deaf, suggests, a positive response is needed: "The parents," he says, "should be taught to accept and *enjoy* their child's deafness and development."

The Socioeconomic Status of Deaf People

Generally speaking, deafness as a handicap is not associated with social class. However, some conductive hearing impairments are associated with poor living conditions and, as a result, demographic surveys can and do indicate that binaural hearing impairments increase with decreased socioeconomic status in the family (Davis, 1983). These impairments rarely produce the more severe hearing losses characteristic of prelingual profound deafness and, in fact, prelingual profound deafness affects children of all social classes more or less equally. Therefore, it is surprising that when children handicapped in this way become adults, they are overrepresented in the lower socioeconomic classes. In fact, to be deaf is to place one at considerable risk of being socially and economically disadvantaged.

The socioeconomic disadvantage of deafness begins with school placement and continues into adult life. Schein and Delk (1974) concluded that deaf workers are educationally overqualified for the jobs they hold, despite the fact that some deaf people are employed in almost every job that you care to mention that does not specifically require the use of hearing. They also concluded that the "clearest measure of the penalty exacted by deafness is personal income" (p. 9). In 1971, prevocationally deaf workers earned only 72% of the average income of the general population ($5,915, compared to $8,188 per year), and in the case of the nonwhite prevocationally deaf worker this fell to 62% of the earnings of the unimpaired nonwhite population. Schein and Delk also point out the vulnerability of deaf people to predicted shifts in the economy resulting from technological advances—they are disproportionately represented in clerical and service occupations where the replacement of people by machines is most likely to occur.

Although deafness can frequently be more important than the social class origins of the parents of the deaf student, this does not mean that the social class of parents has no influence. We have already discussed the social values of hearing people that may have a considerable influence on excessive commitments to oral education. It also is interesting to note that these influences have an impact on the school placement and type of education received by a hearing-impaired student. Quigley, Babbini, and Marshall (1969) noted that lower socioeconomic status students were more likely to be placed in residential schools, and conversely, day school students had a higher proportion of fathers in white collar occupations. However, the variables are interactive, because day students also had better oral communication skills, skills influenced not only by degree of hearing loss (itself a major influence on placement), but also by the social class of parents.

The disadvantages faced by lower socioeconomic groups in receiving services is well known. As long ago as 1958, research established that psychiatric therapy was only essentially successful with middle-class value systems (Hollingshead & Redlich, 1958). Similarly, in the mid 1950s, the British Psychological Society published an excellently documented synopsis of the failure of selection for secondary education to remove social class bias in the British educational system, an argument that continues to this day and that is particularly relevant to scholastic aptitude testing in the United States The complicated relationships between these variables and deafness has been explored by Schroedel (1976), and Fig. 2.4 is developed from his original thesis (p. 247). It has been modified to take account of more recent research and to clarify some of the interactions between the different influences.

Schroedel's research developed a number of interesting relationships. First, it confirms that the father's hearing ability and educational achievements interact to determine the father's occupational status, which in most two parent families in our society also determines the socioeconomic class as well. In turn, the communication milieu is also determined largely within the family setting, but it clearly relates to socioeconomic class, as well as being influenced by the age of onset of impairment, parental attitudes, and the age of the respondent. The communication milieu then interactively determines the oral skill and type of schooling the child receives which, coupled with the manual skill (determined in part by whether or not sign language is learned at home), sets the respondent's eventual level of educational achievement.[10] Educational achievement, in turn, determines the occupational status achieved when the child becomes an adult, although the influence of the attitudes of the employer and general social attitudes almost always mean the occupational status will be lower than for a hearing person of equivalent aptitude. Nevertheless, the general dilution of occupational status in the deaf population shows a significant correlation with the communication milieu of the family, and while causality cannot be assumed, it seems to us that it is probable that poor parent/family communication with the deaf child is one of the primary reasons for this relationship.

In fact, the breakdown in the family communication milieu is often, but not only, associated with a rigid commitment to oralism

---

[10]Total communicators in the United States do seemingly reach higher average levels of academic, social, and economic achievement, but access to Gallaudet College could be a significant factor in determining this relationship.

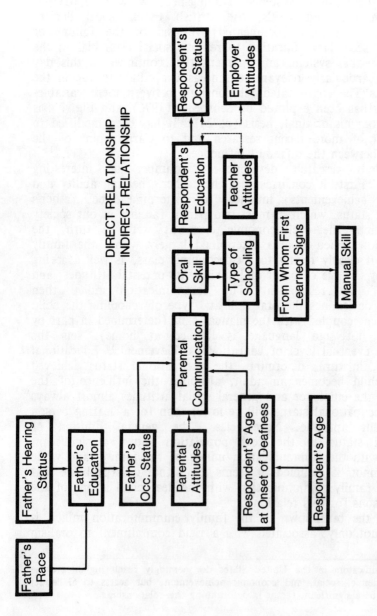

FIG. 2.4.   Variables affecting educational and occupational attainments of deaf persons in the United States.

Source—J.G. Schroedel (1976), *Variables related to the attainment of occupational status among deaf adults*, p. 247, unpublished doctoral dissertation, New York University. Adapted with permission of the author.

for students for whom this method is not suitable. As a result, such a commitment becomes one of the major causes of the marginal status and poor self-esteem of many deaf adolescents and adults, a status that can often border on or be below the poverty line (see Rodda & Carver, 1983). A cycle is established in which educational underachievement becomes linked with lower socioeconomic status, and breaking the cycle becomes ever more difficult as lower and lower expectations are set for deaf students. In our opinion, deaf students are not born to be poor achievers—it is the belief that they are that continues to propagate educational disadvantage, particularly when this belief is coupled with a failure to develop adequate language skills because of inadequate exposure to appropriate communication methods.

Marginality and Self-Esteem

Provided disabled people and nondisabled people relate together as equals, proximity and contact do seem to produce some reduction of prejudice in nonhandicapped persons (Gniadzowsky, 1977). Therefore it is desirable that we provide greater opportunities for deaf students and adults to interact with their hearing peers. Unfortunately, in doing so, we have often failed to carefully enunciate the needs of the deaf student. We have also failed to consider that the degree of marginality affects the degree of acceptance. Prelingual profoundly deaf students invariably cannot communicate easily with their hearing peers (particularly from adolescence onwards). Therefore, they are in a state of *marginality* (see Sussman, 1966; Vardy, 1980). Marginality in turn, prevents both enculturation and socialization, and many deaf students seem to develop poor self-esteem and derogatory attitudes toward themselves. These attitudes are reflected in low academic achievements and also in the increased prevalence of behavior problems in deaf students (see Schein, 1980).

When we come to explore the concept of self-esteem in deaf students in more detail, we need to be cautious in interpreting the existing data (Leblanc, 1983). As Leblanc suggests, a major problem is, how is self-esteem to be measured? One way is through self-report, and there is general agreement that self-report acts as a mirror to our feelings about ourselves (Coombs & Snygg, 1959; Kelly, 1967; Rogers, 1951). Unfortunately, self-report is dependent on fluent communication between observed and observer, and deaf respondents are frequently placed at a disadvantage when studies of this type are undertaken. A very specific example of the problem is found in the research of Garrison, Tesch, and DeCara (1978). They found a strong positive relationship between the scores of deaf students on a reading test and on the Tennessee Self-Concept Scale, but interpreted their results as showing low levels of self-esteem resulted from the inability of the deaf students to read adequately, rather than from poor self-esteem.

Rudner (1968; see also Leblanc, 1983) has discussed the syntax of the English language, and concluded that there are 6 structures that produce serious item bias when testing deaf students. These biases affect any written test, but have particular significance when we are administering self-esteem inventories. They are: (a) Conditionals, *if/when*, (b) Comparatives, *greater than/the most*, (c) Negatives, *not/without/answer not given*, (d) Inferentials, *should/could/because/since*, (e) Low information pronouns, *it/something*, and (f) Lengthy passages. Language problems and differences are not always obvious, and the need for clinicians to be fluent in communicating with and understanding deaf people is obvious if we are to avoid seriously biasing our assessments with language difficulties.

The problems deaf respondents may have in understanding written English in tests of self-esteem can be compared with some insight to the problems that deaf students have in writing English. Levine (1981) has an excellent summary of work such as that of Myklebust (1964), Kates (1972), and Quigley, Power, and Steinkamp (1977). A less well known, but equally important treatise is by Vandenberg (1971). We discuss this research in more detail later, but, for the moment, Levine's (1981) eloquent description of the written English of deaf students will suffice:

> "Deaf language" has a strong "rubber-stamp" quality, rigid in style and loaded with stereotypic repetitions suggesting memorized units rather than generative productions. The simple, short sentences resemble the patterns of much younger hearing children, and the narrowed vocabulary (Cooper & Rosenstein, 1966) is characterized by a large proportion of everyday nouns and verbs at the expense of many other parts of speech. Among the common errors are omission of essential words, use of wrong words, addition of excessive words, and incorrect word order. (p. 80)

This description closely parallels that of the supposed personality structure of deaf students and adults—"egocentricity," "compulsivity," and "absence of thoughtful introspection" are commonly used expressions (see Altshuler, 1962, 1963). Maybe when we describe deaf people in this way, we are assessing English language competence rather than personality characteristics.

There are in fact two alternate theses to explain the congruence between descriptions of the personality and the written English language of deaf students. The first is that receptive and expressive language deficiencies and emotional instability have a common basis in language as a vehicle of both thought emotion (see Lewis, 1968; Rodda, 1985). The second more pragmatic approach is the one to which we referred at the end of the last paragraph and elsewhere. It is that language difficulties invalidate the diagnostic process for deaf students and adults and that the tests used are producing misleading results. The latter thesis has become more acceptable in recent years and as Moores (1982, p. 171) states: "An impressive number of competent researchers with experience in the area of deafness (Donoghue, 1968; Heider & Heider, 1941; Jensema, 1975; Levine, 1948; Myklebust, 1964; Schlesinger & Meadow, 1972; Trybus, 1973) have questioned the results obtained and/or the extent to which the findings reflect actual deviancies in the deaf population." As we shall see later, perhaps even the reading tests given to deaf students produce unreliable data, but the suggestion that English language difficulties explain much of the recorded data on deaf students and adults does not invalidate the assumption that poor language skills are also interactive with emotional difficulties or retarded emotional development. Perhaps both explanations are correct, each for a different group of deaf students or adults, or each for the same group under different conditions.

Communication and Social Support

Stokoe and Battison (1982) approach the problem discussed in the previous section from another pespective—that of the linguist, with psychological overtones. They identify the frustration for hearing people which arises because of the inability to communicate effectively:

> A person who does not respond to verbal commands or questions unless they are finally directed to his or her face arouses ill feelings for not playing the communication game as hearing people do. In our society, the question 'What's the matter, are you deaf?!' is an expression of frustration, accusation, and anger—not an inquiry into the processing capacity of the person's ears. Deaf or hearing, someone who is not perceived as using or understanding language appropriately creates a tension that inhibits smooth social interaction. (p. 189)

The frustration is compounded by the fact that deafness is an invisible handicap; therefore we expect deaf people to behave as if they hear and are unprepared to cope with the realities of communicating and interacting with a person who does not hear.

One of the areas that causes problems for deaf-hearing person-to-person interaction is in the interpretation of facial gesture and eye contact. Stokoe discusses this problem in some detail. Facial gestures and eye contact are integral parts of the sign language communication system (see chapters 3 and 8). The meanings of gestures and the rules governing their use are as formalized and stereotyped as the semantic/syntactical rules of spoken English. Raised eyebrows may express surprise as a natural gesture, but they are a question form in sign language. A statement may become a question, if accompanied by the correct eyebrow movement. A shaking head may similarly negate a statement, and change the whole grammatical structure of a sentence. The sophisticated deaf adult develops an awareness of the problems of conflict between different communication systems and, in many cases, he or she is able to switch from one system to another. Younger deaf people and children and those who are less well endowed by intrinsic ability or education may not accommodate so successfully to the two worlds. For children in particular, failure to respond to the differences in visual cueing may lead to a loss of positive interactions with adults and peers and may even generate situations which reinforce a poor self-image. Some of these children become social and emotional casualties and, as a result, may reinforce the prejudices that are creating the problem in the first place.

Many deaf students leave school ashamed of their culture and their language; some later achieve a more balanced perspective, but others never do. Carbin (1983) explores the problem in detail and emphasizes the need for a more supportive environment for deaf students if we are to overcome the feeling of alienation from their own and, possibly, hearing culture. What happens when the environment is supportive of deaf people in this way has been extensively documented by Groce (1982) in her description of Martha's Vineyard, an island off the southeastern coast of Massachusetts, where, until the late 19th century, the prevalence of deafness increased. In the 20th century, increased population mobility diluted the effects of a recessive genetic strain of deafness, and prevalence rates declined substantially, but Groce has estimated that probably about 1 in 15 residents of the island were deaf during the 1800s. The deafness was total and was not associated with other handicapping conditions. The phenomenon is interesting—a minority handicapping condition is no longer a minority handicap when the large majority of the general public have contact with it.

In a careful analysis of the socioeconomic status of deaf people when they are accepted as social equals, Groce (1982) reports:

There seems to have been little or no social barriers placed on deaf islanders. From earliest childhood they were included in all work and play situations. They seem to have married freely both hearing and deaf partners. Tax records indicate they generally earned an average or above average income (indeed, several were very wealthy). They frequently participated in community and church affairs and several even held public office.... In addition to being self-supporting, all the deaf were legally responsible for their own affairs and many of them were active in church activities, the local militia, and town government. Several held minor town offices and were re-elected regularly. (pp. 111, 116)

She attributes the elevated status of these deaf citizens (by present day standards, let alone the standards of the 19th century) to the fact that communication was not a barrier. She documents the fact that from early childhood, the use of sign language was a normal part of the everyday environment. Indeed, in certain settings (e.g., on fishing boats) it would sometimes be used as a preferred communication method between hearing people. She makes little reference to the importance of deaf role models for deaf young people or to the empathy for both hearing and deaf people that came from personal experiences, although it is probable that these factors also were of major influence. Nevertheless, her documenting of a natural experiment in which barriers to deaf people were reduced, if not removed entirely, is an important contribution to the research literature, and contrasts with the current practice of mainstreaming deaf students in hearing schools.

Educational Policy and Mainstreaming

Kaufman, Gottleib, Agard, and Kuric (1975) state that "Mainstreaming refers to the temporal, instructional and social integration of exceptional children with normal peers. It is based on an ongoing individually determined educational needs assessment, requiring clarification of responsibility for coordinated planning and programming by regular and special education administrative, instructional and support personnel" (p. 40). Despite the jargon, the idea is not a new one in the education of deaf students. Early unsuccessful experiments are fully reported by Bender (1981), McLaughlin (1980), and Pritchard (1963), and Brill (1978) describes more recent methods used for the selection and placement of mainstreamed students. Interestingly, at the turn of the century, one of the early North American experiments involved placing deaf students in a classroom with hearing students in a regular industrial training school. Unfortunately, we do not know if it was successful—the school (the Fredericton Institution for Education of the Deaf and Dumb in New Brunswick, Canada) closed, and the students were transferred to the Halifax School for the Deaf in Nova Scotia (see Rodda, Ellis, & Chaddock, 1983).

Provided students are appropriately placed in a mainstreamed setting, there can be advantageous results, but when mainstreaming reflects a desire to deny the experience of deafness and to assimilate rather than integrate, the practice can and does become counterproductive. It is a continuation of those values associated with the extreme oral position (see pp. 70 to 74). In particular, it frequently rejects the use of sign language, and even when it does not, it provides few opportunities for deaf children to use it intensively and in a large variety of different settings. A language does not make a culture or a subculture, but it is an important aspect of it. Similarly, a culture or a subculture does not make a person, but it is an important aspect of his or her development. As Barbara Kannapell (1980) has said: "I believe my language is me. To reject a language is to reject the person himself or herself" (pp. 11-12).

The common North American model for mainstreaming is the Cascade system. Much of the impetus for this system came from Wolf Wolfensberger (1972), particularly in his classic book, *Normalization: The Principle of Normalization in Human Services*, although Wolfensberger's main thesis had more to do with the acceptance of handicapped people as equals than with a particular educational policy. If we contrast the diagramatic representation of the Cascade system with the less well known model developed in Britain by Gunzberg and Gunzberg (1973), an interesting difference emerges (see Figs. 2.5 and 2.6). The Cascade system is invariably drawn in an administrative or structural mode, and where the student fits in the system is of lesser importance than his or her level of achievement in educational and social skills. The regular class merges into residential provision and then into a hospital or some other kind of provision. The Gunzbergs' model is drawn in a developmental or functional mode. The two are not, of course, necessarily opposed, but they can be if we assume that a hierarchically structured pattern of services enables us to make judgments about "the least restrictive environment" required by classic legislation mandating mainstreaming such as PL 94-142 in the United States and Bill 82 in the Province of Ontario in Canada. The least restrictive environment is defined by the match between students and the programs of the institution, not by predefined but by arbitrary criteria.

Perhaps because of the influence of the Cascade model, we have often concluded that schools for the deaf are institutions and that,

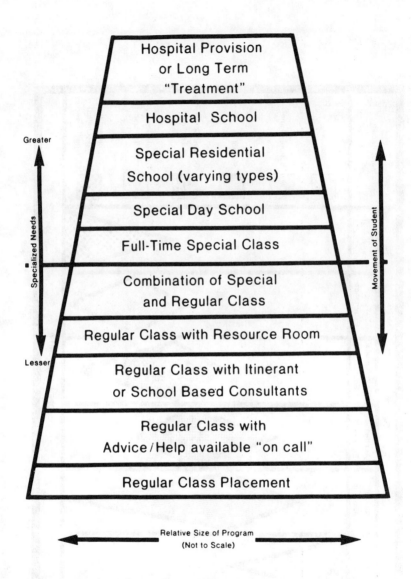

FIG. 2.5.   The Cascade System of special education.
Based on Deno, 1968.

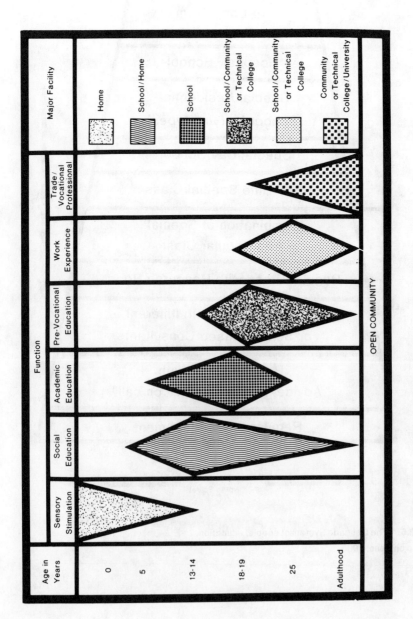

FIG. 2.6.   A social and educational program for deaf students.
Based on Gunzberg and Gunzberg, 1973

de facto, institutions are undesirable. Both premises are suspect. Miller and Gwynne (1973) in their seminal study *A Life Apart*, concluded that institutions using a "warehousing" ideology, based on humanitarian values, and institutions using a "horticultural" approach, based on liberal values, both provided a mechanism to avoid confrontation with the feelings of staff about the perceived inadequacies of the inmates. They suggest that the whole process of admission (or intake) and discharge (graduation in schools) places the recipient of services in a passive role and regards the students (residents or inmates) as throughput—like units to be slotted into a flow diagram. Miller and Gwynne argue that a major shift is needed in which the students become part of the human resources that are focused on a work oriented throughput, and instead of focusing on helping students or clients to achieve their potential, we should shift our values toward specifying specific remedial or educational objectives. The student or client would become an integral part of the process by which these objectives are achieved, not a passive recipient of services. Without these changes:

> Membership of the institution prescribes the dominant role as physical dependency—which in the warehousing setting extends to complete psychophysical dependency. This, on the one hand, pre-empts the possibility of conflict with other roles and, on the other, entails delegation to the institution of many of the decisions that the able-bodied adult would have to make for himself. The resulting pattern of behavior is not one that is likely to foster the development of a mature personality. (Miller & Gwynne, 1973, p. 160)

Perhaps neither humanitarian nor liberal values are the right ones, and perhaps Miller and Gwynne are right. Perhaps we need to stop developing programs for deaf students and their parents, and start working with them and the deaf community to develop better alternatives.

The confusion of values discussed in the previous paragraph is a severe problem, but it is further complicated when we examine how students are selected for mainstreaming. The state of the art has been well documented by Bunch (1977). Of the development of a mainstreaming program in British Columbia Bunch states that "Neither the government nor its critics could suggest acceptable and useful methods of assessing which children were suitable candidates for mainstreaming and what degree of support an individual mainstreamed child required" (p. 11). He goes on to discuss three of the most developed instruments for making such selections in deaf education—the Transitional Instrument for Selection of Hearing Impaired Students for Integration (Rudy & Nace, 1973); the

Integration Profile of the Lexington School for the Deaf (Blumberg, 1973); and the Mainstreaming Placement Question/Check List (Nix, 1977). Bunch rightly criticizes the weighting and scoring of the tests used in the selection process, and comments on the areas of assessment that are not, and should be, included. In addition, it also should be noted that the reliability of the tests described by Bunch, and of others, is usually too low to permit their use in selecting individuals, unless one is prepared to accept very high failure rates. Finally, in judging the suitability of selection methods, there are a number of concerns about the validity of the selection criteria, particularly because these criteria tend to reinforce existing biases within the educational system.

The reinforcement of existing biases means that, generally speaking, the student selected for mainstreaming will be the academically higher achieving student who has good language and communication skills, who is socially well integrated, who is of higher intelligence, and who is drawn from a supportive and intact home environment (Karchmer & Trybus, 1981). An additional problem is that most of the selection criteria used will measure hearing loss as much as any other factor (see Ross, 1976), although some unpublished research by Rodda, Grove, and Denmark (1983) questions this procedure when the sample is limited to severely prelingual deaf students. The effect of these practices is to remove from the mainstream of deaf education the less educationally handicapped deaf child. They leave a demoralized segment of the educational system to cope with the more severely handicapped students, even though teachers, clinicians, and administrators rarely have the necessary training or background. Moreover, the students remaining in schools for the deaf will now lack contact with the good role models provided by successful deaf children, and their self-esteem is likely to diminish further.

In its anxiety to respond to a reasonable and clearly articulated demand, the educational system has generally failed to adequately plan the whole spectrum of services and programs that are needed if mainstreaming is: (a) to be a successful facet of a total system; (b) is to retain and advance the support which students receive from group identity and role modeling in the deaf culture; and (c) to enable integration to be a two-way process—hearing students integrating with deaf students as well as vice versa. To rectify these defects will require a fundamental reassessment of the place of deaf culture and, in particular, of sign language in the curriculum of the regular school.

If deaf students are to be placed in regular schools, then their experiences have to relate realistically to their needs, but, as presently practiced, mainstreaming is mostly the ultimate neo-oralism. It either asks the student to adopt only oral communication methods, or limits his or her manual communication to interaction with only a very small and highly selected group of fellow students and staff. It says again to the deaf child—you must accommodate to the hearing culture, for it will not accommodate to you. Of course, all children, hearing or deaf, have to learn to accommodate to the wider society. The question is how much and how quickly, and we certainly do not expect hearing children to enter into a one-way contract. We expect to accommodate to them as well, but such an accommodation requires a similarity of social background and cultural experiences. Most hearing people and students do not have this empathy for and understanding of the deaf student, and rarely, if ever, do we attempt to provide it in the mainstream setting. The consequences are an increasing number of mainstream failures.

Role of Parents in Mainstreaming

One of the problems with mainstreaming is that it owes much to the clearly articulated demands of the parents of some handicapped children and some parents of deaf students. It is an excellent example of the importance of parents as determinants of educational policy. In the United States, such demands culminated in PL 94-142 mandating the education of handicapped students in the "least restrictive environment." Nevertheless, despite recent changes in educational policy, the paternalism of professionals toward parents still exists (see, for example, Schlesinger & Meadow, 1972, for documentation of this phenomenon, and Harris, 1983, for a highly personal account). It parallels paternalism to deaf people and deaf children. It is even sometimes reinforced by the procedural protections that exist for parents, for example under PL 94-142, procedures that can place parents in an adversary rather than a partnership relationship with professional educators.

In fact, the unwillingness of professionals to accept parents as equal partners has meant that seemingly innovative legislation such as PL 94-142 is circumvented. As Garretson (1981) points out, the deaf child spends a mere 8% of his or her 8,760 hours per year in the classroom, but school systems have effectively insulated themselves from the full effects of PL 94-142 by defining appropriate as meaning "not inappropriate" (Large, 1980). Therefore, the provision by a school district of only one form of mainstreamed education is seen to be acceptable, and the parents of deaf children are forced to accept the local program, irrespective of its suitability for their child. Large (1980) crystalizes the dilemma by saying "Congress and the commentators have blithely assumed that regular placements were always more beneficial. Parents and teachers, who have to deal with the practical aspects of handicaps after the theoreticians finish congratulating themselves, are not so sure ... Parents fear that their children will lose an effective education to be part of an ill-advised experiment in socialization" (p. 270).

The mainstreaming experiment is an important one and has much significance for the education of deaf students. But it is an experiment, and it should not be forgotten that it began in its present form as a reaction against the institutionalization of mentally retarded students and adults, not as an advocated practice for deaf students. As Moores (1978) points out, "educators of retarded students are proclaiming major advances on the basis of (a) beginning to abandon practices which they themselves initiated; (b) mainstreaming children who should never have been in special classes; and (c) they have revised their psychometric definition of mental retardation to that employed 50 years ago" (p. 12). Although we are frequently critical of the education of deaf children, we do not on the whole believe the same criticisms can be made of it as can be made of the education of retarded children. Nor do we advocate the unthinking retention of schools for deaf students in their traditional form. We do believe that deaf students and deaf adults will gradually enter more and more into the mainstream society. They should; for they have much to offer as individuals and as a culture. Nevertheless, we do argue caution, and we do express concern that most mainstream programs do not benefit the deaf child. They often isolate rather than integrate.[11]

In the case of education of deaf students, it is easy to forget that the issue of mainstreaming is complicated by the fact that one of the primary effects of the handicap is to interfere with the communication processes between deaf and hearing people and students. In this sense, deafness is somewhat, but not entirely, different from other handicapping conditions. It is also different because the deaf culture is stronger and more established than other subcultures of handicapped groups, and there is considerable attachment to this subculture on the part of deaf adults. This situation has long been recognized—Higgins (1980, p. 64ff) discusses the influence of Alexander Graham Bell and his considerable concern to prevent deaf people interacting with other deaf people and

---

[11]In the U.K., cuts in educational spending have recently enforced the closure of many schools for the deaf, and imposed on deaf pupils and their parents a kind of unconsidered mainstreaming, resulting in painful and unnecessary controversy.

maintaining their subculture (see also pp. 67 to 69). As a result, Bell opposed residential schools, sign language, school reunions, adult deaf societies, and publication of the literature of the deaf community.

Given the attitudes to deafness that characterized education in the past and their replication in much of modern practice, it is not surprising that deaf people feel threatened by mainstreaming. Many of the social and political achievements of deaf people have come about through a concerted and collective action on their part, not through the efforts of hearing society, and the deaf community is an important and vital agent for changing the status of deaf people. If it were ever destroyed, it would probably regenerate naturally. So if mainstreaming of deaf students is to be successful, it has to be done in cooperation with deaf people. They are supportive of its general principles, but also understand how difficult it can be to be "Outsiders in a Hearing World" or to be enclosed in a "Plate Glass Prison." Extreme neo-oralism and mainstreaming can be, often are, but do not have to be, the ultimate rejection of the deaf culture and of sign language.

Summary

The evolution of sign language and finger spelling has a history spanning several centuries, and the use of manual methods by deaf people has long been recognized. In the 19th century the educational technique known as oralism emerged as a formal system. The oralists rejected the use of signing by deaf people and precipitated a bitter controversy. Today, dissatisfaction with the outcomes of oral education, and new research into manual languages, have led to a revival of the use of sign language in schools using total communication. The oral-total communication controversy is largely a cultural clash between middle-class specialists who have a high regard for verbal skills, and the deaf culture which is continually evolving. Recent attempts to integrate normal and special education (mainstreaming) carries considerable risks where deaf children are concerned. These risks should be considered very carefully, although we do not suggest that no deaf students should be mainstreamed. We do suggest that the unselective application of mainstreaming may weaken deaf culture and if it does so, it will ultimately harm deaf students. In fact, one of the most effective ways for a deaf student to obtain a positive self-image and to aspire to middle-class values is through the support and role modeling that is only available from deaf adults. Therefore, not surprisingly, most deaf adults choose to associate with a deaf subculture, whether one using total communication (most often) or oral communication (less frequently).

Further Reading

Jean Hough's (1983) *Louder than Words* gives a good introduction to the field of manual communication and its history. Harlan Lane (1984) has an edited treatise on the history of deaf education, *The Deaf Experience*, with some fascinating excerpts translated from the originals by Franklin Philip. Peter Trudgill's (1974) *Sociolinguistics* gives a readable account of the social aspects of language use. Jerome Schein's (1983) *A Rose for Tomorrow* is a moving account of the influence of "Fred" Schreiber and his transformation of the National Association of the Deaf into an organization of major political significance—a transformation that had much to do with the recent improvements in the status of deaf people in the United States. One of the best surveys of the problems of communication in deaf children is by Douglass Savage, Lionel Evans, and Fiona Savage (1981), *Psychology and Communication in Deaf Children*. It also includes information drawn from the Newcastle Survey, one of the more significant research studies to be completed on the United Kingdom side of the Atlantic. Paul Higgins (1980) has written a rare sociological text on deafness, *Outsiders in a Hearing World*, and presents a refreshingly different perspective.

3

THE LINGUISTIC STATUS OF SIGN LANGUAGE

We have seen that the use of sign language in the education of deaf students has often been the focus of heated controversy in North America and in the United Kingdom. Educators supporting the oral tradition have typically opposed the introduction of total communication for two basic reasons. First, because the use of manual media is thought to retard oral language development with, to them, obviously undesirable educational and social consequences. Second, because sign language is held to be a deficient linguistic system, and hence can have no valid role in communication or in promoting cognitive development.

Until about 1970, the linguistic status of sign language was regarded as highly controversial; but the consensus appeared to be that, irrespective of the pragmatic value of manual methods of communicating, signing did not exhibit the formal properties of a "natural"—i.e., spoken—language. Visual-gestural communication systems were thought to be linguistically primitive, lacking in vocabulary, grammatically confused, and incapable of expressing subtle and abstract concepts (Bonvillian, Charrow, & Nelson, 1973; Myklebust, 1964). Witnesses appearing before the Lewis Committee in Great Britain (see p. 73) claimed that sign language users relied on "forms which are ungrammatical and bear little relationship to normal usage ... where good and fluent signing is used it is not, in fact, a self-sufficient language but parasitic on well developed mastery of conventional language" (Lewis, 1968, para. 72). The same paragraph goes on to list the supposed deficiencies of signing: (a) Sign order does not follow "normal word sequence"; (b) verbs are used infrequently and without inflection; (c) symbols are lacking for certain parts of speech; and (d) signs may represent words, ideas, feelings, or attitudes.

Even if we agree that the fourth point is a defect of signing, the general thrust of such arguments is clear: Sign language is regarded as inferior *because it does not reflect the syntactical structure of English*. If some of these criticisms were taken seriously, many existing spoken languages could be equally validly regarded as intrinsically nonlinguistic. But despite their transparent absurdity, such claims have continued to dominate the thinking of researchers in the field. Even Furth's (1966) generally favorable attitude to total communication methods was colored by his assumption that hearing-impaired people lack language in some fundamental sense (Gordon, 1977). In fact, before 1970, Stokoe and his associates (Stokoe, 1960; Stokoe, Casterline, & Croneberg, 1965) were almost alone in attempting to assimilate deaf sign language studies into mainstream psycholinguistics.

In this chapter, we discuss the question "Is sign language really a language?" After reviewing some of the widely differing approaches to the study of language, we summarize recent studies of American Sign Language (ASL), that seem to imply that at least one major manual communication system possesses many—if not all—of the vital attributes of spoken language.

Approaches to the Study of Language

It is impossible to summarize adequately the complex fields of linguistics and psycholinguistics in a few pages, but to place the study of communication with deaf people in its proper context such a summary is clearly essential. Therefore, in this section we attempt to trace the development of various approaches to the investigation of spoken language, using this framework to introduce concepts of particular relevance to the study of visual-gestural languages.

Some Basic Concepts

Natural language can be conveniently divided into several levels of analysis which, to some extent, can be discussed and studied independently:

Phonetics is the discipline concerned with the most basic language data—the sounds of speech and the manner of their production.

Phonology is the description of broad classes of speech sounds (*phonemes*) functionally important for a given language.

Morphology is the study of the smallest meaningful speech segments, or *morphemes*, of a specific language. Two types of
morphemes are distinguished: bound morphemes, such as *un-*,
which can exist only as a supplementary unit; and free
morphemes such as *tie*, which can either be joined with other
morphemes (e.g., *untie*) or stand on their own.

Syntax refers to the rules underlying the construction of phrases
and sentences in a specific language.

Semantics is the study of the meaning of morphemes, words, and
sentences.

The traditional term *grammar* covers the syntactical and morphological levels and may incorporate semantic elements.
   Languages may be broadly classified into four basic types:

Flexional languages, such as Latin, which make extensive use of
inflections in modifying words according to their grammatical
function. Inflections are bound morphemes that are attached to
other morphemes to systematically vary their meaning. For example, the addition of the inflection *-ab-* to *amo* (*I love, am
loving*, in Latin) changes it to *amabo* (*I shall love*). Inflections
may also prefix words (e.g., *unusual*) or appear as suffixes (e.g.,
going).

Isolating languages, such as Chinese, shun inflections completely,
employing words that *never* alter to show number, possession,
tense, and similar aspects of grammar.

Agglutinative languages form very long words from strings of
morphemes; Turkish is the most extreme example.

Incorporating languages, such as the Nahuatl language of the
Aztecs, rely heavily on complex verb forms that incorporate the
grammatical roles taken by other parts of speech in the European
family of languages.

Isolating languages are sometimes referred to as *analytical*, in
opposition to the other *synthetic* types.
   Modern English is highly analytical, although originating in a
synthetic language, a Low German dialect spoken by the Frisian
tribes who founded the Kingdom of Mercia in the Midlands of
England. During the Middle English period (circa 1200-1500 A.D.)
systematic changes took place in vowel sounds, especially at the ends
of words, and most verb and noun inflections were lost. These
changes, combined with extensive borrowings from French, Latin,
and other languages that could not readily be incorporated into the

inflectional structure of Old English, resulted in an increasingly isolating morphology.

Early Studies

Traditional approaches to language comprised basically the detailed
description of the vocabulary and grammar of a particular tongue.
They date back to about the 4th century B.C., when Panini prepared
a comprehensive analysis of Sanskrit, the language of ancient India.
In Europe, the first grammars were written in Greece in the 1st century B.C., and the methods and terminology of the Greek
grammarians were rapidly adopted by Roman scholars for the study
of Latin.

The extensive use of Latin for scholastic and religious purposes
encouraged medieval students of language to adhere to the Greco-
Latin model. Latin, a strongly flexional, intricate language, was regarded as a kind of ideal, and its study was deemed to be central to
the educational process; hence the appearance of "grammar" schools.
Languages such as English, with powerful analytical tendencies, were
nevertheless forced into the Latin mold. Many of the prescriptive
dogmas of traditional English grammarians, although valid for Latin,
simply did not reflect everyday English usage. In fact, it is worth
noting that virtually all the parts of speech that still dominate the
teaching of grammar derive directly from Latin forms. The arguments of certain philosophers searching for the universal, logical
principles underlying all natural languages were similarly influenced
by the high status accorded the classical literature.

Relying as it did on a highly restricted set of data, the early European study of language was, inevitably, less an objective science
than an enclosed system of logic. The resurgence of interest in science in the 17th century led to a number of novel approaches (such
as those of Wilkins, Leibnitz, and others), but on the whole such
developments were the exception.

Crystal (1971) has discussed the weaknesses of the traditional approach, which are worth briefly listing: (a) It was tied too closely to
the Latin model; (b) The prescriptive attitude adopted by its practi-
tioners is now seen as inappropriate; the use of terms such as right,
wrong, and incorrect, which are associated with the grammarians' interest in rhetoric and higher literary forms, has no place in objective
study; (c) The grammarians failed to distinguish between spoken and
written forms of language, and regarded written language as the
focus of their studies. In particular, they showed no concern for
prosodic aspects of speech (such as accent, tone, and emphasis), nor
for styles of language (formal vs. casual, for example), nor for

everyday usage (which exhibits constant change); and (d) Their methods were essentially subjective, and they made no explicit statements about criteria and methodology. Partly, this reflected the unavailability of appropriate research techniques; they had no recorders, voice analyzers, and the like. But it also resulted partly from an attitude of mind which preferred armchair thinking to practical study.

Linguistics in the 19th Century

The emergence of linguistics as a scientific discipline is generally associated with the lecture made to the Asiatic Society in Calcutta, on September 27, 1786, by Sir William Jones, at that time Chief Justice in Bengal. Jones, who had been studying Sanskrit, made the dramatic claim that sufficient similarities existed between Sanskrit, Greek, and Latin—and, perhaps, Germanic, Celtic, and Persian languages—to justify the belief that they "have sprung from some common source which, perhaps, no longer exists" (quoted in Potter, 1960, p. 146). Although foreshadowed by the observations of missionaries such as Sassetti and Coeurdoux, who were working in India, Jones' remarks had an immediate impact on European scholars. The outcome was the development of *comparative philology*, the systematic study of the evolution of languages. In the hands of capable workers such as Rasmus Rask, Franz Bopp, Jakob Grimm, Karl Verner, and Max Muller, the philological movement came to dominate 19th century linguistics. An attempt was made to reconstruct the "common source" postulated by Jones, which became known as *Proto-Indo-European* (PIE). The work spanned phonetics, vocabulary, syntax, morphology, and orthography, and suggested that PIE was a highly inflected language compared with its offspring.

Although much of their work was, of necessity, highly speculative, and was limited to the study of languages with surviving orthographic records, the philologists introduced a new dynamic conception of language that threw into sharp relief the inadequacies of the traditional approach. It encouraged linguists to examine a wider variety of languages and to develop new methods and concepts (for example, that of systematic vowel changes). The discovery that, in effect, half of the world's existing languages could be traced back to a common ancestor stimulated a vast quantity of research. Language was seen in a wider context (Table 3.1).

One of the most famous triumphs of 19th century scholarship carries an interesting commentary on attitudes to unfamiliar methods of communication. For several hundred years, Europeans had been fascinated and mystified by the hieroglyphs—pictorial symbols—

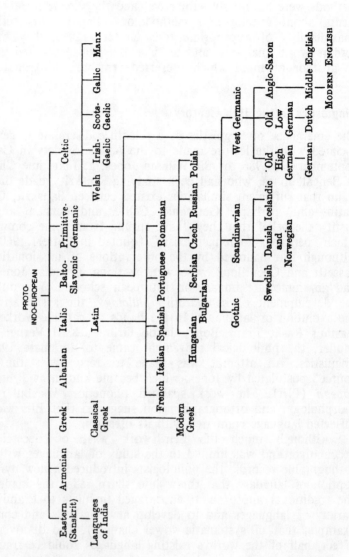

TABLE 3.1

A "Genealogical Table" Showing
the Evolution of Modern English from Proto-Indo-European

PROTO-
INDO-EUROPEAN

Eastern
(Sanskrit)

Languages
of India

Armenian

Albanian

Greek

Classical
Greek

Modern
Greek

Italic

Latin

French Italian Spanish Portuguese Romanian

Balto-
Slavonic

Hungarian   Serbian Czech Russian Polish
          Bulgarian

Primitive-
Germanic

Celtic

Welsh Irish-   Scots- Gallic Manx
      Gaelic   Gaelic

Gothic

Scandinavian

Swedish Danish Icelandic
       and
     Norwegian

West Germanic

Old
High
German

Old
Low
German

German Dutch

Anglo-Saxon

Middle English

MODERN ENGLISH

Source—F. Wood (1941), *An outline history of the English language*, London: Macmillan.
Reprinted by permission of the publishers.

found on the surviving monuments and buildings of Ancient Egypt. Following the wildly fanciful interpretations of Athanasius Kircher, a noted Jesuit scholar, the consensus of opinion held that the hieroglyphs represented a complex esoteric symbolism at best, or were merely overelaborate decorations at worst. Moreover, the writings of classical authorities such as Herodotus and Herapollo were in firm agreement with these conclusions. Undoubtedly the Egyptians' development of two further distinct yet related scripts, hieratic and demotic, contributed to the confusion.

Following the discovery of the Rosetta Stone—a large slab covered with carved inscriptions in hieroglyphic, demotic, and Greek—in 1799, the solution was considered to be within reach. But it took another 20 years for the "best minds of the day," culminating in the linguistic genius Jean-Francois Champollion, to overcome the prevailing beliefs about the hieroglyphs. Champollion was able to demonstrate that the symbols were nothing less than the letters of a *fully phonetic alphabet*. Ceram (1952) gives two reasons why the overwhelming majority of specialists failed even to consider this seemingly obvious possibility: the high regard felt for classical authors, and the visual impact of the hieroglyphs themselves, which looked like pictures and therefore must have been nothing more than pictures. It is tempting indeed to draw a parallel between the case of the hieroglyphs and more recent attitudes to sign language. As we have seen, respect for the established viewpoint and superficial judgments about visual modes of communication still continue 160 years after Champollion's brilliant breakthrough.[1]

Linguistics in the 20th Century: 1900-1957

In the early part of the century, linguistics developed a more rigorous approach to its subject matter and ceased to be closely identified with philology. Saussure (1915) emphasized the distinction between *synchronic* linguistics (the study of a language at a particular stage in its development) and *diachronic* linguistics (the study of the evolution of languages); and interest shifted from the diachronic to the synchronic, and has remained there ever since.

A number of factors contributed to this change. One was the invention of technological aids to speech analysis. Another was the need for new ways of transcribing the thousand or so Amerindian languages, that were found to differ considerably from the Indo-

---

[1]For an account of the deciphering of an abstract script which proved to be hopelessly nonphonetic (the cuneiform writing of Babylon) see Ceram (1952, chaps. 16-17).

European family, and that were rapidly becoming extinct under the pressure of European settlement. A further factor was the combined influence of the logical-positivist school of philosophy and the behaviorist movement in psychology, that emphasized the supposed need for researchers to restrict their interest to observable features of behavior. The outcome of these influences was *structuralism*, an approach that was tied to the surface features of language, and that tended to focus on specific levels of analysis separately. The lower levels of analysis, phonetics, and phonology, received more attention than syntax, whereas semantics often was ignored. The structuralists seemed to feel that the levels of analysis should be kept conceptually isolated, in the sense that it was not considered proper to define a noun, for example, in terms of its semantic properties. Therefore, it is not surprising that the structuralists made many highly detailed descriptions of the fine grain of language, but failed to develop comprehensive models of language production and comprehension.

Phonology

A major point of controversy in this period was the status of the phoneme. How it was to be defined came to be a fundamental question, even though phonetic studies have clearly identified the mechanisms underlying speech production. The air stream generated by the lungs may be modified in four basic ways to influence oral output: (a) The vocal cords may be relaxed to produce a *voiceless* sound, or tensed and vibrated to produce a *voiced* sound; (b) The air stream may emerge through the mouth to produce a *buccal* (or oral) sound, or through both nose and mouth to produce a *nasal* sound, depending on the position of the soft palate or *velum*; (c) The action of the tongue also plays a major part in speech production by varying the resonance characteristics of the mouth to modify vowel sounds, and by checking or constricting the air flow at various locations to produce consonants; and (d) The lips further influence vocal output through variations in tension and in size and shape of the labial opening. Nevertheless, it is important to note that, although the phonetic mechanisms known to be implicated in the production of specific sound in isolation can be readily described, the control systems responsible for coordinating the complex integrating activities of these mechanisms during natural speech remain mysterious (Laver, 1970).

Given the flexibility inherent in the mode of operation of many of these mechanisms, it becomes plain that the human vocal apparatus is capable of generating a near-infinite number of speech sounds. *Plosive* sounds, for example, which are produced by a brief interruption of the air stream, may result from movements of the lips (*bilabial*, [p] and [b]) or of the tongue against the roof of the mouth (*velar*, [k], [g]) or against the teeth, or near the gums (*alveolar* [t], [d]). Even if we adopt the model of Roman Jakobson (Jakobson & Halle, 1956) and make the simplifying assumption that all the parameters involved can be regarded as binary (for example, voiced vs. voiceless, nasal vs. buccal)—the *distinctive features* theory—the potential number of different speech sounds is still immense: 4,096 to be precise. No natural language employs more than a small fraction of the possible speech sounds: English uses around 44, French and German around 36 sounds. No language appears to possess less than 20 or more than about 75 basic sounds, or phonemes, as they are termed.

To appreciate fully why humans are so sparing in their use of the productive capacities of the speech system, we must exploit the conceptual framework provided by Information Theory (pp. 115 to 119). But some of the reasons are self-evident. One is that the production, transmission, and reception of sound waves is inevitably a mechanically imperfect process. It therefore makes sense to employ only a subset of potential phonemes that are relatively hard to confuse with each other. If all the possible sounds were used, a large number would be perceptually similar (i.e., would share many distinctive features) and hence easily confused; choosing the right sound out of over 4,000 during continuous discourse would impose an excessive cognitive load.

A second reason is that speech sounds vary as a function of factors external to the language system: the speaker's own characteristic vocal apparatus; his or her mood; minor physiological changes (e.g., a cold or a sore throat); desire to communicate emotional and paralinguistic cues (e.g., sarcasm); social group; regional dialect, and so on. Because the speech channel carries so much "non-systemic" information, many of the potential speech sounds are not going to be available for incorporation into the language system. Third, it is intuitively likely (although impossible to test) that any language using all the possible sounds would take an impossibly long time to acquire.

So the phoneme is a natural feature of language, a basic element or building block, and it is difficult to envisage any communication system that does not employ a restricted set of elements. The binary system, used in computers, makes do with only two (0 and 1), and is being increasingly introduced into advanced electronics systems. At the other extreme, the ideographs used in Chinese orthography number many thousands; but this is a very atypical case. And yet the seemingly innocuous concept of the phoneme has generated some vigorous debates. Fudge (1970) has defined four distinct ways of viewing it: (a) the psychological view of the phoneme as the "ideal sound" aimed at by the speaker; (b) the the physical view of the phoneme as a family of sounds; (c) the functional view, that the phoneme is the product of minimal sound differences (the distinctive features approach); and (d) the abstract view, which rejects phonetic criteria, and focuses on morphology, distributional constraints, and syntax. However, none of these views, considered separately, can fully account for phonological variations within the language system: Language is essentially arbitrary in many repects. In this book we adopt an eclectic view of the phoneme, although we generally use the terminology of the physical approach.[2]

Grammar

Beginning with the work of Leonard Bloomfield, whose major book, *Language*, was published in 1933, the structuralists adopted a severely constrained methodology. They argued that the levels of analysis should be considered in strict sequence; first identifying the phonemes of a language, then defining the morphemes to reveal syntactical structure. Semantics was not only ignored, but explicitly rejected. For example, structuralists condemned appeals to semantics in defining word classes; it was considered wrong to define, say, a noun, as "the name of an object, person, place, quality, etc." It is easy to find counterexamples: *purple* is certainly the name of a color, and there are numerous abstract words which are sometimes regarded as nouns, sometimes as verbs, and so on. The semantic or *notional* definition of the noun is clearly imprecise and insufficient.

To define word classes, therefore, the structural linguists restricted their definitions to those using only morphological and syntactical criteria. Any native English speaker, for example, would be capable of identifying the elements of the nonsense string *The grabes bloaded scaffily* as noun, verb, and adverb. With a sufficiently large language sample (*I like grabes, The grabe runs, Where is the grabe?* and so on), the linguist can confidently identify *grabe* as a noun because it consistently occupies certain positions in the sentence (and likewise other word classes). The meaning of the word plays no part in the process.

In fact, the structuralists went further and rejected even the concept of *word*, preferring to deal with morphemes. But it soon became

---

[2]It is conventional to distinguish between phonetic and phonological transcriptions using brackets and slashes respectively; e.g., [k] (phonetic) or /k/ (phonological). Morphemes are transcribed thus: {ed}.

evident that this approach carried with it as many problems as did the traditional conceptions (see Palmer, 1971, pp. 110-124) and often more. Morphemes proved to vary widely. The plural morpheme {-s}, for example, is sometimes realized phonologically as /s/ (as in *books*), sometimes as /z/ (*pens*), and sometimes as /iz/ (*glasses*). These *allomorphs* represent the influence of phonetic environment: They happen to be the easiest to pronounce in each case. Harder to deal with are special cases such as *oxen*, which are not phonetically determined.[3]

To attack the problem of syntax, Bloomfield developed the method of Immediate Constituent (IC) analysis. Each sentence was divided into two segments, then four, and so on, on the basis of substitution: If a specific string of morphemes can be replaced by another string, and the sentence remains grammatical, it follows that it can be regarded as a functional unit in discourse (see Fig. 3.1).

There were many reasons why IC analysis could not cope with the complexities of grammar. For one thing, the segmentation process often was arbitrary. Why divide sentences into halves? Why not into three basic parts (Noun Phrase—Verb Phrase—Noun Phrase)? Were the segments genuinely objective, or did they reflect the linguist's implicit knowledge (in practice, the first cut inevitably reflected the traditional grammarians' division into subject and predicate)? How do we deal with sentences such as *She made the whole story up* (Palmer, 1971) where *made ... up* is split between segments? The basic weakness of IC analysis lay in its inability to recognize the hierarchical structure of language. Human speakers can too easily switch around the structure of sentences. Altering the order of verbs and adverbs, changing active into passive, and using similar techniques, they totally disrupt the tidy segments of the structuralists that fundamentally depend on sequential contingencies. Attempts by Pike, Lamb, and others to resolve these problems continued into the 1950s but by then the weaknesses of the extreme structuralist approach had become increasingly obvious.

---

[3]The structuralists undoubtedly created many pseudo-problems of this kind by refusing to draw on their philological heritage. The *-en* suffix is derived from the regular plural form (*-an*) of Southern Old English; the *-s* inflection derives from the East Midland dialect. The mutated plurals *men*, *mice*, *teeth*, etc., can similarly be traced back to an early stage in the evolution of English. Other "irregular" forms such as *-ae* reflect Latin borrowings.

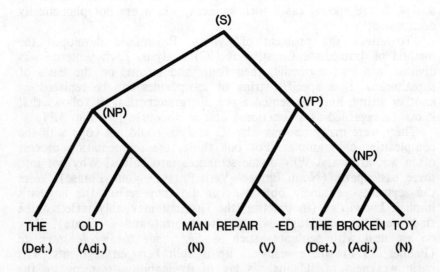

THE   OLD   MAN   REPAIR   -ED   THE   BROKEN   TOY
(Det.)   (Adj.)   (N)   (V)   (Det.)   (Adj.)   (N)

The labels attached to the tree diagram are secondary to IC analysis and alternatives are available.

S=Sentence, NP=Noun Phrase, VP=Verb Phrase, Det.=Determiner, Adj.=Adjective, N=Noun, and V=Verb (comprising a stem and a past tense inflection).

A labeled diagram of this type is known as a *phrase marker*.

FIG. 3.1.   Immediate constituent analysis of a simple sentence.

Early Psychological Approaches to Language

Before the early 1950s relatively few attempts had been made to study language from a psychological perspective.

In Russia, Lev Semenovich Vygotsky initiated a series of experiments aimed at establishing the functional role of language in simple learning situations. This approach, associated with the "conditioning" theories of Ivan Petrovich Pavlov, has continued until the present time, through the work of Aleksandr Romanovich Luria and his colleagues. Although valuable in highlighting the controlling function of simple self-directed commands in relatively uncomplicated tasks, usually with children or clinical patients as subjects, the Soviet research rarely deals with complex syntactical structures and is relatively unconcerned with theories of language per se (Luria, 1959).

In America the behaviorist school of psychology also evinced little interest in language, although the rote learning of verbal materials played a prominent role in experimentation. Osgood (1952) and his associates have made extensive use of the *semantic differential*, a means of measuring connotative meaning through ratings on bipolar scales such as *active-passive* and *kind-cruel*. Factor analyses (see p. 311) of such ratings suggest that there are just three basic dimensions used by human subjects: *evaluation*, *potency*, and *activity*. This research, which finds application in a clinical context, covers precisely the ground that structural linguists find most distasteful: the meaning of highly abstract and/or emotion-laden words. Osgood works generally within the behaviorist tradition, regarding language as an internalized set of stimulus-response (S-R) elements, but it is not essential to accept this model to agree that the semantic differential is a theoretically and practically valuable technique. Perhaps the most ambitious attempt to explain language in S-R terms was undertaken by Skinner (1957); and his views were summarized in the book, *Verbal Behavior*, which provoked a highly critical response from the linguist Chomsky (1959). In practice, a number of researchers in North America continue to draw on concepts of verbal mediation (notably Paivio, 1971) but the majority of psycholinguists consider the behaviorist account of language to be formally and empirically inadequate.

Of considerable interest to students of the psychology of deafness is the continuing debate, associated with the speculations of Benjamin Lee Whorf, about the relationship between cognition and language. Whorf, a specialist in the study of American Indian languages, proposed the concept of *linguistic relativity*, which broadly asserts that thinking and conceptual process are determined by linguistic factors: that one's language predisposes one to look at the world in a particular way. This was not an altogether novel idea when Whorf first put it forward in the 1940s; many philosophers had argued that the development of language was the most important difference between man and other species. However, Whorf was able to provide numerous specific examples of Indian, mainly Hopi, grammatical structure which appeared to reflect modes of thought very different from the Western (Whorf, 1940, 1956). Attempts to confirm the Whorfian hypothesis employing concept formation and naming techniques have had varying degrees of success (see Brown, 1958, chap. VII; Radford & Burton, 1974, chap. 7, for reviews). The methodological problem is of distinguishing between the general communication function of language—which provides the developing child with a rich source of conceptual information—and a specific effect associated with particular grammatical and lexical systems. It would be strange, perhaps, if language had no specific effects on cognition, but few researchers today would share Whorf's view that linguistic structure is the *major* determinant of one's mode of thought. Certainly nobody would claim—as was once the case—that "language *is* thinking," or that "thinking is independent of language." The relationship between the two is obviously very complex.

In the early 1950s, one of the most significant contributions to the problem of syntax came from the neurophysiologist Karl Lashley. Common to both the structuralist and the behaviorist accounts of language was the assumption that the structure underlying speech performance was essentially sequential in nature. Words, morphemes, and phonemes could be regarded as chains of elements, produced one at a time. The connections between these elements were analyzed by the behaviorists into "simple" S-R units. In a powerfully argued paper, Lashley (1951) asserted that, far from explaining syntax, the serial ordering of language behavior posed profound difficulties. The structuralists had concerned themselves chiefly with the analysis of verbal materials after they had been produced. Hence they had never confronted the problem of language production directly. By giving examples of errors in production, and by considering the extraordinarily precise timing required to coordinate speech (and other skilled acts), Lashley showed that highly complex mechanisms must be involved.

Although it was ostensibly concerned with memory, Bartlett's studies of the repeated transmission of narrative materials (Bartlett, 1932) anticipated much later research. He found that when short stories were recalled by subjects, systematic errors were produced. In particular, the syntax of the original material was lost. Subjects tended to recall the meaning of the stories, not the exact form of words, and to reconstruct, rather than recall, the material. When the theme of the story was culturally unfamiliar, and even when it was not, and subjects repeated it to each other in an "oral tradition" paradigm, the strange or unexpected elements tended to be lost, often with amusing consequences. For humans, semantic factors are more important than syntax. It is puzzling why linguists thought otherwise.

Information Theory

One of the criticisms that could be directed at the early linguistic and psychological investigation of language was that it was non-quantitative. Nobody had tried to apply mathematics in any systematic way. The first researcher to make this effort was Claude Shannon, a mathematics and electronics specialist. During World War II, Shannon was given the task of developing a mathematical model of *cryptanalysis*—codebreaking. Given the amazing complexity of modern codes and ciphers it is surprising that cryptanalysis works at all. But however convoluted the cipher, the basic tool of the cryptanalyst is *his or her knowledge of the language in which the secret message is written*. Without this, the cryptanalyst's chances of success are slight.[4] If the message is in English, he or she will know that the most frequent letter appearing in it will be E, almost certainly, followed by T (the approximate ranking for the more common letters is given by the mnemonic "ETAOIN SHRDLU"), while letters such as X, Z, and Q may not appear at all. Certain digrams (pairs of letters) such as *th* and *he* will be more likely to occur than others such as *on* and *to*; some (such as *qt*) will not occur at all. As his or her reconstruction of the message proceeds, the cryptanalyst will meet segments such as SE-DREI-FOR-EME-TS (rarely in such an obvious form) that make demands on his or her syntactical and semantic knowledge. In short, the *organization* of the language provides the cryptanalyst with multiple clues about the structure of the message (Kahn, 1968).

Although these techniques had been in use for several hundred years, Shannon was alone in recognizing in them the key to a fundamental characteristic of language and developing a mathematical representation of it. He pointed out that all human languages exhibit *redundancy*: They transmit far less information than they could, given the number of basic elements (letters) available. *Information*, in

---

[4] During the Second World War, the U.S. forces in the Pacific employed native Navaho speakers to transmit radio messages. It was known that no German or Japanese scholars were familiar with this language.

this definition, he expressed in terms of *bits* (short for *binary digits*). A bit of information is a reflection of the probability of each specific signal: A highly unlikely signal carries more information than a common or frequent signal (Shannon, 1948; Shannon & Weaver, 1949).

The basic formula developed by Shannon are as follows (non-mathematical readers can go on to the next paragraph):
(1) If $P =$ the probability of the signal and $H =$ the information carried, then:
$$H = \log_2 (1/P) \text{ bits}$$
(2) The average information carried by N signals of differing probabilities P_i, where $\Sigma P_i = 1$, is given by:
$$H = \Sigma P_i \log_2 (1/P) \text{ bits}$$
(3) Redundancy is defined by comparing the maximum information possible in a set of signals, H_m, with the actual information observed, H_o:
$$\text{Redundancy} = [1 - (H_o/H_m)]$$
We can represent the communication situation schematically in two ways. Figure 3.2a shows a transmitter and receiver of information. The channel through which the information travels is thought of as having limited capacity; only a certain number of bits can be forced through it per second. In psychology, we are interested in the information-transmitting characteristics of the human subject who can be regarded as the channel; information may be input (the stimulus) and output (the subject's response). In Fig. 3.2b the circle on the left represents the input, and the circle on the right the output. The overlapping area (B) represents the information correctly registered. Some of the information is lost (area A), and the subject's response will also contain information not present in the stimulus, *noise* (area C).

This model explains clearly why natural languages exhibit constraints on their use of the available speech sounds and on the combination of these sounds. If all the possible phonemes were employed in discourse, the listener would be required to process the incoming information at a rate of around 12 bits per phoneme. Restricting the number of phonemes to about 40, and permitting some to occur more frequently than others, reduces the information load to just 4 or 5 bits per phoneme. Constraints on the combination of phonemes and morphemes resulting from phonological, syntactical, and semantic rules reduce the load further. An average sample of English text, for example, is about 70% redundant. The corresponding estimates for languages with additional constraints (case, verb inflections, gender, and so on) may be even larger.

(a) *Transmission and reception of information*

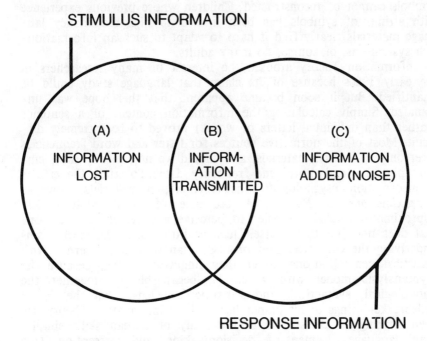

It should be noted that the size of the circles is not proportional to the total amount of information. To calculate (A), (B), and (C) a stimulus-response matrix is employed; see Fitts and Posner (1967, pp. 88-90)

FIG. 3.2.   The Information Theory representation of the communication process.

Increasing the redundancy of a language, therefore, reduces the processing demands made of the listener. If information is lost, or if noise is present, in the sense of Fig. 3.2b, the hearer can readily reconstruct the missing or distorted segments of the message. Neisser (1967) has argued that speech perception is largely a reconstructive process. We "hear" mostly what we expect to hear. This is why the native speakers of a language tend to be unaware of differences in the pronunciation of specific phonemes in various phonetic environments. Perhaps the nearest approach to a nonredundant communication system familiar to most people is algebra. In an expression such as $2(a+b)+b-3a-4b$, the basic elements occur almost equally often and are subject to few sequential constraints. Lost or distorted symbols cannot be reconstructed. Children whose previous experience with strings of symbols has been limited to high-redundancy language materials clearly find it hard to adapt to such an information-rich system—as, of course, do many adults.

Information Theory aroused the interest of many researchers in the early 1950s because of its claim that language study could be quantified. But it soon became apparent that this hope was unfounded. Simply calculating the information content of a sentence (rather than individual letters or words) proved to be extremely difficult. Most of the normative sources for letter and word frequencies refer only to written materials; and should we not, in any case, employ phoneme and morpheme frequency data? To study the effects of information, psychologists constructed written materials known as *approximations to English*. A sequence of words that closely approximates English is easier to perceive and remember than one that does not. But this in itself tells us little about the mechanisms underlying the comprehension process. Shannon was concerned with statistical generalizations rather than linguistic theory, because the cryptanalysis model with which he began blurred together the phonological, syntactical, and semantic knowledge that the skilled codebreaker brings to his or her task. Where Information Theory has been strikingly successful is in the study of human skills simpler than language, elementary decisionmaking and perception (see Broadbent, 1965; Fitts & Posner, 1967; Treisman, 1965; Welford, 1968).

The most valuable contribution of Information Theory to linguistics was the concept of a language *generator*, a device for producing strings of symbols by following certain explicit rules. Shannon's theory takes into account only the transitional probabilities connecting the symbols employed by the system; a generator following such rules can only mimic the surface features of language. But the notion that a finite set of elementary rules can, in principle, generate an infinite sequence of symbols, led directly to the most significant modern linguistic theory: *transformational-generative grammar*.

Generative Grammar

The theory of generative grammar made its first appearance in Noam Chomsky's (1957) book *Syntactic Structures*. Chomsky, a linguist at Massachusetts Institute of Technology, had studied philosophy and was aware both of the new approach to language associated with Information Theory and of recent trends in mathematics dealing with transformational rules. For Chomsky the central aim of a linguistic theory was to account for language productivity: How do we have the potential for generating an infinite number of unique and often novel sentences? It is intuitively obvious that models of language employing only "left-to-right" constraints on word sequence— the "beads-on-a-string" approach (Matthei & Roeper, 1983)—fail to capture vital characteristics of syntax (see Miller, 1967b; Miller, Galanter, & Pribram, 1960). Chomsky was able to demonstrate formally the inadequacy of such models. His own theory drew on two basic concepts, generation and transformation, and is generally referred to as transformational-generative (TG) grammar.

Many excellent introductions to TG grammar are available (see Greene, 1972, 1975; Lyons, 1970; Matthei & Roeper, 1983; Palmer, 1971; Postal, 1964), and the finer details of the theory have changed over the years, so we give only a bare outline of Chomsky's approach. Unfortunately, it is impossible to evade the fact that his theory is immensely complex and highly abstract. Readers who care to do so may therefore skip the following section, although as it is *the* major linguistic theory of recent years (while not necessarily the best) it is worth getting a basic grasp of its overall structure.

Chomsky begins with a fundamental distinction between linguistic *competence* and *performance*. Competence is the speaker/hearer's knowledge of the finite set of rules that govern grammatical processes. Performance is the observable language behavior of an individual or group, the output of the psychological mechanisms which apply the rules. To take an obvious analogy, knowledge of the rules of chess constitutes competence in that game. Both a third-rate amateur and a Grand Master will possess competence in this sense, but there will be an immense difference between the two in terms of performance. The Master will possess greater qualities of foresight and strategy than the casual player, but this does not imply that he has a better grasp of the rules of the game: It means that he applies these rules more effectively. In the same way, Chomsky argues, two language users may have equal levels of competence, but factors extraneous to the rule system—such as perceptual distortion, limitations on short-term memory and channel capacity—will place severe constraints on their observed levels of performance (Chomsky, 1965, p. 10).

Chomsky therefore rejects the structuralist school's insistence that only the surface features of language behavior can be the legitimate subject matter of linguistics. And Chomsky is interested only in competence; he is trying to make explicit the rules underlying the language system, not attempting to design a comprehensive model of the language user. However, he does follow the structuralist tradition in restricting his interest to syntactical rules: semantic rules he regards as, in some sense, secondary.

Figure 3.3 summarizes Chomsky's theory as it was presented in his 1965 book *Aspects of the Theory of Syntax*. By that date it had been significantly changed, compared with the earlier (1957) version, and was even then in a state of flux. However, the overall organization of the grammar has retained its distinctive character.

The *Syntactic Component* of the grammar comprises two major subcomponents, the *Base* and the *Transformational Subcomponent*. In turn, the Base consists of two further subcomponents: the *Categorial Subcomponent* and the *Lexical Subcomponent*. The construction of a sentence begins when the categorial component generates a string of abstract symbols by the application of *rewriting rules*. These are complicated expressions, rather like the formulae for chemical reactions, which show how sentences can be broken down into successively smaller constituents. For example:

(1) S —> NP ^ Aux ^ VP

Which generates a sentence S composed of noun phrase (NP), auxiliary (Aux), and verb phrase (VP); then

(2) VP —> V ^ NP

Which asserts that the verb phrase contains a verb and a further noun phrase;

(3) NP —> Det ^ N

Which defines one NP as a determiner and a noun;

(4) NP —> N

Which means that the other NP comprises only one noun; and finally

(5) Det —> *the*

(6) Aux —> M

Further rules are required to specify the characteristics of the nouns (for example, whether common, animate, or abstract) and the verb (which may take a wide variety of roles, and that is defined as a specific symbol Q), with the result:

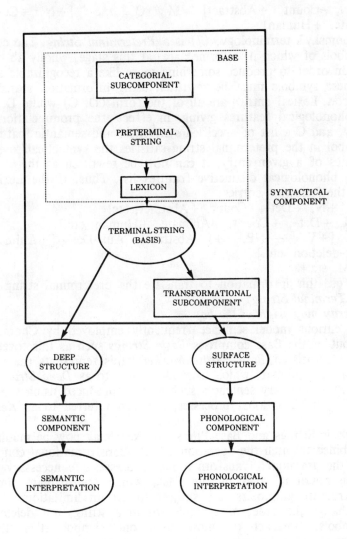

FIG. 3.3.   Chomsky's Theory of Transformational-Generative Grammar.

(7) [+N, –Count, +Abstract] ˆ M ˆ Q ˆ *the* ˆ [+N, +Count, +Animate, +Human]

In Chomsky's terminology, (7) is a *Preterminal String*. The complex symbols of which it is formed are, at this stage, wholly abstract entities. In order to produce something more like a recognizable sentence, these symbols must be rewritten using information stored in the Lexicon. Lexical entries are all of the form (D, C) where D is a list of phonological features giving, in effect, the pronunciation of the entry, and C a list of specified syntactical and semantic features. If a symbol in the preterminal string satisfies the syntactical/semantic features of a given entry, it can now be rewritten as the corresponding phonological distinctive features list. Thus, if the Lexicon includes the following entries:

sincerity [+N, +Det–, –Count, +Abstract, etc.]

boy [+N, +Det–, +Count, +Animate, +Human, etc.]

frighten [+V, +–NP, +[+Abstract] Aux–Det [+Animate], +Object–deletion, etc.]

may [+M, etc.]

we may use this information to translate the preterminal string (7) into the *Terminal String*:

(8) *sincerity may frighten the boy*,

a rather curious model sentence frequently employed by Chomsky. The output of the Base comprises *Basic Strings* such as this together with their associated *Base Phrase Markers*; this represents the basis of generative grammar, which Chomsky refers to as *Deep Structure*. Particularly elementary sentences such as (8), produced using a minimum of transformational processes, are also referred to as *Kernel Sentences*.

The Basic Strings and Base Phrase Markers may now be modified and combined through the operation of the Transformational component of the grammar. Transformational processes are necessary because the rewriting rules of the Base, which approximate simple phrase-structure grammars, are subject to certain limitations. They cannot change the order of symbols within a string, nor delete or add symbols, nor act on more than one symbol at a time. Transformational rules enable the grammar to generate sentences which rewriting rules could not handle. Some examples are passives, negatives, questions, embedded phrases, and imperatives.

In Chomsky's (1965) theory, the transformational process begins in the Base. The Categorial Subcomponent contains rules which rewrite S as a string including, say, a marker calling for a passive transformation. The Base Phrase Marker produces, in this case, an active Terminal String together with the passive notation. To take an example given by Palmer (1971), the terminal string *the man read a book* would be accompanied by the symbols (by + passive). The Base Phrase Marker thus modified would enter the Transformational Component, which would effect the transformation:

$NP_1 + Aux + V + NP_2 + by + Passive \longrightarrow$
$NP_2 + Aux + be + en + V + by + NP_1$

resulting in the passive surface structure:

The book was read by the man.

In this case, examples of deletion and adding (the determiner of "book" changes from "a" to "the," and the auxiliary "was" is added), and comprehensive reordering, are observed.

We can summarize the whole process as follows: (a) the generation of a set of abstract symbols representing the underlying syntactical structure of a sentence; (b) the translation of this expression into a simple sentence using information from the lexicon; (c) the optional application of various transformational processes to produce a syntactically more complex version of the sentence; and (d) the output of the finished version via the speech organs, again using information stored in the lexicon.

It should be clear from this brief and (believe it or not) highly simplified account that Chomsky's theory, especially in its later versions, is wide in scope and intricate in detail. Against the background of sterile structuralism and behaviorist dogma, it appeared to offer a radical new approach to linguistics and stimulated a great deal of research. But the theory has proven extraordinarily difficult to evaluate, and it has failed, to some extent, to fulfill its early promise. Both formal and empirical criteria point to significant deficiencies in the theory.

Formal criticisms of transformational-generative grammar can be summarized under five interrelated headings:

Testability.   Chomsky's distinction between competence and performance, although natural, leads to severe methodological problems. If competence cannot be observed directly, due to the distorting effects of performance characteristics, it is difficult to see how the theory can be disproved. If the language behavior of an experimental subject appears to contradict the predictions of the theory, the way is open for Chomsky to claim that we are only describing the subject's performance, whereas the theory is concerned with competence. At the same time, the theory is "psychological" in form, and Chomsky explicitly states that any model of the language user would include generative grammar as a basic component (Chomsky, 1965, p. 9). Criticism of this type has been most forcibly voiced by Herriot (1970, pp. 56-58). Other researchers such as Miller have tried to test the theory on the assumption that competence can be investigated if sufficiently good controls on performance factors can be achieved.

Rules.   There is no doubt that employing formal rule systems makes Chomsky's theory far more explicit and potentially powerful than traditional or structural grammars. But is the distinction of kind or of degree? Given any sufficiently complex system of rewriting and transformational rules it ought, logically, to be possible to describe any language or language-like system. Is there any reason to prefer Chomsky's specific choice of rule; and is this approach any different in principle from a less formal, traditional description of grammar? Going back to our analogy with the game of chess, it is clear that there is no single "right" way to express a set of rules. For example, the move of a knight might be expressed either as "move two squares forward and one square to the side" or as "move one square forward and one square diagonally." Both are equally valid descriptions. Even for a simple example like this, one can imagine numerous systems of notation which could equally well express the underlying rule. But aside from personal preference, there would be no formal reason for favoring one particular system, and no way of testing them experimentally or by observing people playing chess.

Semantics.   Perhaps the strangest aspect of Chomsky's approach lies in his attitude to semantics. It is obvious that the initial stage in the generation of a sentence must comprise an idea which the speaker wishes to communicate. Meaning must precede syntax, logically and temporally. And yet Chomsky's model states that sentence production is initiated in the categorial component of the Base. It is not until a Terminal String and Base phrase marker have been produced that the semantic component can produce a "semantic interpretation" of the sentence. Any possibility that Chomsky is using the term interpretation in some special technical sense seems to be dispelled by remarks such as: "Both the phonological and semantic components are therefore purely interpretive" (Chomsky, 1965, p. 16); "the syntactic component ... constitutes [the grammar's] sole 'creative' part" (Chomsky, 1965, p. 136); and "[The phonological and semantic components] are purely interpretive; they play no part in the recursive generation of sentence structures" (Chomsky, 1965, p. 141). Moreover, many of the lexical entries, which do play a key role in sentence generation, undoubtedly contain information that can be described as semantic (for example, whether the lexical entry is abstract, animate or human). And Chomsky candidly admits at many points that it is often not possible to decide whether a particular aspect of grammar should be considered as syntactical or semantic in nature.

Subjectivity.   A criticism that can be directed against many linguists is that their arguments are often built on a highly selected sample of sentence types. Language is such a rich source of varied grammatical forms that it is easy to find examples of sentences which support one's theoretical posture. Conversely, it is also easy to find examples of sentences that contradict rival linguists' theories. The problem becomes more acute when the linguist makes subjective judgments about the "grammaticality" or "comprehensibility" of his or her sentence examples. Chomsky is usually cautious in deriving generalizations from his instances, but it is often difficult to agree with his interpretations of them. For example, Chomsky (1965, pp. 195-196) cites the sentence: "Anyone who feels that if so many more students whom we haven't actually admitted are sitting in on the course than ones we have that the room had to be changed, then probably auditors will have to be excluded, is likely to agree that the curriculum needs revision." He remarks: "Though hardly a model of felicitous style, it seems fairly comprehensible, and not extremely low on the scale of acceptability." Opinions might differ!

Rationalism. The general tone of Chomsky's approach has offended many researchers, notably Herriot (1970), who argue that Chomsky is a rationalist rather than an empiricist. Much of his writing is essentially dialectic, and not only does he not rely on experimentation, but he rarely cites the experimental results of others. He also employs concepts that many psychologists would regard as mentalistic. In Chomsky's defense it should be noted that linguists traditionally have rejected the experimental method as psychologists would understand it, and have usually preferred to debate crucial points of linguistic theory rather than to subject them to objective testing. Moreover, much of Chomsky's support derives from his enthusiastic espousal of mentalistic and cognitive constructs and his powerful attacks on behaviorism. It seems inconsistent for Chomsky's critics to say that because his theory is dialectic in nature it can be dismissed dialectically.[5]

Despite criticisms such as we have just discussed, many psycholinguists have attempted to test aspects of Chomsky's theory experimentally. Their work has typically focused on the transformational component of the model. The classic study of Miller and McKean (1964) required subjects to transform a given sentence in various ways (active into passive, for example) and to press a button (calling up a search list and recording transformation time)

---

[5]Interestingly, many psychologists have rejected Piaget with somewhat similar arguments, but this has not prevented him from having a major impact on both theory and practice.

when they had done so. They found that the passive transformation took on average 0.9 seconds, negatives took 0.4 seconds, and both together took 1.5 seconds. The implication was that to get from an active sentence to a passive negative, subjects were making the two constituent transformations in sequence, as Chomsky's theory predicts. Studies using other techniques (e.g., Savin & Perchonock, 1965) also seemed to support the reality of the transformation as a psychological construct, although the relative difficulties of the transformations examined often did not agree.

A number of researchers questioned the validity of such results on two basic grounds. First, asking subjects to perform transformations to order does not tell us how sentences are normally generated. Second, no account is taken of semantic factors. Meaning is clearly confounded with type of transformation. Passives focus attention on an alternative sentence subject; negatives change the meaning completely. When experiments are run in which meaning and the "truth value" of verbal materials are systematically varied, syntactical factors cease to dominate. In recall experiments, subjects remember the meaning of sentences rather than their syntax (Sachs, 1967). Indeed, when the semantic structure is unambiguous, or when one particular interpretation is highly probable, even the active-passive difference exerts no effect on performance (Herriot, 1969; Slobin, 1966). Similarly, when judgments of truth value are made of simple visual displays matched with descriptive sentences, response time varies with aspects of the display, even though the truth value of the sentences is unchanged (Cornish, 1971). Finally, the difficulty of passive-negative transformations can be shown to vary as a function of the order in which test sentences are presented, and as a function of verb tense (Wright, 1968).

Taken together, such results cast doubt on the psychological validity of transformational-generative grammar, and also strongly support the claim that Chomsky's neglect of semantics weakens the theory. Semantics is not an additional factor to be grafted onto syntactic theory at some later date; all the evidence available implies that for human language users, the semantic content of a sentence governs its comprehension and may even overrule, or bypass completely, syntactic processes if they appear faulty. Proponents of Chomsky's theory might argue that this is merely an example of the idiosyncracies of human performance obscuring the underlying competence. But it seems that semantic processes are fundamental, not only for humans, but for machines: Attempts to program computers to process natural languages that are syntax-based (and often derived from the Chomsky theory) tend to be unsuccessful (Thorne, 1964); programs based on semantics, that treat syntactic processing as secondary, have been markedly more successful (see for example, Quillian, 1967, 1969). This is not to say that attempts to describe the rule system underlying language are misguided or unnecessary, merely that they are less important than was once thought.

Case Grammars

As a result of what might be thought of as the rediscovery of semantics, some linguists have attempted to formulate grammars which are rooted firmly in the semantic relationships within the sentence, and so mark something like a return to the spirit of the traditional grammars of the 19th century. *Case Grammars*, as they are known, are most closely identified with the work of Fillmore (1968) and Chafe (1970). "Case" comes from the Latin *casus*, "a falling (away)," and refers to the various roles of a noun-concept within a sentence, as they depart from the basic "Nominative" (naming) function. Latin nouns may fall into any of six cases, and are mostly inflected differently for each; for example, in the famous phrase "Et tu, Brute?" Brutus is in the "Vocative" case, being "a thing or person addressed." In English nearly all case-related inflections have been lost (with a few exceptions such as possessives and a few pronouns). Modern case grammarians have extended the concept to cover all the possible semantic roles of the constituent elements of sentences. Fillmore's (1968) grammar includes cases such as the "Agentive," the animate instigator of action, the "Instrumental," the object or force causally involved in the action of a verb (e.g., "He opened the door with a *key*"), and the "Dative," the animate being affected by the action of a verb, and so on. Chafe (1970) uses a slightly different terminology ("Agent," "Experiencer," "Instrument," and other similar concepts). Halliday (1970) has further extended the notion by defining types of language function associated with different grammatical structures. For these writers, semantic function and syntactic structure are necessarily inseparable: If animate and nonanimate concepts are constrained by certain syntactical rules, why not regard this fact as primary rather than as something which creates a problem for a purely syntactical theory? Case grammars have proven valuable in studies of the acquisition of language (Brown, 1973; Wells, 1974) and may well provide the basis for a unified psychological and linguistic model of language.

The Nature of American Sign Language

The brief summary of language research given in the previous sections serves to emphasize the diversity of approaches employed by linguists, psychologists, and information theorists. It is intended to place the following survey of sign language research into some kind of historical perspective. Each of the approaches seems to us to provide a valuable contribution to the field; none of them, in isolation, provides a comprehensive answer to fundamental questions about the nature of language. In fact, research interest in the structure of American Sign Language (ASL) has increased dramatically in the last decade. Until about 1970, only a handful of workers such as Stokoe (1960) and McCall (1965) concerned themselves with the linguistics of ASL. Specialists in the field of deafness merely *assumed* ASL was, or was not, a language, depending on their stance within the oral-manual controversy. But the stimulus for more recent research was not a concern for the plight of the hearing-impaired. Rather, the main factor seems to have been a remarkable series of studies by Allen and Beatrice Gardner, who, beginning in 1966, attempted to train an infant chimpanzee in the use of ASL (Gardner & Gardner, 1969). As described in some detail by Linden (1975), the apparent success of this experiment prompted an entertaining debate among linguists, psychologists, and zoologists: Had the chimpanzee, Washoe, learned to use language? The complex issues raised by Washoe's manual performance clearly revolved about the linguistic standing of ASL. If ASL was *not* a language, Washoe could not have acquired language.

Ursula Bellugi, a psycholinguist specializing in the acquisition of language, was originally highly critical of the Gardners' claims (Bronowski & Bellugi, 1970), in part on the basis of the lack of consistent sign order in the utterances attributed to Washoe. Realizing that next to nothing was known about the acquisition of ASL by deaf children, Bellugi and her associates at the Salk Institute initiated a series of studies that has evolved into a major ongoing program of research into the grammatical structure of ASL. Because the Salk program remains to a great extent the nucleus of present sign language research, the following summary is based on Klima and Bellugi's (1979) own account of their findings, *The Signs of Language*.

The Structure of Signs in ASL

Stokoe (1960) proposed the use of the term *chereme* to refer to aspects of the formation of signs in ASL that closely parallel the phonemes of natural language. Like English and other spoken languages, ASL employs a restricted set of formational elements to convey information: Only a small percentage of the almost infinite number of possible hand/arm configurations are actually employed by native ASL users. Stokoe's scheme defined three basic sign parameters, which he termed *Dez*, *Tab*, and *Sig*; Klima and Bellugi's terminology is easier to grasp and we shall use it in preference to Stokoe's:

1. *Dez* (in Bellugi's system, *Hand Configuration* abbreviated HC), the shape adopted by the signer's hand or hands. Stokoe identified 19 "primes," or characteristic HCs, employed by ASL users.

2. *Tab* (*Place of Articulation*, PA): the location of the sign relative to the signer's body. Stokoe identified some 12 PA primes in ASL.

3. *Sig* (*Movement*, MOV), the motions made by the signer's hand(s) during execution of a sign. ASL employs about 24 MOV primes.

Summing the numbers of primes in each formational category, we find a total of about 55 major cheremes employed in ASL, which compares well with the numbers of phonemes typically associated with spoken languages (see p. 109). However, a few signs in ASL are distinguished by certain minor parameters of HC: *Contacting Region* (where part of the hand touches part of the body); *Orientation* of the hand, relative to the body; and *Hand Arrangement*, which is a distinction between signs made with one hand only (40% of known ASL signs), with two hands (35%), and cases in which one hand uses the other as a passive "base" (25%). Moreover, as we see, grammatical processes in ASL make use of a variety of additional patterns of movement and location as well as qualitatively different formational components. We ignore this complication for the moment and focus on the individual signs in their *citation form*—that is, bereft of syntactical context.

Stokoe observed the strict criterion of "minimal contrasts" employed by functional linguists in identifying phonemes (p. 110); to count as a prime, a particular feature had to be used to distinguish at least one pair of signs. Minor differences (e.g., in HC) between signs that did not reliably distinguish them he defined as *subprimes*. Although Stokoe's classification is open to criticism (Tweney & Hoemann, 1973), it is a convenient way of organizing data about signs, at least initially (Wilbur, 1979).

Figure 3.4 illustrates the major HC primes together with examples of subprimes. Typically the HC is assumed before the onset of MOV components, and remains unchanged throughout the production of a sign (with a few exceptions; see Klima & Bellugi, 1979, p. 45).

The 12 PA primes described by Stokoe are identified with distinct parts of the body which the signer's hand nears or touches at some stage during execution of a sign: (a) the forehead; (b) the cheek; (c) the mid-face region; (d) the lips and chin; (e) the whole face; (f) the neck; (g) the trunk; (h) the upper arm; (i) the forearm; (j) the wrist; (k) the base hand; and (l) the neutral space in front of the signer. As Bellugi has observed, this aspect of Stokoe's scheme requires modification. It is by no means clear that the neutral space should count as only one prime: In fact, it appears that ASL users divide the signing space into a set of orthogonal planes, which are the preferred regions for various types of movement (Fig. 3.5). Some pairs of signs, such as JUDGE and EXPLAIN, are distinguished solely by the plane of movement—vertical, in the first instance, horizontal in the second.

The most complex sign parameter is MOV, which may be subdivided into several distinct classes of movement: movements of the fingers or wrist; linear movements in one of the signing planes; circular movements; interactions of the two hands; simultaneous clusters of basic movement components; and extremely complex sequential and/or simultaneous combinations of movement. An especially complicated example is given by Klima and Bellugi (1979, p. 59): CIRCUS comprises six discrete MOV elements combined into two sequential clusters. In some cases a single sign may possess the characteristics of two separate signs.

No completely satisfying system for the categorization of MOV components has yet been devised. Some signs are distinguished only by very subtle qualities of movement, such as tension/laxity. In addition, the MOV elements of a sign may be reduced or modified by the operation of grammatical inflections.

The formation of a sign in ASL does not result from the random combination of primes from each of the three major parameters. Just as sequential constraints function within spoken languages, effectively ruling out phoneme combinations such as *thxl* in English, so do physical and systemic constraints limit the numbers of potential ASL signs. Two major constraints have been recognized in ASL. The *Symmetry Constraint* applies to two-handed signs, and asserts that both hands must adopt the same HC and MOV components, and that they must be produced in the same PA or signing plane. The *Dominance Constraint* affects signs comprising an active and a base hand, and indicates that the base hand must adopt an HC either matching the active hand or selected from a subset of six common HCs. Two additional types of constraint have also been

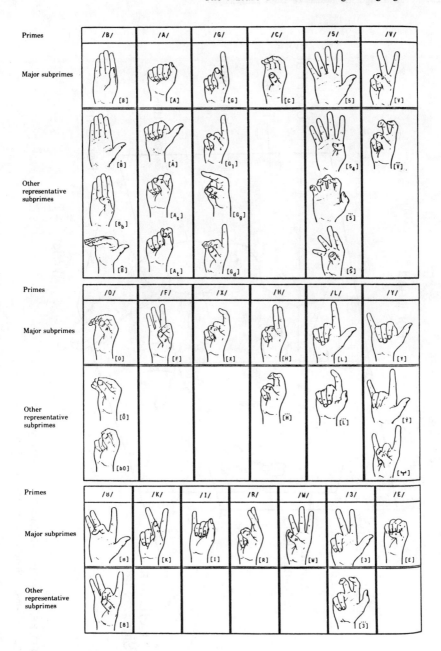

FIG. 3.4.   Hand configuration primes shown with representative subprimes.

Source—E.S. Klima and U. Bellugi (1979), *The signs of language*, p. 44. Copyright and reprinted by permission of Harvard University Press.

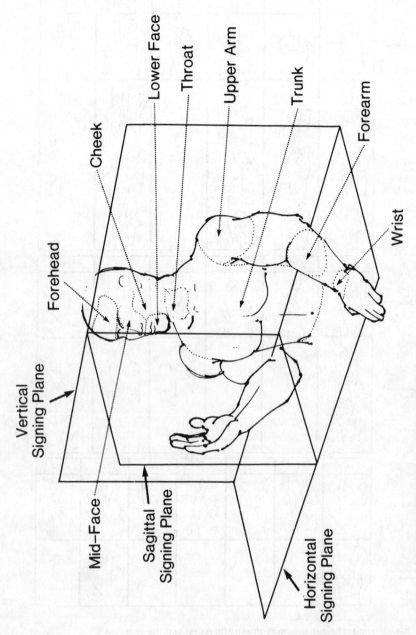

FIG. 3.5.   The place of articulation signing parameter.
Source—Instructional Technology Centre, University of Alberta.

identified: constraints on the kind of HC making contact with specified parts of the body, and complex restrictions governing MOV elements such as manner of onset and their interaction with other
parameters.

Iconicity of Signs

One of the factors influencing the outsider's view of sign language is
the obviously pantomimic origin of many signs. This *iconicity*, or
pictorial quality, has been widely regarded as an indication that
manual languages are in some way primitive, linguistically inferior,
and crudely concrete. (At this point, we may recall the episode of
the Rosetta Stone recounted on p. 107.) Critics of manual media
have contrasted iconic aspects of sign languages with the essentially
arbitrary relationship between phonetic and semantic factors in natural language.

Klima and Bellugi (1979) describe a study of iconicity in ASL,
the results of which confirmed the adage about "appearances being
deceptive." They showed 10 hearing subjects 90 common ASL signs
and asked them to guess their meaning. If ASL were no more than a
set of elaborate pantomimes, one might expect this to be a relatively
simple task. In the event, not one of the subjects correctly identified
81 of the 90 signs. The other 9 signs were guessed correctly by only
a few subjects. When a further 10 subjects completed a multiple-
choice test using the same list of signs, their success rate remained at
the chance level. Only a handful of signs possessed sufficient
transparency to enable non-ASL users to guess their meaning.

Ten other subjects were shown the signs and given their
meanings: This time they were asked to guess the origin of the sign.
Over half the signs were found to be, in Bellugi's terms, *translucent*:
That is, the subjects could give a reasonably accurate account of the
relation between sign and meaning. It seems that signs in ASL do
possess significant iconicity, but that for the most part it is insufficiently prominent for non-ASL users to be able to exploit it in
grasping the meanings of signs.

Etymology of Signs

Historically, ASL is related to Old French Sign Language (OFSL)
which was introduced into the United States around 1817 (see
chapter 2) in a modified form. Klima and Bellugi (1979) drew on
three major sources of historical data about signs: a French manual
by l'Epée, dated 1784, giving details of the citation forms of Old
French signs; a manual of ASL signs compiled in 1918 (which we
will abbreviate to Old ASL); and Stokoe's modern ASL dictionary

(Stokoe, Casterline, & Croneberg, 1965). Comparisons of the three sources led Klima and Bellugi to several interesting conclusions about the nature of etymological change in ASL:

1. Over time, pantomimic aspects of signing such as body and head movement, facial gesturing, and environmental contact, are lost, and their roles taken over by movements of the hands (Fig. 3.6).

2. Signs originally made at the periphery of the signing space tend to migrate into the center of the space over time. Two-handed signs contacting the face either become one-handed or are displaced from the central region of the face. One-handed signs made below the neck either become two-handed or move toward the center of the signing space.

3. Two-handed signs tend to follow the symmetry constraint described earlier; either they become symmetrical in HC and MOV or, when one hand acts on the other as base, the base hand adopts the HC of the active hand. A recently invented sign, VIDEO-RECORDER, originally mimicked the circular motion of two videotape spools; very quickly the MOV component became wholly symmetrical (Fig. 3.7).

4. The creation of new ASL signs is accomplished through five basic types of process: (a) iconic or mimetic processes, which are rapidly superseded by systemic assimilation; (b) the finger spelled initial of an English word combining with a semantically similar sign; (c) the figurative extension of an existing sign, corresponding to a familiar process in natural language; (d) the formation of nouns from existing verbs; and (e) the compounding of two or more signs. Of these, the fifth process—the creation of multipart signs such as BLUE-SPOT (for *bruise*)—is the most important. Compounds function as units in discourse: The constituent signs cannot independently take on syntactical modulations or be separated by adjectives. The movement components of the first constituent are greatly reduced, whereas the second sign loses repetitive movements, and various operations smooth out the transition between the two. Some compounds of fairly recent origin cited by Klima and Bellugi include DIRTY-AIR (*pollution*) and NUDE-ZOOM-OFF (*streaker*). As the merging process continues, iconic features of the multipart sign are overridden, multiple repetitions are replaced by simple, fluid movements, and the duration of the sign approaches that of unipart signs. Ultimately the sign bears little or no trace of its dual origin.

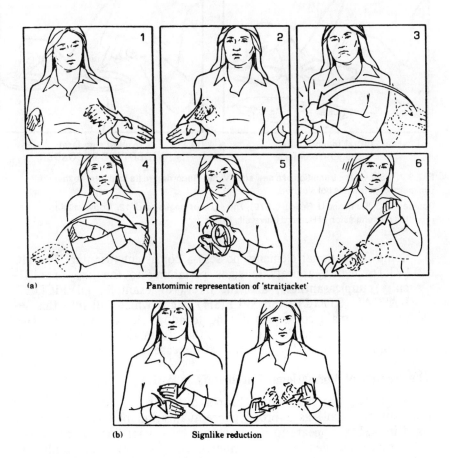

(a)   Pantomimic representation of 'straitjacket'

(b)   Signlike reduction

FIG. 3.6.   The progression from pantomime to sign.

Source—E.S. Klima and U. Bellugi (1979), *The signs of language*, p. 16. Copyright and reprinted by permission of Harvard University Press.

(a)   Initial invention for   (b)   Evolved sign form
           'videotape recorder'   VIDEOTAPE-RECORDER

FIG. 3.7.   Shows the transition of a new sign, Video-Recorder, to its final form so that the symmetry constraint is not violated.

Source—E.S. Klima and U. Bellugi (1979), *The signs of language*, p. 12. Copyright and reprinted by permission of Harvard University Press.

5. Some formational elements possess a consistent meaning. The HC [V] frequently appears in signs pertaining to the idea of difficulty, unpleasantness, and the like (for example, DIFFICULT, RASCAL, STRICT, and SELFISH). Signs which fall into this semantic domain consequently tend to adopt this characteristic HC. Thus, over extended periods, the formational similarity of semantically related signs tends to increase.

The Reality of Formational Parameters in ASL

Although the chereme model proposed by Stokoe remains open to criticism of detail, as a broad conceptualization of the structure of signs in ASL it appears to be supported by several lines of evidence.

Formational elements in perception and memory. A number of experiments (to be reviewed in chapter 4) have shown that deaf ASL users employ the formational parameters as a basis for encoding items in memory. Moreover, there is evidence from a study of confusions made between HCs perceived under conditions of visual noise that one parameter, at least, can be decomposed into a set of "distinctive features" similar to those identified for spoken languages (Lane, Boyes-Braem, & Bellugi, 1976).

The eclipse of iconicity. As we have seen, iconic elements in ASL signs are invariably suppressed by the operation of systemic constraints. This is true historically—as the lexical forms of signs change following the rules described previously—and grammatically—

as inflectional processes modify individual signs during communication. The residual, obvious iconicity, which was once thought to characterize all signing systems, is actually very rare.

Slips of the hands.   Although unusual, errors made during the production of signs provide further support for the reality of formational processes. Of 131 errors collected by the Salk researchers, most involved the substitution of one or two primes, most often in HC. Only in 9 cases was the entire sign incorrect. The overwhelming majority of errors (126) conformed to the formational rules of ASL—that is, they were potentially valid ASL signs.

Comparative studies.   Klima and Bellugi reported a comparison of ASL and Chinese Sign Language (CSL) that identified three major categories of CSL signs: signs similar to existing ASL signs; signs that are possible ASL signs; and signs that clearly violate the formational rules of ASL. Of the final category some of the "impossible" CSL signs comprised primes different from those in use in ASL; others combined valid ASL primes in nonpermitted ways. However, even the "similar" and "possible" CSL signs differed in subtle ways (such as stiffness and angularity) from their ASL equivalents. These "phonetic" differences parallel variations between the same phonemes in different spoken languages. Chinese signers, asked to produce ASL signs, did so using their own signing accent.

Puns in signing.   Poetry and theatrical productions among the deaf population employ a variety of techniques to produce "plays on signs," jokes, puns, and the like, precisely similar to the creative uses of spoken language. By substituting specific primes into a normal sign, the ASL user derives a novel form. For example:

> After watching a lengthy explanation of a technical linguistic point, a deaf person was asked if he understood. The signer replied "UNDERSTAND," but instead of making the sign with the index finger normally used, he substituted his little finger ... (which) occurs in a symbolic way in some signs where it conveys the notion of thinness or extreme smallness (SPAGHETTI, THREAD, SKINNY-PERSON, INFINITESIMAL) ... The substitution in UNDERSTAND clearly carried the meaning "understand a little." (Klima & Bellugi, 1979, pp. 324-5)[6]

---

[6]At a rather more basic level, future researchers may have difficulty in understanding a dialectical version of WEEKEND, in HAVE A GOOD WEEKEND, as used by the staff of the Western Canadian Centre of Specialization in Deafness at the University of Alberta. It literally translates "weak backside," a pun developed by a deaf colleague who is fluently bilingual ASL/English.

Signs for Class Membership

In order to deal effectively with relatively abstract ideas, language must develop ways of communicating concepts lying at different levels in the semantic hierarchy. A fundamental distinction can be made between basic-level concepts such as *chair* and *apple* that correspond closely to our experience in everyday life, and superordinate concepts such as *furniture* and *fruit* that refer to wider classes possessing fewer concrete, obvious attributes. A further type of category, the subordinate, refers to subclasses that are distinguished on the basis of relatively small details of appearance and function (*kitchen chair, snow plow*).

English is quite well equipped with lexical terms for basic and superordinate categories, but subordinates often tend to be compounds. At first sight, ASL appears to possess adequate numbers of basic level signs, but fewer superordinate or subordinate signs relative to English (Rosch, Mervis, Gray, Johnson, & Boyes-Braem, 1976). However, Klima and Bellugi found that ASL employs a variety of syntactical devices to overcome deficiencies of vocabulary. To represent superordinate categories, ASL permits signers to string together 3 (rarely, 4) basic level signs, selected from a very short list of 5 or 6 prototypical exemplars, together with a sign for ETC. Thus APPLE-ORANGE-BANANA-ETC. stands for *fruit*. The items constituting the set are not fixed or ordered, in contrast to normal compounds (e.g., KNIFE-FORK, meaning *silverware*), and the MOV primes of the three signs are all equally compressed.

To represent subordinate concepts, ASL employs three methods: simple compounding, as in English (e.g., COOK-CHAIR, *kitchen chair*); compounds employing size/shape specifiers, which are bound forms such as -RECTANGULAR tagged on to a simple sign (e.g., PICTURE-RECTANGULAR, *photograph*); and conjuncts of basic signs with individualistic mime (e.g., one of Bellugi's informants represented *grand piano* by signing PIANO, then a gesture tracing the peculiar shape of a "grand," followed by OPEN-UPWARD).

The Grammar of ASL

The findings just described go a long way toward dispelling the allegation that sign languages rely wholly on mimetic/iconic representational processes. At the level of lexical signs, ASL exhibits a formal structure quite as sophisticated and subtle as that of any oral language.

However, until very recently, the view was widespread that sign languages conformed to no systematic syntactical structure. Not only did manual languages fail to reflect the grammatical rules of any familiar spoken language, but the variation observed in sign order fostered the belief that they lacked any form of syntax. Judith Greene (1975), discussing the Washoe experiment, remarked on the "crudity" of ASL and its "lack of subtle grammatical inflections." Tweney and Hoemann (1973, p. 56) claimed that "ASL lacks, to a very great degree, not only order constraints but sign-level inflection markers to indicate grammatical role. The absence of both ordering and morphological inflection has been used to argue that sign languages lack linguistic structure (Tervoort, 1968)." Dale (1974), a strongly oralist writer, talks about "the grammatical syntax (if one can call it that) of signed language" (p. 14). Signing was generally regarded as a kind of random listing of immutable elements, highly analytical in character.

But this view was utterly wrong. ASL has proven to be an extremely inflected language. How could so many experts have been so mistaken for so long? Klima and Bellugi (1979) remark:

> We found that the way deaf people signed to us was radically different from the way they signed to each other ... they arranged their signs in English word order, mouthed English words, and eliminated the most distinctive properties of their own language.... Sometimes when something different came into our view, one deaf person would say to another, "Don't show them that—that's slang." When they were signing among themselves, however ... the so-called slang was pervasive: there were all kinds of embellishments that they earnestly shielded us from. (p. vi)

So, remarkably, it seems that the critics of ASL *were so successful at portraying it as linguistically deficient that even its users were convinced of its inferiority.* The result was a self-fulfilling prophecy: The "experts" were now shown only what they expected to see. Only when the Salk researchers began to run controlled experiments did the true complexity of ASL syntax emerge.

General Features of ASL Grammar

It seems to have been established beyond doubt that ASL is a highly inflected language. More specifically, it strongly resembles the family of *incorporating* languages that invoke complex manipulations of verb forms to carry a wide variety of meanings. However, whereas most natural languages inflect using sequential[7] rearrangements of morphemes, ASL employs *simultaneous* inflections: A basic sign structure is embedded within a complex pattern of movements that

---

[7]Of course, spoken languages do employ pitch and stress superimposed on standard syntax to modify meaning; sometimes a meaning can be wholly reversed (e.g., "*Charming!*" "I like *that!*"). Is this inflection? Linguists disagree.

systematically modify its meaning. This exploitation of spatial parameters enables the ASL signer to achieve an economy of expression which eludes the English speaker. Lane, Boyes-Braem, and Bellugi (1976) cite a 7-word sentence, "Three of them came over to me," which can be compressed into a single inflected ASL sign.

Besides compression of meaning, ASL shares another feature with incorporating languages such as Navaho: Many of the meanings transmitted lack any simple English mapping. We refer in chapter 5 (p. 229) to the classifiers that can also incorporate ASL "size-and-shape specifiers" and transmit certain physical data about objects (Kegl, 1976; Kegl & Wilbur, 1976; Wilbur, 1982). Other subtleties of meaning encountered in ASL grammar include distinctions between categories of verb object, manner of verb operation, and aspect. Some of the associated inflections are obligatory in a given syntactical context, and some are optional.

Finally, a characteristic feature of all inflected languages is a relative lack of concern for item order. Whereas word sequence is frequently crucial in disambiguating sentences in English and other analytical languages, synthetic languages possess considerable flexibility in this regard. Hence, early observations regarding the lack of word order in sign language were correct. It was the conclusion that this meant that they were not languages that was unjustified—they were merely reflecting a characteristic of all inflected languages. In the following sections we explore these inflectional characteristics in more detail.

Aspectual Modulations

Some adjectival signs in ASL are regarded as *mutable* in the sense that they may be modified by certain inflections of *aspect*. In certain syntactical environments, aspectual modulations may be obligatory on ASL users. In the case of nonmutable signs, such inflections are not appropriate. Typically, aspectual features are signaled by movement tempo and manner. Klima and Bellugi have identified the following major aspectual inflections:

1. *Predispositional aspect*, meaning "is prone to be ..." or "tend to be ..." are characterized by the Circular Modulation, three smoothly executed circular movements. Repetitive movements constituting the basic form of the sign reduce to a single element embedded within the inflection. Certain features, such as hand-internal movements, are severely curtailed or lost altogether. In certain contexts, the circular modulation is obligatory: thus, following Klima and Bellugi, the sentence:
BOY TEND ^ (HIS) ALL-HIS-LIFE SICK [M:predispositional]

("that boy has tended to be sickly all his life") is grammatical in ASL, but the uninflected version
*BOY TEND-(HIS) ALL-HIS-LIFE SICK [uninflected]
is regarded as incorrect by ASL signers.

2. *Susceptative aspect*, meaning "easily" or "susceptible to," is carried by a single thrusting motion combined with loose HC: the Thrust Modulation.

3. *Continuative aspect*, indicating an enduring quality; "for a long time," and similar terms are signaled by three or four elliptical movements, slow and irregular in tempo, known as the Elliptical Modulation.

4. *Incessant aspect*, defining multiple occurrences of a state, "incessantly," and the like. The Tremolo Modulation comprises several repetitions of tiny, tense, uneven movements.

5. *Frequentive aspect*, denoting "frequently" or "often," carried by the Marcato Modulation, which consists of four to six regular repetitions.

6. *Intensive aspect*, signifying, for example, "intensely," and "very," is carried by the Tense Modulation: a long, tense hold, then rapid movement followed by a final hold.

7. *Approximative aspect*, meaning "slightly," "somewhat," and so on, is characterized by a lax HC and minimal reiteration: the Lax Modulation.

8. *Resultative aspect*, used when some process has led to a complete change of some sort. The Accelerando Modulation has a tense start, slow acceleration, and a long final hold.

9. *Iterative aspect*, signifying "repeatedly," has a tense movement followed by a slow return.

10. *Protractive aspect*, "constantly," comprises an extended hold.

11. *Susceptative/frequentive aspect*, meaning "frequently susceptible to," combines (2) and (5) to produce four steady repetitions of a brief thrusting motion.

Figure 3.8 gives examples of each modulation applied to the basic sign SICK.

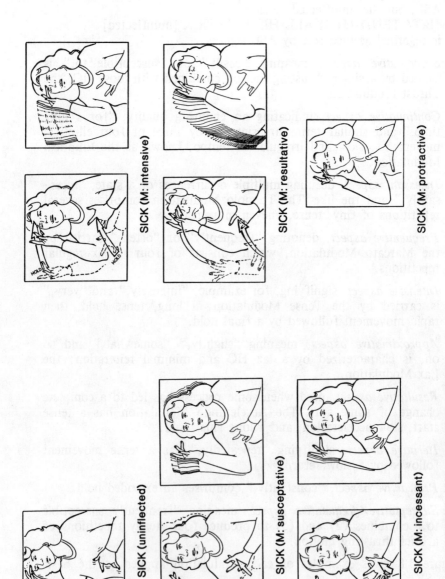

FIG. 3.8.   Aspectual modulations of the ASL sign SICK.

Source—E.S. Klima and U. Bellugi (1979), *The signs of language*, pp. 246-263. Copyright and reprinted by permission of Harvard University Press.

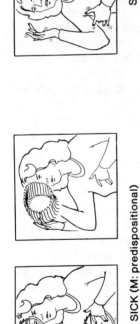

SICK (M: approximative)

SICK (M: iterative)

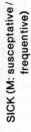

SICK (M: susceptative / frequentive)

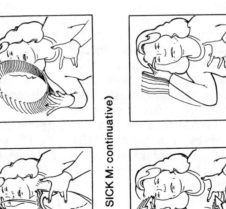

SICK (M: predispositional)

SICK M: continuative)

SICK (M: frequentive)

Fig. 3.8 (cont.)

Verb Inflections in ASL

In ASL, as in other incorporating languages, verbs are employed to carry information which in English would be expressed through a variety of syntactical devices. Some verb inflections in ASL are obligatory, and some are optional. Some are identical to those applied to adjectival structures. Once again, many of the semantic distinctions signaled by verb marking in ASL would, in English, either be ignored, or expressed through quite long phrases.

Verb number is obligatory in most instances and takes on the role of noun inflection in English. Number marking exploits the spatial indexing system used by ASL: To express pronouns and nouns referred to anaphorically, the signer assigns locations in the horizontal signing plane. Movements directed toward one of these locations will refer to the person or object "placed" there previously. Thus a slight modification of a verb sign removes the need to employ a standard form of noun or descriptive phrase to remove ambiguity and achieves a remarkable economy of effort. Moreover, interactions between the objects present on the signing plane can be expressed directly by movements from one to another; and references to indeterminate or generic concepts can be established at correspondingly higher planes. It seems as if the signer is creating a spatial model of the semantic elements in his narrative, strikingly reminiscent of the "memory theaters" invented by Renaissance mnemonic writers such as Camillo and Fludd. To remember numerous or difficult ideas, one was advised to mentally place vivid and striking images on an imaginary stage (Yates, 1966). The ASL signer goes further and "places" his concepts at specific loci in full view of his audience (Bellugi & Klima, 1982a).[8]

Conventionally, actions made in a forward direction signify "you," whereas movements directed to one side signify "him"; but body and head shifts can reassign the locations in systematic ways. Number in ASL can be signified within the context of this scheme: singular verbs as in MAN, (ME) ASK ("I asked the man") are produced with a single movement toward one locus; multiple verbs, as in MAN, (ME) ASK [N:multiple] ("I asked the men"), are produced with a sweep along the signing plane. In addition, dual and triad verbs can be signified by two or three movements toward different loci. Further distinctions (between concepts known to the

---

[8]It is interesting to speculate about the capacity of the place system. How many characters and things can be positioned on the signing planes before the memories of the observers (and perhaps even the signer) are overloaded? Do confusions occur between adjacent loci?

signer and those not known) are expressed through the height and length of movements.

Distributional Aspect is a verb inflection in ASL with no parallel in English. We list the basic forms very tersely (see Klima and Bellugi, 1979, pp. 284-91, for a detailed description). The *Exhaustive* form signifies actions relating to all the members of a group, and comprises a series of arcs. The *Allocative Determinate* refers to actions directed toward specified individuals at different times: Both hands make a series of "random movements" directed at different loci. The *Allocative Indeterminate* signifies actions to unspecified individuals: Both hands produce large spiral patterns. The *Apportionative External* inflection signals actions distributed around a closed group and is made by circular horizontal iterations. The *Apportionative Internal* refers to actions distributed over all the parts of a whole and comprises vertical circling movements. The *Seriated External* modulation refers to objects in the same generic class: Iterated movements of a sign are overlaid by a single horizontal shift. The *Seriated Internal*, referring to some of the internal features of objects, is similar, but with a downward vertical shift.

Temporal Aspect and Focus of verbs includes many of the Aspectual Modulations applied to adjectival predicates (protractive, incessant, continuative, and iterative). In addition, there are the *Habitual* inflection, a series of rapid, non-tense repetitions, to act "regularly"; the *Facilitative*, a single fast elongated movement, meaning "with ease"; the *Inceptive*, "the onset of a change of state," and the *Augmentive*, three or four iterations on an upward line, meaning "more and more," "increasingly," and similar concepts.

A set of selected verb inflections listed by Hanson and Bellugi (1982) is shown in Fig. 3.9. In general, aspectual modulations are marked by temporal and stylistic patterning; distributional inflections are spatial in character.

Derivational Processes

A number of processes in ASL govern the derivation of one type of sign from another. As in English, nouns and verbs are frequently very similar, except that nouns are made in a more restrained manner (failure to distinguish the two may have led observers to claim that ASL is syntactically deficient in this respect): for example, SWEEP and BROOM. Nouns can be formed into adjectives (e.g., CHINA-CHINESE) by using a fast, tense movement. Verbs may be formed into gerunds or adjectives, and consistently applied rules similarly control the figurative extension of the signs for concrete concepts.

TEMPORAL ASPECT

PREACH (habitual)
'preach regularly'

PREACH (iterative)
'preach over and over again'

PREACH (continuative)
'preach for a long time'

DISTRIBUTIONAL ASPECT

PREACH (exhaustive)
'preach to each of them'

PREACH (apportionative
internal)
'preach all over'

PREACH (apportionate
external)
'preach among members of a group'

PREACH (allocative
determinate)
'preach to certain ones'

PREACH (allocative
indeterminate)
'preach to any and all'

FIG. 3.9.   Aspectual modulations of signs.

Formational Components

Morphological processes in ASL may be decomposed into a limited set of formational features. Klima and Bellugi (1979) have identified 11 such components. Some are spatial, some temporal in form; some are bipolar, some are multidimensional:

1. *Planar locus*: location of the inflection with respect to the major signing planes;

2. *Geometric pattern*: movement with respect to points, arcs, circles, or linear motion;

3. *Direction*: lateral, downwards, or upwards;

4. *Manner*: nature of offset (hold, continuous, or restrained);

5. *Rate*: relative speed of articulation;

6. *Tension*: tense or lax;

7. *Evenness*: even or uneven movement;

8. *Size*: spatially elongated or curtailed;

9. *Contouring*: multiple articulations are patterned in various ways— e.g., straight, circular, or elliptical;

10. *Cyclicity*: number and type of repetitions;

11. *Doubling of hands*: some inflections employ two hands for signs that use single hands in their citation form.

These dimensions of inflection are qualitatively different from those underlying the formational parameters of basic signs and those employed in the indexic system. In general the inflectional processes exploit a wider range of movement qualities than the lexical parameters. During discourse, the simpler lexical movements are embedded within the morphological patterns, mutatis mutandis, and their meaning modified accordingly. Sometimes the dimensional values of lexical forms are changed; sometimes the inflections are simply added to the basic signs; sometimes a movement inherent to a sign is nested within the inflectional movement. As the intended meaning of the signer increases in complexity, inflections may themselves be embedded within other inflections in an extraordinary spatio-temporal kaleidoscope. In fact, the nature of morphological processes in ASL suggest that we need to revise our views about the simple sign: Perhaps we should regard it not as an elementary combination of parameters that may be modified under inflection, but as an underlying abstract form which is realized in one way under citation conditions, and in another way during the operation of inflections (Supalla & Newport, 1978; also see McDonald, 1983).

The Acquisition of ASL

A major focus of the Salk Institute's ASL research has been the acquisition of sign language by the deaf child of deaf parents. We briefly summarize the initial results of these studies as described by Bellugi and Klima (1982b) in their first major paper on the subject (also see Bellugi & Klima, 1982a). Further data on the acquisition of sign language is reviewed in later chapters.

Deictic Reference

Whereas names and simple nouns carry a one-to-one correspondence with concrete objects in the environment, personal pronouns such as *I* and *you* change in meaning depending on who is speaking. For this reason, hearing children make frequent errors when using them, and complete acquisition of the personal pronoun system does not appear before about 3 years of age. In ASL, I and YOU are signaled by pointing, and it might be expected that deaf infants would experience less difficulty than their hearing counterparts in grasping the structure of the system.

In fact, the performance of deaf children matches that of hearing, both qualitatively and chronologically. Deaf children of less than 3 years of age typically make errors in distinguishing "self" from "other" in situations involving I and YOU. Mothers with children in this age group prefer to use personal names or standard signs (e.g., MOTHER) in signing to them. Deaf children seem unable to exploit the (to us) obvious iconicity inherent in the act of pointing; rather, the formal properties of ASL signs direct their behavior from a very early age. One of the Salk team, Laura Petitto, has identified four stages in the acquisition of deictic reference: (a) At 10 months, the deaf child points freely at himself/herself and others; (b) from 11 months to 1:9 years this ceases altogether, although objects may still be pointed at. Lexical signs are used to refer to self and others. (c) Around 1:10 years, the child again starts to point toward addressees, but when referring to himself/herself; in this stage, attempts to correct the child's ASL, even by direct manipulation of his/her hands, are ineffective. (d) Finally, at around 2:3 years, the pronoun system is fully acquired. This pattern, remark Bellugi and Klima (1982b), "suggests very strongly that the same strategies are being employed by deaf and by hearing children" (p. 9). Their errors, in both cases, may result from the overgeneralization of linguistic rules that are modified or reversed in a few specific situations.

Verb Agreement

As we have seen, verbal indexing is spatial in character: The action of a verb is directed toward or away from specifically assigned locations in the signing space. Some ASL verbs are transitive and require a compulsory indexing component; others are intransitive and do not; some can be optionally indexed; others have limitations of various kinds, as in English. Another Salk researcher, Richard Meier (1980), has described 2 phases in the acquisition of verb agreement. At about 2 years, deaf children do not employ any inflectional processes and fail to mark verbs appropriately. To convey "you give me," they will sign GIVE in its uninflected form, which normally reads "I give you." Again, parental efforts to correct the child's actions invariably fail. In a second phase, between 2 and 3 years, the child slowly acquires the correct inflectional forms. Morphologically complex forms are more slowly acquired, even though they may be simpler iconically. Errors of overgeneralization such as *SAY[x:1 to 2] ("I say to you"), which is ungrammatical in ASL, occur frequently. Clearly the deaf child is learning the rules of language and applying them to the irregular forms as well as the regular.

Noun-Verb Distinction

The behavioral basis of the ASL user's discrimination between nouns and related verbs is muscle tension; nouns have more restrained manner and somewhat smaller movements. Non-ASL speakers find the visual distinction very difficult to spot. Bellugi and Klima (1982b) have reviewed the work of Patricia Launer, in the Salk laboratory, concerning the acquisition of noun-verb derivational processes; Launer gathered extensive observational and test data on 32 deaf children of deaf parents and identified three significant periods. At ages 1-2 years, no distinction is made between nouns and morphologically related verbs. In this period, mothers' signing to their children is characterized by highly exaggerated signing movements that obliterate noun-verb differences and emphasize iconic aspects of signs. "Motherese" is nongrammatical in ASL, and bears comparison with the "baby talk" of hearing parents. At 2-3 years mothers begin to employ appropriate noun-verb marking, and their children start to apply these distinctions slowly and inconsistently. Often the children spontaneously develop idiosyncratic ways of distinguishing nouns and verbs, as though aware of the need to differentiate the two syntactic classes but not yet able to cope with the subtleties of ASL morphology. Finally, at 3-5 years, deaf children acquire the noun-verb distinction and apply the markers to all kinds of noun-verb pairings irrespective of iconicity or concreteness. They even begin to apply the markers creatively, in deriving novel verb forms from nouns, and apply the morphological rules in irregular ASL forms (overgeneralization).

Anaphoric Reference

Evidence that verb-agreement and anaphoric reference, although structurally similar, are different systems within ASL, comes from studies of the acquisition of anaphoric indexing. Ruth Loew analyzed the stories told by deaf children. She found that at 3 years, the children fail to make consistent reference to nonpresent entities in their narratives. At 3:6 years they begin to index the characters in their discourse, but instead of allocating separate locations for each they "stack" all the referents in one place! At 4:4 years different locations are assigned correctly but changed unexpectedly at intervals. Finally, by 4:9 years, something close to an adult level of usage is attained.

ASL in the Linguistic Context

Taken together, the data just described provide striking support for the proposition that ASL is acquired in much the same way as is any oral language: Children acquire increasingly complex sets of linguistic rules in a systematic fashion. Iconic and pantomimic features play only a minimal role, even in the earliest stages of development. Moreover, deaf children seem to acquire ASL at the same rate as hearing children acquire spoken language (see pp. 236 to 237). However, a conclusive answer cannot be given to naive questions about the linguistic status of sign language until oral language itself is defined. Clearly, we could define language by reference to its surface features: oral output, acoustic transmission, and aural reception. Such a definition, which was adopted by the structuralists, would automatically exclude all sign languages, including ASL, from the linguistic domain. Signing could then be regarded as an instance of some more general phenomenon such as "communication" or "semiotics" (symbolic behavior). But this is a trivial response to the problem. ASL shares many of the underlying features of spoken languages, even if its surface form is radically different. Moreover, the orthography of "societal" languages is nonacoustic but clearly conforms to precisely the same grammatical and structural patterns as oral communication: It is obviously absurd to accept one as "language" while disqualifying the other.

To attempt to answer questions about the linguistic status of sign language, we briefly summarize the empirical and conceptual questions raised by the study of ASL. These remarks do not provide any easy answers but, we hope, will serve to place ASL in a linguistic context.

Levels of Analysis

ASL clearly exhibits a structural hierarchy of features akin to the "levels of analysis" that are applied in the study of oral languages. Corresponding to the phonetic level we have a gestural level; then there is a cheremic level (phonemic); a morphological level and a syntactical level; and finally a semantic level. Where ASL differs from oral language is in its preference for spatial over serial modes of production: Inflections are applied simultaneously with the lexical roots they modify. This is probably an inevitable consequence of operating in a visual, rather than an acoustic, modality: Spatial features are more salient than sequential and make more efficient use of transmission time. Perhaps, too, simultaneous nesting of the elements of a message reduces visual short-term memory load (Bellugi, 1980); we return to this topic in chapter 4.

Iconicity

One of the defining characteristics of natural language is thought to be arbitrariness in the relationship between lexical form and semantic reference. Sign languages, which at first sight appear to be highly iconic or pantomimic, seem to violate this rule. But it is clear from the evidence just reviewed (also see chapter 5, pp. 195 to 199) that iconicity in ASL is a weak and transient characteristic. Historically, the citation forms of signs tend to lose transparency; grammatical processes regularly obscure or contradict iconic features of signs; and during the acquisition of ASL, iconic characteristics of signs seem of little help. Moreover, it may merely be an evolutionary accident (see chapter 6) that man developed a form of communication in a medium that offered few opportunities for pantomimic symbolism: How could a spoken word mimic concepts such as *rock* and *tree*? It is notable that where spoken language enters a modally compatible lexical area—dealing with sounds—examples of echoicity abound: for example, *crash, bleat, bang, moan,* and *whisper.* Moreover, there is evidence for regular relationships between phonetic and semantic factors across a wide variety of languages (Brown, Black, & Horowitz, 1955). Perhaps we should regard arbitrariness, therefore, as a tendency in both spoken and signed languages, rather than an immutable characteristic of language behavior.

Grammar

Far from being inherently ungrammatical, and therefore non-linguistic, ASL conforms to a grammatical form that appears in the typology of spoken languages (McDonald, 1983). Synthetic languages differ from the analytical type in being relatively unconcerned with word order. Observing this lack of consistency in the sequencing of signs in ASL, and observing little else, critics of manual languages concluded until very recently that signing had no syntax. Ironically, European classicists for centuries regarded their own native tongues as inferior to Latin or Greek, because their more stringent rules of sequence gave them less expressive power. Analytical languages were thought of as degenerate.[9] We have already referred to the tendency of scholars to fall into superficial thinking when discussing different types of language, and we do so again. In so doing, we emphasize the fact that judgments about the linguistic quality of sign language are frequently arbitrary and based more on a lack of knowledge than on objectivity.

Semantic Power

Another frequently voiced comment on ASL was that it lacked expressive power. As we noted in chapter 2, adjectives such as "concrete," "crude," "primitive," and worse were often applied. It should be clear even from a cursory review of ASL grammar that recursive inflectional processes provide the ASL user with an expressive instrument of extraordinary capacity. Distinctions that are not drawn in English, or which cannot be concisely expressed, appear to present no difficulties to the experienced signer (and also, incidentally, contradict claims that the deaf are tied to an impaired form of cognition). ASL provides the means for categorizing and subclassifying phenomena and for deriving abstract and metaphoric representations from concrete signs (see Klima & Bellugi, 1979, on ASL puns, poetry, and theater). Tweney remarked (personal communication, March 1980): "As for the supposed inability of sign to carry an abstract message, I can offer you an anecdote. While at the Salk Institute I had the humbling (and revealing) experience of losing an argument about a sticky point in psycholinguistic theory to a deaf

---

[9]Comparing Latin and English, Kinchin Smith (1948, p. vi) remarks: "Latin is terse and accurate; it is content with one word where we use three. Every sentence is a mosaic in which the words are intricately fitted; alter one and the pattern is destroyed.... A Latin sentence is ... all neat and tidy, every part in due subordination to the whole, no straggling phrases, no unnecessary words, and all clearly rounded off under the undisputed leadership of a main verb."

graduate student who argued entirely in ASL. It takes very few such incidents to persuade one!"

Redundancy

In common with oral language, and not in common with other semiotic systems, ASL introduces a high level of redundancy into its messages. As we see in chapter 4, signs and inflections can be identified by the ASL receiver even when the information presented to him or her is no more than a fraction of that available in a complete visual display. The systemic constraints imposed by the formational and morphological rules of ASL ease the job of perceiving signed messages. Although Information Theory was developed to quantify the information content of sequentially constrained materials, there is no mathematical reason why we should be unable to apply the same logic to spatially organized elements.

Evolution

ASL has had a relatively short history compared with any known natural language. And yet during the period for which records exist— no more than 2 centuries—it has shown tremendous evolutionary change; and this despite the fact that deaf individuals have often been socially and intellectually isolated from one another, and in the face of widespread hostility to visual gestural languages among the hearing community. Perhaps one reason for the rapid change was the need to accommodate and resolve differences between Old French and original American signing systems. Another reason may be that ASL lacks an orthography that would function as a stabilizing factor. A third reason may be the need for deaf children in many schools to recreate the creolization of their language in each successive generation (chapter 5, pp. 265 to 266).

Acquisition

Deaf children of deaf parents appear to learn ASL using essentially the same cognitive strategies employed by hearing children acquiring oral languages. Iconicity at the lexical and morphological levels seems to be of little assistance to the deaf child; he or she is primarily concerned with understanding and applying the rule system underlying ASL. We may perhaps draw a rough parallel with etymological factors in spoken language: Knowing that words in English, for example, share a common Latin root, should make it somewhat easier to acquire them. But it is unlikely that such lexical redundancy contributes significantly to their acquisition by hearing infants.

The evidence, therefore, overwhelmingly supports the hypothesis that ASL is a variety of language rather than a mimetic or semiotic communication system. The internal structure of ASL differs little from that of spoken language; only its external manifestations appear atypical. Clearly, our ability to integrate ASL into mainstream psycholinguistics depends on our theoretical stance. The structuralists would have found it impossible to assimilate manual methods of communication (see Bonvillian, Charrow, & Nelson, 1973, p. 333, citing the views of Bloomfield). However, current schools of linguistics could bring ASL "into the fold" with very little difficulty. Generative grammars, which are fundamentally abstract in form, might readily be adapted to deal with simultaneous production of manual signals: Referring back to Fig. 3.3 and the associated discussion, we see the major modifications required would be (a) changing the categorial rules for generating preterminal strings; (b) altering the lexicon by substituting cheremic features for phonological and adjusting the syntactical/semantic entries; (c) entering ASL rules of grammar into the transformational subcomponent; and (d) changing the phonological component into a cheremic component. Such a task would be immensely complex, but in principle the formal constituents of a Chomskian model of ASL would be identical to those of the standard version. Whether such effort would be justified, given the problems associated with such approaches, is another question. Case grammars, suitably modified, could also handle ASL. Other possibilities have been discussed by Tweney and Hoemann (1973), and by Deuchar (1983), regarding BSL. But perhaps any elaborate theory building ought to await a more complete informal description of sign language syntax than is currently available.

Summary

A brief history of the development of linguistics and psycholinguistics suggests that we can define six basic approaches to the study of language: (a) traditional grammar, which is essentially descriptive; (b) comparative philology, concerned with the evolution of language; (c) structuralism, which deals only with surface features of language; (d) Information Theory, which attempts to quantify linguistic content; (e) transformational-generative grammar, which seeks to make explicit the rules underlying the production of syntax; and (f) case grammar, which emphasizes the primacy of semantic intent in language generation. Each approach focuses on a different aspect of language behavior; as yet no comprehensive model of natural language has been presented.

Studies of ASL conducted at the Salk Institute indicate that ASL possesses many of the vital attributes of language: (a) hierarchical organization; (b) use of a limited range of distinctive features to enhance redundancy; (c) a tendency to arbitrariness; (d) complex morphology; (e) systematic rules of derivation and compounding of signs; (f) means of communicating nonpresent and abstract concepts; and (g) rule-governed acquisition in children. However, it differs from spoken language in exploiting the opportunities visual media offer for simultaneous presentation of lexical and syntactical layers of manual movements.

Further Reading

The best recent summary of research into the psychology of language is E.H. Matthei and Thomas Roeper's (1983) excellent *Understanding and Producing Speech*. A readable introduction to the general field of linguistics is David Crystal's (1971) *Linguistics*. Simeon Potter's (1950) entertaining survey of the evolution of English, *Our Language*, provides an insight into the findings of philology, and *The Study of Language in England, 1780-1860* by Hans Aarsleff (1983) is a fascinating "intellectual journey" up to the time of William Jones. An awesome example of a traditional grammar, originally published in 1898, is J.C. Nesfield's (1930) *Manual of English Grammar and Composition*. Noam Chomsky's (1965) *Aspects of the Theory of Syntax* summarizes the theory of generative grammar but is not easy reading. The major source of information on ASL is Edward Klima and Ursula Bellugi's (1979) *The Signs of Language*; excellent summaries of the Salk researchers' findings are to be found in the papers by Bellugi and Klima (1979) and Bellugi (1980). Also of current interest as a general overview is Jerome Schein's (1984) *Speaking the Language of Signs*. An excellent practical text focused on the application of psycholinguistics and developmental psychology to teaching deaf students is by David Wood, Heather Wood, Amanda Griffiths and Ian Howarth (1985), *Teaching and Talking with Deaf Children*. It is refreshingly different from the traditional deaf education textbooks.

4

COGNITIVE FACTORS IN COMMUNICATION

In the previous chapter we discussed ASL from a linguistic viewpoint. In Chomsky's terminology, we were concerned there with those factors that constitute competence in the ASL user. Here, however, we are more interested in performance. We attempt to describe the cognitive mechanisms that underpin various methods of communication used by hearing-impaired people. By cognitive we mean those aspects of mental activity concerned with the processing of information, using the term in its broadest sense—perception, memory, and thinking.

Table 4.1 lists the major methods of communication and the cognitive channels utilized by each. In subsequent discussion, we neglect "aural only" methods that prohibit the use of any receptive channel other than amplified sound: These are employed very rarely and have never been properly investigated. We also omit consideration of the various forms of "cued speech" that exploit a restricted set of manual phonetic signs to supplement lipreading; the Rochester Method, which relies on finger spelling, and the Danish System, which is a primitive form of cued speech. The use of such systems is restricted to a few schools for the deaf, and the numbers of deaf adults relying on them is miniscule. Also missing are any of the artificial sign systems based on the formal structure of English. These systems are important, but almost nothing is known about their cognitive and linguistic bases.

We have seen that at least one major visual-gestural language, ASL, possesses many of the structural characteristics of a natural language. The four major methods of communication listed in the table therefore exhibit, on a formal level, linguistic competence:

157

TABLE 4.1
The Receptive Channels Utilized by Various Methods of Communication

Channel / Method	Amplified Sound	Lip Movements	Finger Spelling	Manual Phonetic Cues	Sign Language[a]	Non-Verbal Cues[b]	Writing
AURAL	X					X	
ORAL	X	X				X	
MANUAL			X		X	X	
TOTAL	X	X	X		X	X	
CUED SPEECH[c]	X	X		X		X	
READING							X

[a]This category does not distinguish natural sign languages from artificial systems modeled on English syntax

[b]Informal gesture, facial expression, postural cues, and similar

[c]Including Rochester and Danish systems

competence in either English, or ASL, or both (in the case of Total Communication). But, as many critics of Chomsky's theory have pointed out, it is very difficult, perhaps even impossible, to assess competence in isolation. What we can measure is performance—the communicative effectiveness of each method under controlled conditions. A high level of performance can be taken to imply the existence of an underlying competence. However, errors in performance may result either from impaired competence or defects in the peripheral processing mechanisms involved in the reception of language. In this chapter we attempt a preliminary approach to this problem, by decomposing the receptive process into its constituent elements.

Figure 4.1 illustrates the main features of an integrated approach to the cognitive organization underlying receptive communication. Visual (and residual aural) information enters the receiver's system via perceptual and memory encoding mechanisms, and a preliminary (and perhaps incorrect) reading of the start of the message passes to the natural and sign language "competence mechanisms." These mechanisms interact with semantic memory to generate an initial context for the message; in turn, output from semantic memory biases the lower level cognitive structures to recognize lexical units associated with the context. As the sample of message information increases, the receiver will be able to make increasingly good guesses about its meaning.

As in all such information-processing diagrams, there is considerable doubt about which subsystems are directly connected with which others; for example, do some perceptual analyzers provide a direct input to semantic memory? And some questions are unanswerable at the present stage of knowledge: for example, (a) should semantic memory be incorporated into the competence structure? and (b) should lexical storage be represented separately? Nevertheless, the approach provides a convenient framework for organizing research findings and gives some impression of the complexity of the communication process.

In this chapter, we begin by summarizing evidence concerning the short-term memory, semantic memory, and knowledge of syntax of the deaf communicator: the basic apparatus which he or she brings to the communication task. Then we review comparisons made between various methods of communication. Finally, we try to account for the relative performance of the major methods in terms of central and peripheral cognitive factors.

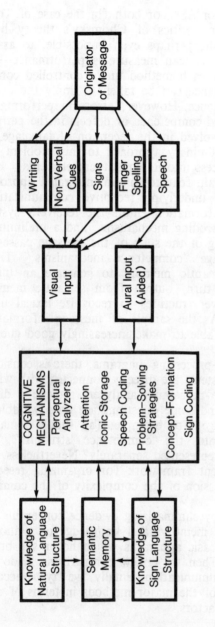

FIG. 4.1. A framework for the communication process.

Cognitive Skills and Deafness

Certain early investigators, such as Pintner, took the view that deafness itself exercised a permanent, crippling effect on intellectual function. Summarizing the results of studies of the intelligence of hearing-impaired children measured by performance tests, Pintner, Eisenson and Stanton (1941) concluded that the deaf child has an Intelligence Quotient (IQ) score 10 points lower, on average, than that of the hearing child. In contrast, Vernon (1968, 1969) reviewed some 50 independent estimates of the nonverbal intelligence of deaf respondents published between 1930 and 1967 and concluded that deaf and hearing populations show substantially the same distribution. What difference there is can be accounted for plausibly in terms of factors confounded with deafness: the greater incidence of neurological damage found among deaf people; their poorer social and vocational status; their propensity for greater emotional problems; and difficulties in explaining task requirements to them (see e.g., Chess, Korn, & Fernandez, 1971). But when we consider measures of verbal English manipulative skill, a very different picture emerges: Not surprisingly, deaf students and adults are clearly unable to perform in the same way as the hearing on such measures.

Short-Term Retention

The first major attempt to compare the visual short-term memory characteristics of deaf and hearing children was by Blair (1957). Severely and profoundly impaired children were matched with hearing subjects on the basis of intelligence, age, and sex. On both the Knox Cube test (in which subjects are required to remember the order of the stimuli) and Memory for Designs, the deaf subjects significantly outperformed the hearing. On the Object Location test, common objects were displayed in a number of different positions on a card, with subjects required to remember where they had appeared. Deaf subjects again achieved higher scores than the hearing, although the difference was not statistically significant. Only in the Span test, in which subjects had to recall sequences of stimuli, digits, pictures, dominoes, or reversed digits, did the scores of the deaf subjects consistently fall below those of the control subjects. In other words, deaf subjects were found to have a slightly smaller capacity for short-term retention. Blair conjectured that this reflected a specific deficit in auditory memory and found that deaf children's scores on the four span tests correlated significantly with their reading ability. Later researchers, notably Conrad, whose work is described in more detail (pp. 199 to 201) have confirmed these findings, showing in addition that measures of acoustic short-term encoding are highly correlated with individual lipreading and speech skills. It seems that the short-term memory (STM) deficiency is specifically associated with the amount of verbal encoding and processing demanded by the test employed. In the light of such findings, Belmont and Karchmer (1978) have questioned whether we should describe deaf people as having a "memory" deficit per se. But whatever the theoretical interpretation we place on the evidence, its pragmatic significance is plain—in learning situations, deaf children will experience more problems than hearing in holding several verbal items in working memory. (Also see Belmont, Karchmer, & Pilkonis, 1976, on the effects of rehearsal.)

Free Recall of Word Lists

Koh, Vernon, and Bailey (1971) compared the recall of word lists by deaf and hearing subjects in two age groups, 13-14 years and 18-20 years. Two types of lists were employed: *mixed*, in which words were selected randomly; and *categorized*, in which the words belonged to specific semantic categories. Hearing subjects generally exploit their semantic knowledge in memorizing verbal materials, which makes it easier for them to recall categorized or associated lists of words. Would deaf subjects have the same ability? Over the whole experiment, hearing subjects performed more efficiently than deaf; but the older deaf subjects did nearly as well as the older hearing subjects in recalling the categorized lists. Both groups appeared to be exploiting their conceptual knowledge in coping with the task, but the hearing subjects were doing so more effectively. We look at this problem in more detail in the next section.

Semantic Organization

The basic "world knowledge" which humans possess—their semantic memory—is increasingly regarded by researchers as central to the communication process. Deficiencies in input and output channels may be corrected or bypassed, but unless the human communicator has at his or her disposal the central cognitive mechanisms that make understanding of messages possible, the situation is hopeless. As we see, prelingual hearing loss exercises a devastating effect on the ability of the deaf child to acquire competence in the syntax of oral language. But does it similarly inhibit the acquisition of semantic structures necessary for comprehension? To answer this question, basically three lines of enquiry have been followed.

Bonvillian, Charrow, and Nelson (1973) reviewed studies of deaf individuals employing word-association techniques, in which these individuals had to state which words they associated with various stimulus words. They concluded that deaf and hearing subjects show significant differences in the number and type of associations given. The deaf subjects tended to give fewer responses, expressed a greater number of "visual" associations, and were less effective in matching the syntactic class of the stimulus than hearing subjects. The authors suggested that the results might be attributable to (a) associations being influenced by sign language syntax; and (b) excessive formality in the English instruction given to deaf pupils. Expanding on their second point, it is important to note that deaf children, more so than hearing, have less experience in dealing with tasks involving open-ended or undirected responses. Such techniques are used less frequently because communication difficulties between adult and child encourage the adult to use questions which require pointing, monosyllabic or very brief answers (see pp. 222 and 248).

The studies reported in the previous paragraph are interesting, but they confound syntactical and semantic factors so that interpretation is difficult. Two important papers reporting data on the semantic organization of deaf adolescents in which syntax and semantics are clearly separated are worth describing in some detail because they draw out some interesting conclusions about semantics. Tweney, Hoemann, and Andrews (1975) reported two experiments in which subjects were required to sort words into categories. In the first study, 63 deaf and 63 hearing subjects (16-18 years) were presented with a mixture of (a) common nouns and (b) words relating to sound (such as *hiss, roar, whine*). As expected, deaf subjects often placed the sound words in a "don't know" category. The remaining word selections were analyzed to detect clusters of words regarded as similar by each group of subjects. Consistency of choice within the groups was assessed by means of an "overlap coefficient." For common nouns, the deaf and hearing subjects showed about the same degree of semantic consistency; for sound words, both groups were less consistent overall, with the deaf slightly less consistent than the hearing.

In a second study employing the same basic design, Tweney, Hoemann, and Andrews compared the sorting patterns of deaf and hearing subjects for concrete (high imagery) and abstract (low imagery) words. The two lists were very carefully controlled with respect to frequency, signability, and normative vocabulary measures. In addition, the common nouns employed in the first experiment were included to assess reliability. For the high imagery words, both deaf and hearing groups achieved overlap scores of 0.500. For low imagery words the overlap scores were again about the same (0.611 for deaf subjects, 0.666 for hearing). The only differences observed between the groups were matters of detail: In the high imagery condition deaf subjects tended to classify *magazine* with *avenue*; hearing tended to class it with *chair*. The deaf subjects grouped the low-imagery word *length* with *style*, where hearing subjects linked it with *hour*. The authors concluded that "the present studies provide strong evidence for equality of hierarchical semantic structure in deaf and in hearing subjects" (Tweney, Hoemann, & Andrews, 1975, p. 72). The result is particularly interesting because it contradicts the frequent assertion that deaf people are tied to concrete modes of mentation. In fact, the response of deaf and hearing subjects to abstract verbal materials is very similar *when no demands are made on syntactical skills*. Further support for this contention is also found indirectly in studies such as that of Poizner, Bellugi, and Tweney (1981) showing that deaf and hearing persons' ratings of word imagery are highly correlated ($r = 0.92$). In view of the limited verbal experience of hearing-impaired children, such findings pose interesting questions concerning the acquisition of semantic information, questions we attempt to address in some detail throughout the rest of this chapter.

A similar technique, more usually employed in a clinical context, has been applied to deaf adults by the late Angus Gordon (1977). They were asked to rate eight people (father, teacher, and others) on 10 constructs such as *like-dislike*, and *happy-sad*. Once again, analyses of the data showed no difference in complexity of personal construct systems between the deaf group and a hearing control group. Moreover, in terms of the major evaluative component detected in such studies, the pattern of loadings observed for the two groups correlated highly ($r = 0.86$). The few puzzling differences that did emerge seemed to reflect emotional adjustment rather than cognitive complexity. Nevertheless, the study revealed that deaf people organize their conception of the social environment in as complex and sophisticated a manner as hearing people, even though they are lacking in auditory language input and in speech competence. Semantic competence can seemingly exist independently of syntactical skill in a spoken language (and perhaps even a signed language), and once this distinction is understood and accepted, many seemingly puzzling aspects of deaf persons' behavior become intelligible. Although raising awkward theoretical problems, this finding is a hopeful sign, implying, as it does, that knowledge of the world even of a highly abstract kind can be acquired and utilized by hearing-impaired people.

Linguistic Skills

In vivid contrast to the results obtained for semantic skills, the many
studies of the syntactical abilities of prelingually deaf respondents are
unanimous in concluding that prelingual profoundly deaf persons
*rarely, if ever, attain high levels of proficiency in spoken language
structures.* Because this area is very thoroughly documented our review is brief: Good summaries have been published by Myklebust
(1964); Bonvillian, Charrow, and Nelson (1973); Russell, Quigley,
and Power (1976); and by Levine (1981).

Normative surveys of the reading skills of the deaf provide the
least optimistic picture (Reynolds, 1976). For example, the classic
and widely quoted study conducted by the Office of Demographic
Studies at Gallaudet College in 1971 employed the Paragraph
Meaning Subtest of the Stanford Achievement Test (SAT) (see
DiFrancesca, 1972; Reynolds, 1976). The results of this survey,
shown in Fig. 4.2, indicated that although the reading skills of deaf
students increase steadily from 6-20 years, they peak at a reading
level equivalent to Grade 4 in the United States school system (approximately chronological age 9 years). In another major survey of
over 13,000 deaf children, Silverman-Dresner and Guilfoyle (1972),
looked at the vocabulary scores of respondents aged 8-17 years.
Multiple choice criteria were used to assess the deaf pupils' understanding of English words known to be familiar to hearing children
of a younger (6-11 years) age range. Deaf children aged 8-9 years
recognized only 18 out of the pool of 7,300 words on average (about
0.25%), but scores increased rapidly with age, and subjects in the
16-17 years group responded correctly to 2,545 (35%) of the test
words. Estimates of the spoken vocabulary sizes of hearing children,
although not directly comparable, suggest average scores of 19 for
15-month-old hearing infants, and around 2,600 for 6-year-olds (see
p. 17; Mussen, Conger, & Kagan, 1969, p. 247). Taking these results
at face value suggests that the English vocabulary of deaf students at
the end of their school career is only equivalent to that of a 6-year-
old hearing child. In fact, as we have already seen, the deaf student
has a conceptually complex world, and, for many, their internalized
or sign language vocabulary is significantly greater than their spoken
English vocabulary.

More detailed studies of the acquisition of relatively complex
spoken language syntactical structures suggest that some of the
grammatical processes of these languages also present extreme difficulties for prelingually deaf students. Identifying these problems has
not, unfortunately, suggested effective remedial techniques, but it
does give us some insights into the problems facing students who are

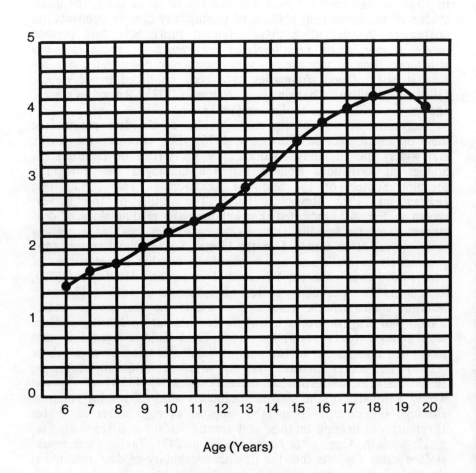

FIG. 4.2.   Reading skills of deaf students: Grade equivalent scores on the Paragraph
Meaning Subtest of the SAT.

Data from H.N. Reynolds (1978), Perceptual effects of deafness, in R.D. Walk and H.L. Pick
(Eds.), *Perception and experience*, New York: Plenum Press.

trying to code temporal order using a visual-spatial system. The basic paradigm was set by Heider and Heider (1940); it uses four methods to assess syntactical skills: (a) classifying and analyzing written materials produced by deaf and hearing-impaired subjects; (b) requiring students or others to complete a partial sentence or phrase (the 'cloze' procedure); (c) multiple choice techniques of various types; and (d) asking subjects to give judgments of the grammaticality of grammatical and deviant sentences.

Although potentially the most informative method, the analysis of written materials generated by deaf respondents has proven extremely difficult (Arnold, 1978a). For example, the most extensive data on written language materials, those of Myklebust (1964), were obtained using the Picture Story Language Test (PSLT). They deal only in relatively gross measures of syntax, such as counts of the relative frequencies of basic word classes. Doubts about the syntactical categorization proposed by Myklebust have been expressed by a number of researchers, including Vandenberg (1971), O'Sullivan (1977), Kretschmer and Kretschmer (1978) and Arnold (1979). One of the problems is that it is difficult to apply formal criteria of grammaticality to materials so deficient in English language structure. Lacking any kind of linguistic framework, judges inevitably have to make guesses about the subjects' intended meaning (see Table 4.2 which uses the method of analysis proposed by Kretschmer and Kretschmer) and, as a glance at the examples given in Table 4.2 shows, this is by no means easy. The validity and reliability of such procedures must be seriously questioned, particularly when they focus on English language (or another spoken language) syntax to the exclusion of others. It is reasonable to regard them as assessments of English language competence. Unfortunately, they have also been equated with assessments of language competence, which results in a very misleading view of the achievements of deaf children. Analysts have frequently failed to recognize the possibility that some deficiencies in the English productions of deaf children may reflect a confusion between English and Sign Language syntax.

Taking account of the reservations just expressed, some of Myklebust's findings are of considerable interest. He found that over the age range 7-17 years the lengths of stories produced by deaf and by hearing subjects both showed regular increases, with the hearing subjects producing essays almost twice as long as those of the deaf subjects at each age level. By 17 years, the deaf and hearing groups both averaged around 10 sentences per essay, the sentences of the deaf respondents being shorter and simpler. An overall measure of syntax showed that the hearing subjects tended to reach their ceiling by age 11 years; deaf respondents were still showing a slight

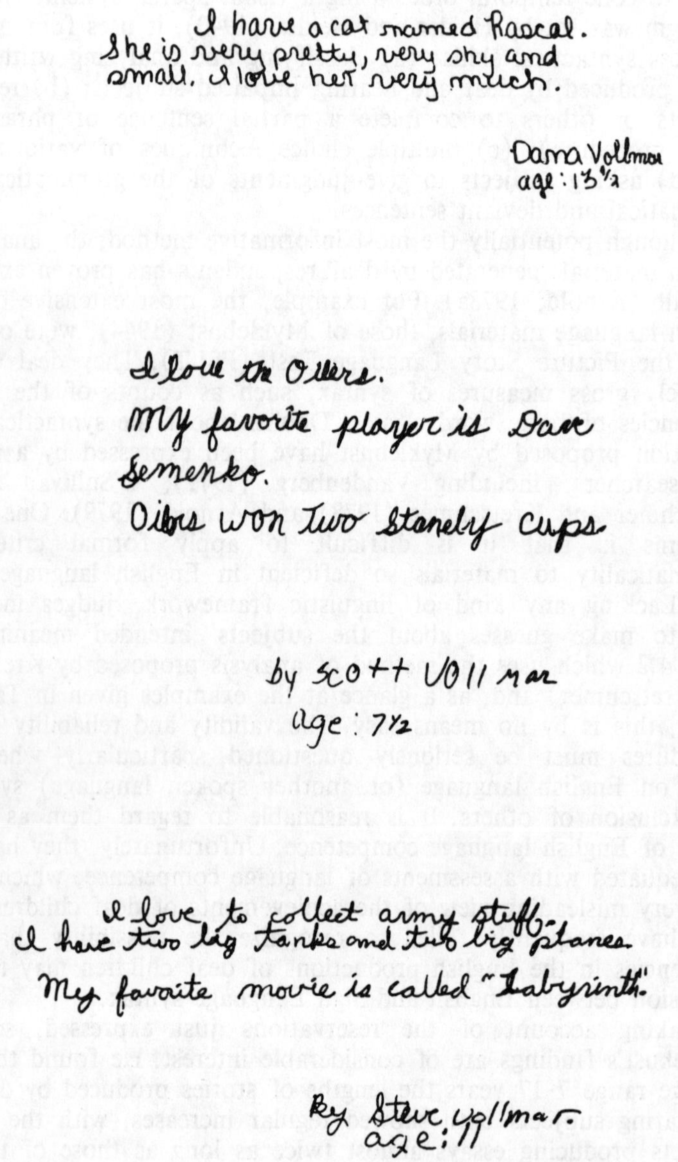

I have a cat named Rascal.
She is very pretty, very shy and
small. I love her very much.

Dana Vollmer
age : 13½

I love the Oilers.
My favorite player is Dave
Semenko.
Oilers won Two Stanely cups

by Scott Vollmar
age : 7½

I love to collect army stuff.
I have two big tanks and two big planes.
My favorite movie is called "Labyrinth."

By Steve Vollmar.
age: 11

FIG. 4.3   Examples of good language produced by some deaf students.

TABLE 4.2

Language Sample Analysis

Name: Lyn   Age: 11-10   Hearing Status: Hearing-Impaired

Context: This sample was elicited in response to the LeBoeuf Picture Story Sequence "Teatime." The subject was asked to produce a story about the pictures. The utterances collected were produced by the child in sign and oral language form.

Sample: The girl asked Mother I want to pour the coffee. And the girl was happy to pour in the cup. And the girl did not watch pour. And the table. And Mother was cross with mother girl.

Analysis:

Sentence 1:   The girl asked Mother I want to pour the coffee.

Direct discourse question:	The girl asked mother ( )*	agent, action-causative, patient
Pronominalization:	The girl want to pour the coffee	
Nominalization:	The girl wants ( )	experiencer, process-causative, complement
	The girl poured the coffee	agent, action-causative, patient

*Kretschmer and Kretschmer (1978, p. 195) give the following explanation of their use of parentheses. "The parenthesis represents an elaborated node. Because the node has been filled by an entire proposition, it was felt that this fact could be represented best by employing a null or empty position represented by a set of parentheses." In the first sentence Lyn has produced an utterance which includes one elaborated node, thus, the use of the parenthesis in the analysis undertaken is appropriate.

Comment:

Sentence 1 is a complex production where Lyn conveys the meaning very well. However, the conventions of direct discourse are such that the verb "ask" is used with a modal, e.g., 'The girl asked her Mother, "Can I pour?"' The verb "said" could be used here, e.g., "The girl said to her mother..." In direct discourse the sentence would have become "The girl asked her mother if she could..." Kretschmer and Kretschmer would describe this as a pragmatic violation (p. 192).

This sentence might include a personal pronoun or definite article. If she is making the assumption that the girl is related to the woman in the picture "pronominalization—genitive" would be appropriate, e.g., "her" in reference to the mother. If the woman, in Lyn's conception, is any mother, the definite article modulation "the" would be appropriate. Lyn has used past tense morphemic modulation appropriately in this sentence "asked."

Analysis:

Sentence 2:	And the girl was happy to pour in the cup.	
Coordinating conjunction:	The girl was happy to pour in the cup	
Nominalization infinitive:	The girl was happy ( )	experiencer, stative-dynamic, condition
	The girl poured (the tea, coffee) in the cup	agent, action-causative (patient-omitted) locative-action

Comment:

Again, Lyn has appropriately caught the semantic loading in the pictures since the girl did indeed look happy and did begin to pour the tea in cup. She omits the object (patient) node in this sentence. This might be because she was not sure what the liquid in the pot was—this might not be within her experience and this is understandable as teapots are not as common as they used to be and Lyn is an Inuit girl, too!

The syntax of "happy to pour" could be an example of a "violation of transformation selection restrictions" (p. 191). Thus Lyn might have used "happy to be pouring," "happy that she is allowed to" or something of this nature.

"In the cup" is categorized as "locative action" because this would seem to be the most appropriate semantic description. Kretschmer and Kretschmer do not provide an example of the use of "in" plus action. They might categorize "the girl" in "the girl was happy" as "entity" while "experiencer" would seem quite appropriate (see p. 107).

Analysis:

Sentence 3:	The girl did not watch pour.
Coordinating conjunction:	The girl did not watch pour
Negation:	The girl did watch ( )
Do-support:	The girl watched (when she was pouring) agent, action-causative

Comment:

In this sentence the modality change (negation) and the do-support transformative have been used appropriately.

Lyn's use of "pour" to convey the meaning "when she was pouring" or "as she poured" shows that at the semantic or deep structure level she is aware of quite complex propositions. She does not as yet have the surface forms to convey this meaning in English (or signed English).

Analysis:

Sentence 4:	And the table.

This is not a sentence form and should be labeled a fragment or an utterance. Lyn seems to have omitted a sizeable chunk of surface form here. Her meaning was probably "and the tea spilled on the table."

Coordinating conjunction:	And (the tea spilled on) the table locative action

Comment:

Kretschmer and Kretschmer's analysis techniques depend a great deal on syntactic structures actually being present. This writer would like to see changes made in the analysis format with less stress on the sentence and more on single word production, etc. being incorporated.

Analysis:

Sentence 5:	And the mother was cross with mother girl.
Coordinating conjunction:	The mother was cross with mother girl (possessive 's' omitted?)

Possessive: The mother has a girl (daughter?)

                     The mother was cross with the girl   experiencer,
                                                             stative-dynamic
                                                             recipient
Comment:

Lyn has conveyed her meaning but has used a semantic/syntactic form "mother girl" not used in English. The present writer has guessed at Lyn's meaning of "mother girl."

Summary:	*Semantic Summary:*

Summary:

No. of prepositions: 7
No. of sentences: 4

Syntactic Summary:

Modality
  Negation 1
  Direct Discourse 1

Elaborated Nodes
  Possessive 1

Conjunctions
  Coordinating 4

Transformations
  Pronominalization 1
  Do-support 1

Nominalization/infinitive 2

Semantic Summary:

Verb Categories
  action-causative 4
  process-causative 1
  stative-dynamic 2

Modifier Categories
  condition 2

Noun Categories
  agent 4
  experiencer 3
  patient 2
  recipient 1

Adverbial Categories
  locative action 2

The analysis in this table was prepared by Ceinwen E. Cumming of the University of Alberta. It uses the technique developed by Richard Kretschmer (Kretschmer & Kretschmer, 1978), but like all such analyses, it is a best attempt rather than a definitive statement. The analysis is also complicated by the fact that there are a number of syntactical intrusions.

improvement with age at 17. In contrast, a semantic measure, abstraction, showed a strong and consistent gain with age, and the correlation between syntax and abstraction scores dropped rapidly over the 9-17 years range, to 0.16 at age 17. The correlations between intelligence and abstraction, and intelligence and syntax remained low over the entire age range. Finally, Myklebust noted that the essays of deaf students contained more nouns, fewer verbs, pronouns, and adjectives, and fewer adverbs and conjunctions than the essays of hearing students.

Other studies have seemingly employed more "objective" tests of syntactical skill. Perhaps the most impressive research in this area is that conducted by Stephen Quigley and his associates at the University of Illinois, and summarized in their book *Linguistics and Deaf Children* (Russell, Quigley, & Power, 1976). Over 400 deaf school children were given a battery of tests (known collectively as the Test of Syntactic Abilities or TSA), including sentence completion, correction, conjoining, and judgments of grammaticality. The subjects were all profoundly prelingually deaf and of average intelligence, with an age range of 10-18 years. Hearing controls, aged 8-10 years, were also examined. The tests were designed within the framework of transformational grammar, with the aim of detecting typically deaf language errors ("deafisms"). In the following brief survey of the Illinois team's findings, we concentrate on the empirical data and omit the extensive Chomskian interpretations that they tend to favor.

Phrase Structure. The fundamental Noun Phrase (NP)+Verb Phrase (VP) pattern that underlies English sentences is acquired very early by hearing children (Brown, 1973). Two-word utterances begin around 2 years. By kindergarten age most of the basic structures have been acquired. Subject noun phrases and pronouns are rarely used early on, and the complexities of the verb system are absorbed more slowly. In contrast to hearing children, deaf children do not acquire the English NP+VP construction until about 10 years: Before this semantic rules predominate (Power, 1973). A sentence such as "The cat chased the dog" might be interpreted as "dog chasing cat" because this is the more likely situation (Russell, Quigley, & Power, 1976).

Sentence Conjunction. The joining of two simple sentences using *and, but,* or *or* is acquired by hearing children before 3 years, although failures to match the tense and number of the relevant verbs are common. Deaf children frequently apply conjunction procedures but make a number of characteristic errors. Wilbur, Quigley, and Montanelli (1975) defined "Object-Object Deletion" as the omission of an object word from the second conjoined sentence (e.g., "John threw the ball and Mary dropped"). "Object-Subject Deletion" likewise involves the omission of the subject from a second sentence ("The boy saw the turtles and ate the fish," where the turtles were eating the fish). Deletion of *and* is also common. Wilbur (1977) found that although judgments of grammaticality of deaf students' language rose to 80% correct at 18 years, the production of correctly conjoined sentences scored only 50-70% at this age. The frequency of Object-Subject Deletion actually increased slightly with age, perhaps because (as in the example cited) deaf children are likely to be misunderstood rather than corrected if their statements are not obviously wrong.

Relative Clauses. Relativization, the process of embedding a clause within a sentence (e.g., "The man *who is eating a cookie* is angry"), is one of the more difficult syntactical acquisitions. Menyuk (1969) found that some 40% of 10-year-old hearing children experienced problems with relative clauses. Quigley, Smith, and Wilbur (1974) reported the performance of deaf subjects on three TSA subtests: (a) a processing test, which required yes/no judgments concerning simple sentences that were or were not congruent with a complex sentence; (b) an embedding test, in which subjects made yes/no choices about complex sentences, given two simple sentences; and (c) a copying test requiring a grammaticality judgment and rewriting. Deaf children showed only a small improvement in processing scores with age (from 60% to 75%); in contrast, hearing 10-year-olds scored over 80%. The deaf subjects (and, to a lesser extent, the hearing) performed most poorly when the clause was medial—that is, in a fully embedded position. Their scores remained around 50% for all ages, 10-18 years. The deaf children tended to associate the closest NP and VP instead of the NP and VP separated by the embedded clause. Performance on the embedding subtest was also poor (50% to 60% for the deaf, around 80% for the hearing 8-10-year-olds). Both Object-Object and Object-Subject deletions caused problems for the deaf, as did sentences containing deviant possessives. The deaf subjects showed significant improvements with age in their ability to reject redundant repetitions of the clausal noun ("copying").

The Verb System. Unlike languages such as French or Latin, English employs only a few inflections to modify verb stems in the expression of tense, voice, and mood. Extensive use is made of auxiliary verbs (*have, be, shall, will, may* and *do*) combined with a few simple inflections. In hearing infants, the verb first appears in its root (unmarked) form, and is subsequently modified using the *-ing* suffix, or *-ed* to represent the past tense. Auxiliaries are acquired later. In general the present progressive (continuous) appears before past tense. Quigley, Montanelli, and Wilbur (1976) report that analysis of written language samples indicates that deaf children make four basic types of error in handling verbs: errors involving auxiliaries; inflections; copulas (such as *seem*); and often the complete omission of the verb. They found that deaf subjects' judgments of the grammaticality of auxiliary verb constructions improved from around 50% correct at 10 years to 70% at 18 years; least improvement occurred for passives (only 61% correct at 18 years). Some 40% of deaf 18-year-olds failed to notice missing auxiliaries; about 30% failed to spot missing inflections or *by* when used in passives. Only 50% of the oldest subjects noticed that of the two verbs employed in conjoined sentences one did not match the appropriate tense. However, they found it quite easy to spot missing verbs, and showed rapid improvement in their ability to detect the misuse of *be* and *have*.

Employing a controlled production technique, Ivimey (1981) has identified three stages in the acquisition of verbs. In Stage 1, deaf children employ *unit verbs*—a verb form, not necessarily simple present—combined with external markers indicative of tense, rather than the appropriate inflections or auxiliaries. The specific form of the verb seems to be idiosyncratic. In other words, in this stage deaf children appear to treat English as if it were a wholly isolating language like Chinese (do Chinese deaf children therefore find it easier to acquire their own language than do English-speaking deaf children?). Then, in an intermediate stage, regular future marking appears, but unit verbs are retained for past and present. By about 14 years of age, Stage 3 is reached, in which threefold time marking (often nonstandard) appears, but no distinction is made for aspect.

Parasnis and Lylak (1985) employed a sentence completion technique to compare deaf and hearing subjects' understanding of modals (auxilary verbs such as *can, should*, etc.). Judging which is most appropriate in a given context depends on a subtle blend of syntactic and semantic factors. To facilitate responding, two complete sentences were presented to provide a context, then an incomplete sentence. Subjects ranked the five given modals for their aptness in completing each test sentence. Differences between deaf and hearing groups emerged for items requiring an understanding of *could* used for opportunity and probability, and *should* used for future completion. In general, the deaf students tested were able to apply modals in social contexts but had difficulty when "logical decision-making" was involved (e.g., when *must* is used for logical deduction).

In fact, there is no doubt that deaf students find extreme difficulty in coping with the minutiae of the English verb system—its complicated mixture of inflections, auxiliaries, and copulas, which map on to a subtle range of temporal and conceptual meanings. Passives, which reverse the "normal" English word order, and which are acquired relatively late (up to 9 years) by hearing children, pose especially severe problems for deaf students.

Pronouns.   The pronoun system in English is complicated by the retention of case forms that have generally ceased to function within the noun system. Hearing children generally acquire the distinction between first and second person rapidly; neutral pronouns are acquired before masculine and feminine; singular before plural. More complex forms (e.g., reflexives) are more slowly acquired, and hearing children continue to make errors of use into their tenth year. Wilbur, Montanelli, and Quigley (1976) employed a multiple choice sentence completion method to assess deaf subjects' understanding of pronoun structures. Over the 10-18 year age range, correct use of pronouns showed a strongly linear gain from a generally low level (about 40%) to a moderately high level (70-80%). Possessives (*yours*, 54%; *ours*, 53%; and *theirs*, 61% at 18 years) and reflexives (e.g., *yourself, yourselves*, 55% at 18 years) proved especially difficult. In contrast to the results for hearing students, the deaf students found third person pronouns easier than second person. Relative pronouns (*which, who, that*, etc.) proved hardest of all (27% correct at 10 years improving to 56% at 18 years), but this finding is qualified by the presence of interactions with case and human versus nonhuman pronoun types (subject pronouns easier than object pronouns and human easier than nonhuman). A supplementary analysis of written language samples showed that the deaf subjects did attempt to use pronouns at appropriate times and made relatively few mistakes of case and number; person mistakes occurred more frequently. Wilbur and her colleagues concluded that deaf children probably acquire pronouns one at a time, and that some (e.g., *whose*) are often misused.

Negatives. Hearing children appear to master negation by about 8 years or sooner. Very young deaf children occasionally appear not to respond to negative markers in English, but comprehension of negative sentences is good over the period 8-17 years (Schmitt, 1968). Russell, Quigley, and Power (1976) report that the development of the negation system in deaf students follows the pattern found for the hearing, although somewhat delayed. Misuse of *do* continued to occur 30% of the time at 18 years, but deaf subjects acquire contractions (e.g., *don't*) easily and often overapply the principle.

Questions. Correct formation of questions is acquired as late as 9 years by hearing children. In their study of deaf children, Quigley, Wilbur, and Montanelli (1974) analyzed responses to simple multiple choice questions and to right/wrong-rewrite test items. Their subjects showed steady gains in comprehension of yes/no questions, Wh-questions (those beginning *who, what*, etc.), and, to a lesser extent, in tag-questions ("It is you, isn't it?"). Interestingly, grammaticality judgments showed a smaller increase with age than comprehension scores. Grammaticality scores also varied as a function of the location of *who*; higher scores resulted when *who* was the subject, rather than the object, of the question. Acceptance of deviant forms (e.g., with "copying" or redundant repetitions) showed a slow but steady decrease with age.

Complements. A traditional grammarian defines the complement as follows: "Some verbs take *one* object only, but still require some other word or words to make the predication *complete* ... (these) are called the complement" (Nesfield, 1930, p. 40). Modern psycholinguists regard complementation as one of the recursive processes in English by which simple sentences are combined into more complex structures (the others being conjunction and relativization). Quigley, Wilbur, and Montanelli (1976) define three basic types of complement: *clausal* ("John knows that *Mary is my sister*"); *infinitival* ("Horace wants Harriet *to wear a kimono*"); and *gerundive ("John's watching TV* annoys me"). The latter is also known as a possessive complement and extends the traditional definition of complementation.[1] There are complex and often arbitrary constraints on the use of specific verbs in complement formation. In hearing children, the process of complement acquisition is slow and irregular: basic forms are employed soon after first use of a permitted verb, but some forms (those involving *ask* and *promise*, for example) may not be mastered until 9 years. It is not surprising that deaf children rarely attempt to introduce complements into their written productions. Quigley, Wilbur, and Montanelli again employed a right/wrong-rewrite method to assess understanding of infinitives and gerunds. Scores on this test showed only a moderate improvement with time (50% at age 10 to 63% at 18 years) compared with hearing controls' score of 88% at 10 years. Possessives were found to be easier than infinitives for both hearing and deaf. Overall, the deaf subjects scarcely exceeded a chance level of scoring, which implies that the complementation process is by far the most difficult feature of English syntax for hearing-impaired children to acquire.

The easiest way to summarize the data obtained by the Illinois team is to graph the average scores obtained for each syntactical structure. Figure 4.4 shows the scores for the youngest (10 years) and oldest (18 years) subgroups for (a) judgments of grammaticality, and (b) the scores obtained in various production tests (multiple choice and/or cloze procedures). Two syntactical categories (questions and conjoined structures) appear in both charts. The graphs could be misinterpreted for two reasons: First, they camouflage a great deal of variation between subtests and

---

[1]Traditionally, a gerund functions as a noun, not a complement.

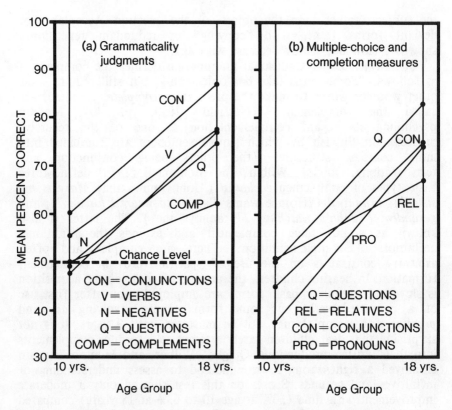

FIG. 4.4.   The performance of deaf subjects on selected tests of syntactical skill.
Data from S.P. Quigley, M.W. Steinkamp, D.J. Power, and B.W. Jones (1978), *Test of syntactic ability*, Beaverton, OR: Dormac.

between items; second, it is not clear whether the results obtained using various different production methods, often designed specifically to pick up certain characteristic processing errors, are directly comparable. With these reservations we may note the following points:

1. For virtually all the subtests represented, 10-year-old hearing control subjects were scoring in the 90% range (i.e., at the test ceiling).

2. All the test scores of the deaf subjects tend to increase with age. The relationship between mean score and age is usually strongly linear (in one case a quadratic relationship was also noted). In

other words, *the deaf subjects showed no signs of reaching a definite ceiling significantly lower than the ceiling for hearing persons*. But at the age of 18, the overwhelming majority of deaf persons are removed from full-time education and left to fend for themselves. If we make the assumption that their *potential* level of linguistic ability is far higher than is usually supposed, we can conduct an interesting experiment. If we extrapolate the percentage scores shown in Fig. 4.4, most will intersect the 100% ordinate in the age range 22-25 years. The two syntactical structures showing a smaller gradient are relativization (achieving 100% at 32 years) and complementation (42 years, for judgments of grammaticality). We are not, of course, arguing that intensive full-time language training continued for 10 or 20 years past regular school leaving age will enable all deaf persons to acquire perfect syntax. But these data do throw into doubt the claim that the English grammatical skills of deaf students and adults can only be improved to a limited extent, and strongly support the arguments of writers such as Ivimey (1976) and Wood (1984) who assert that the English language skills of the deaf are developmentally delayed rather than qualitatively different from the skills of the hearing child.

3. Taking into account the detailed pattern of scoring, we can tentatively identify two very general "problem areas" for the deaf language user. First, the deaf user finds it difficult to cope with the "fine grain" of English grammar: The complex rule systems underlying the use of inflection and auxiliaries within the verb system and the associated subtleties of tense, mood, and passivization; the case structure of the pronoun system; the seemingly arbitrary rules governing the selection of *be* and *have*, and various kinds of prepositions. These kinds of structure, known collectively as *functors*, are acquired by hearing children more slowly than the *contentive* words (nouns, verbs, adjectives and so on) which have a relatively direct semantic function (Brown, 1973). Second, processes such as relativization and complementation, which involve the reordering and transformation of whole segments of discourse, appear extremely difficult. In view of the specific auditory short-term memory processing problems noted among the deaf population (see pp. 204 to 205), it is tempting to account for this difficulty in terms of insufficient processing capacity. An alternative explanation is that of interference from ASL syntax because sign languages seem to lack equivalents of functor words, embedding the functor role within inflected verbal signs. However, it should

be stressed that such difficulties affect orally educated deaf children as well as those allowed to use manual methods. Our examination of the written materials produced by deaf students from various backgrounds leads us to suggest that it is very difficult, if not impossible, to distinguish between orally and totally educated students solely on the basis of the types of grammatical errors they make.

4. The close correspondence between the scores of deaf subjects on the TSA and the results of normative reading surveys suggests that the latter are primarily measuring syntactical factors. This point becomes important later in the chapter, when we contrast the survey findings with data relating to pragmatic measures of communication. Despite their poor syntactical skills, deaf people seem to be able to comprehend the *meaning* of messages addressed to them in a variety of modalities. Consider a series of (relatively) complex syntactical structures such as: "I would like to go"; "I might want to go"; "I would have liked to go"; "I will want to go"; "I shall like to go," and so on. Provided the receiver detects the three key elements *I, like/want,* and *go,* he will have a fairly good grasp on the semantic content of any of these forms. Given a specific context, his interpretations will be even more accurate. According to Brown (1973), this is broadly how hearing children function at an early stage of language acquisition: The "telegraphic" nature of their utterances in this stage reflects the primacy of semantic over syntactic factors.

5. Quigley, Smith, and Wilbur (1974) describe the sampling procedures employed to select over 450 deaf subjects in the TSA program: A selection controlled with respect to day versus residential programs and geographical region. However, detailed data on the educational background of the subjects, and in particular data regarding methods of communication, are not given. In chapter 5 we see that scores on the TSA are significantly influenced by educational regime (Brasel & Quigley, 1975), again reinforcing the need to distinguish English skills and skills in other languages, particularly sign language.

Higher Cognitive Skills

By "higher" skills we mean thinking, reasoning, problem solving, and concept formation: cognitive skills that may draw on "lower level" resources but that fall into the broad category of "intelligent behavior." Studies of the performance of deaf persons in this area are especially interesting because they go some way toward resolving the hoary question about the relationship between thinking and language. The most outspoken proponent of this viewpoint, Hans Furth, has argued that the deaf population provides the experimenter with a way of distinguishing verbal and conceptual influences on behavior. In his reviews of cognitive studies of the deaf, Furth (1964, 1966) has emphatically rejected the views of the Russian School and of the neo-associationists in favor of a position similar to that adopted by the Swiss developmentalist, Jean Piaget.

A number of studies listed by Furth (1964) have examined the ability of hearing-impaired subjects to learn and utilize concepts. Furth (1961) employed three experimental tasks: The *sameness* task required subjects to select a stimulus possessing certain characteristics; the *symmetry* task required subjects to select a figure possessing symmetry; the *opposition* task required subjects to pick the opposite size (smallest or largest) of the one specified by the tester. The results showed that deaf and hearing subjects aged 7-12 years performed equally well on the sameness and symmetry tests but that deaf subjects performed slightly less well than the hearing on the opposition task, which could have been supported by verbal mediation. Other studies have shown the deaf students to be inferior on analogies and alternation but, overall, the differences are not dramatic.

Transfer tasks require subjects to learn a concept and to apply it with a dissimilar set of stimuli. Writers such as Luria have claimed that verbal mediation is of crucial importance in such tasks: By saying to himself, in effect, "Pick the biggest one," for example, hearing children are able to break free from the constraints of concrete stimuli and generalize their behavior. However, deaf subjects appear to perform roughly on a par with hearing controls in this paradigm. O'Connor and Hermelin (1971) compared the performance of deaf, blind, mentally handicapped, and normal children on three different transfer tasks. The initial task required subjects to discriminate between a short and long tactile stimulus (touch). The *scalar* transfer task employed a different stimulus strength (a softer touch); the *dimensional* task employed a stimulus in the same tactile modality (a puff of air); the *crossmodal* task used a stimulus in a different modality (light or sound). They found that the deaf subjects *performed better than the other subject groups on all three tasks*, although they were less able verbally to describe the concept than the others. Similiar results were reported by Blank and Bridger (1966) using a cross modal transfer design.

Furth (1963) employed a pictorial choice task in which subjects had to respond to a "part-whole" concept hidden among distracting visual features. No differences emerged between deaf and hearing children aged 6-10 years and 14-15 years. Once again, oral ability to verbalize the solution was not strongly related to performance; intelligence and age were the only significant variables.

A further series of studies has examined the performance of deaf children on tests of the kind devised by Piaget. Piaget proposed that the child achieves a series of intellectual equilibria with his environment, corresponding to observable stages of development. Language does not play a central role in Piaget's theory: Direct experience of the world is the vital factor, although critics have pointed out that linguistic knowledge is a prerequisite to understanding task instructions and may therefore influence his results. The kind of task employed by Piaget tests the subjects' understanding of sequence, invariance of physical properties, and set membership properties. In general, the deaf subjects in Piagetian experiments by Furth (1964, 1966) and others showed a slight retardation, between 6 months and 2 years, compared with hearing controls. However, it is likely that this difference partially reflects difficulty in communicating the task instructions. Darbyshire and Reeves (1969-70) took care to ensure that all their subjects understood the task requirements for six Piagetian tests, and found no differences in performance between deaf and hearing children. In view of the poor English skills of deaf students, these findings run counter to the hypothesis of a causal link between verbal ability and cognitive development. Rather, as Furth argues, cognitive deficits on the part of the deaf probably result from a generalized lack of stimulation which is secondary to deafness. The reduced social communication, poorer reading skills, and restricted educational opportunities characteristic of deaf children clearly militate against cognitive development. In this respect, it is interesting that Darbyshire and Reeves found that socioeconomic variables had only a slight effect on performance within their hearing control group (average correlation $r=0.17$) but a fairly strong effect within their deaf group ($r=0.49$). And as Vida Carver has pointed out to us in personal discussion, the deaf child has fewer opportunities than the hearing to interact fully with his or her physical environment: He or she must spend a high proportion of his or her time visually scanning for social stimuli.

Two interesting studies by Paul Arnold and his associates are worth mentioning at this point. In contrast to some other researchers, Arnold and Walter (1979) found 19-year-old deaf students significantly inferior to hearing controls on tests of abstract and mechanical reasoning as well as in verbal reasoning. However, in a study in which subjects had to mentally rotate complex stimuli through either 90 degrees or 180 degrees, deaf 15-year-olds outperformed hearing subjects (Arnold, 1978b). In another study, Bolton (1971) factor analyzed the results of several tests given to deaf subjects. Four major factors emerged: nonverbal reasoning, manual communication, oral communication, and psychomotor skill. The relative independence of these factors goes some way toward accounting for the diversity of findings in this area, but in many cases it seems that specific aspects of cognitive tasks create unexpected difficulties for deaf people.

We can sum up the results of this brief review in the following way. First, in many aspects of cognitive skill, deaf respondents are equal to or even superior to the hearing. In some areas, they are retarded compared with the hearing, but only slightly so. Therefore, allowing for the depressed scores on nonverbal intelligence tests, and taking into account other factors likely to reduce the test scores of deaf subjects, it seems reasonable to conclude that the cognitive abilities of deaf children, students, and adults are essentially normal.

However, second, in two specific areas, short-term memory storage and English language skill, deaf subjects consistently score below hearing controls. As we see later, there is strong evidence that the relationship between the two is direct and linked with the ability of deaf children to develop phonological codes. Indeed, it is worth noting that inability to acquire phonological encoding has also been implicated as a factor in English language deficits in hearing populations (see Jorm, 1983, for a review), and in this instance, we can confidently ascribe the deficient performance of deaf students to a specific effect resulting from their inability to hear, a disability that can be overcome by the use of alternative visual coding strategies.

Experimental Studies of Communication

Considering the central role of the issue of "communication method" in the education of deaf children, it is surprising that only a few experimental studies have attempted to assess directly the relative efficiency of the various communication media. The research in this area falls into two broad categories: (a) comparative studies of overall receptive performance; and (b) studies of communication processes in situations approximating to natural use.

Some of the more recent studies of receptive communication skill are described in Table 4.3, which summarizes details of the samples, the tests used, and the mode of response, with results expressed as percentage scores. None of the experiments listed has included all possible communication channels or combinations of channels. Nevertheless, regarding the four major methods of communication— those most commonly employed in social or instructional contexts— the evidence is unequivocal:

1. Oral reception is *always* found to be inferior to manual communication, total communication, and reading.

2. Reading is *always* found to be superior to all other methods of communication.

3. Total communication is usually found to be superior to signing alone, but one major study (White & Stevenson, 1975) suggested that manual methods were superior to total communication (a difference that was not statistically significant).

These conclusions are also supported by the work of Moores, McIntyre, and Weiss (1972), Puthli (1977), and Denmark et al. (1979), and as far as we know, no contrary findings have been reported.

As one might expect, the absolute percentage scores obtained in such studies vary as a function of variables other than method of communication. Mode of response is clearly a crucial factor: Pictorial multiple choice, which makes no demands on the poor expressive skills of deaf subjects, generally leads to higher scoring than verbal multiple choice or written response paradigms. Length and complexity of messages must also influence performance, although this variable has never been systematically investigated. Age (Grove & Rodda, 1984; White & Stevenson, 1975), intelligence (White & Stevenson, 1975), and syntactical structure (Grove, O'Sullivan, & Rodda, 1979; Grove & Rodda, 1984) have also been shown to exert significant effects.

Some of the data obtained for reception using oral media are of particular interest. White and Stevenson (1975) found that the lipreading comprehension scores of orally educated subjects were not significantly higher than the scores of control subjects who answered the test questions without receiving the messages. Conrad (1977) and Arnold and Walter (1979) found that deaf lip-readers performed no better than hearing lip-readers with no previous experience. And Johnson's (1976) extensive data for students entering the National Technical Institute for the Deaf in Rochester (NTID), and the studies of Erber (1972, 1979), show that the aural component does play a significant role in oral reception.

Several researchers have focused on the communication process rather than overall measures of performance, employing pairs of deaf subjects familiar with each other's method of communication

TABLE 4.3

Reception Scores (%) for Various Methods of Communication: Some Recent Studies

AUTHORS	White & Stevenson (1975)		Conrad (1977)		Johnson (1976)	Arnold & Walter (1979)		Grove, O'Sullivan & Rodda (1979)	Grove & Rodda (1984)
SAMPLE	45 deaf pupils from TC regime (Maryland sample) BEA 88 dB Av. age 14:8	36 deaf pupils from oral regime (Michigan sample) BEA 88 dB Av. age 14:8	67 deaf pupils from oral regime BEA>94 Age 15-16.5	118 hearing controls Age 15-16	245 deaf students (1975 intake of NTID) BEA 95 dB	25 deaf students BEA 105 dB Av. age 19:2	21 hearing controls skilled in signing age 20-30	26 severely and profound deaf pupils from oral regimes aged 16-21	113 severely and profound deaf pupils from TC regimes Av. age 14:2
TEST	Passages from school readers		Modified Donaldson Lipreading Test		Written response score based on 50 "key words"	Everyday Sentence List		Test of Communication Skills	
MODE OF RESPONSE	Verbal multiple-choice		Pictorial multiple-choice					Pictorial multiple-choice	
SOUND ONLY	—	—	—	—	(0)	—	—	—	—
LIPREADING ONLY	—	—	—	—	40.1	36.2	34.6	—	—
LIPREADING AND SOUND	43.5	48.2*	70.9	66.6	53.1	—	—	70.7	56.5
MANUAL	70.9	65.9	—	—	63.2	65.7	54.3	84.2**	64.2
TOTAL	65.9	63.7	—	—	78.7	—	—	79.0	68.4
READING	76.0	69.1	88.2***	96.6	—	—	—	—	72.7

Notes: *Not significantly greater than the baseline score
**Based on only two subjects
***Subjects in the reading condition had been tested previously with the same items presented orally

(often matched with hearing controls). Although less rigorous than the comparative experiments, this technique does allow greater flexibility of design and provides valuable insights into the nature of interaction between deaf people in a semirealistic context.

A number of such studies have examined the capacity of sign language for transmitting grammatical relationships. Schlesinger (1971) studied the structure of communications between deaf adults using Israeli Sign Language (ISL). Subjects had to describe simple pictures embodying basic syntactical forms. Their overall performance was poor, and Schlesinger observed that ISL seemed to lack any consistent sign order and failed to transmit certain syntactical structures: Sometimes verbs were lost completely. Bonvillian, Charrow, and Nelson (1973) have suggested that recent high levels of immigration in Israel have not favored the development of a homogeneous signing subculture. In North America, where ASL has evolved consistent grammatical mechanisms over a 100-year period, a study by Bode (1974), similar to Schlesinger's, showed that ASL users performed at a relatively high level.

Tweney and Hoemann (1973) and Hoemann and Tweney (1973) have shown that ASL is capable of transmitting complex message structures. Their first study employed the method of back-translation, whereby an English message was given to a deaf adult subject to transmit to a second subject using ASL. The receiver then wrote out an English interpretation of the ASL signal. Eight very complex classes of English syntactical structure were employed, "chosen to render the set of sentences as difficult as possible" for ASL users. Various types of expletive (*that, it, to*) and inflections known to present special problems for the hearing-impaired were included. It was found that for 63% of the sentences, the back-translation substantially captured the meaning of the target message, despite minor syntactic and lexical changes; in 27% of the trials, the message was recovered with no structural changes at all. The message types that seemed hardest (around 50% correct semantically) were: Expletives (verbal), e.g., "It worries Stephen that John is reckless"; Expletives with it-deletion (verbal) ("That John is reckless worries Stephen"); Derived nominalizations ("John's recklessness worries Stephen"); and There-constructions ("There is a good movie playing tomorrow").

Although suggestive, such experiments are subject to a number of methodological and conceptual uncertainties. One problem lies in the selection of deaf subjects who must be skilled both in English and ASL; none of Tweney and Hoemann's subjects had acquired ASL as a native language, and although they had been using signing socially for an average of 30 years, many made extensive use of finger spelling and may have employed a form of ASL influenced by English grammar (Stokoe, 1973). To answer this criticism, Hoemann and Tweney (1973) repeated the study with deaf subjects born to deaf parents, and prohibited finger spelling; longer English texts were also employed. Substantially similar results were obtained.

A potentially more complex problem is that of distinguishing between information losses resulting from (a) the generally poor oral language skills of deaf persons; and (b) the processing of messages through an ASL channel. In the Grove and Rodda (1984) study referred to previously, no interaction was observed between communication method and syntactical structure. This implies that the effects of transmission through a signing medium are uniform on different types of English language structure. Clearly further research into this question would be valuable.

Some studies have employed a more pragmatic approach to the communication issue. Hoemann (1972) asked deaf children (8 and 11 years) to teach each other a simple game using ASL and finger spelling. Their performance was poorer than that of hearing control subjects, largely because they tended to get lost in detail and failed to explain the general aims of the game. In contrast, Jordan's (1974) experiment involved the relatively concrete task of describing a picture for multiple choice selection. Here deaf adolescents performed better than hearing controls. In a later study, Jordan (1983) compared the communication scores of hearing and deaf children aged 6-15 years. Deaf subjects using manual methods outperformed those using oral methods at all ages except 13-15 years. "For the six and seven year old oral children," remarks Jordan, "interpersonal communication was virtually nil" (p. 241). Hearing children gained higher scores than deaf at all ages. Interestingly, dyads comprising a teacher of the deaf and a hearing-impaired student scored at a consistently high level. English glosses of the BSL messages from the "senders" revealed ambiguity in sign ordering and a seeming inability to see things from the receivers' viewpoint. Often the members of a pupil-pupil dyad could not agree initially on which method to employ. In contrast, teachers communicating with pupils, using Signed English, established the specific medium very rapidly. Jordan felt that recent changes in educational regime at the Scottish schools which provided his subjects may have contributed to their relatively poor performance.

Breslaw, Griffiths, Wood and Howarth (1981; see also p. 263) reported two experiments comparing groups of 6- to 10-year-old deaf and hearing subjects. In the first, the sender had to direct the receiver to place colored blocks of eight basic types on the appropriate token on a board. In terms of numbers of attempts prior to solution, deaf subjects proved to be more efficient than hearing, and more often transmitted complete information in one utterance. In the second experiment, these authors employed a picture selection task similar to that of Jordan. Deaf subjects were selected from three oral schools: Children from one school performed on a par with hearing subjects, but those from the other two schools were inferior to the hearing group. Utterances were classified in terms of *features* (any attribute of a picture), *actions* (roughly equivalent to verbs) and *relationships* (defining the relationships between features). Although significant differences in the absolute numbers of such utterances were observed between the groups, the proportion of utterances falling in each category showed less variation. The deaf subjects produced about 76% features, with 13% actions and 11% relationships; for the hearing group the corresponding figures were 76%, 6% and 18%. Clearly, the deaf groups employed relatively more actions and correspondingly fewer relationships than hearing subjects. It is unclear whether this finding reflects a lack of understanding of relationships—unlikely, perhaps—or a failure of communication. As we noted previously, deaf children seem to experience considerable difficulty in dealing with the fine infrastructure of English syntax—verb auxiliaries, case, number, subtleties of mood and voice, and similar aspects. Many of the terms used to describe relationships undoubtedly fall into this category.

A different method of investigation has been employed by Kyle (1983) to assess the production of signing. Subjects were asked to describe the action in silent movie clips. It was found that signed narratives differed from spoken in that they gave a more accurate account of the sequence of events: only 5% chronological errors in the signed discourse compared with 17% in spoken. However, the overall level of recall after one hour did not differ (29% correct in the deaf group; 28% in the hearing). This runs counter to the assumption that deaf people have difficulties dealing with sequence, and suggests, in Kyle's terminology, that sign language may be intrinsically "event-structured." Edmondson (1983), using Bartlett's (1932) story-chain technique, found that deaf children using sign language made *more* errors of interpretation than hearing children using speech, and argued that "in the school context it is likely to be not entirely successful" (p. 231). Because these conclusions are based on observations of only five deaf boys in an oral school that was only just beginning to tolerate manual methods, it is uncertain whether such generalizations are justified.

Cognitive Processes Underlying Communication

The controlled studies of receptive communication process in deaf individuals described in the previous section are in substantial agreement concerning the relative efficiency of the four major methods of communication: Reading is more effective than Total Communication which is, in turn, more effective than signing alone; and lipreading is the least efficient method of communication. They also show that when pairs of deaf students or adults are permitted to communicate in fairly naturalistic situations, a variable but generally high degree of functional effectiveness is attained, often matching that of hearing control subjects. In fact, we now have a reasonably good picture of the cognitive and communication skills of the hearing-impaired population. What is lacking is a detailed account of the process of communication. Can we explain the differences in performance between the major media in terms of the operating characteristics of the cognitive mechanisms underlying each?

In this section, we trace the inflow of information through the processing stages summarized in Fig. 4.1 (p. 160). At each stage we compare the major methods of communication (oral, manual, total, and reading) with respect to the demands each places on the deaf person's cognitive abilities. In this way we are able to isolate the bottlenecks and sources of distortion affecting the reception of messages. However, we are relatively unconcerned with the skills underlying expressive communication, although these are clearly of vital importance.

Perception of Basic Elements

At the lowest level of analysis, all systems of communication employ a relatively restricted set of basic elements, which are combined (sequentially or simultaneously) to create more complex units. In the case of aural reception, the basic elements are phonemes; for lipreading the elements are the oral analogs of phonemes; for manual reception they are various patterns of movement, location and hand orientation; and for reading they are printed letters. The redundancy of oral and sign language systems ensures that a high level of receptive performance can be maintained even without identification of all of the basic elements. Nevertheless, performance will deteriorate if recognition of these stimuli is impaired. We can distinguish two types of impairment: first, a generalized increase in "noise" level, resulting in a lower signal/noise ratio; and second, a specific deficit associated with the perception of certain elements.

In the case of English, we know that most information is carried by consonants. Loss of vowel information has a less damaging effect on word recognition than loss of consonants; for example, the missing letters in -A-I-A-E are harder to guess than in N-V-G-T-. And by definition, frequently encountered consonants such as T carry less information than those of lower frequency (e.g., B). Less is known about the relative importance of the various formational parameters of signed languages.

Reading, under normal conditions, clearly presents elements that can be identified with near 100% accuracy. That is, a printed text, with few typographical errors, viewed under good illumination, and with unlimited reading time, provides a very high-grade input.

Obviously, when handwritten rather than printed messages are employed, or limitations placed on visual acuity or reading time, the perception of individual letters will be impaired. As far as we know, no research to investigate the reading performance of deaf subjects under such conditions has been conducted. In any case, we can assume that information loss due to these factors will, in most practical circumstances, be kept to a minimum.

In contrast, lipreading presents the receiver with a rather low grade input. Numerous physical, physiological, and psychological variables have been shown to influence oral reception; unless all are at near optimal levels, perception of lip movements is likely to be degraded. Moreover, many of these variables may interact in a complex fashion. We briefly review the major findings of studies in this area; for more detailed discussions see Erber (1975), Farwell (1976), and Parasnis and Samar (1982).

Much of our knowledge of the effects of physical variables on lipreading comes from the work of Norman Erber of the Central Institute for the Deaf at St. Louis. In an important paper, Erber (1974) systematically examined the effects of changes in illumination and the relative positions of the speaker and the profoundly deaf lip-reader. He found that *distance* has a consistent linear effect; for every additional foot separating speaker and lip-reader reception scores diminish by about one percentage point. Similiar effects have been obtained by simulating an equivalent reduction in visual acuity through the use of lenses (Romano & Berlow, 1976) and of roughened plexiglass (Erber, 1979). *Illumination* of the speaker's face has a relatively small effect, provided that it exceeds 0.03 footlamberts (a measure of luminance), and provided that the speaker is not framed against a very bright background (a situation that may occur when, for example, a teacher stands with his or her back to a window). *Angle of illumination* also has a small effect: Reception is at its best when the speaker's face is lit from the front or from 45°, but is reduced when the light source is directly overhead. *Angle of regard* has a more potent effect. Oral reception is good when the reader views the speaker from the front or 45° to one side, but falls off by about 15 percentage points when he has a side view. Small (30°) changes in vertical viewing angle have no significant effect on lipreading scores.

A further series of studies has investigated the contribution of residual auditory and visual gestural channels to lipreading performance. There is much evidence that residual hearing plays a significant part in the oral reception process (Erber, 1972, 1979; Johnson, 1976). For severely deaf subjects, the addition of acoustic information (via a hearing aid or amplification system) may raise lipreading scores by up to 20 percentage points. As we would expect, the corresponding figure for profoundly deaf subjects is much lower: around one percentage point. Erber (1972), studying the perception of eight spoken consonants, estimated the information transmitted by auditory, visual, and combined auditory-visual channels (see chapter 3). For severely deaf subjects, the auditory channel transmitted 1.06 bits of information, the visual channel 1.29 bits, and the two channels combined 2.35 bits (out of a maximum of 3 bits). For profoundly deaf subjects, the corresponding figures were 0.17 bits, 1.32 bits, and 1.54 bits. In each case, the information transmitted in the auditory-visual condition equalled the sum of the information transmitted through the two component channels separately. This implies: (a) There is virtually no overlap in the phonological information obtained through the two channels: Lip movements give cues to place of articulation, frication, and duration, while residual hearing provides data concerning nasality and voicing—and, happily, the two input channels complement each other perfectly; (b) Deaf people are able to exploit this situation in a strikingly efficient fashion; and (c) The oral superiority of severely deaf over profoundly deaf subjects largely reflects the contribution of residual hearing; there is no difference between the two groups in Erber's study in pure lipreading skill, both transmitting about 1.3 bits of information in this condition (cf. Fry, 1966).

Berger and Popelka (1971) used hearing subjects to determine the contribution of informal gesture to lipreading performance. They presented sentences constructed around highly familiar gestures—for example, "I agree with what you said," which goes with nodding the head—either with or without the accompanying gesture. In the "no gesture" condition subjects scored on average 29.4%. When gestures were added, the scores increased to 58.6%. Although this obviously reflects the maximum possible contribution of gestural information, and although it might have been preferable to use deaf rather than hearing subjects, such a result does indicate the extent to which everyday "oral" communication might exploit nonverbal media, possibly at an unconscious level.

Another important factor determining the success (or otherwise) of lipreading is the individual speaker. Some people simply open their mouths wider than others, and these are easier to lip-read (Lowell, 1957-1958). But there is evidence that familiarity with a particular speaker is also important. An early study by Day, Fusfeld, and Pintner (cited by Farwell, 1976, p. 21) showed that the lipreading scores of 400 deaf children improved 50-60 percentage points if a familiar teacher, rather than an outside examiner, presented the test material. There was no correlation between the two conditions of the test, suggesting that the effects of speaker familiarity were not uniform on different types of sentence structure. Grove and Rodda (1984) found that lip-readers, unlike subjects using other methods of communication, showed a small but consistent increase in scoring through the course of a 120-item test. It seems that deaf persons relying on oral reception require time to "tune in" to the characteristic lip movements of each newly encountered speaker. Brief verbalizations from unfamiliar speakers are likely to be especially difficult for the lip-reader.

The studies reviewed above provide information about the kinds of variable that exercise generalized effects on oral reception. But additionally, and more critically, lipreading also suffers from a specific sensory deficit. Only a few English phonemes can be reliably identified *even when all of the variables determining the overall signal/noise ratio are set at optimal levels*. Table 4.4 lists the sounds that can easily be perceived and those that can be perceived with difficulty. As one would expect, only the labial phonetic elements— those articulated with lip closure and opening—can be consistently detected. And of these, only a handful uniquely identify specific phonemes.

To illustrate the difficulties that the specific deficit imposes on the lip-reader we can imagine a simple sentence in a printed analog of the form in which he or she would perceive it under ideal conditions (Table 4.5). Even a skilled cryptanalyst might require some time to identify the message with the aid of pen and paper; and time, of course, is what the lip-reader lacks. When we remember that less will be perceived under less favorable conditions and that the message[2] is represented in its maximally intelligible form, it becomes puzzling that oral communication works at all. In view of

---

[2] "Paris is the capital of France."

TABLE 4.4

Patterns of Lip Movement Associated with Specific Sounds and
Groups of Speech Sounds

Sounds	Phonetic transcriptions	Associated lip movements
A. Easily Perceived Consonant Sounds		
P, B, M	[p], [b], [m]	"Bilabial" sounds (full closure of lips). P and B are plosives, M nasal.
F, V	[f], [v]	Both are "labio-dental"—i.e., upper teeth make contact with lower lip.
Th	[θ], [δ], [ð]	"Dental"—tongue makes contact with both upper and lower teeth
W	[w]	A labial semivowel—the lips pucker but do not completely close
Sh, Ch, J (& soft G), Z	[ʃ], [tʃ], [dʒ], [ʒ]	For all these sounds the mouth is open with the lips slightly protruding
B. Consonant Sounds that are Hard to Perceive		
R	[r]	A semivowel produced by lightly flicking the tongue behind upper teeth
L	[l]	A liquid semivowal; similar production to R with mouth wider and tongue visible
T, D, N, S, Z	[t], [d], [n], [s], [z]	Two subtly different sets of lip shapes which are easily confused with each other and also with L (when tongue hidden)

Table 4.4 cont.

C. Long Vowel Sounds

Ah	[ɑ:]	Mouth wide open
Aw	[ɔ:]	Somewhat smaller opening
Er	[ɜ] or [ɚ]	Narrower lip shape
Oo	[u:]	Lips puckered
Ee	[i:]	Elongated (smiling) mouth

Short vowels provide little or no useful lip movement information. Diphthongs (double or changing vowels) may sometimes be detected. Some short vowels are realized, especially in rapid speech, in a neutral or undifferentiated form, and so provide no help to the lip-reader.

TABLE 4.5

Elements of an English Message
Perceptible Through Lip Movements

$$
\begin{Bmatrix} P \\ B \\ M \end{Bmatrix} \text{-R-S-STh-} \begin{Bmatrix} K \\ G \\ \text{-ng} \end{Bmatrix} - \begin{Bmatrix} P \\ B \\ M \end{Bmatrix} - \begin{Bmatrix} T \\ D \\ N \end{Bmatrix} -L- \begin{Bmatrix} F \\ V \end{Bmatrix} \begin{Bmatrix} F \\ V \end{Bmatrix} \text{RA} \begin{Bmatrix} T \\ D \\ N \end{Bmatrix} \text{S}
$$

The message contains six words, although this will not be obvious to the lip-reader. Curved brackets represent sets of phonemes which look similar on a speaker's lips (in this case, they do not represent morphemes). The reader may determine how long he takes to understand the message, remembering that, in normal conditions, the deaf lip-reader will have no more than about three seconds to complete the task.

the findings of Erber (1972) and of Berger and Popelka (1971), we are forced to conclude that perhaps as much as 50% of the nominal "lipreading" scores obtained by severely and profoundly deaf subjects actually measures the reception of information through acoustic and gestural channels. Other cues may play a small part in the process; for example, some highly skilled lip-readers claim to be able to exploit small but meaningful neck and cheek movements that aid the detection of K, G, and H sounds (Martin, 1981, p. 38). The evidence regarding facial expression, "body language," and other similar variables is as yet somewhat inconsistent. A great deal more research is required before we can say just how much information is being transmitted via each input channel.

In addition, little is known about the ability of the lip-reader to detect elements of pitch, stress, and rhythm, which play a significant role in speech perception and which may be crucial in comprehending the more subtle dimensions of language (e.g., sarcasm, irony, and humor). Perhaps the alleged "concreteness" of deaf cognition, and the failure of many deaf children to grasp the metaphorical and analogical content in verbal messages partly reflect processing difficulties of this type. Perhaps this comprises a special form of experiential deprivation. Isolating and measuring such effects is likely to be difficult.

There is no doubt that the basic structures of sign language are far more easily perceived than are patterns of lip movement. This is scarcely surprising because, as we have already seen, the evolution of manual systems has been directed by the need to employ highly visible perceptual elements. In the case of ASL, signs tend to be made in the central zone of the "signing space" (for maximal visual acuity), two-handed signs tend to be symmetrical in terms of hand configuration, location, and movement (to increase redundancy), and historical changes in ASL signs invariably increase their perceptibility at the expense of a loss in iconicity (Klima & Bellugi, 1979, chaps. 2-3). However, experimental studies of the perceptual process are still rare. We look at three major techniques that aim to assess sign perception by systematically obscuring or reducing the visual input available to subjects.

Tweney, Heiman, and Hoemann (1977) have employed the method of repetitive interruption developed by Miller and Licklider (1950) for the study of speech perception. The intelligibility of spoken English broken up by regular interruptions depends on both the frequency of the interruptions (being at its poorest at around one interruption per second) and the total percentage of speech transmitted in a given time period (the Speech-Time Fraction, or STF). Tweney and his co-workers compared the receptive performance of deaf and hearing subjects for matched sets of signs and spoken words respectively. In their first experiment random, unrelated sign/word lists were presented for three STFs (25%, 50%, and 75%) and four rates of interruption (0.5, 1.0, 2.0, and 4.0 interruptions per second). Both variables generated significant effects on reception scores, but the deaf group (52% average score) outperformed the hearing group overall (30%).

In two further experiments, Tweney, Heimann, and Hoemann examined the perception of three types of stimuli: *grammatical strings* (length 5 items), judged to follow ASL syntax; *anomalous strings*, syntactically correct but with no semantic validity; and *random strings*, lists of items unrelated either syntactically or semantically (abbreviated GS, AS, and RS respectively). At a rate of two interruptions per second (STF 50%) the deaf group again outperformed the hearing group (reception scores of 81% and 23% respectively) and performed significantly better in the GS condition (88%) than in the AS condition (79%) or in the RS condition (77%). No significant effects were observed between the different conditions with the hearing subjects. In other words, the deaf subjects were able to exploit the increased message redundancy provided by ASL linguistic structure, just as hearing subjects have been shown to do utilizing English structure (Miller & Isard, 1963). Reasoning that the poorer performance of the hearing group might in this case be due to inappropriate interruption rate, the authors repeated the experiment with hearing subjects alone and higher rates of interruption. At 10 interruptions per second, the hearing group's performance closely matched that of the deaf group at 2 interruptions per second.

In their final experiment, Tweney, Heiman, and Hoemann compared performance in both an interruption condition (2 interruptions per second) and no-interruption condition for GS lists and scrambled sentences (SS) composed of randomized GS strings. An RS condition was also employed. In terms of items recalled correctly, both subject groups gained near perfect scores in the no-interruption condition, indicating that short-term memory losses were negligible. Linguistic structure exerted a significant effect within both groups, with mean scores ranked GS>SS>RS, as predicted. However, in terms of items recalled in their correct order, deaf subjects performed particularly poorly in the SS condition. This was due to their tendency to impose ASL syntax on the scrambled messages, confirming that sequential constraints do play a significant role in the perception of signs.

A rather different technique for investigating the perception of ASL messages containing embedded structures has been employed by

Tweney, Liddell, and Bellugi (1977). An ASL sentence such as "RECENTLY DOG CHASE CAT COME HOME" can be disambiguated by means of changes in facial expression (Liddell, 1978). A specific expression (comprising raised eyebrows, raised upper lip, and a tilting back of the head) accompanying the sign sequence "RECENTLY DOG CHASE CAT" will give the total message the unambiguous meaning *The dog which recently chased the cat came home*. Analogous methods in speech include changes of pitch and emphasis. Tweney, Liddell, and Bellugi examined the perception of such ASL messages by presenting them on a TV screen obscured by "snow," an electronic form of interference taking the form of a rapidly changing pattern of random dots. Deaf ASL users had to view the resulting display and to write down English glosses of each message. It was predicted that clauses would tend to be perceived as units, and that transitional errors would increase at the boundaries of clauses rather than within them. The results were generally in line with this hypothesis, although many of the sentences were rather easy and generated too few errors. As the authors point out, this technique possesses considerable potential for future research.

Perhaps the most promising method of studying the perception of dynamic displays was developed by Johansson (1973), who attached sets of small lights to peoples' bodies and filmed them in a darkened room. Subjects viewing the films could readily identify the pattern of moving lights as a person and specify the behavior in which he or she was engaged. Subsequent research has shown that subjects can also recognize gender, facial changes of expression, and even specific individuals from the movement of the lights.

Poizner, Bellugi, and Lutes-Driscoll (1981) adapted Johansson's technique by presenting three-dimensional video films of an ASL signer. Lights were placed on top of the signer's head, on each shoulder, and on each elbow, wrist, and index finger. Congenitally deaf ASL users served as subjects in four separate experiments. In the first, subjects were required to match the movement primes (not the overall signs) shown in the point-light display with movements shown in a normal video display. First the normal video was presented, then the point-light display, after which subjects had to respond "same" or "different." In a control condition, two normal videos were presented. It was found that the accuracy of the responses to point-light displays was not significantly different from that in the control condition (81.4% correct and 82.4% correct respectively). Moreover, the relative difficulties of the various (14) movement primes employed was the same for both conditions.

In a second experiment, Poizner, Bellugi, and Lutes-Driscoll studied the perception of six ASL inflections of temporal aspect superimposed on the sign LOOK-AT. Again, the subjects were required to make same/different judgments. This time, accuracy was so high (93%) that comparison with a control condition was unnecessary. Poizner and his colleagues next investigated the identification of 50 ASL signs, all made with a /G/ hand configuration, and of 10 inflections occurring on two basic signs. Point-light displays were presented in both three-dimensional and two-dimensional formats for sign identification, and in only a two-dimensional format for the inflections. Identification of signs was again remarkably efficient: 83.1% in three-dimensional, 78.8% in two-dimensional displays. Identification of inflections was also highly accurate (77.6% in two-dimensional only).

A final experiment studied the contributions made by separate elements in the point-light display. Thirty-two ASL signs that had proven especially easy to identify in the preceding experiment were presented either without the fingertip lights, the wrist lights, the elbow lights, or the head and shoulder lights. With no lights removed, subjects averaged 85.6% correct in identifying the signs; with head and shoulder lights removed, the mean score dropped to 76.6%; with elbow lights removed, 71.9%; wrist lights removed, 68.8%; and with no fingertip lights, only 23.4%. As the authors point out, the information carried by each of the joints of the arm is directly related to the number of *degrees of freedom* (df) available to it. The shoulders do not move and so have no degrees of freedom, but control the elbow with 3 *df*, the wrist with 5 *df* and the fingertips with 7 *df*. The freedom of movement of each joint incorporates the movement degrees of freedom of all the joints less distal to it (i.e., closer to the shoulder). Thus most information is carried by the fingertips, and loss of fingertip motion is particularly detrimental to sign perception (Fig. 4.5).

Tartter and Fischer (1983) employed a similar technique to assess the perceptual saliency of hand location, orientation, movement, and hand shape. Small pieces of reflective tape, rather than lights, were used: one on the nose and 13 on each hand. Nine pairs of ASL signs, differing only in one feature, were selected for each parameter, and subjects had to choose one of two drawings corresponding to the stimulus presented. The point-light condition was slightly less effective than a video presentation condition, and for both the methods of presentation location was easier to perceive than orientation, and movement and hand shape somewhat harder. Hand shape scored at only a chance level in the point-light condition. The authors suggest that removing redundancy from a manual display might make it possible to transmit signed messages over standard telephone lines.

Despite procedural differences, the experiments just described are in agreement regarding the intelligibility of ASL signs. It is clear that signs are far more perceptible than lip movements, and are less readily disrupted by low frequency temporal interruptions than spoken words. In information theory terms, a visual sign is more redundant than a speech signal and far more redundant than the pattern of labial movements associated with speech. Redundancy operates at three levels:

1. In a given time period, a visual display emits far more information than an auditory stimulus. Yet with only a meager sampling of the available information—in particular, data regarding the motion of the signer's fingertips and hand shape— the receiver can identify individual signs with a high degree of accuracy (Poizner, Bellugi, & Tweney, 1981).

2. As we noted previously, systematic constraints on sign formation artificially enhance signal redundancy (Klima & Bellugi, 1979).

3. Sequential constraints on signing, previously thought to be relatively inconsequential, definitely function in the production and perception of ASL, as they do in the perception of aural language (Tweney, Heiman, & Hoemann, 1977).

In fact, it is a measure of the overall redundancy of signed messages that they are so extraordinarily resistant to disruption under "noisy" conditions. Neither does signing exhibit any specific sensory deficits akin to those of lipreading.

Short-Term Retention

We have already reviewed evidence suggesting that the hearing-impaired perform less well than the hearing on tests of STM capacity. In this section we consider the results of experiments designed to assess the nature of the STM encoding process in deaf subjects, compared with that normal for hearing persons. We also summarize data that directly compare the STM characteristics of information acquired via the four major modalities (oral, manual, total, and reading).

Beginning with the work of Conrad (1964), investigations of STM in normal subjects have generally concluded that short-term traces are acoustic in nature. The pattern of errors made in immediate recall for verbal material is typically found to parallel confusions made between similar sounding stimuli under "noisy" listening

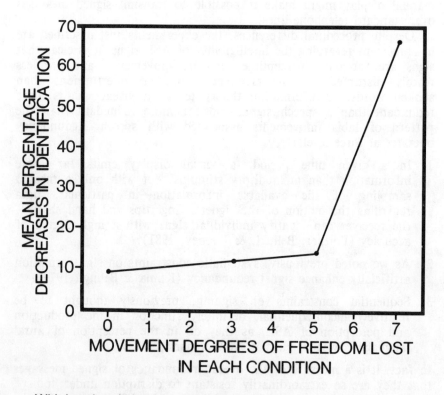

With head and shoulder lights removed: zero d.f. are lost;
with elbow lights removed: 3 d.f. are lost;
with wrist lights removed: 4 d.f. are lost;
and with fingertip lights removed: 7 d.f. are lost.

FIG. 4.5.   Mean percentage decrease in ASL sign identification as function of the degrees of freedom on movement lost when point lights are removed.

Source—H. Poizner U. Bellugi, and V. Lutes-Driscoll (1981), Perception of American Sign Language in dynamic point-light displays, *Journal of Experimental Psychology*, 7, 430-440, p. 439. Copyright 1981 by the American Psychological Association. Reprinted by permission of Dr. Ursula Bellugi, Salk Institute.

conditions. Visual short-term memory tends to decay very rapidly and visually presented material is recoded into an acoustic form (Sperling, 1967). Do deaf subjects, lacking normal auditory experience, also employ acoustic recoding, or do they utilize some radically different strategy?[3]

Conrad (1970a) studied the immediate recall of 5- and 6-letter sequences drawn from the ensemble B, C, H, K, L, T, X, Y, and Z. Orally educated male deaf students (BEA hearing loss over 75dB) and normally hearing controls were compared. Among the deaf subjects, three confusion clusters were found: BCT, KXYZ, and XH. For hearing subjects only BCT and XH generated significant confusions. K, X, Y, and Z are visually similar and B, C, and T are acoustically similar; XH is harder to account for. However, a closer examination made by deaf subjects revealed that different types of error were being made by different individuals. Two subgroups could be distinguished. Out of 36 subjects, 21 exhibited confusions among B, C, and T, and so appeared to be employing acoustic (or articulatory) recoding strategies. The remainder (15) showed clustering of errors only for the visually similar letters (KXYZ).

Conrad attempted to correlate this between-subject difference with other subject characteristics. It was not related to age, intelligence, or hearing loss (although the latter variable was restricted in range). However, it correlated highly with teachers' ratings of the subjects' speech quality. All but one of the articulatory group were judged to have good speech relative to the deaf population, but only 5 of the visual group had good speech. Overall, the visual group made more recall errors, but this finding was qualified by an interaction of the group and input conditions. When subjects read the stimulus letters silently, articulators and visualizers performed equally well; but when subjects were required to read the stimuli aloud, the performance of the visualizers deteriorated. Because reading aloud would involve articulatory mechanisms, it either interfered with, or competed for capacity with, processing in the visual modality. Conrad (1971) extended these findings using a comprehension task: here reading aloud increased the scores of articulators and reduced the scores of visualizers.

Conrad has confirmed and extended these findings in various ways (Conrad, 1970b, 1972, 1973a, 1973b, 1979; Conrad & Rush, 1965), and it appears to be clearly established that deaf people can be divided into subgroups, one having and the other lacking a

---

[3]Recently Besner and Davelaar (1982) have suggested that normally hearing persons possess two independent phonological coding systems.

significant level of articulatory STM coding. About half possess articulatory coding skills and, therefore, function similarly to hearing persons; the remainder have poor speech coding. Articulatory coding correlates with oral skill (speech and speech reading) and, less strongly, with residual hearing. Clearly, over the entire range of hearing impairments, there must be a strong causal influence of hearing loss on coding, but the relationship with oral skill is more problematical. Do deaf children receiving oral education develop better speech coding than others? There is no evidence to support this hypothesis; in fact, Conrad's subjects span the range of educational regimes, including intensively oral-educated English pupils, and American subjects using Total Communication. It seems that irrespective of educational background, a significant number of deaf persons will inevitably lack the ability to process speech and lipreading stimuli in short-term memory. In this case, they have two possible ways of encoding in STM: They may use a visual code based on the structure of written letters and words, or they may employ codes derived from manual communication (finger spelling or signing) which may be visually or kinesthetically mediated. A number of studies have focused on this issue, with confusing results.

Locke and Locke (1971) examined confusion errors for lists of consonants designed to be phonetically, visually, or dactylically similar (dactylic refers to the shapes of finger spelling). Hearing subjects made most phonetic errors, followed by deaf subjects with good speech; deaf subjects with poor speech skills made very few. For both visual and dactylic confusions this ranking was reversed. Deaf subjects with poor speech were more likely to show overt signs of dactylic rehearsal, testifying that they were indeed actively recoding stimuli into a finger spelled form. Wallace (1972) obtained broadly similar results: Oral deaf subjects exhibited visual and acoustic confusions; manual subjects showed signs of visual and dactylic coding but almost no acoustic coding. Interestingly, the manual group outperformed the oral group in recall of letter sequences, but oral subjects did better in a face recognition test. Both deaf groups proved better at facial recognition than hearing controls: It seemed that verbal coding of features by hearing subjects (e.g., "wears glasses") led to errors, whereas the deaf subjects retained a more vivid image of the target photograph.

Wallace and Corballis (1973) reported similar data for the recall of 4- and 5-letter sequences by hearing, oral deaf, and manual deaf subjects. All the deaf subjects used visual coding; only the oral subjects employed some acoustic coding. Wilson (1975) examined the recall confusions of lists of letters presented by finger spelling. The letters were drawn from two dactylically similar ensembles: Only one ensemble generated significant dactylic confusion (AEIOU, which in the U.K. two-handed finger spelling system are produced by placing the right hand index finger against the thumb and fingers of the left hand in sequence). It remains unclear whether the STM trace in such a case comprises a visual image of the stimulus or a kinesthetic recoding.

Carey and Blake (1974) employed the Sperling paradigm (see pp. 200 and 417) for examaining very short-term visual retention. The stimuli were letters or shapes in a two-dimensional display. Both hearing and deaf subjects exhibited visual letter confusions. Recall of position information was similar for the two groups, but hearing subjects showed better letter recall. This contradicts the notion that deaf subjects rely on purely iconic short-term traces: It seems instead that they recode into a mixture of visual and kinesthetic representations. Because all deaf persons rely on visual input channels for communication, it makes sense that these channels should be "cleared" as rapidly as possible to permit further processing.

So far we have considered only the recall of simple alphabetical stimuli. In a recent series of studies, Bellugi and her associates have investigated short-term memory processes involved with the retention of ASL signs. Bellugi, Klima, and Siple (1975) and Klima and Bellugi (1979) prepared matching lists of ASL signs and their English equivalents. Deaf subjects were presented with video displays in which signs were shown at a rate of one per second, the signer wearing a neutral facial expression. Their performance was compared with that of hearing persons listening to the matched word lists read aloud. It was found that the average recall of hearing subjects (memory span) was 5.9 items (recalled in the correct order). Deaf subjects did slightly less well: 4.9 items. The authors considered that because signs take longer to process than words, the results were consistent with the hypothesis that deaf subjects in the experiment had less rehearsal time than did the hearing. Error analysis revealed that the hearing subjects were using phonological encoding. The deaf subjects' errors were all derived from confusions between the functional parameters of ASL: In most cases only one parameter (e.g., the MOV prime) was changed. No evidence of phonological, iconic, or semantic confusions was found.

Klima and Bellugi (1979) systematically varied the formational similarity of ASL lists. There were 18 lists of five signs: In six lists, all of the items within a given list shared a specific PA prime; in another six lists, the items shared an HC prime; in the final set of six lists, items shared MOV primes. To assess the effects of formational similarity, the same items were also presented in random lists, and the average recall of each item under the two conditions compared. The results indicated that similarity of HC primes slightly enhances recall; MOV has no significant effect; similarity of PA leads to reduced recall. This finding is consistent with our earlier speculations about the role of place of articulation in signing: Presenting several signs in the same signing zone seems to overload the memory-place mechanism. However, two reasons for caution should be noted: First, there was wide variation between different primes within each condition; second, the average rated similarity of signs within the lists (derived from hearing raters unfamiliar with ASL) was not precisely matched. Although these data are equivocal in detail, they do confirm that native ASL users employ the structural characteristics of ASL in memorizing lists of signs, and the kinesthetic/visual attributes of sign language may take over the role taken by phonological processes in the short-term memory of hearing persons.

Poizner, Bellugi, and Tweney (1981) extended these findings by comparing deaf subjects' short-term memory for lists of random signs with their recall of lists of similar signs. In hearing subjects, phonological similarity has the effect of reducing recall through the confusion effect. Three types of sign-similarity were defined: *iconic, semantic,* or *formational*. It was found that iconic similarity had no effect on recall; semantic similarity had only a slight effect (specifically with lists of countries); but formationally similar signs were recalled significantly less well than lists of random signs. Once again, these data strongly support the conclusion that deaf persons decompose signs into their structural components prior to entering them in short-term memory.

Further evidence for the effect discussed in the previous paragraph comes from a study of the immediate recall of ASL inflections (Poizner, Newkirk, Bellugi, & Klima, 1981). The subjects were both deaf and hearing adults born to deaf parents, for whom ASL represented natural language. They were required to recall lists of ASL verbs with or without any of eight different inflections. Each list contained four signs, of which two, three, or all four might be inflected. For all subjects, average recall decreased with increasing numbers of inflected signs, indicating that inflections were requiring additional storage space, and hence that signs were not being stored as whole units. Analyses of errors were also made. If whole items comprised basic STM units, one would expect the majority of errors to involve the transposition of complete signs. In fact, only 6% of errors fell into this category. About 18% of errors involved the transposition of morphological components between sign stems; 20% involved the loss or addition of inflections; 32% consisted of intrusions of other signs or inflections; and 16% of the errors involved the scrambling of sign components. Clearly signs are broken down into their formational and morphological components at an early stage of processing. Similar phenomena have been observed for the processing of English, despite its isolating character (Kempley & Morton, 1982; Murrell & Morton, 1974). Here again we have evidence for a continuity between spoken and signed languages, particularly since Poizner, Bellugi, and Tweney (1981) emphasize that the componential decomposition does not merely reflect surface features of the signed input; incorrectly transposed inflections were all recalled in the allomorphic form appropriate to the verb stem on which they were superimposed.

Sequential versus Spatial Memory

In a series of elegant experiments designed to assess the role of stimulus ordering in recall, O'Connor and Hermelin have compared the performance of groups of deaf, blind, mentally handicapped, autistic, and normal children. We briefly summarize their results for comparisons of deaf and hearing subjects (Hermelin, 1972; Hermelin & O'Connor, 1975; O'Connor & Hermelin, 1972, 1973a). Their basic paradigm involved presenting subjects with three-digit stimuli for which spatial and temporal orders did not correspond (Fig. 4.6), and assessing their preferences for each.

Presented with such a display, hearing subjects tended to recall the digits in their temporal order. Deaf subjects recalled the digits in their spatial order. Similar results were obtained for recognition tasks (O'Connor & Hermelin, 1973b), but not for a task in which subjects were required to choose the "middle" digit of three (O'Connor & Hermelin, 1972). Moreover, deaf subjects showed improved recall for stimuli presented to them spatially rather than sequentially (Hermelin & O'Connor, 1975). Spatial preferences were not correlated with oral skills or short-term encoding (O'Connor & Hermelin, 1973). These results appeared to provide very strong evidence for atypical modes of input organization and short-term retention on the part of deaf children. Apparently lack of acoustic stimulation may result in a qualitative change in the way in which deaf children process incoming stimuli. If hearing impairment somehow inhibits sequential modes of processing, this might explain the extreme difficulties deaf persons experience in acquiring the syntax of English.

Unfortunately, a more recent study by Beck, Beck, and Gironella (1977) has upset this tidy picture. In attempting to replicate O'Connor and Hermelin's (1973b) key experiment, these authors failed to confirm either the hearing subjects' preference for temporal

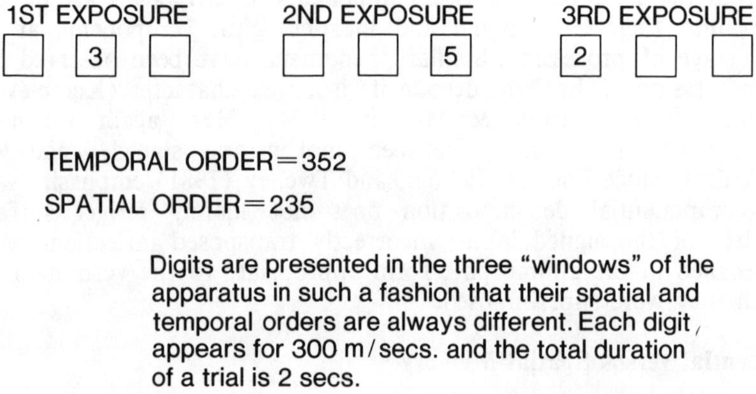

1ST EXPOSURE   2ND EXPOSURE   3RD EXPOSURE

□ 3 □   □ □ 5   2 □ □

TEMPORAL ORDER = 352

SPATIAL ORDER = 235

Digits are presented in the three "windows" of the
apparatus in such a fashion that their spatial and
temporal orders are always different. Each digit
appears for 300 m / secs. and the total duration
of a trial is 2 secs.

FIG. 4.6. Stimulus displays employed by Hermelin and O'Connor to assess spatial and
temporal coding preferences.

processing strategies or the deaf subjects' tendency to use spatial
processing. The divergence between the two sets of results is striking
(Fig. 4.7). In a comprehensive review of studies of sequential
processing in the deaf, Cumming and Rodda (1985) suggest that
hearing-deaf differences in cognitive processing emerge only when
linguistic materials are employed. Their conclusion is that further
research is required. If it should be confirmed that deaf children
suffer a specific difficulty in coping with materials for which
sequential ordering is essential, this would tie in very neatly with
their syntactical problems—passivization and embedding in particular.
We return to this topic in chapter 5.

Short-Term Memory and Communication Method

The STM encoding studies previously reviewed have generated many
interesting and valuable findings. But considering memory systems in
isolation, decoupled from their normal role as a component in more
complex cognitive processes, can give us a misleadingly incomplete
view (Reitman, 1970). What are the STM characteristics associated
with specific methods of reception? As yet, no experiments have
dealt directly with this issue; however, we have indirect evidence

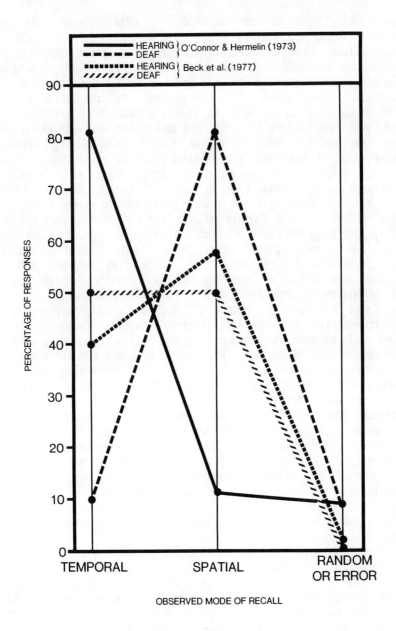

FIG. 4.7.   Spatial or temporal modes of recall: Preferences of matched deaf and hearing subjects.

concerning the short-term retention of data acquired via oral, manual, total, and reading input channels. The data in Table 4.6 come from two experiments referred to previously (Grove, O'Sullivan, & Rodda, 1979; Grove & Rodda, 1984) in which English, Canadian, and American subjects from a wide range of educational backgrounds were given a 120-item pictorial multiple choice test (the Test of Communication Skills or TCS). Subjects were presented with brief messages varying in syntactical and conceptual complexity, and were required to choose a picture matching the message from an array of eight drawings. The total time spent on the test by each subject gives us an estimate of the average time taken to communicate each item. This, in turn, tells us how long the subject had to retain items in short-term memory before giving a response. Clearly, this estimate directly reflects temporal components common to all the subjects (such as item difficulty and presentation time) and also components unique to each individual subject (comprehension and search time). Differences between subjects' average communication times will therefore provide a rough measure of differences of times spent in short-term storage.

Table 4.6 provides details of the relationship between mean communication time and total receptive communication scores for four basic methods of communication. The most interesting statistics are the gradient of the best fitting regression line and the coefficient of correlation. In the Reading condition, it is misleading to refer to "short-term memory," because subjects in this group were presented with messages typed on small cards and were permitted to keep them in view while searching for the target picture. The gradient of the regression line is therefore close to zero, and the correlation coefficient is not significant. Both Oral and Manual conditions, in contrast, show significant short-term memory loss effects, as manifested in negative regression functions and correlation coefficients. In other words, as the average time spent per item increases, overall communication score drops. Subjects who are slower to respond, therefore, tend to gain lower overall receptive scores.

Perhaps the most unexpected finding is that subjects in the Total Communication condition, like subjects in the Reading condition, appear to show no significant short-term losses, as assessed by the best fitting regression line. Apparently, the presentation of a combined oral and manual signal results in a more robust memory trace. Whether this is achieved by having dual speech and manual STM codes, or by accelerating the transfer of information into a semantic form, or whether it results from the strategic distribution of attention during input, is a matter for further experimentation.

TABLE 4.6

The Relationship Between Total Reception Score and Mean Communication Time for Four Methods of Communication

SAMPLE:	ENGLISH				U.S./CANADIAN				COMBINED			
Method of Communication	Grad.	r	n	P	Grad.	r	n	P	Grad.	r̂	N¹	P
Oral	-2.30	-0.61	10	0.03	-1.32	-0.43	17	0.04	-1.68	-0.50	24	0.006
Manual	—	—	—	—	-1.39	-0.40	22	0.03	—	—	—	—
Total	-0.44	-0.31	15	n.s.	-0.10	-0.08	26	n.s.	-0.22	-0.16	38	n.s.
Reading	—	—	—	—	-0.02	-0.03	23	n.s.	—	—	—	—

Note: The table shows (1) The gradient of the best–fitting regression line of total reception score (%) on mean communication time per test item (secs.); (2) The associated coefficient of correlation; (3) The number of subjects in the sample; and (4) The significance level of the correlation as assessed by a one-tailed z-test. Data from English subjects (see Grove et al., 1979) and U.S. and Canadian subjects (see Grove & Rodda, 1984).

Irrespective of the precise mechanism underlying this finding, it does provide strong support for the philosophical position traditionally adopted by proponents of total communication methods. Deaf people are able to cope with messages presented simultaneously in two separate modalities, and, moreover, a combined input appears to facilitate the storage of the message information. Further research to measure the STM traces associated with different input channels more directly would clearly be desirable.

Rate of Information Processing

The finding that receptive communication scores depend on speed of response for oral and manual methods of communication, but not for total communication methods or reading, suggests that comparisons between communication methods employing only overall percentage scores might be misleading. Perhaps the higher scores noted for reading and total methods relative to oral and manual methods might partially reflect differences in communication speed.

Klima and Bellugi (1979, chap. 8) have reported studies of the production rates for oral, manual, and total communication. Hearing adults of deaf parents were asked to tell stories in English, ASL, or combined communication. Signs were produced at a rate of 2 to 2.5 signs per second in both manual and total conditions. Speech-only was produced at a rate of 4 to 5 words per second; during total communication the speech production rate dropped slightly to around 3 to 4 words per second. Since the information transmitted by words and signs cannot be directly compared, Klima and Bellugi also estimated the time required to generate propositions in ASL and speech. This time no consistent differences between speech-only and manual conditions and speech-only and total communication were apparent. However, deaf ASL users produced propositions and signs at a slightly faster rate than hearing signers, and for all subjects, about 1 to 2 seconds were required to produce an elementary proposition. Interestingly, a given proposition could be expressed using far fewer signs (less than half) than words.

To examine the relationship between response time and communication, Grove and Rodda (1984) compared the four basic receptive methods using a measure of Information Transfer Rate (ITR), defined as the average number of messages correctly transmitted per minute of testing time. For subjects of average age 13.8 years, mean ITR in the Reading condition was 2.39 items/minute. Oral communication, as assessed by the ITR metric, was again least effective: 1.36 items/minute. Interestingly, Total and Manual Methods gained identical ITR scores: 2.07 items/minute. The data also strongly confirm the superiority of reading over oral methods of reception: Reading is not only more efficient overall, in terms of gross percentages, but is significantly faster. The relationship between manual and total methods is more complex. Reference to Table 4.3 (p. 185) shows that in percentage terms, the manual-total difference derived from several studies varies considerably. If these two methods transmit approximately the same amount of information per unit time, the reason for these fluctuations may lie in the differing temporal demands of the specific tasks involved. These results also imply that the manual component of total communication is more important than the oral component. The addition of an oral signal slightly improves reception but at the expense of a reduction in transmission rate. The "trade off" is a sensible compromise, and we have to assume that, for students, it plays a vital role in facilitating the development of receptive and expressive speech skills. We realize that this conclusion will dismay proponents of "pure" oral or manual methods, but from a purely pragmatic viewpoint total communication does, it seems, have significant advantages over both.

Semantic Recoding

A further stage in the reception of information is the transfer of input data from short-term memory into a semantic form. Here two factors are involved: task requirements and processing time. If the subject in a communication experiment is required merely to recall or recognize a recently presented stimulus, transfer into a long-term semantic store is unnecessary. The subject can gain a high "communication" score by exploiting short-term storage mechanisms, whether speech- or sign-based. Some of the receptive studies cited previously undoubtedly fall into this category (e.g., Johnson, 1976), while experiments employing a pictorial multiple choice technique (Conrad, 1977; Grove, O'Sullivan & Rodda, 1979; Grove & Rodda, 1984) clearly demand a certain amount of semantic processing. The White and Stevenson (1975) study involved the presentation of complete passages and a subsequent comprehension test, and, therefore, was probably drawing on semantic processing skills of a relatively high order.

The major study of semantic recoding dealing with hearing persons is by Sachs (1967), who showed that after a delay subjects could not remember the surface form of English sentences, only their meaning. A replication of this type of study using deaf subjects has been reported by Hanson and Bellugi (1982). ASL sentences were presented for immediate or delayed (45 seconds) recognition. The test sentences were changed in four ways: *formal* changes involved alterations in sign order with no change in meaning; *lexical* changes altered the specific signs and/or their morphology, but again the meaning remained constant; *inflectional* changes involved switching inflections between sign stems in the sentence; *semantic* changes altered sign order. Thus formal and lexical changes affected only surface structure; inflectional and semantic changes altered both surface structure and meaning. The subjects, native ASL users, had to say whether the test sentence was "exactly the same" as a sentence seen previously. When an immediate recognition test was made, there were no differences between scores in the four conditions. However, after 45 seconds, semantic and inflectional changes were noted more readily than formal and lexical changes. Average ratings of confidence made by the judges dropped significantly after a delay for all conditions except the semantic one. In other words, just as hearing subjects forget the surface form of English sentences and recall only their meaning, so deaf subjects rapidly lose information about the surface structure of ASL messages.

The Receptive Process: A Working Hypothesis

Having sketched out the performance characteristics of the perceptual and cognitive mechanisms underlying the reception of information by deaf persons, we try to develop some hypotheses about the processes of reception associated with each of the four major methods of communication. In so doing, we hope both to increase our understanding of the communicative abilities of hearing-impaired people and to provide a plausible framework for further research.

Oral Communication. It should by now be obvious why oral communication is invariably found to be the least effective receptive method. It combines too many areas of weakness at the sensory and short-term memory levels:

1. The signal-noise ratio for visually perceived lip movements is poor, unless a wide range of physical and physiological variables are fixed at optimal levels.

2. Too few basic elements (phonemes) can be perceived at all, and of these only eight can be unambiguously recognized under ideal conditions (i.e., less than 20% of all English phonemes).

3. Short-term encoding skills of deaf people are known to vary considerably: Around half have poor speech coding skills.

4. Some evidence suggests that deaf people may have more problems than hearing people in coping with sequentially ordered materials.

Given, therefore, a fragmented and ambiguous input, how does the lip-reader proceed to reconstruct the original message? As we noted earlier, the lip-reader does have access to significant nonlabial cues to meaning: amplified residual hearing and informal gesture. For the severely deaf lip-reader, these cues may actually contribute more to the reception process than the lip movements themselves. Nevertheless, combining these diverse signals into a coherent whole must be an acutely difficult task. To use the terminology of Information Theory and cryptanalysis, the lip-reader is in a real time situation akin to that of a codebreaker confronted with a mixture of code and cipher representing a message in an only vaguely familiar language. Most of the cipher is missing, and much is distorted. The number of contextual cues depends on the precise circumstances: in the classroom, with friends, or meeting strangers on the street. The lip-reader must be engaged in a complex interpolatory process, guessing those parts of the message which he cannot perceive, exploiting each and every available clue. How does the lip-reader accomplish this extraordinary mental feat?

Dynamic studies of the lipreading process have so far been lacking; but we do have quite a lot of correlational information concerning the relationship between individual cognitive skills and lipreading ability (see Farwell, 1976, for a brief review). We have already referred to one very important correlate of oral skill, namely speech coding. If the deaf person is unable to develop internal representations of acoustic stimuli, his or her chances of developing good oral skills are slight. But, in this case, as with all correlational evidence, we could turn the argument around and say instead that people develop speech coding as a result of having good lipreading abilities. Potentially more valuable are studies employing variables that are more likely to be innately determined (e.g., the various factors of intelligence, general cognitive skills, and so on).

Perhaps surprisingly, the Intelligence Quotient (IQ) has only a small (albeit consistent) effect on oral reception scores. White and Stevenson (1975) found that reception scores depended on both IQ and educational background: Students from a Total Communication school showed a small but linear relationship between IQ and oral reception; subjects from an oral school performed better if they were of average IQ rather than of low or even high IQ—a very puzzling result. The picture changes when we consider specific cognitive skills: Farwell (1976) notes that several tests yield moderate to high correlations with lipreading scores, notably Visual Synthesis, Visual

Closure, Concept Formation, Rhythm, and some tests of Visual Memory. Myklebust (1964) also cites a number of significant correlations, between lipreading and scores on the "Draw-a-Man" test, and also with various verbal measures such as Vocabulary, Syntax, Abstraction, and Sentence Length. Arnold and Walter (1979) reported a small correlation between lipreading and a test of Verbal Reasoning.

The most comprehensive single study of the correlates of oral skill is that of van Uden (1983), who factor-analyzed the results of 15 cognitive and behavioral tests taken by orally educated deaf children aged 7-11 years. Three factors were identified: Factor I, labeled *eupraxia*, loaded on tests measuring fine sequential motor control in both oral and manual (in the general sense) skills. Memory for simultaneously presented visual stimuli negatively loaded on this factor. Factor II measured *activity*, and distinguished between tests as a function of the total amount of motor behavior demanded by each. Factor III measured the *memory demand* of each test. The fact that Factor I, which increased in importance with age, loaded on both oral and manual skills, suggests that both reflect the workings of a more general cognitive mechanism. The importance of manual sequential skills as determinants of lipreading ability is dramatically revealed when we look at the four major correlates of oral reception for the oldest age group in van Uden's experiment (10-11 years). They are: (a) repeating lip-read words five times from memory— essentially an extension of the basic lipreading test employed in our studies—which yields a correlation of $r=0.92$; (b) imitating successive paper folding movements, $r=0.89$; (c) imitating complex hand and finger configurations, $r=0.82$; and (d) imitating finger movements outside one's field of vision, from memory, $r=0.77$. In short, the tests most strongly predictive of oral receptive skill (not including the first test) all measure relatively complex *manual* abilities. Also surprising, in view of the findings reported previously in this chapter, is the fact that short-term memory (as assessed by a combined lipreading and digit recall test) is not strongly correlated with lipreading scores at age 10-11 years, despite achieving a high correlation ($r=0.81$) at age 8-9 years.

Attempts to mold such data into an information-processing model of lipreading have been rare (Parasnis & Samar, 1982). The only serious attempt reported to date, that of Risberg and Agelfors (1978, cited by Parasnis & Samar, 1982, p. 69), found, as we would expect, that two major psychological processes are involved: sensory and conceptual memory processes. However, this general scheme tells us little about the dynamics of the system. A further problem, noted by Farwell (1976), is that many of the correlational studies have failed to control for the effects of residual hearing, gesture, and other significant variables. The cognitive mechanisms involved in extracting meaning from residual hearing, gesture, and lip movements, are probably quite different. The definitive study—one examining the effects of many different variables on the reception scores obtained when each of these input channels is operating—has yet to be run. Nevertheless, we can put forward hypotheses about the process.

It seems likely that, in order to make sense of the partial input on which the lip-reader is forced to rely, he or she is obliged to interpolate; that is, the lip-reader must reconstruct the missing or distorted elements of the message. Complete reconstruction is not necessary: The redundancy of spoken language ensures that the meaning of an utterance can be deduced even when parts have been lost. If this were not the case, lipreading would never have proven viable for any deaf person. However, much of the redundancy of natural language is syntactical in nature, and we have already seen that the syntactical abilities of deaf people, and particularly deaf children, are generally poor. A natural implication of this is that much lipreading is semantically based—that is, the lip-reader must rapidly identify the semantic context of the message, form hypotheses about possible alternative meanings, and constantly update these hypotheses as more information becomes available. It is clear that this task represents a cognitive effort of major proportions.

Much of the correlational evidence just reviewed is broadly consistent with this model. We would expect variables such as verbal reasoning, concept formation, visual memory, vocabulary, syntax, and so on, to play a part in the reconstruction process. Moreover, the data cited in Table 4.6, showing that oral reception is subject to short-term memory losses, are consistent with the notion that the reconstruction process draws heavily on short-term retention mechanisms. This explains why, as message length increases from simple sentences (Grove & Rodda, 1984) to long passages (White & Stevenson, 1975), lipreading scores decrease dramatically.

It is somewhat surprising that message length has never been systematically varied in any major study of lipreading: the model proposed here predicts an "inverted U" function, with scores increasing as messages grow from one word to short sentences (as the amount of contextual information increases) and then decreasing as the numbers of sentences rise (because of memory overload effects). At first sight, the 84% lipreading score obtained by profoundly deaf subjects aged 13-16 years for the reception of single common words in the study of Erber (1974), raises difficulties for the model. We would not expect such a high level of performance.

However, Erber primed his subjects by showing them a list of the stimuli prior to each testing session. Less importantly, the subjects selected were all described as "good" lip-readers.

If oral skill covaries with many cognitive factors, we would expect wider intersubject variation in lipreading scores than that associated with other methods of communication. This is precisely what Grove and Rodda (1984) found; in their study the youngest oral subject group proved to contain both the lowest scorer and the highest scorer in the entire experiment.

Finally, the data on transmission speed (also from Grove & Rodda, 1984) cited previously (p. 210) also tend to confirm the reconstruction model. Lip-readers are much slower to respond to messages than are subjects employing other media, implying that their responses are contingent on the outcomes of more, or more complex, cognitive processes than are required in other communication methods.

The data reviewed in this chapter not only broadly support the model of oral reception presented here, but also cast considerable doubt on the utility of lipreading as a general purpose method of communication for deaf students. If so little information is transmitted so slowly that neither brief everyday messages, nor more complex discourse, are communicated effectively, then one must conclude that oral methods are inherently inferior. We subscribe to this view *as a statistical generalization.* There are undoubtedly many deaf persons whose lipreading skills are more than adequate; and many more partially hearing people who with an effective hearing aid can comprehend oral/aural messages. But on the whole, severely prelingually impaired respondents, in a number of experimental tests, perform significantly worse in oral conditions than for all other methods of communication. We know of no published or unpublished studies that show lipreading to be superior to other receptive methods. Until such evidence is forthcoming, the conclusion just reached is inescapable.

Nevertheless, in a recent closely argued series of papers, Ivimey (1977a, 1977b, 1977c) has presented an alternative viewpoint. Reviewing studies of speech perception in the hearing, Ivimey (1977c) points out that:

> Every perceiver has at his command a number of cognitive models and perception involves the application of these models to sensory inputs. These sensory inputs are typically fragmentary, debased and fleeting. Thus the case of the deaf, relying ... on lipreading, should not be set off against the hearing.... Both media provide debased and fragmentary data ... both are exactly equally fleeting. (p. 90)

Ivimey (1977c) goes on to claim that lipreading failures reflect the deaf person's acquisition of a nonstandard form of English: "A major constraint on the interpretation of language by the deaf is to be found in the impoverished and defective systems of knowledge that they have both of the language in which messages are coded and of the probable content of the messages" (p. 94).

Although Ivimey's views are interesting and stimulating, and although he is clearly correct in emphasizing the role of the cognitive models underlying the communication process, we feel that his defense of lipreading overlooks two vital points. First, although both speech and lip-read inputs are fragmentary and debased, they are by no means equally debased. A hearing person is potentially able to identify all the phonemes of natural language; as we have seen, the deaf person is not. Secondly, although there is a logical similarity between the tasks confronting the hearing listener and the deaf lipreader, the cognitive processes employed in each case may not be comparable. The hearing child is genetically programmed to identify and utilize the phonological structure of any natural language; we cannot assume that the deaf child has a corresponding innate ability to exploit lip movement patterns. There is evidence that hearing people do learn to employ lip movements in speech perception as they grow older; however, younger children rely mostly on acoustic signals (McGurk & MacDonald, 1976). Presumably this developmental trend stems from the need both to adapt to small hearing losses occurring later in life and to compensate for acoustic attenuation under unfavorable listening conditions. In either case, the ability to assimilate lip movement information is probably contingent on a basic competence in spoken language; and it is this competence that the young deaf child lacks.

In our opinion, the evidence regarding performance during oral reception should make disturbing reading for those specialists who continue to support a strictly oralist position. Even under optimal conditions, it is unequivocally the least efficient method of communication for deaf children and adolescents. To reconstruct lip-read messages, the deaf person must devote so much of his or her working memory capacity to the task of disambiguating a highly degraded input that his or her ability to attend to and comprehend the "higher level" conceptual content of the input is severely compromised. And yet lipreading is advocated as an educational method. To reconstruct messages, the lip-reader must also possess a high level of competence in English, which the deaf student does not have. And yet lipreading is alleged to be an effective way of learning English. To reconstruct messages, the lip-reader requires a well defined set of conditions: a familiar speaker, optimal levels of illumination and angle of regard, and close physical proximity. These conditions are rarely met (and we have not even considered the situation in which the speaker is another deaf person with poor speech skills). And yet lipreading is presented as an effective everyday mode of communication.

If we take into account the facts that "pure" lipreading—not supplemented by residual aural or gestural information—does not vary as a function of severity of hearing impairment (Erber, 1972), and that hearing people with no prior experience of lipreading perform on a par with orally educated deaf persons (Arnold & Walter, 1979; Conrad, 1977), we are also led to question the value of intensive oral training. It almost seems as though lipreading is an individual skill more dependent on innately determined cognitive factors than on experience and training (see chapter 8). It is possible that the small gains in language test scores associated with intensive oral regimes reflect more the environmental enrichment and increased personal attention that they entail rather than any specifically linguistic effect (chapter 5).

Lipreading is a complicated and difficult processing task even for the mature learner with a developed spoken language system; it is even more difficult for the child or student who has failed to internalize English language syntax. Why, therefore, should it be the only method of receptive communication (with or without aural input) permitted to some deaf children?

Manual Communication. It is clear both from studies of the structural characteristics of sign language and from evidence concerning receptive efficiency that manual communication is a more effective medium of reception than lipreading for a majority of severely prelingually deaf people. For hearing-impaired persons for whom sign language is their native mode of communication, signs are easier to perceive and process than lip movements. But it is notable that manual reception is not the most effective method. It is somewhat less effective, overall, than total communication; and significantly less effective than reading. In the light of these data, the oral-manual controversy seems a little absurd. Neither method is best. Indeed, both are inferior to combined methods and reading.

How can we account for the poor overall performance of the manual method? First, we need to be certain that the comparison is a fair one. Very few of the subjects in the manual conditions of the comparative experiments fall into the category of "deaf children born to deaf, manually proficient parents." Many acquire sign language in the classroom, or, secretively, outside it, at a relatively late stage of their intellectual development. Until we can be sure that all our manual communicators have acquired sign language at an early age, our measures of manual efficiency will consistently underestimate the receptive potential of the method (Mayberry, Fischer, & Hatfield, 1983). On the other hand, relatively few deaf children (no more than 20%) are born to parents with any knowledge of signing (Harvey, 1982). The comparative findings may therefore be regarded as valid de facto measures of receptive efficiency. Secondly, we turn again to the data on short-term memory. Table 4.1 suggests that both oral and manual methods are associated with rapid short-term information loss. Although articulatory coding of lip-read signals, and sign parameter coding of manual input, may to some extent take over in the deaf person the role played by acoustic coding in the cognitive system of the hearing person, these findings imply that they fail to fully compensate for hearing handicap. Perhaps this is not surprising, but further research is required to test the hypothesis.

Unfortunately, few studies have systematically investigated the cognitive skills underlying manual communication. "Communication" may be a general skill of which more specific abilities such as lipreading and signing are isolated manifestations. Undoubtedly, the possession of an adequate semantic base is a prerequisite for communication in any modality, and deaf people are not strongly deficient in this respect. The chief difference between a lip-reader with poor English skills and a manual communicator with an imperfect knowledge of ASL (or its equivalent) lies in the quality of the peripheral processing involved. The lip-reader has to cope with a low quality input; the manual communicator has a high grade input.

Total Communication. Total or combined methods of communication are, it is frequently asserted, the ideal receptive technique. Because several channels of information are open to the subject, he or she can monitor all of them, switching his or her attention rapidly between them. Thus, ambiguity in one channel may swiftly be resolved by reference to another channel. This is a very plausible argument, but it has never been systematically investigated: Most research has been directed toward oral *or* manual methods. Even Klima and Bellugi's (1979) excellent comparison of rates of communication during manual or total communication phases was based on only a small number of subjects. Moreover, some supporters of pure manual methods have questioned the ability of total communicators to correctly express sign language syntax while simultaneously using spoken language forms. We discuss one aspect of this problem in chapter 8.

What is clear, however, is that a total communication message is more redundant in Information Theory terms (see chapter 3, p. 116 and Fig. 3.2b) than either an oral or manual message on its own. Moreover, there is evidence that, in some situations, quality of redundancy may play a more vital role than quantity: Nicolaci-da-Costa and Harris (1983) found that hearing children's comprehension of spoken sentences was enhanced when redundancy was produced by presenting number information in more than one syntactical form. However, redundancy produced by repetition of the same syntactical marker had no effect at all on comprehension. The parallels with total versus oral communication are obvious: Total communication creates redundancy by employing two qualitatively different types of input. In instructional and informal situations, lipreading tends to make extensive use of repetition of the same basic elements (usually those that are difficult if not impossible to identify reliably). Remember also that "lipreading" itself relies heavily on gestural and aural components.

Apart from the study by White and Stevenson (1975), all the major comparisons of different receptive methods do confirm a superiority of total over manual communication. However, Grove and Rodda (1984) found that total and manual methods transmit about the same amount of information per unit time. Considering the data on putative short-term loss, the most sensible interpretation of these findings is that total communicators, having access to a more reliable memory trace, can afford to operate at a more leisurely rate than manual communicators. They therefore gain higher accuracy scores than the manual subjects, who are quicker to respond but make more errors. If this hypothesis is correct, delays of recall should adversely affect manual reception scores, but have little effect on combined scores. And if communication is defined collectively as reception, comprehension, and long-term storage, total communication methods would be established as a qualitatively better mode of reception than oral or manual techniques alone.

Unfortunately, we have been unable to locate any significant studies of Total Communication in which attempts have been made either to assess the contribution of each channel to overall receptive scores or to analyze the dynamics of the process. Thus many key questions have remained not only unanswered but also unasked. For example: How does the receiver divide his or her attention between the component channels (aural, oral, manual)? What determines the decision to monitor one channel rather than another? What happens when two channels give conflicting signals? How does the transmitter combine the syntactical structures of English and sign language? Do different transmitters combine the linguistic components in different ways? And so on. Clearly, this is an area demanding further research.

Reading. Perhaps the most remarkable, and yet neglected, outcome of the comparative studies is the finding that reading *consistently emerges as the most efficient receptive method.* When rate of information transmission is taken into account, the superiority of reading is enhanced. Puthli (personal communication, 1980) has suggested that the low status of signing may tend to depress the scores for manual and total methods relative to reading, but the observed rankings apply both to subjects taken from oral regimes and those educated using combined methods. We are obliged to conclude that reading is the optimal receptive medium, certainly for purposes of instruction, and arguably for interaction between the deaf child of average oral skills and the hearing community. Even within the youngest age group studied by Grove and Rodda (1984), 9-11 years, reading scores exceeded oral scores by about 20%. This suggests that greater emphasis on the systematic use of written materials and visual displays in schools for the deaf might lead to corresponding gains in attainment.

One reason why reading has been afforded little attention by educationalists as a potential mode of instruction is that the results of normative surveys of reading skills among the deaf have overwhelmingly convinced educators and others that hearing-impaired children possess extremely poor reading ability. But there are several reasons for questioning the pessimistic conclusions of normative studies:

1. Much of the variation in test scores nominally measuring reading skills may reflect the technique used to assess comprehension. It is reasonable to assume that multiple choice methods are likely to generate higher scores than free response methods, and that pictorial choice will produce higher scoring than verbal multiple choice (compare, for example, the reading scores presented by White and Stevenson, 1975, with those of Conrad, 1977). However, there have been no systematic studies along these lines, and no serious attempts to consider how they may result in misleading conclusions being drawn from the existing data.

2. Deaf children are known to posses recognition vocabularies (assessed by verbal multiple choice) far smaller than those possessed by hearing children (Silverman-Dresner & Guilfoyle, 1972). They are thus seriously handicapped in respect of a basic component of the communication process, and it may be inferred that at least some proportion of the poor "reading" scores of deaf students reflects not a failure of comprehension but deficient sight vocabulary.

3. There is no doubt that almost all prelingually deaf children experience profound difficulty in grasping complex English

syntactical structures, and the extent to which remedial education can be employed to improve syntactical competence is still in doubt (see Brasel & Quigley, 1975; Thompson, 1927). Some percentage of the observed deficiency may stem from the problems deaf subjects exhibit in coping with sequential information, which may in turn be an unavoidable consequence of lack of aural input during a critical stage of development. The work of Quigley and his associates suggests that the acquisition of basic English syntactical structures by deaf children may be delayed by more than 10 years relative to the hearing. Much less is known about semantic processing. Although communication is concerned essentially with the transmission of meaning, it is notable—and surprising—that very few studies of communication with the deaf have concerned themselves with this variable. Most experiments have been limited to a comparatively gross rating of abstraction (e.g., Myklebust, 1964) and have concluded that the deaf find it hard to handle abstract ideas. But abstraction is a difficult concept to define, and its assessment by means of ratings is clearly risky. For example, abstract concepts tend to be associated with longer, more complex, and less frequently used words than do concrete concepts. Mode of response also becomes crucial in distinguishing syntactical from semantic factors. It is possible that many of the studies that show reading comprehension in deaf students to lag dramatically behind the reading performance scores of the hearing have employed scoring criteria biased too heavily toward the syntax, rather than the meaning, of the materials involved. Maeder (1980) compared the performance of two groups of deaf children presented with the same conceptual information, either in a 720-word passage containing complex syntactical structures or in a 550-word passage composed of short, active declarative sentences. When a semantic criterion (verbal multiple choice) was applied, syntactical complexity was found to exercise no significant effect on comprehension. Cumming, Grove, and Rodda (1985) report a similar finding.

4. There is evidence that deaf and hearing children employ radically different strategies in answering reading test questions (Davey, LaSasso, Macready, & Swaiko, 1982; Webster, Wood, & Griffiths, 1981; Wood, Griffiths, & Webster, 1981). In particular, deaf students are more likely to attempt very difficult items than are hearing students of the same putative reading age, and are more likely to respond on the basis of semantic association or spatial position rather than to develop effective

linguistic strategies. Webster, Wood, and Griffiths (1981) conclude that: "It seems clear that the reading age estimates of deaf children are *not* reliable guides to their functional linguistic skills. A deaf child's score may resemble that of a younger hearing child, but the performance and processes that lead to that score are likely to be different.... This clearly raises questions about the value of reading estimates of the deaf child, using norms based on studies of the hearing" (p. 13). The assessment of such test scores is made doubly difficult by the lack of control exercised by the test constructors over their materials. Frequently the numbers of distractors in multiple choice tests vary, and the semantic and syntactical relationships between target words and distractors are permitted to change in an unsystematic fashion. Wood, Griffiths, and Webster (1981) concluded that only tests such as the Test of Syntactic Ability (Quigley, Steinkamp, Power, & Jones, 1978), based on observations of deaf children's grammatical performance, can be validly employed with hearing-impaired respondents. And it is notable that scores on the TSA do not indicate a fixed ceiling on the syntactical skills of deaf people.

There is no question that the English syntactical skills of deaf children in receptive and, especially, expressive communication are extremely poor. Nevertheless, hearing impairment does not incapacitate their central comprehension processes. Provided deaf readers can grasp the semantic context of a message, they seem to be able to exploit the syntactical redundancy of natural language and to comprehend its contents with a surprising degree of efficiency. Given a low but consistent level of grammatical ability, cognitive theory would predict that a printed input should generate higher receptive performance scores than oral or manual stimuli: first, because of its superior signal/noise ratio, and second, because it is not subject to rapid fading. The reader is free to return to words that he or she might feel unsure of; hence, fewer demands are made on his or her perceptual and short-term retention mechanisms. Perhaps the spatial nature of the printed message also contributes to its greater effectiveness. There seems to be little doubt that this is so for deaf students; but the potential of reading as a method of communication has been obscured by the finding that deaf students have very low levels of achievement on conventional tests of reading. If cognitive processing theory can assist in the education of deaf students, perhaps it can do so by shifting our focus from a negative to a more positive stance. Rather than emphasizing low reading achievements, should we not be emphasizing the value of reading as a vehicle of communication?

Summary

Despite their handicap, hearing-impaired persons retain essentially normal cognitive capacities. Deafness does not, as was once thought, directly impair intellectual functioning. But, not surprisingly, it does have specific effects on specific cognitive functions associated with audition: short-term memory encoding and the acquisition of natural language syntax. A review of experimental studies of receptive communication in various modalities suggests that, despite their poor English grammatical skills, deaf persons perform most efficiently when provided with a written input. Lipreading appears to be inferior to all other receptive methods; manual and total communication come between lipreading and reading. The efficiency of each method appears to be related to its *peripheral* processing characteristics: the perceptibility of sensory elements, short-term storage, type of display and other similar factors.

Further Reading

Excellent introductions to the general psychology of communication are George Miller's (1967a) *The Psychology of Communication*, and, also edited by Miller (1973), *Communication, Language and Meaning*. A more advanced treatment is to be found in Raynar Rommetveit's (1974) *On Message Structure*. The higher level cognitive skills of the deaf are reviewed by Hans Furth (1966) in his *Thinking Without Language*; specifically linguistic skills are extensively documented in *Linguistics and Deaf Children* by W.K. Russell, Stephen P. Quigley, and D.J. Power (1976). David Martin (1986) has edited an excellent summary of the present status of research into a number of topics related to cognition and deafness, *Cognition, Education and Deafness*. Finally, Robert Conrad's (1979) book *The Deaf Schoolchild* is vital reading for anybody interested in this topic.

5

LANGUAGE DEVELOPMENT
AND EDUCATIONAL ISSUES

We saw in chapter 3 that sign language is commonly misconceived as a primitive or inefficient language. We are exploring the nature of sign language in many ways in this book, and by doing so, we hope, refute this myth. In fact, even though the rate of production of sounds in conversation is about twice the rate of the production of signs, sign language can, by a variety of methods, communicate meaning as efficiently and quickly as speech. Unfortunately, that this is so is not always appreciated by people either unfamiliar with sign language or those whose sign language skills are limited to the use of manual English. The following quotes illustrate very clearly some of the prejudices and misconceptions common among opponents of sign language:

> It is believed that because manual communication can be used in a grammatical form that does not follow the rules of English language, the child will not acquire the ability to express himself in an acceptable way. Another argument ... is that it is associated with the stereotype commonly referred to as "dummy." ... It has been said that the child who uses it would end up in ... "ghettoes." ... Faced with these views, it is not surprising that parents believe a rigid adherence to oral means is vital if their child is to achieve "normality." (Verney, 1976, p. 69)

> The argument against the traditional sign language, that it is nongrammatical and impedes the development of correct language forms, is valid, and this has probably stimulated the introduction of the Paget-Gorman systematic sign language and other techniques. (Reeves, 1976, p. 12)

> It is impossible to recognise the acquisition of a sign language as a good alternative [to spoken language]. It is not a verbal language. (Ewing &

Ewing, 1964 as cited by Gregory, 1976, p. 124)

The main argument of the pure oralists is that deaf children have to live in a hearing society, and so must use the methods of communication of that society. (Denmark, 1976, p. 76)

Natural gesture is permitted because this is used in teaching normal children and in society generally, but it must be used with caution ... and for this reason its use tends to be restricted more to the least orally competent pupils in the older age ranges. (Reeves, 1976, p. 14)

On this point, I would suggest that frustration over difficulty with communication is not restricted to the orally-trained deaf child. It bothers the manually-trained deaf child as well. (Lowell, 1976, p. 31)

If we were considering the use of sign language in hearing children, the equality of sign systems and spoken English suggests that either could facilitate language development. Unfortunately, our focus is deaf children, children who cannot hear, and who, if they are to develop language using spoken English, have to use an inefficient visual code based on lipreading. Therefore, it seems to us (and many others) a fairly logical conclusion that sign language is a better way of developing a first language in young deaf children. The question of which sign language to use (particularly American Sign Language or some form of manually coded English) is more complex, but the choice between a visual code and a quasi-auditory code seems to be fairly obvious (Brennan, 1975).

It certainly seems to us that it is wholly unreasonable for many people in the hearing community to seek to impose on the deaf community a method of communication—oralism—which is known to be functionally ineffective, purely because hearing persons cannot understand the language of the deaf community—American Sign Language or its equivalent. It is rather like insisting that paraplegics should only be allowed to use crutches, because wheelchairs create a nuisance for pedestrians. The controversy between oral approaches and total communication approaches was discussed in chapter 2, and it cannot be ignored in any discussion of the development of language in deaf children or educational policies for such children. Experience and research more than justify the use of total communication in the education of prelingual deaf children; and this is a specific premise that underlies this chapter and others.

Brill (1970) has an insightful review of the oral versus total communication controversy. He discusses eight *invalid* assumptions that have been used in the past to support the use of oral only methods in the education of deaf students. These invalid assumptions are a concise summary of the oralist philosophy. They are:

1. Expressive and receptive communication are a common generic skill.

2. Individual differences in the ability to learn speech and lipreading are of lesser importance than the need to learn such skills.

3. Learning language through speech and lipreading is the same as learning speech and lipreading with an existing language base.

4. Using manual communication creates confusion in language skills, and "deafisms" result from sign language rather than from the use of different coding processes in short-term and long-term memory.

5. The use of manual communication impairs the development of speech and lipreading skills.

6. Motivation to use speech declines if a person also develops manual communication skills.

7. Developing speech and lipreading is more important than avoiding frustration at the lack of communication or dealing with the negative attitudes of some hearing people toward sign language.

8. Good oral skills cannot be developed in an environment where the use of sign language is permitted or encouraged.

After exploring these assumptions, Brill concluded that the use of other methods of communication in programs for deaf students was not only justified but absolutely necessary. At the same symposium Vernon (1970) also echoed this position. He listed a number of myths that exist in deaf education, presented objective evidence to refute them, and reached similar conclusions to those of Brill.

The assumptions described by Brill and the myths cited by Vernon have one common factor. They have become incorporated into the value systems of ardent supporters of oral only methods of educating deaf students. Therefore, they are rarely questioned, and when they are questioned, the questioning is counterproductive, because it is difficult for proponents of these methods to accept that a commitment to the development of oral success, may, in fact, have precluded the development of adequate language in their students.

The Milan Conference (see p. 68) ensured that oral methods dominated the education of deaf students for almost a century, particularly in Europe, and during that time "sign language" had a secondary status in education and elsewhere. As a result, it was not until 1960 that Stokoe's seminal work provided a method of recording sign language and the first evidence of its fully fledged status as a language began to emerge (Stokoe, 1960, and chapter 3). The result was a slow growth in the study of "deaf" sign language as a special branch of semiotics and linguistics, and an increasing awareness of its status and characteristics as a language. In time, this knowledge filtered through to the educators of deaf students, and in the early 1970s the phrase "Total Communication" was popularized by Denton (1972). Increasingly, from 1972 onwards, the argument between oral communication and sign language is being perceived as a non sequitur. Even staunch advocates of the oral education of deaf students (such as Daniel Ling, 1984, and van Uden in Holland) are beginning to accept that sign language and finger spelling may be of some value.[1] Unfortunately, this grudging acceptance of sign language still excludes many deaf students from the educational and social benefits of an early and consistent experience of sign language and masks equally contentious arguments about what is the best sign language to use in the classroom.

Overall Characteristics of Sign Language

Stokoe's original breakdown of signs by shape (dez), place (tab) and movement (sig) has been widely reported and is also described in chapters 2 and 3. Wilbur (1979) has one of the most detailed accounts, illustrating the various facets of signs and their analysis and development in the period following Stokoe's first publication. To reiterate, the primary discriminating features of American Sign Language are the hand shape, the movement of the hands, the relationship between the two hands, and the place of the sign (Bellugi, Klima, & Siple, 1975; Friedman, 1977). It is interesting to note that in this system, the errors that young children make in learning sign language are consistent with the emergence of the adult language form (see for example Collins-Ahlgren, 1975).

Wilbur (1982) also draws attention in another paper to the confusion which ASL causes for the uninitiated by its use of hand shapes and classifiers. First, the hand shapes used in sign language are not the same as the finger spelled letters of the American one-handed alphabet, although they may have some approximation to these letters. In some signs, particularly those of more recent origin, a finger spelled symbol may even be used to give greater isomorphism with English, but these are not to be confused with the hand positions that increase the visual discriminability of signs. Second, the process of pronominalization in ASL makes considerable

---

[1]Many people do not realize that the Instituut voor-Doven in Sint Michielsgestel in the Netherlands has separate oral and sign language programs.

use of "classifiers." Wilbur states that there are classifiers for vehicles, hollow containers, solid objects that are extended in one direction (e.g., trees, poles), smaller objects that are extended in one direction (e.g., pencils, pens), objects that are flat and immovable, people, objects with legs that do not move (e.g., easel, barbecue grill), objects with legs that do move (e.g., people walking) and animal legs (Kegl, 1976; Kegl & Wilbur, 1976). Once an object has been identified in a conversation, a classifier may take over and act as a pronoun, but in doing so it can also incorporate many adjectival components.

In fact, the sophistications of sign language are such that a single sign can be used to map a seven-proposition English sentence (see p. 140). Another interesting example is given, for example, by Levine (1981, p. 97). She compares sign language translation with the translation of Japanese Haiku. She gives an example of the translation of a Haiku from Henderson (1959, p. 7):

Word-for-word transcription:	Tower / on / when-I-climb / cryptomeria's / top-twig / on / butterfly / one
Order-of-thought translation:	The tower high I climb, there, on that fir top sits a butterfly!

A similar translation of sign language is cited from Fant, (1974-1975, p. 2):

Sign-for-sign expression:	NOW MORNING / SUNRISE / I-LOOK-AT / THRILL
English equivalent:	It was a thrill to watch the sunrise this morning.

Levine concluded that there "is a striking similarity in feel and expression between Henderson's and Fant's examples," and raises the very important question of whether or not "expression, hence grammar, is governed by order of thoughts or events."

In addition to their failure to adequately record sign language, many of its detractors also based their judgments on the sign language of children. Apart from the obvious illogic of judging a language from its use by people who are learning it, such judgments also fail to consider the influence of lack of adequate English skills on the language use. We discussed this problem in more detail (pp. 165 to 180), but as we have already suggested, English language delay is widely recognized as a problem for prelingual profoundly deaf students. Whether there is delay in the use of ASL (given suitable opportunities to learn it) is less certain, and in fact, the evidence seems to indicate that there is not. Nevertheless, many observers of sign language in deaf children choose to base their judgments on the English coded structure of the sign language, not on the more appropriate ASL code or its equivalent.

In discussing these problems it is easy to forget that, for many years, ASL was a suppressed language. Outside of Gallaudet College and a few selected schools, its use by an educated intelligentsia was frowned on and discouraged. Therefore, it had little opportunity to develop more formal structures and was used primarily as a vehicle of ordinary conversation in specific social settings. It is questionable if the semantics and syntax of English would have developed to their present levels if to do so had required us to greet our neighbor with statements such as, "The quadruped is being subject to considerable excessive physical stress on its external surfaces by John, the offspring of my wife and myself. This stress is causing considerable emotional upheaval for the quadruped." What we may say is "[My son] John, is hitting the dog; The dog is barking." Therefore, the question is: Do deaf children say or write "John hit dog" because they cannot form any other syntactical structure or because they have not been given the opportunity to learn to do so?

Perhaps, as in English, deaf students need exposure to higher level syntax and semantics than are found in conversational signs. Schein (1980) points out the absurdity of the present position of many educators of hearing-impaired students:

> In my experience, deaf children are often poorly informed about matters important to their daily living. They know little about hearing impairment! Causes, types, proper auditory hygiene. They seldom know much, if anything, about deaf society, deaf history, deaf culture. You are experts on deafness. Can you identify Cadwallader Washburn, Rex Lowman, Konstantin E. Tsiolkovsky?
>
> What about coping strategies? How to handle market place situations; what to do about insults; where to learn about helpful gadgets—all of these can be taught. Are they?
>
> How many schools teach typing as routinely as handwriting, so that deaf children can efficiently use teletype attachments for their telephone? Few, if any, to my knowledge.
>
> There is more. You have the idea, however, from the examples. The curriculum for hearing-impaired students needs to be designed for hearing-impaired students. (p. 7)

There is general agreement about language delay in deaf students, but why do we assume it results from deafness? Could it be merely experiential deprivation?

Development of Language in Hearing-Impaired Children

In two widely reported studies (Gregory, 1976; Schlesinger & Meadow, 1972) and a number of others (e.g., Collins, 1969; Goss, 1970; Greenberg & Marvin 1979), it has been established that hearing parents (mothers) of deaf children adopt characteristic interactive patterns with their deaf children approximating to those of lower socioeconomic class hearing mothers:

> Of course it would be almost impossible to get an accurate idea of the amount that a mother talked to her child. Rather we tried to ascertain the situations in which she talked to her child and whether she told stories, said nursery rhymes, etc. Sixty per cent (72) of the mothers said that they read stories, or said nursery rhymes with their child.... A further 33 per cent (40) did talk fairly constantly to their children, not taking into account whether the child was listening to them or not, while the remaining 8 per cent (10) only talked if their child was attending to them. None of the mothers said that she did not talk to her child at all. (Gregory, 1976, p. 119)

A number of the social aspects of mother/child interaction referred to by Gregory are not immediately germane to a book on language and cognition, except insofar as the absence of a stable and affectionate environment can itself cause language delay (see Connor, 1976; Luterman, 1984; Norden, 1981, for insightful comments on the need to deal with the maternal or paternal anger and guilt that may be associated with having a deaf child). Nevertheless, sensory coding processes and memory develop very early in life, and the boundaries between the general well-being of the child, the development of these processes, and the development of language are not very clear. Therefore, some general discussion is needed as a preface to a more specific discussion of the development of sign language in young children.

In discussing the development of language in deaf children, it also is important to note that they can accommodate to the communication needs of other individuals. For example, older deaf students can adopt conversation patterns suitable for interacting, say, with an 18-month-old baby. In doing so, the students use simplified syntax and heightened patterns that are adapted to the baby's level of performance. In fact, in an important study of early language development, Wilbur and Jones (1974) noted that the vocabularies of hearing children of deaf parents developed separately for sign language and spoken language. This finding suggests that they were probably located in different memory stores and could be used independently in different situations demanding different language systems.

Prelinguistic Communication

Language forms a part of purposive behavior (see Robinson, 1972 for an excellent introduction to language behavior in this context). So it is frequently difficult to separate verbal and nonverbal aspects of communication, and interfering with one can seriously impair communication using the other system. The growth and development of language in young children is part of a sequential process that gradually increases the verbal repertoire of the child, but it does so on the basis of a highly developed nonverbal and prelinguistic communication system. Even before the development of verbal communication these prelinguistic aspects are affected by deafness, and hearing parents learning manual communication are not able to compensate fully for their limited ability to communicate with their deaf children (Meadow, Greenberg, Erting, & Carmichael, 1981; Wedell-Mannig & Lumley, 1980). Essentially, as we suggested in the previous section, the process of parent-child communication in such situations remains more autocratic (although less so than with oral communication) and lacks the spontaneity found in deaf parents with deaf children and hearing parents with hearing children.

Day (1982) has reported a major observational study of mother/deaf child interaction that provides considerable insight into the development of these communicative processes. The study was of young (35-43 months old) deaf children who were using "primarily one- and two-word sign utterances." He used a modification of Dore's (1977) classification system and described the nature of the communication patterns as follows:

Description was the most frequently used attribute of communication (26.8%), particularly of event, identity and location. These types of communication "demonstrated both symbolic and social sophistication in that the children indicated they expected the conversational partner to understand the imaginary use and to join in the imagined context" (p. 10).

Requests formed 20.2% of utterances and most frequently required action by the receiver or requests for objects. However, even at this stage, *Wh*—questions and *Yes-No* questions were emerging. Pointing was an important attribute of the communicative behaviors in this category and such behavior has been studied longitudinally by Kantor (1981). Kantor noted in particular that modulated *wh* forms in young children only occurred when the referent is present (see Hoffmeister, 1982).

Conversational Devices were a common aspect of communication (18.2%) and devices, such as pointing, were used as "attempts to begin or continue social contact rather than to express specific informational content." Again, about one in 5 communicative occurrences were of this type, and they could take the form of checks, comments, or offers; could direct attention to an object or to the person communicating, or they could be "polite" responses or requests.

Responses (15.5%) illustrated the interaction between language delay in deaf children as both a cause and effect. The questions asked by the mothers tended to focus on *Yes-No* questions, which, as Day points out, is a characteristic of mothers of hearing children when their children are at the one word utterance stage (Rogden, 1979). *Wh-* questions were limited, rarely included *Why* questions, and never included *When* or *How* questions. This problem continues in the school, and Wood (see, for example, Wood, 1982) has shown that teachers of deaf students tend to monopolize the classroom conversation. They prefer to exercise a directive control, rather than fostering natural interactive language development.

Statement and Performance (16%) constituted the remaining responses (except for the 3.3% that could not be interpreted). They included nonformal and formal linguistic expressions and sensorimotor activities.

Day (1982) points out the following:

> In general, the deaf children in the present study appeared to communicate frequently and with considerable success with their signing, hearing mothers. In spite of the short utterance length of the signing deaf children, the set of communicative intentions they generated was more like that reported for hearing 3-year-old children.... Parents and deaf children acquire a mutually comprehensible language system. Future efforts may also assist the parents in establishing effective interaction patterns and in building their children's awareness ... of ... useful functions which linguistic communication systems serve. (p. 19)

Without such a system, language will not develop and deaf children will be severely delayed in academic achievements and in social-emotional development.

Language Development

The classic studies of Bloom (1970) and Brown (1973) have done much in setting the scene for our understanding of the process of language development in young children. Berry (1980) has summarized the early stages of acquisition in hearing children as follows:

STAGE 1: Beginning Oral Language

1. *Phonotary Markers*:   These are illustrated by statements such as "More-more" and "Go-go." These *action percepts* are the perceptions that the child has concerning his interaction with his environment and they are related to the prosodic features of language; the melodic, visual, and kinesthetic patterns of language that permit transmission of meaning.

2. *Action Percepts and Attention Focus*:   A good example is the use of the same term with two quite different meanings, such as "*My truck!*" or "My truck?" At this age, the child is limited in vocabulary, but rich in communication. Single word, *holophrastic* sentences use postural, facial and intonational changes to indicate many grammatical aspects such as an agent, a recipient, or a possessor of an attribute. It is interesting that deaf people using only oral communication frequently make considerable use of these aspects of language to overcome their limited spoken vocabulary.

3. *Emergence of Word Order (Presyntax)*:   "More milk" is a good early example of this stage. The child functions at a sensori-motor level, but even so, two-word sentences with a specific order pattern are emerging. They indicate word order has achieved significance.

STAGE 2: Early Intermediate Stage of Language Development

1. *Expansion of Interaction*:   "Mommy go" vs. "Go Mommy" is an inconsistent example of order relationship. Such sentences form the basis of later syntactical development. They involve irregularity of word order, but sequences of agent-action-object tend to be regular and consistent and provide for social interaction. Berry graphically calls this the "grasping stage."

2. *Prosody and Syntax*:   The use of *more* as an *operator word* that changes meaning with inflection and intonation illustrates the growing skill of the child in using the patterns of sound and gestural support systems to give different meanings to the same words.

3. *The Early Sentence*:   Typical early sentences are "Mary go home" and "I not crying." However, Berry suggests that the early appearance of nouns and nouns phrases in children's language reflect the influence of parents. She feels that predication is the form that is of importance to the child, resulting in development of (a) action verbs/verb phrases, (b) subject-verb-

object-sentence and (c) declarative, *Yes-No* and *Wh-* questions, negations, imperatives and directives. Nevertheless, in the early stages children are still very dependent on word order, and changes of word order will confuse them.

The later developments of language also are described by Berry, but it is the early stages that are of interest in the present context. It is during these stages that many deaf children begin to branch into a visual-kinesthetic language system, whereas the hearing child opts to develop a sophisticated oral/aural system. Table 5.1 provides a synopsis of our knowledge to date, and shows the development of manual communication skills in deaf children. It clearly establishes that the natural development of spoken language in the hearing child and of sign language in the deaf child follow similar patterns, provided the experiences of the children are similar and differ only in the language to which they are exposed.

The similarities between deaf children and hearing children are hardly surprising if we adopt a Chomskian view of language (pp. 119 to 127). The emergence of the deep structure of language is not dependent on the use of one modality of communication. Therefore, if deaf children are exposed to appropriate and adequate language models from a very early age, they have equal opportunity to develop skills in this language. In contrast, if the adult user of language lacks proficiency in sign language or if children cannot properly process oral/aural language, they will not be able to internalize syntactical or other features. They will not have sufficient language samples from which to generate a conventional surface structure, and they will have great difficulty in learning the transformational rules that allow them to achieve communicative competence.

A useful way of identifying where and how the divergence between oral and visual-kinesthetic language takes place is to consider what Berry describes as "early signs of linguistic retardation" but what, in our context, are more correctly described as early signs of oral/aural language retardation. If a child is able to hear normally, there is often a high correlation between oral/aural language skills and linguistic retardation, but even so there are a number of conditions, such as cerebral palsy, where even a normally hearing child may have good language and deviant speech (see chapter 1). In the case of deaf children, this is even more likely. Table 5.1 is based on Berry's system: It compares the symptoms described by Berry with what we know of the development of language in deaf children. As we have already indicated, it shows that deaf children who are not handicapped in other ways and who receive appropriate language

TABLE 5.1

Berry's (1980) Symptoms of Linguistic Delay
Applied to Deaf Children

Symptom	Deaf Children
Stage 1	
i) Lack of awareness/reaction to environment.	Show normal awareness.
ii) Delay in a) gestural language, or b) prosodic patterning of sound.	a) Earlier than hearing. b) Show babbling and non-aural patterning normal
iii) Lack comprehension of simple direction.	Only if communication method is inappropriate.
iv) Limited emotional/social interaction	Normal until child becomes frustrated by communication problems.
v) Failure beyond one or two word vocabulary.	Failure for speech, but not for manual communication if given an opportunity.
vi) Delay in comprehension of agent-action or action-object.	Comprehends, but may not have an appropriate symbol system to represent.
vii) At three years do not ask where or what?	Do, but recipient does not understand.
viii) Do not imitate talk of parent or peers.	Parents are didactic which limits imitation. Better with peers, but may be a slight delay.
ix) Extends word naming.	Does in speech, but not in other forms of communication.

Table 5.1 cont.

Symptom	Deaf Children
Stage 2	
i) Perceptually and semantically retarded. Does not explore; monosyllabic; limited use of where/what; no use of why/who.	Evidence indicates some slight delays, but probably these result from major difficulty which is environmental deprivation. Deaf children who show these symptoms have lost or limited ability to communicate because it has not been reinforced.
ii) Body language is uncoordinated resulting in stereotyped oral and/or gestural communication.	Motoric delay seems to be a problem with *some* children. Etiology is probably an important factor.
iii) Vocabulary and structural forms are limited.	For English, but a rich "concept" store which may or may not have been developed into ASL or a similar language. In the absence of other input, deaf children will develop an idiosyncratic sign language.
iv) Distortion of speech and other auditory prosodic patterns.	Normal for a deaf child, but results in some deaf children being diagnosed incorrectly.
v) Does not imitate speech, but auditory prosodic reinforcement increases retention.	Normal for deaf child. Articulation drill is not as effective as prosodic reinforcement, but often this fact is not used in remediation.

experience, are not linguistically retarded. In fact, there is no obvious reason from our understanding of the development of deaf children why they should not develop good language, provided they are diagnosed early enough and given appropriate educational experiences.

In practice and despite the promising prognosis for good language development, some early language delay is almost inevitable for most deaf children. As yet, we are rarely able to make an immediate diagnosis of deafness at birth; our techniques are lacking reliability and our screening programs are often inadequate (Lyon & Lyon, 1981-1982). As a result, deaf children miss many of the beneficial experiences that are necessary to facilitate early language development. The resulting delays, regrettable and serious though they are, should not be confused with a language deficit. If deaf children are diagnosed early, and if they and their parents receive appropriate help, we should be able to overcome the problems that arise during the period when the parents are not aware they have a deaf child, and, therefore, cannot develop alternative strategies for communicating. Our failure to do so reflects on the inadequacy of educational and parent counseling programs, not on the ability of the child to benefit from appropriate instructional and learning experiences.

Conversely, present findings on the development of sign language in deaf children give additional reinforcement to the need for early identification of hearing losses so eloquently argued by those with a more oral/aural perspective (classically Ewing & Ewing, 1961 in Great Britain; and Northern & Downs, 1978 in America). Whatever the educational experience of the deaf child and despite some muddled thinking about so-called critical periods for the development of language in young deaf children,[2] it is clear if we do not know the child is deaf or hard of hearing, we cannot modify the form of the language input to enable him or her to develop a naturally based language. At least on this point, supporters of oral education or education using total communication are in clear agreement.

Sign Language Acquisition in Hearing and Deaf Children

We have already summarized some of the early findings of the Salk Institute researchers on the acquisition of sign language (chapter 3). In addition, Kretschmer and Kretschmer (1978) have an excellent review (chapter 4). The latter authors concluded early gestural language in younger deaf children develops from a symbolic organization that does not replicate the characteristics of spoken English. Unfortunately, while correct, this conclusion is misleading because, as noted earlier, sign language acquisition in children follows a similar pattern to the way in which spoken English is acquired. The form of the language differs, but not the competence. Finally, Hoffmeister's (1982) synopsis of the studies of natural language acquisition in deaf children of deaf parents and deaf children of hearing parents is an important addition to the literature and to

---

[2]See Sluckin (1972) for an impressive analysis of the evidence for and against the concept of critical periods and Sluckin, Herbert, and Sluckin (1983) for an equally impressive analysis of similarly confused concepts about "maternal bonding."

our understanding of this problem.

Wilbur (1979) describes current knowledge about the developmental process involved in sign language acquisition and reinforces and summarizes Table 5.1:

> Semantic relations seem to develop in parallel fashion in spoken and sign language. Syntactic structures in ASL require several developmental stages before the child learns the correct adult form, as shown for verb inflection by Fischer, and for noun indexing, possessives, plurals, etc., by Hoffmeister. Overgeneralization of rules (e.g., "camed" and "wented" used by children learning English) is documented, demonstrating that the child learning sign language adopts similar acquisition strategies to the child learning to speak. Of interest also is the "fall back" seen in both Kantor's and Hoffmeister's studies. In Kantor's study, the child "fell back" on motorically simpler handshapes when faced with the necessity of making semantic and syntactic decisions in the use of the classifiers. (p. 170)

It also seems probable when opportunities are given to learn a manual language, the first sign tends to be learned about 8 to 12 weeks earlier than the first word is spoken by a hearing child, and during that 12-week period the child learns approximately 20 signs (McIntire, 1974).

Hoffmeister (1982) concludes that as children develop language, the hearing children of deaf parents develop two separate lexicons for the sign and the spoken vocabulary. In the early stages these two vocabularies complement rather than replicate each other, and the existence of two lexicons does not seem to be related to the difference between visual and auditory processing characteristics. For example, Hoffmeister, basing his arguments on those of Meier and Bellugi, argues that iconicity is not a major factor in the order of acquisition of signs in children. In fact, the order of acquisition seems to follow the approximate chronological sequence described by Brown for spoken language, and this sequence, in itself, seems to have a fairly wide degree of generalizability. However, one note of dissent to this general conclusion is sounded by Supalla and Newport (1978) who suggest that iconicity is contained within the movement of a sign, and that movement frames form the basis for the development of the language in children. They suggest an important aspect of this process in sign language learning is the recombination of the movement patterns that emerge from the static hand positions, patterns that include sequential as well as simultaneous recombinations.

It is also interesting to note that deaf children develop early in life a facility in code switching similar to that developed by children who learn two spoken languages. For example, Priesler (1981) found that Sava, a 4-year-old Swedish deaf child, could switch and vary language codes depending on the recipient of her communication and their skill in either Swedish Sign Language (equivalent to ASL) or Signed Swedish (equivalent to MCE). Schlesinger (1978) makes an important distinction in this discussion. She refers to the bimodal acquisition of language as the use of signs in association with parallel speech. Acquisition in this way is different from what she regards as truly bilingual acquisition (i.e., the acquisition of speech after the acquisition of ASL). There is, however, a third possibility, which is the simultaneous acquisition of ASL and MCE, and Priesler's research seems to indicate that it is possible for children to carry both English language syntax and ASL syntax simultaneously—even when the English is in a manually coded form.

An important study by Greenberg (1980) described the differentiated use of speech, vocalization, gesture, and sign in 28 hearing mother/deaf preschooler dyads, where half the pairs used simultaneous oral and manual communication, and the other half oral communication only. Greenberg (1980) found the simultaneous use of sign and oral communication was associated with a higher level communication skill and with the use of certain pragmatic contexts, such as the presence of the subject of the conversation. Greenberg (1980) reaches a provocative conclusion, suggesting that:

> Parents, teachers, and therapists might selectively choose goals that reinforce bimodal communication for progressively more difficult or advanced forms of communication. However, when use of a second mode adds little, for example, when a head nod, voice, or sign alone would be sufficient, it *would appear unnatural and overbearing to require a bimodal message.* (p. 77; italics added)

Greenberg's suggestion is contrary to the popular belief (although not necessarily practice) that total communication programs emphasize the continuous and simultaneous use of all modalities of communication. Interestingly, the traditional perspective also ignores the reality of most conversation within hearing groups and deaf groups. Conversational interaction makes a great deal of use of pragmatics and of nonverbal cues, so that verbal cueing is often omitted or short-circuited. Following Greenberg's suggestion will not only make conversation more natural for children, but also for parents and teachers. Finally, it is worth noting that Greenberg showed a clear relationship between communicative competence and length of preschool experience, confirming the importance of early diagnosis and appropriate preschool placement if deaf children are to make good progress in any language.

Language Deficiencies and Language Coding

Donaldson (1978) has questioned the results of early cognitive test-ing on two grounds. First, it is by no means clear that young chil-dren understand precisely what is required of them in a given task. There is a paradox in expecting infants to understand the physical meaning of verbal forms such as "bigger," "longer," and "more" in order to test their understanding of the underlying concepts. They may know the concepts, but not their verbal equivalents. And, sec-ond, the medium in which a conceptual task is embedded is of cru-cial importance. A problem presented in an unfamiliar context will be failed, whereas the same problem, in an everyday context, may be trivial. A good example is found in children who seemingly exhibit egocentricity by their inability to imagine what a group of toy mountains would look like from another viewpoint, but who readily solve the problem when it is presented in terms of a naughty boy hiding from the gaze of a policeman.

As we pointed out earlier, terms such as *abstract* and *concrete* can be dangerously misleading. A child may be able to apply relatively abstract logic to a superficially concrete situation. Conversely, an im-pressive level of abstract performance may be based solidly in a matrix of concrete images and originally acquired through the study of concrete instances; this is the way we commonly learn difficult concepts, and it is the most efficient (see Paivio, 1971). Some of our greatest thinkers, such as Einstein, Feynman, and Gamow, have ad-mitted making significant use of visual and other imagery. (Feynman, in fact, gained a Nobel Prize for theoretical work in quantum mechanics based directly on his observation of a boy throwing a plate Frisbee-fashion.) It should be clear, therefore, that assessing the concreteness of a mental process by external criteria— such as a count of the number of abstract words used by a deaf child—is a dubious procedure. Devising means of accurately deter-mining the conceptual abilities of hearing as well as deaf children re-mains a stiff challenge, and, undoubtedly, some of our judgments about concept formation in deaf students and others are colored by the inadequacy of our methods of assessment.

Nevertheless, and whatever the reasons, the English (or other spoken language) deficiencies of deaf children are clearly established (see chapter 4). In addition to the many general surveys of the problem, Levine (1981) draws an interesting comparison between written language errors identified by Smith in 1897 and the recent classical study of language errors in deaf students conducted by Quigley, Power, and Steinkamp (1977). The latter authors identified the following as difficult structures for deaf students: "the verb system, the use of pronouns, infinitives and gerunds; and the use of relative pronouns, phrases and clauses" (Levine, 1981, p. 79). Levine compares this to Smith's (1897) description of errors of construction in the written examination response of deaf students:

> Misuse of the verb,
> Misuse of the adjective and adverb,
> Misuse of the relative clause,
> Confusion of direct and indirect quotations,
> Careless use of pronouns, especially in lack of agreement with antecedent,
> Misuse or omission of the articles,
> Transposition of adjective and noun,
> Transposition of letters in familiar words.
> (J.L. Smith, 1897, p. 205; edited by Levine, 1981, p. 79)

The comparison shows little change in the intervening years, and confirmation of the magnitude of this problem is provided not only by the work of the Center for Demographic Studies discussed in chapter 4, but by studies in the United Kingdom by Ives (1976), Morris (1978), and Montgomery and Montgomery (1981). Ives collected extensive data on 1,598 students in England and found that 11% of them were functionally illiterate. Morris, in a later analysis of the data, found that a similar percentage (10%) showed no improvement in their reading skills with age. Finally, Table 5.2, reproduced from Montgomery and Montgomery, shows a somewhat similar percentage of illiteracy (7%) in Scottish students, and also shows that at the end of their school career only 10% of profoundly deaf students can produce "good written work and grammatical sentences" in English.

A major part of the problem of spoken language illiteracy results from the use of an inappropriate method of language input. Vernon and Koh (1974) have pointed out the non sequitur in the use of lipreading as a vehicle for learning language and other concepts, particularly with younger deaf students. It is that if a person is to use it efficiently, lipreading requires a knowledge of language (see pp. 212 to 219). The evidence that effective lipreading requires good language skills comes from two sources. First, studies such as that of Grove, O'Sullivan, and Rodda (1979) and Savage, Evans, and Savage (1981) have shown that the performance of deaf students using lipreading falls below their performance when using manual or total communication. Indeed, the language level of such students exceeds that of

TABLE 5.2
Academic Achievement of Scottish School Leavers

Virtually illiterate—few simple written words only	5
Produces many written words and phrases but does not write in sentences	8
* Many errors of spelling and grammar but tries to write in sentences	20
** Writes in simple sentences with many grammatical slips	27
Can produce good written work in grammatical sentences	10
Total	70

* mean 15-year-old deaf pupil
** median 15-year-old deaf pupil

Source—J. Montgomery and G.W.G. Montgomery, 1981, Integration and the communication gap. In G.W.G. Montgomery (Ed.), *The integration and disintegration of deaf in society* (p. 80), published by Scottish Workshop Publications.

their lipreading skills, but given the cognitive and perceptual difficulties associated with oral communication (see chapter 4), this result is not surprising. Second, Conrad (1977), in a well known study, has shown that hearing respondents do better at a lipreading task than hearing-impaired students, and an unreported study, in Holland, found similarly that hearing subjects performed better than deaf subjects in a visual spatial tracking task that required the use of some form of internalized temporal code. Another problem faced by teachers of lipreading is the question of linguistic style. Natural languages such as English comprise a wide variety of styles, differing in terms of formality and technical content (Strevens, 1964). If you teach deaf children orally employing a formal English style, their ability to lip-read people speaking informal or "vulgar" styles will be limited; conversely, instruction in informal modes will perhaps create difficulties in appreciating the more formal styles. Finally, to these problems can be added the lack of an environment conducive to good lipreading, such as good lighting with no glare and clear visibility of the speaker's face, the deaf student's inability to benefit from the pragmatic factors that assist in decoding the lip movements, and poor knowledge of syntax and lexical factors.

In contrast to lipreading, Siple, Fischer, and Bellugi (1977) have suggested that signs may be stored in long-term memory on the basis of semantics. Evans (1981) relates this to Coltheart's (1980) discussion of "deep dyslexia" in which reading for some learning disabled students becomes progressively more difficult as semantic content is increased; the order of difficulty is (a) nouns, (b) adjectives and verbs, and (c) articles, prepositions, and conjunctions. Such a distinction can be related to right hemispheric processing in the cerebral hemispheres, the hemisphere with spatial coding functions (see chapter 6). Evans goes on to suggest that this distinction is also important in the distinctive functions sign language and finger spelling have in manual communication. He suggests that the "different media might have complementary roles—signing to represent content words and finger spelling to convey the function words—which together synthesize into a form that closely represents, or has syntactic compatability with, spoken or written English" (p. 88).

In support of the suggestion made in the previous paragraph, Evans cites, among other sources, his own study (Evans, 1978) in which the addition of finger spelling improved the intelligibility of the lipreading of syntactically refined variations in English by 50%, a study which incidentally offers considerable support for the use of Cued Speech (Cornett, 1967) in oral programs. Furthermore, in identifying finger spelling as a supplementary coding process in manually coded English, Evans (1981) also points out that the initialization of a generic sign allows for a more specific correspondence between the concepts of sign language and the concepts of spoken English (see Fig. 5.1, for example). Unfortunately, such a process is not so easy in British Sign Language. Apart from the intrinsic awkwardness of the two-handed alphabet when used in conjunction with sign language, a fundamental (possibly universal) rule of sign language is that two *moving* hands must approximate to the same movement (Battison, 1974). However, it seems that BSL users do occasionally violate the symmetry constraint, and do use unitialization at times (see chapter 8).[3]

Evans also found that adding signs to speech, lipreading and finger spelling to give "total communication" led to a further 40% increase in performance. He relates this finding (p. 102) to Brill and Fahey's (1971) observations on the sign vocabulary of preschool deaf children. As Evans points out, such vocabulary is primarily semantic

---

[3]Deaf people frequently oppose the process of initialization, but it seems that such opposition is more the result of the association of the process with signed English and with the way in which such systems violate ASL grammar. They will and do use the process when it is of value.

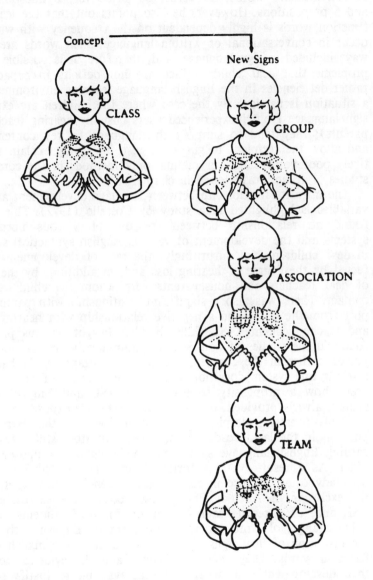

FIG. 5.1.   Creating new signs by initialization.

Source—L. Evans (1982), *Total communication: Structure and strategy*, p. 66. Reprinted by permission of Gallaudet College Press, 800 Florida Ave., Washington, DC 20002, USA.

in content—276 words, 35 verbs, 32 adjectives, 6 question forms, and 5 prepositions. However, he also points out that the learning of function words is highly dependent on the frequency with which they occur in conversational or written language. Such words are not always included in sign language, and, therefore, it is possible that the problems that deaf children face are not deficits in capacity, but rather deficiencies in the English language learning environment. Such a situation is particularly the case where the children are exposed to sign language from inexperienced users (usually hearing teachers and parents); they tend to simplify the language to key content words and allow the recipient to guess the rest. This may explain the relatively poor performance of manual only methods in the comparative studies of reception reviewed in chapter 4.

The intricate relationship between language development and other variables is highlighted in a study by Costello (1972). This research found no relationship between the use of various normal sign systems and the development of various English syntactical structures in deaf children. Not surprisingly, the rate of development was affected by the degree of hearing loss and, in addition, by the number of deaf teachers and houseparents with whom the child came into contact. There was also a significant relationship with parental support from the home and a negative relationship with hearing parents and teachers lacking ASL skills. Further insight on this problem is found in the studies of adult-child communicative interaction we reported earlier in the chapter, and it is important to emphasize that learning one system does not preclude the learning of another. Children show a propensity to learn both ASL and English language syntax, always provided, of course, that they are exposed to both.

Unfortunately, despite some moderations of the extreme oral position in the last decade or so, many educators still insist on regarding English language syntax and ASL syntax as opposed to each other. As a result, various forms of manually coded English have been advocated for use in schools (and even formally approved) to the exclusion of ASL or BSL. These codes make extensive use of ASL and, as a result, cause confusion for deaf students. They involve changes of word order, development of English verb endings, the invention of new signs, and the introduction of English language function words. They cause confusion, and the evidence to justify their development is as meager as that available to justify oral only methods for educating deaf students. In fact, hearing children rather easily learn two codes and to code switch, and doing so has only moderate and short-term effects on other academic skills. Unfortunately, we seem unwilling to conclude that deaf children could have similar abilities.

Conceptually Signed English, a system developed by Christensen (1981) and described by Cumming (1982b), may have some relevance in resolving the difficulties of policy referred to in the previous paragraph. The intent and the ideas are, perhaps, of more importance than the method itself. ASL is a visually based separate language, and when it is used as a reinforcer for English, it may create some linguistic confusion for deaf students. Cumming gives an example of the use of the same ASL sign in Signing Exact English for "run" in "Your nose will run" and "run" in "You will run." Conceptually Signed English attempts to remove this problem by allowing meaning to decide which sign is used, and also by taking account of idiomatic uses in both English and ASL. As Cumming suggests, it may "provide one answer to the concern expressed by Stokoe (1975): 'the reduction or cannibalization of a sign language to serve as an imperfect code for English may fail in its purpose and leave the child with little competence in either language' " (p. 419). It may also represent to some degree a return to semantics in sign language, similar to the return in the 1970s to semantics in spoken languages.

In a rare study of adolescent language, Steutenburgh (1971) explored the development of language in hearing and hearing-impaired students, ages 9 to 14 years. He found that during this period hearing-impaired students failed to develop more complex sentence structures, whereas hearing children succeeded. He also noted the semantic poverty of the language used by hearing-impaired students when they were compared to hearing students. In this context, Kretschmer and Kretschmer (1978) make an interesting comparison with the Fitzgerald Key, an early device for teaching deaf students. They point out that the sentence pattern used by deaf students tends to follow the highly structured format used in the Key. At least part of this pattern has to do with classroom organization. Deaf students are rarely exposed to free flowing and interactive communication, even in total communication settings,[4] and in an orally dominant classroom, the physical ecology still places considerable restraint on such communication. These constraints have been somewhat reduced for children with useful residual hearing since the advent of radio frequency transmission systems in classrooms for deaf children in the mid 1960s, but they still exist and hinder the development of adequate language structures.

---

[4]However, total communication is a big improvement over oral classrooms. For example, an important study by Wolff (1977) established that classes using total communication had more teacher/student communication than classes using oral communication or oral communication with finger spelling.

By definition, it is not surprising that teachers are didactic in their classroom organization. As we noted earlier, parents show similar patterns but unfortunately, by being didactic, both teachers and parents tend to monopolize the conversations and limit the interaction between the children and themselves. Craig and Collins (1970) have studied these patterns and found that teacher-initiated conversations were by far the most dominant form of communication in classes of deaf students, and that, as we have suggested, the teachers also tended to ask direct questions or provide the information that the students needed in order to perform appropriate tasks. Wood (1982) made a similar observation in the United Kingdom. Lawson (1978) did not obtain the same results with intermediate age students, but he still noted a considerable amount of reactive behavior by students to teacher initiated activities, and a failure by teachers to incorporate new ideas into the cognitive framework of the student.

Again, such approaches do not facilitate language use by deaf children and, therefore, language development; and this has had considerable implications for teacher training, teaching inservicing and classroom practice. Perhaps one of the most important implications is that the poor development of English language in deaf students may result from our failure to provide them with opportunities to experience language in any form, let alone in English. It may be the linguistic poverty of their total environment that causes language delay and retardation, not their lack of exposure to English. If we changed this environment by systematically exposing deaf students to both ASL and English, perhaps we might begin to see rapid improvement in English language competence without attempting to impose on deaf students an arbitrary manually coded English form of sign language. Perhaps signs and finger spelling are sufficient by themselves; they certainly seem to be in much of the adult deaf community. However, exposure to written English is also of vital importance, both in view of the research findings reported in chapter 4, and in the opinion of deaf people who are highly proficient in English (Carver, 1985).

Successive and Spatial Processing

Debate as to whether deaf respondents show preference for spatial over temporal processing when given the opportunity to choose was referred to in chapter 4 (pp. 205 to 206). Cumming and Rodda (1985)[5] have provided a major review of this topic, and much of

---

[5]We are grateful to our colleague, Ceinwen Cumming, for giving us permission to

this section is based on their paper. It is worth referring again to the study of O'Connor and Hermelin (1973b) who found spatial preference in their deaf subjects. Although, as we described earlier, this finding was not repeated in the studies of Beck, Beck and Gironella (1977), and a study by Das (1983) also produced contradictory results. However, the subjects of Beck, Beck and Gironella had hearing losses as low as 45dB BEA in some instances, and because subjects with this level of hearing would normally be able to use a phonological code, the divergent results may be because experimental controls were inadequate. Similarly, in the Das study, the subjects attended a school for the deaf where the formal policy of the school is to use Signed English, whereas the orally trained children in the O'Connor and Hermelin (1973b) study had not been systematically exposed to any sign system. Therefore, differences in educational treatment may be a factor. Finally, it is worth noting that a developmental trend has been detected in hearing children in the use of successive or temporal coding, and as a result, further research is needed using orally only and manually taught children of differing ages before we can reach definitive conclusions about the effects of auditory deprivation on the successive processing of sensory input. It seems that a number of factors will determine how children will function and if they use a phonological or a visual code, although, in practice, we suspect the most important one is the degree of residual hearing.

In fact, in auditory based languages such as English, the retention of temporal order in short-term memory is essential for the completion of syntactical processing, and interestingly, it is spoken language syntactical difficulties that are mainly reflected in the general language delay of deaf children when recorded on academic achievement tests and in their poor reading achievement (Quigley, 1982). Possibly, as van Uden (1983) emphasizes, experiences in sequencing at the motoric and iconic levels as young children will help deaf children to apply successive processing appropriately to language tasks requiring such processing when the tasks are not critically dependent on the ability to hear. If so, we are again presented with evidence to support the use of sign language at as early an age as possible, and with evidence that supports the use of ASL rather than a more artificial, manually coded English system.

---

[5](cont'd) incorporate the material, even though only one of us co-authored the paper and although she is not designated as an author of this text. Furthermore, certain paragraphs in the next section also owe a great deal to this paper and another, as yet unpublished, paper by Cumming and Rodda.

Despite the suggestions made in the previous paragraph, Quigley (1982) states unequivocally that there is not, as yet, enough valid research information available concerning successive processing in deaf children. To a degree, he is correct in his assertions, and researchers do need to look at individual differences in successive processing in individuals with differing degrees of hearing loss, as well as at trends in different groups of children. Research is also needed using tasks at the enactive, iconic, and symbolic levels of representation, particularly because Das (1983) has found that his "marker" tests for successive processing do not factor out together when used with deaf students. Interestingly, this is the first time that this has happened, but we cannot accept Quigley's conclusion without some comments. As should be clear from chapter 4, we know a great deal about cognitive processing and deafness, and what we know leads us to conclude that the concepts of general cognitive psychology have considerable applicability in understanding how deaf students and others process sequential material.

In discussing the concepts referred to in the previous paragraph, our view is that hearing ought to be given much less emphasis than has been the case in the past. As is clear from the Beck, Beck, and Gironella study, much of our difficulty has arisen from a failure to understand that not all "deaf" children in schools or programs for deaf students are deaf. Many have milder levels of hearing impairment, many are hard of hearing; and it is our contention that the academic failures of deaf students result from five main factors that have little to do with the need for more research. They result from: (a) the use of tests of reading that fail to provide context for the reader, (b) the failure to develop the adequate language levels (in any language) that are a prerequisite to any satisfactory testing, (c) specifically, the failure to use ASL as a language of instruction, (d) the failure in the education of deaf students to follow the lead of cognitive theorists and rediscover semantics and, (e) finally and most importantly, the failure in training and practice to adequately prepare teachers of deaf students to teach reading skills (see pp. 252 to 260). All of these problems can be remedied now. They do not require further research, and it is unwise to assume that the academic deficits of deaf children reflect anything more than the inadequacies of their educational experiences: the failure to provide them with rich language experiences in an intelligible form.

Despite the failures, it seems deaf individuals are able to use successive processing and, therefore, if taught in an appropriate way, their English language skills should be more than adequate. However, the processing of language may be different in deaf children and adults than in hearing. The spatial bias of deaf individuals, as illustrated in ASL, seems to result in a de-emphasis on temporal ordering. Appreciation for such ordering, which is important in an auditory-oral language like English, may develop later in deaf children (MacDougall, 1979) or may develop simultaneously if they are raised bilingually. When spatial rather than temporal coding predominates, reading performance may be adversely affected, and the differences in successive processing skills that are found between deaf and hearing populations may stem from changes in neurological organization, from bias in materials or from poor teaching techniques. Any complex combination of these factors may affect performance in any one child, but until the variable of poor teaching techniques is systematically controlled or removed, any assumptions that deaf students have an intrinsic deficit in academic abilities cannot be justified. In fact, present research seems to suggest that audition does not appear to be necessary for the appreciation of successivity. When linguistic factors relating to either English or ASL are kept to a minimum, deaf students and adults function as well as the hearing on successive tasks (McDaniel, 1980). It is when linguistic factors are involved that apparent qualitative differences between deaf and the hearing groups emerge (Conrad, 1979).

Writing and ASL

Sperling (1978) has discussed in detail some of the major issues in any discussion of developing language and communication skills in deaf students. Of particular interest is his discussion of Japanese and Chinese ideographic writing, and the implications this may have for a written form of ASL. At present, sign transcription systems are too cumbersome for use in literary texts, and the only written form of ASL is found in simple kindergarten or first grade readers, where the text is given in print English and pictorial ASL. Figure 5.2 illustrates the hypothetical 10-character ideographic alphabet used by Sperling to illustrate his plausible assertion that it is possible to develop an ideographic system that can also be parsed, thereby combining some of the strengths of an ideographic and a phonetic system. Certainly, if such a system were developed, it would be of considerable benefit to deaf children unable to internalize the phonetic coding structure of speech and who are, therefore, unlikely to read written English fluently and effectively until they have acquired competence in another language. The existence of a written form of ASL would also remove one of the main barriers to a completely bilingual or immersion education of deaf children (see pp. 260 to 264)—the lack of written materials for use in formal class settings with older students.

Some indication of the potential "pay-off" from making sign language available in a written form is found in a study by Vorih and Rosier (1978) of Navaho Indians. After a switch to first language teaching in spoken and written Navaho, later academic achievements of Navaho students in English were considerably higher than those of students whose instructional programs were always in English. However, some caution has to be exercised in generalizing from this study to deaf students—the Navaho students had a well established language before entering school, whereas because of delays in diagnosis, inadequate counseling of parents, and the lack of sufficient good preschool programs, many deaf students enter school with minimal competence in any language. Even so, Moores' classic study of the academic achievements of deaf students in different programs showed fairly conclusively that the addition of sign language to the instructional program increased academic achievement without any reduction in speech or lipreading skills (Moores, McIntyre, & Weiss, 1972). That this is so is not surprising because, whether in oral French (Genesee, 1976) or in deaf adults (Kensicki, 1980), literary skills in a second language can exist independently of the ability to speak or understand the spoken form of that language (see Luetke-Stahlman, 1982).

Reading

We made some reference to reading skills when discussing successive and temporal processing in deaf students. Interestingly, reading is perhaps the most neglected area of study in the education of deaf students, despite the fact that it is the primary method of communicating academic material to such students. Indeed, as we suggested in chapter 1, reading is now of increasing importance in social and leisure activities as Telephone Devices for the Deaf (TDDs) and caption TV decoders become universally available. And as we pointed out in chapter 4, every comparative study in the literature that includes reading as a receptive channel shows it to be the most efficient vehicle of communication. Nevertheless, communication through oral or manual methods is given much greater emphasis in the educational system, and the lack of interest in reading is even more striking when normative studies of the reading achievement of deaf students in many different countries paradoxically show such students to be so limited in their attainments (see chapter 4 and, classically, DiFrancesca, 1972, in the United States, and Rodda, 1970, Conrad, 1979, and Savage, Evans, & Savage, 1981, in Great

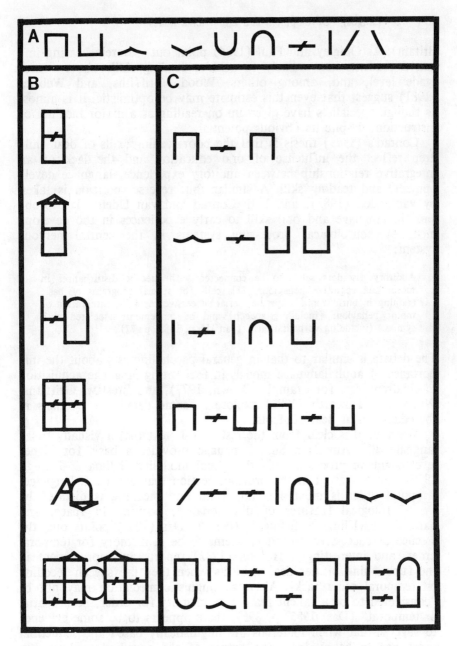

FIG. 5.2. A hypothetical alphabet of 10 characters (A) for transposing ASL into ideographs (B) and (C) letter by letter transcription showing parsings of B.

Source—G. Sperling (1978), Future prospects in language and communication for the congenitally deaf. In S. Lieben (Ed.), *Deaf children: Developmental perspectives*, New York: Academic Press.

Britain). As Quigley and Paul (1984) point out, severely hearing-impaired students are unlikely to achieve reading skills above fourth grade level, and, among others, Wood, Griffiths, and Webster (1981) suggest that even this estimate may be optimistic. It is almost as though specialists have given up on reading as a major medium of instruction, despite its obvious potential.

Conrad's (1979) thesis is that the poor reading skills of deaf children reflect the influence of oral education and the lack of an integrative relationship between auditory experience, language development, and reading skill. A similar, but reverse, position is taken by van Uden (1983), and both Conrad and van Uden relate problems in language and oral skill to early experiences in the development of neurological processing systems in the central nervous system:

> Auditory disorders seem to be connected with specific disturbances in motor and cognitive behaviour. This calls for special programs of basic training in eurhythmia, eupraxia, serial successive memory, integration of motor behaviour (including speech) and of movement associated with symbols (including verbalisations). (van Uden, 1983, p. 77)

The debate is similar to that in general psycholinguists about the importance of adult language models in facilitating language acquisition in children (see, for example, Brown, 1977), and Breslaw, Griffiths, Wood, and Howarth (1981) explore in some detail the parallels in the education of deaf students.

We hope it is clear from the rest of this text that a visually based language like American Sign Language provides a basis for higher level cognitive processing via the visual modality (Klima & Bellugi, 1979). We suggested in the previous section that in such a language, temporal order is much less important and meaning is dictated by the cherological features of directionality, position in space, and hand shape (Klima & Bellugi, 1979). As Das (1983) points out, the essence of successive processing seems to be in memory for temporal order, and interestingly, Hanson (1982) reports an improvement in the functioning of her deaf subjects when they use speech recoding on temporal order tasks. Although linguistic mediation may not be "considered to be a salient feature of memory for order, be it spatial or temporal" (Das, 1983, p. 895), there appears to be some evidence to suggest that when materials are linguistically based and sequential order has to be retained, the nature of the encoding medium becomes a relevant factor (Conrad, 1979; Hanson, 1982).

Conrad (1979) has also discussed the role that phonetically based languages such as English seem to play in the retention of temporal order. He concludes that, when tasks and materials are better handled through phonological recoding, deaf students are at a disadvantage. Therefore, any qualitative differences in the performance of deaf subjects in successive processing may stem from the mismatch between the task and the encoding medium rather than from any basic problem in dealing with material at a symbolic level (p. 249). Thus, the tentative conclusion referred to earlier in this chapter concerning difficulties deaf students and adults seem to have with successive processing at a symbolic level (p. 251) seems rather too simplistic. It would seem that a complex interaction of factors may be taking place.

We referred in the earlier section (p. 251) to age differences in the use of spatial and temporal coding processes, and Altom and Weil (1977) have shown that young hearing children prefer spatial orders of recall, whereas older hearing children choose temporal orders. As we suggested, preference for spatial or temporal order in both deaf and hearing children may reflect a developmental trend, although no research evidence is available to resolve this question with deaf children. It is also possible that increasing skills in English, a sequentially based language, make temporal ordering more salient as deaf children become older (Conrad, 1979). In fact, on temporal matching tasks, Arooshian and Bryan (1979) did detect a developmental trend in the performance of their deaf subjects, and if this places temporal ordering for deaf children within a developmental framework and relates it, at least in part, to the language experiences of the students, then again we have evidence that the differences found in temporal functioning need not necessarily be irremediable.

Kirby (1980) mentions that successive processing is used by normally hearing beginning readers, but MacDougall (1979) found that young deaf beginning readers focused on visual information. Some of his older deaf subjects did integrate visual and auditory processing on reading tasks, but with his hearing students, MacDougall identified a trend in the opposite direction. Hearing readers progressed from auditory or successive processing to integration of the visual with the auditory, and it would seem that deaf beginning readers are comparable in some ways to Altom and Weil's preschool hearing children in their visual bias. Furthermore, successive processing in deaf children may develop more slowly than in hearing children when the materials to be processed are symbolically encoded in the English language, but develop at the same rate when these skills are divorced from their use in this language.

As an alternative to the hypotheses just discussed, it has been suggested that deaf individuals may have both spatial and temporal orders available to them, although they may prefer spatial orders of recall on short-term memory tasks (Conrad, 1979; Das, 1983). Hanson's (1982) subjects, being bilingual in English and American Sign Language, would have both orders available to them, and that deaf children have both orders available is also suggested by the research of Beck, Beck, and Gironella (1977) and Das (1983). In fact, spatial preference in deaf students may be related to choice rather than to any underlying neurological problem. Thus, remediation strategies, where visual coding impedes processing of temporally ordered material such as written English, may be appropriate. They may force deaf students to focus on using more temporally based strategies, thereby improving their reading skills.

An early study by Schmitt (1968) is important in any discussion of reading in deaf students. He established that most of the comprehension errors resulted from the internalization of language structures that were different from those used in English. Breslaw, Griffiths, Wood, and Howarth (1981) approached the same problem more pragmatically, but they did establish that the communicative competence of hearing-impaired students varied between different oral schools—indeed, in one school the children performed at the same level as hearing students. Communicative competence is not reading skill, but it is not unreasonable to infer that oral teaching methods can have both positive and negative influences on the development of reading skills in deaf students.

Some evidence of how this might be achieved is found in a study by Brooks (1978), who investigated reading problems of deaf students and concluded that verbal regulation was an important part of the process. In commenting on the findings, Harris (1978) noted that "certain aspects of the spoken language might be available to the deaf child with appropriate technology" (p. 228) because the phonology and orthography of English are not mirrors of each other. One form of appropriate "technology" could be the use of sign language to provide "ongoing or structural regulation for the reader in that it provides a continuous rhythmic stream with peaks coordinated with the high information part of the graphic message" (p. 227).

It seems from more recent evidence that Conrad and van Uden are somewhat pessimistic in assuming that the achievement levels of deaf students are predetermined by either the nature of the educational handicap or by some fairly permanent interaction of deafness with educational treatment. Furthermore, a number of studies show that reading comprehension is aided by context (Ewoldt, 1981; Luria, 1982; Pearson & Johnson, 1978) and, therefore, it is important that we do not underestimate the skills of hearing-impaired or deaf students. Reading tests are invariably based on short sentences and do not provide the contextual support that deaf children seem to need to overcome syntactical differences between their language structures and spoken English. Our deaf colleague, Roger Carver (1985), has emphasized the importance of reading and pencil and paper communication in promoting English skills. Educated in an oralist regime, yet lacking good oral ability, he was able to immerse himself in written materials, not to improve his knowledge of syntax, but to find out about interesting topics.

The lack of contextual support in many standardized tests of reading leads to underestimation of the ability of deaf people to acquire useful information—as opposed to syntactical skills—from printed material. This may, in turn, produce a self-fulfilling prophecy, so that the pessimistic conclusions of global reading surveys actually cause the "reading deficits" they purport to measure.

Ewoldt (1981) and Pehrssen (1978) have both argued that reading schemes for deaf children are ineffective because they use a basal reading approach that presupposes a knowledge of English language syntax. From different routes, they arrive at the conclusion that the teaching of English to deaf children should be approached as "Teaching English as a Foreign Language" (TEFL). If they are correct (and we believe they are), a whole new spectrum of skills will be required by teachers of deaf children, skills they have not acquired in the past. Learning a second language draws on quite different cognitive resources from those employed in acquiring a first language, and many hearing people (including one of the authors) find it an impossibly difficult task. The problems confronting deaf students are, of course, even more severe.

Moores (1982, p. 293) cites a study by Coley and Bockmiller that confirms that we are right to emphasize the need to improve the skills of the teachers who teach deaf children to read (see Bockmiller & Coley, 1981). Of 395 teachers teaching reading to hearing-impaired students, only 35% had a course in teaching reading. As a result, they relied on basal readers rather than on a diagnostic/prescriptive approach using a number of different methods matched to the individual needs of the child. However, diagnostic/prescriptive approaches are not a panacea, and the reading curriculum of most schools and programs for deaf children needs to be carefully evaluated with the objective of selecting or developing a reading scheme more suited to the visual processing skills of these children.

Some specific suggestions for increasing the language experiences of deaf students can be drawn from Gormley and Geoffrion (1981). They include:

1. Developing a word bank using flash cards,

2. Using the word bank for developing student or teacher generated stories,

3. Using the word bank and a "cloze procedure" to enable the students to develop good semantics and syntax,

4. Adding prediction and retelling to the stories generated from the word bank,

5. Reading to the younger students in their preferred language, and

6. Using letter writing to motivate better reading and writing skills.

In a sense, what these authors suggest is no more than good language teaching, and it is unfortunate it is thought necessary to instruct teachers of the hearing-impaired in these techniques. Indeed, in doing so, it must be emphasized that the purpose of the techniques suggested by Gormley and Geoltrion is to facilitate the free flow of creative language. If they are married to incorrect assumptions of semantic poverty in the deaf student and to highly structured language teaching approaches, they will be no more successful than traditional methods. In fact, under these conditions, no method will be successful because they all will presuppose failure of the deaf child in the reading task.

Another interesting and important association has been noted in the development of speech skills when deaf preschoolers learn to read (Norden, 1981). Children exposed to early reading activities in a total communication preschool program spontaneously began to make the lip movements of speech and even to articulate without voice when reading. If we accept the concept of "inner speech" (Conrad, 1979) as a vehicle for language, and if we accept that at least some deaf children can develop an articulatory code, then this result is not surprising. Nevertheless, the educational implications are obvious and major. They suggest a strong focus on visual communication and reading will facilitate, not impede, the development of both language and speech skills, and the findings offer quantitative support for those teachers who advocate methods based on the use of reading and writing coupled with oral or sign conversational and instructional processes (see van Uden, 1977).

A rare study of deaf students' coding skills in arithmetic throws some further light on the problem (Hitch, Arnold, & Phillips, 1983). When required to judge whether integer addition problems were right or wrong, deaf students, matched for arithmetical achievement with hearing controls, showed similar classification times to the hearing students. The authors suggest, therefore, that neither deaf nor hearing students use subvocalization in the counting process. However, if we accept the arguments of Groen and Parkman (1972) that counting in hearing students involves subvocalizations, it is equally possible to conclude both hearing and deaf students use subvocalization strategies in the same way that Norden found speech was developed as a by-product of learning to read.

Whatever the conceptual underpinning for arithmetical skill in deaf students, the study by Hitch, Arnold and Phillips certainly raises significant questions about educational practices, because it seems we cannot conclude that deaf children's retardation in mathematical skills is an intrinsic aspect of their handicap (Wood, Wood, & Howarth, 1983). Hitch, Arnold, and Phillips suggest two possible reasons for this retardation, and we suggest that both probably apply: (a) the mathematics curriculum is neglected in schools and programs for deaf students, and (b) communication difficulties in oral programs prevent the child from understanding the concepts and requirements placed before him or her. The teaching of basic skills in reading and number will not develop good speech in deaf students, but, contradictory though it may seem, we can at least suggest that in the absence of these skills, work on teaching speech will have more limited results. Therefore, it seems (a) the teaching of speech should be integrated into the other activities of the classroom, but not intrude on these activities; (b) the teaching of speech should not be equated with the teaching of language, and (c) the reading and mathematics components of any school program should start early and should receive continuing and considerable emphasis. It is unfortunate that these practices are foreign to many schools for deaf students. In particular, very few schools or programs have a heavy emphasis on early teaching of reading and math skills, and many schools choose to delegate much of the teaching of speech to individualized instruction by a speech pathologist or a teacher in a setting isolated from the mainstream of the classroom. Both practices are undesirable.

Finally, one important strategy to be considered in teaching reading to deaf students is the degree to which the use of sign language may supplement the written text. A study by Robbins (1976) seems to indicate that even pictorial signs set alongside the written text can facilitate reading comprehension. She concludes that reading schemes used with deaf students should put more focus on the use of semantic cues and enable the students to relate the text to their experiences. As we noted earlier, at present, signed texts can only be used with younger students, and even if desirable, they cannot be produced in the same quantity and variety as conventional texts. Therefore, supplementing traditional orthography with signed material can only be seen as a method of strengthening traditional reading skills. Nevertheless, it may be an important way of overcoming some of the reading deficits characteristic of deaf students of all ages, particularly because English orthography focuses on semantic rather than phonetic groupings.

Bilingual Education

Charrow has undertaken two major studies of deaf students and the use of English as a foreign language (Charrow, 1976; Charrow & Fletcher, 1974). Using the "Test of English as a Foreign Language," Charrow and Fletcher concluded that English seemed to be processed as a second language by deaf students. In the later study, Charrow concluded that ASL did not interfere with language acquisition in deaf children, but rather their English reflected the particular difficulties faced by them in mastering oral language. As we discussed in chapter 4, Ivimey (1976) has similarly concluded that "deafisms" are systematic variations of English structure. A good example of how these differences occur is in the use of adverbs or adverbial phrases to delineate time with a consequent failure to use verb tense for this purpose. Similarly, plurality often is determined by subject determiners rather than by plural inflections. It is possible that such examples reflect the influence of ASL grammar, although, as we pointed out earlier, similar errors are made by oral pupils with no knowledge of sign language. The question is whether learning manual syntax makes it harder or easier to learn the corresponding English syntactical structure; and whether the two languages should be taught simultaneously or separately. Unless teachers have a very clear idea of what they are doing, problems of ASL-English interference may appear.

Some indications of how these problems might arise is found in an early study by Winslow (1973). It related to the use of *deictic* and *specific* gestures and indicated that in hearing-impaired children aged 4 to 5 years, "point statements" were the largest single category of sign. Semantic content was rich, and the point signs invariably functioned as syntactical markers, except that the sign for MORE was used early and consistently. Goldin-Meadow and Feldman (1975) also noted the value of pointing as a linguistic attribute with rather more important characteristics than previously ascribed. In particular, it is the beginning of the classifier system used in sign language, and it has a particular value in the process of pronominalization. Another important observation in the Goldin-Meadow and Feldman study was that the parents used a syntactically less complex gestural system than their children, and in some respects the children taught the parents.

Feldman (1975) extended the analysis of Winslow (1973) to describe deictic and specific gestures in more detail. The former acted as "this" and "that" do in spoken language, and were variations of the point gesture. They were used to identify small objects, and Kretschmer and Kretschmer (1978, p. 90) suggest they are an example of the "striking parallel" between the acquisition of signed and spoken language development" (Bates, 1976). In contrast to deictic gestures, specific gestures seem to reflect a transition into the semantics and syntax of a sign language system. At an early stage transitive action signs emerge, followed by intransitive ones. An important distinction that emerges in this process was discussed in chapter 3—sign language develops as an ergative language with a base in semantics, whereas spoken English develops as an accusative language with a strong base in syntax (see Kretschmer & Kretschmer, 1978, p. 93). Such a difference again lends very strong support to the need to teach English to deaf students as a second language, because the isomorphism between the two languages is limited.

In contrast to the bilingual environment of their home, Erting (1978) has described the situation that faces many deaf children of deaf parents when they enter a school or classroom:

> Typically, these deaf children enter a monolingual classroom in which some variety of signed English is the only language used, and the only language manually presented that is understood by the teachers.... The educational goal for these children is mastery of the signed English variety of PSE [Pidgin Signed English], and their communication is judged on the basis of the appropriateness of its grammatical form to English rather than on its content. From all this the message is clear: their home, their family, their community, their language, and they themselves are not valued—they must change to become acceptable. (p. 143)

The situation for deaf children of hearing parents is no different in the classroom but, of course, such children are in an even more difficult situation because they rarely have a well developed language system in either English or ASL.

The effect of the conditions referred to in the previous paragraph is to deprive deaf children of language experiences appropriate to their handicap, and to impair the development of an adequate self-esteem. A common cry of deaf people is that schools made them ashamed of their deafness or led them to believe that English was a superior language. An interesting variant on this theme is found in an old sign for SCHOOL used in Eastern Canada. It is a hand placed over the mouth in a manner or form that suggests "hiding your talking." A seemingly sensible interpretation of the sign is that it reflects the use of the hidden sign language taking place in almost every oral school when the teacher's back is turned. Signing in such schools was only practiced surreptitiously, and with some risk of being punished.[6] Partly as a reaction against these attitudes (which are not necessarily any better in a school where a form of manually coded English is used) and partly as an outgrowth of increasing ethnocentrism, a number of deaf people and deaf and hearing professionals are beginning to argue that for social as well as cognitive reasons, the education of deaf students should be properly regarded as a form of bilingual education, and the teaching of English to deaf students should be regarded in the same way as teaching of any second language.

In the studies described so far, discussion of bilingualism and deafness usually refers to the languages of ASL and English, and Luetke-Stahlman (1983) has a useful description of the possible different types of bilingual programs, ranging from English immersion to a transitional program that starts with all ASL at Grade 1 and progresses to all English at Grade 12. However, for a surprisingly high percentage of North American deaf students, the problem is compounded by a trilingualism (perhaps 10% according to Moores when cited by Luetke-Stahlman & Weiner, 1982). For example, in many Spanish, Italian, or French ethnic communities, the language of the home is one of these languages rather than English. If, as in the province of Quebec in Canada, the language of the school is the same, then we have the typical deaf bilingual situation. Unfortunately, this situation is rare, and mostly the language of the school is English. The study of Luetke-Stahlman and Weiner (1982) is one of the few that looks intensively at this problem. Not surprisingly, the authors concluded that when three different students were exposed to three different languages, each of the students demonstrated widely different language system preferences. One functioned best with sign alone or with sign combined with oral English or oral Spanish; the second used oral Spanish or sign; the third preferred oral English combined with sign. This diversity of skills led them to conclude that the determination of the appropriate instructional language for a trilingual student should be based on four factors: (a) knowledge of the language system of the home, (b) the exposure to sign language, (c) the amount of usable hearing, and (d) the system that the student seemed to use most effectively in learning. Echoing the claims of advocates of the use of ASL with bilingual or potentially bilingual students, they reject the concept of total English immersion

---

[6]There is still one place in Canada where deaf children are punished for using signs.

as the best method of educating trilingual (or, by implication, bilingual) students.

We discussed in chapter 4 the systematic investigations by Breslaw, Griffiths, Wood, and Howarth (1981) into the referential communication of hearing-impaired students in British oral schools. Like many others (see, for example, Grove, O'Sullivan, & Rodda, 1979), they were surprised by the communicative competence shown by the students when compared with much of the existing published data on the language achievements of deaf students. As they observe, the problem in interpreting these data can be seen in the respective positions of Hoemann (1972) and Schlesinger (1971). In studies in the United States and Israel respectively, these researchers agreed that referential communication was less developed in deaf than in hearing students. However, Hoemann attributed the delay to a lack of adequate and/or appropriate language experiences; Schlesinger attributed it to the inability of sign language to provide adequate cues for various syntactical structures.

Breslaw, Griffiths, Wood, and Howarth considered the problem again by looking at the ability of hearing-impaired children from 6 to 10 years of age to play a game that required them to communicate to another student their moves of blocks placed on tokens of similar size, shape and color (see chapter 4, p. 188). They found some quantitative differences in the performance of hearing and hearing-impaired students, but the study failed to demonstrate "any validity in the hypothesis that the deaf child is unable to take his listener's needs into account" (p. 273). Perhaps a more interesting comment on the education of deaf students was that, "the observation that struck us most forcibly was the lack of enthusiasm and the air of boredom with which all the children approached the task" (p. 274) and in a neatly insightful comment the authors state, "there is something paradoxical in our expecting them to understand us in order that we might demonstrate how they fail to understand each other" (p. 275). Not surprisingly, the researchers developed a more interesting task.

In the second study by Breslaw, Griffiths, Wood, and Howarth, the game consisted of describing pictures in a reading textbook so that the recipients of the information could locate it in their textbooks. The age of the students was similar, but they started at about age 8 years, rather than 6. The general conclusion was, "although some deaf children performed marginally less effectively than hearing peers, the differences were not massive, and the children from one school performed on a par with the hearing sample" (p. 281). Again, as we noted in chapter 4, in the more complex task an important difference was found in the relatively greater use of "action" (roughly equivalent to action verbs) by hearing-impaired students and "relationships" between the features of the pictures by hearing students. However, this difference did not significantly affect the successful completion of the task. Of a number of possible explanations presented by the authors, our opinion is that the most probable one is that "the deaf children were expressing relationships nonverbally in such a way that the hearing transcribers were unable to appreciate" (p. 281). Such an explanation accords with previous failures to understand the complex syntax of deaf sign language (for example, using classifiers to pronominalize). There is certainly no evidence of semantic inferiority in deaf students, and assuming that they are "less sensitive to relationships" is contrary to their successful performance on the task.

An interesting study of ASL/English bilingualism is that of Prinz and Prinz (1979, 1981). These authors studied a hearing female child, Anya, the offspring of a deaf mother and a hearing father. They noted that "babbling" occurred in sign language as well as spoken English, and confirmed other studies, referred to previously, by reporting that the first sign emerged "several months before the first spoken words." Babbling in both languages was combined at an early stage of language development into oral or manual strings that later associated with the development of combinations of oral and manual symbols to allow the child to communicate. The observations on the development of a lexical system showed that, "lexical acquisition in ASL and spoken English progresses through similar stages," and that the results of this study seemed to confirm (see Volterra & Taeschner, 1978) that early bilingualism initially results in the formation of one lexical system into which entries are made separately from both languages. spoken language. Indeed, such gestures seem to be a normal precursor. The study also confirmed the results of Stokes and Menyuk (1975). In the early bilingual acquisition of ASL and spoken English, a construct is encoded in one modality or the other, but only rarely in both modalities. Later this single lexicon separates (in the case of Anya some time between 14 and 21 months of age). When this separation takes place, the use of alternate codes begins and signs and words exist for the same concept. At this point, code switching becomes possible and is shown in the communicative behavior of the child. Finally, it is interesting to note that in a parallel way to the development of the lexicon, early syntax uses structures from both languages in both languages. Presumably, separation takes place at some later age, but this had not occurred for Anya by age 21 months.

Ethnicity and Education

We referred in chapter 1 to the ethnic nature of the deaf community, and much of the concern about language and deafness arises
from this concept (again, see Erting, 1978). Ethnicity associates with
a separate language, ASL, and with the existence of international,
national, and local social, political, and other networks. However, as
Erting points out, the deaf ethnic group differs in one important respect from most other similar groups—membership by birth is rare
because only about 10% of deaf children are born to deaf parents.
Therefore, enculturation by parents is also rare and, indeed, in some
respects parents may have to be enculturated by their adolescent
children or by deaf adults. Erting has also pointed out some other
significant factors of deaf ethnicity: (a) it is in the inability to
speak rather than hear to which the stigma of deafness attaches itself, (b) only a minority (approximately 12% in the United States
and less elsewhere) of teachers of hearing-impaired students are
themselves deaf, and (c) indeed, training programs for teachers of
hearing-impaired students have systematically discriminated against
deaf and hard of hearing applicants. The result has been educational
policies in which English (whether in an oral or a manual form) has
been the dominant language of instruction.

Presenting similar arguments to those of Erting, the parallels between the use of West Indian Creole and British Sign Language in
schools in the United Kingdom have been explored intensively by
Ladd and Edwards (1982), who also draw parallels between negative
attitudes toward deaf and West Indian people, and the derogatory
attitudes shown toward their languages by teachers and educational
administration (see p. 78). They point out that one of the unfortunate effects of this situation is the internalization of these negative
attitudes by the minority group. Therefore, "West Indians, particularly the educated West Indians, are among the severest critics of
their own community's speech. Many deny all knowledge of Creole"
(p. 102). The origins for the "creolization" of British Sign Language,
according to Ladd and Edwards, are found in the first instance in
the verbal and nonverbal cuing that identify for deaf people and
others their low status because they are not fluent at communicating
in the prevailing spoken language. In the orally dominant schools
that have been and are still a characteristic of Great Britain, the
students of each school develop their own idiosyncratic language
structures, and teachers communicate only in a pidgin language
(usually oral, but still pidgin even if supplemented or reinforced by
sign language). Recent developments have complicated the situation
by adding two distinct forms of manually coded English into the

British educational system—the Paget-Gorman Sign System and Signed Systematic English. However, at no point have teachers incorporated into the classroom the formal sign language of the adult deaf community, which has primarily been retained in the institutes (clubs) for adult deaf people (see p. 69). As we noted earlier in chapter 3, the result is that "most deaf people are forced to recreolize BSL in every generation" (Ladd & Edwards, 1982, p. 112).

There are severe educational consequences resulting from the attitudes discussed in the previous paragraphs. Both West Indian and deaf students are severely retarded educationally, and we agree with the view of Ladd and Edwards that this results, at least in part, from "an educational system that is totally predicated on the use of standard English." To support their contention, Ladd and Edwards cite some interesting parallels—(a) when using their own language the students are perceived to be less intelligent and badly behaved; (b) the students are described as "non-verbal and inarticulate," but teachers also complain that they never stop talking in their own language; (c) standard English is the model of use and success, and Creole is often banned in the classroom (and would be elsewhere if possible); (d) when the Creole language is used, attempts are made to ensure that it is used "properly" which means that it is distorted to conform to the syntax of spoken English; and (e) comments are made about the "lack of spontaneity" in written expression without associating this problem with the hypercorrection of spontaneous language structures.

Of particular significance in the present discussion is the effect of the values just described on academic learning. Instead of learning becoming a process of assimilation and comprehension, it becomes one of correcting incorrectly produced speech patterns or manual English. The constant focus by the teacher on English results, for example, in "a child who reads for accuracy of pronunciation and not for meaning" (Ladd & Edwards, 1982, p. 119). The student is not given the opportunity to develop his or her spontaneous understanding of the grammatical rules of language—artificial language structure completely dominates and, as a result, language function is lost. With limited language function, it is hardly surprising that deaf students fail to benefit from academic and other forms of instruction. That they do not is a sad comment on a century and a half of formalized education of deaf students, whether in Great Britain, Canada, the United States, or elsewhere. The problem lies not in the inability to hear, but in the way we choose to educate deaf students.

Summary

In this chapter we look at the use of sign language in the classroom and the community at large and discuss issues that relate directly to sign language and education. We again look at the characteristics of sign language and relate them to the beauty of form as in, say, Japanese Haiku. We discuss the development of sign language in children, and establish that "language delay" in deaf children is a function of language form and lack of language experience. It is not the result of using sign language in the home and the school. We do note that for the deaf child, distinctions between an oral and a sign language begin to emerge early in life. We also suggest that the measured reading achievements of deaf children suffer from a lack of context in the way they are assessed, and that good teaching of reading at an early age would do much to facilitate academic and social development. Finally, we explore the evidence for and advocate that deaf education adopt an official policy of bilingualism with, in North America, ASL as a first language and English (or another spoken language) as a second language.

Further Reading

Two excellent basic texts discussing the education of deaf students have been written by Donald Moores (1982), *Educating Deaf Children: Psychology, Principles and Practice* (2nd ed.), and by Stephen Quigley and Robert Kretschmer (1982), *The Education of Deaf Children*. A good introduction to children's language in general is *Children's Language and Learning* by Judith Lindfors (1980), and Keith Nelson (1979/1980) has edited an extensive two volume research compilation on this topic, *Children's Language*. An important document in precipitating change in the education of deaf children in Britain is found in the published proceedings of the Royal National Institute for the Deaf symposium on *Methods of Communication in the Education of Deaf Children* (RNID, 1976). *Total Communication* as a system, and its importance for deaf people, is neatly presented in a book of that title by James Alon Pahz and Cheryl Susanne Pahz (1978), and Richard Brill (1971) discusses administration in the education of deaf students in *Education of the Deaf*, although, of course, this book was written before recent changes in law, policy, and practice. Finally, Alice Streng and Richard and Laura Kretschmer (1978) have published a practical text of considerable value for practicing teachers: *Language Learning and Deafness: Theory, Application and Classroom Management*.

6

THE PHYSIOLOGICAL BASIS OF
COMMUNICATION

In preceding chapters we have discussed the contribution made by linguistics and cognitive psychology toward understanding and overcoming the problems of prelingually deaf students and adults. In this chapter, we ask the reciprocal question: What do the psychological and linguistic phenomena associated with deafness tell us about fundamental issues in human cognition?

We approach this question in two ways: first, by examining the neurophysiological factors linked with language and communication, and second, by considering the role of communication in the evolution of mankind. If sign language does share the formal distinguishing features of natural language, does this imply that the one is derived from the other, or that they share a common source?

Brain Mechanisms and Language

Innate Language Programming?

Of all the species inhabiting this planet, modern man (*Homo sapiens sapiens*) is the only one to employ language, a fact that has led many writers to claim that language is the critical characteristic of humanity. As we saw in chapter 3, there is a lot of evidence concerning the structural and functional basis of natural language; and the research of the Salk Institute implies strongly that American Sign Language possesses all the formal attributes of spoken communication systems. But is language a special feature of human evolution, or does it merely reflect the generalized increase in cognitive capacity that has led mankind to its present privileged status? The behaviorist

269

school, which dominated psychology in the 1930s and 1940s, inclined strongly to the view that language had no special status: It was simply one piece of behavior among many others that humans could acquire by building up chains of stimulus-response (S-R) connections. It was this typically overstated claim that led directly to the demise of behaviorism as an explanation of language. In particular, Chomsky's (1959) critique of Skinner's language theory so totally exposed the inadequacies of an S-R learning model that behaviorism was dealt a blow from which it was never to recover.

Chomsky's view, shared by the majority of psycholinguists working in the 1960s, was that human beings were equipped with a genetically programmed mechanism for acquiring language (1965), the "Language Acquisition Device" (LAD; McNeill, 1966). Recently, the slightly more apt term *Language-Responsible Cognitive Structure* (LRCS) has been proposed (Chomsky & Walker, 1978; Von Eckardt Klein, 1978).

What evidence do we have that humans possess a separate and distinct LRCS? There are three main interlocking types of evidence: neurophysiological (to which we return shortly), linguistic, and biological. Formal analyses by Chomsky and others suggest that the nature of linguistic processes in man, particularly those involving syntax, are of a form and complexity that sets them apart from cognitive processes of a less specialized kind. The biological case has been most forcibly put by Lenneberg (1964, 1966, 1967, 1973) who lists the following key points:

1. Language function is known to be strongly localized neuroanatomically.

2. All nonhandicapped children acquire their native languages easily and rapidly, in a more or less fixed developmental schedule.

3. Handicapping conditions occasionally delay or inhibit acquisition of language, but in general language is difficult to suppress. Blind children, for instance, clearly lack critical types of stimulation, and typically show cognitive deficits (for example, in acquiring conservation); nevertheless, they score at a "normal" level on language tests, which suggests an extraordinary independence of function. Mental deficiency has to be extreme (an IQ below 20) to completely prevent language acquisition.

4. Language cannot be taught to nonhumans. So far the results of various programs designed to teach chimpanzees ASL or special symbolic communication systems have been equivocal: Chimpanzees are able to match signs and concepts but their use of signs in combination does not seem to reflect a high level of syntactical understanding.

5. The existence of language universals—systemic features common to all terrestrial languages—implies specificity.

Lenneberg (1967, 1973) suggests that human language is probably as species-specific as is birdsong or the "dance" of honey bees, and points to evidence that certain language disorders are hereditary and may be linked to chromosomal abnormality. But his most interesting point relates to brain size. In the rare condition known as *nanocephalic dwarfism*, human children develop into miniature versions of the adult form. They rarely exceed 3 feet in height and are unable to attain a mental age of over 6 years. From 2 to 14 years, the brain weight of normal children increases from 1,000 to 1,300 gm; in contrast, the brain of the nanocephalic dwarf weighs no more than 300 to 400 gm. And yet the sufferers of this syndrome experience little difficulty in acquiring basic levels of language. This argues strongly that language acquisition is mediated by neural structures that function effectively despite gross reductions in overall brain size and the intellectual deficits associated with such reductions. Coincidentally, 400 gm is also about the weight of the chimpanzee brain, which again reinforces the notion that structure and not quantity of neural machinery is the crucial factor.

Chomsky and Walker (1978, pp. 15-16) have defined the issues relating to the LRCS and its acquisition in this way:

1. The person who knows a language L has developed a certain LRCS, which among other things assigns to each sentence of L a full characterization of its [linguistically determined] properties.... If this aspect of LRCS is called LRCS(L), the grammar of L, we can say that to know a language is to have developed a mental representation of its grammar.

2. LRCS(L) results from an interaction of the natural endowment of the child with the environment.... The child starts to acquire language in some initial cognitive state S_0 which is genetically determined and essentially invariant for the species. Some subsystem represented in S_0, call it $LRCS_0$, is the system responsible for language acquisition.... the child passes through a sequence of cognitive states S_0, S_1 ... in which LRCS is correspondingly modified from $LRCS_0$ to the mature state LRCS(L).

3. Each successive cognitive state S_i includes a performance system P (or perhaps several such systems) that incorporates LRCS(L) as one component which interacts with others. Thus putting language to use involves much more than knowing grammar.

As a general description this seems fairly comprehensive, and we could accept it without necessarily adopting a specifically Chomskian model of syntax. Nevertheless, a number of writers interested in language acquisition have questioned the extent to which $LRCS_0$ is capable, as Chomsky has claimed, of driving the acquisition process along when it is fueled by fragmentary and often ungrammatical samples of L and without certain crucial experiential stimuli. Sinha and Walkerdine (1974, 1975) have argued that the acquisition of spatial terms (for example, *in* and *under*) arises out of a complex interaction of children with their environment during which they begin with functional responses; words as well as actions are "embedded within sensorimotor schema" and the child slowly learns to abstract out the perceptual features of a situation and to apply the spatial terms correctly. Wells (1974) has emphasized the social interaction of the child with its mother as a means of directing the acquisitional process. Bruner (1975) has adopted a similar approach, suggesting that "what may be innate about language acquisition is not linguistic innateness, but some special features of human action and human attention that permit language to be decoded by the uses to which it is put" (p. 2). Against such arguments, the special cases posed by blind and mentally handicapped people continue to imply some essentially innate mechanism, capable of decoding and incorporating language stimuli into central processing even in the absence of appropriate perceptual and cognitive scaffolding.

Language Structures in the Cortex

Beginning with the pioneering work of the French physician Paul Broca and the later research of Carl Wernicke, in the 19th century, a great deal of information has been gathered supporting the view that linguistic processes are mediated via specific areas of brain tissue. The areas in question tend, for most people, to be restricted to the left cortical hemisphere of the brain (Fig. 6.1).

Two major methods of investigation have been employed to "map out" the cortical functions associated with language. First, and most important, it is possible to correlate damage to specific parts of the brain with the presence of language disorders, or *aphasias*. The study of aphasia is complex and has generated a huge (and somewhat confused) literature. For reviews and discussion see Geschwind (1965, 1973), Kean (1978), and Saffran (1982); for an attempt to set the problem into a broader communicative context, including deafness and autism, see Rodda (1977). Basically, "Broca's aphasia," caused by damage to Broca's area (Fig. 6.1a), is characterized by slow, ungrammatical, but essentially meaningful speech. Damage to

(a) Areas associated with aphasic disorders

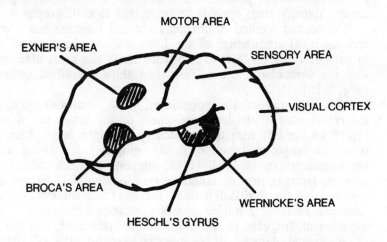

(b) Areas which, stimulated electrically, affect language

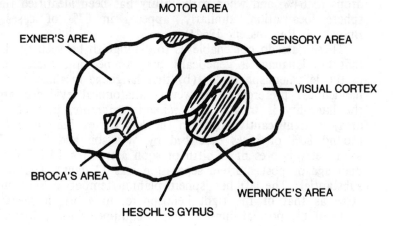

FIG. 6.1.   Cortical language areas.

Wernicke's area, which adjoins Heschl's gyrus, an aural reception area, produces a relatively fluent, modulated linguistic output which contains numerous phonemic and semantic errors. A third part of the cortex, Exner's area, appears to be related to orthography.

The second method of mapping cortical function has involved direct electrical stimulation of the brain and has been shown to result in various types of "language disturbance"; the areas affected in this way are somewhat more diffuse than those identified pathologically (Fig. 6.1b).

In a majority of the population, these cortical language centers are represented in the left hemisphere of the brain. But if very early injury to the left hemisphere occurs, the right hemisphere can take over the language function in its entirety.[1] Reviewing studies of brain maturation, Maxwell (1984) suggests that, in normally hearing infants, lateralization of language may be complete by the age of 3, making this the "critical period" for adapting successfully to neural damage. There is a rather complex relationship between the lateralization of language in the brain, hand preference, and the presence of prelingual damage. It seems that around 90% of right-handed people possess language functions localized in the left hemisphere; among lefthanders without signs of early brain damage this figure drops to 64%, and when early injury has been identified right hemisphere localization, similarly, appears in 67% of cases (Milner, Branch, & Rasmussen, 1964).

These data do not enable us to distinguish between the hypotheses that (a) language is genetically programmed and therefore localized in the left hemisphere, or (b) that language localizes as a result of handedness preferences. However, anatomical evidence argues that the laterality is innate. The *planum temporale*, part of Wernicke's area, is significantly larger in the left cortex than in the right. In around 80% of cases described by Witelson and Pallie (1973) the asymmetry is present at birth or soon after (for 14 infants, the median age of post mortem separation was 12 days). The difference is substantial: The left hemisphere planum temporale is about twice as large as that of the right hemisphere. In short, it seems that the brain of the normal human child is equipped with a distinct physical structure specialized for the processing of linguistic stimuli: the LRCS, in Chomsky's terminology.

---

[1]But not the speech function: Speech defects are more common in children with early left hemisphere damage than in those with early right hemisphere damage (Annett, 1973)

The Lateralization of the Brain

The lateral organization of the human brain is one of its most strik-ing and puzzling features (Fig. 6.2). The two cortical hemispheres carry the evolutionarily most advanced intellectual capacities, but they are anatomically quite distinct. They are joined by a dense bundle of nerve fibres (some 2 million), the *corpus callosum*, which contains the overwhelming majority of neuronal connections of the hemispheres. The two halves of the cortex are primarily linked with the motor and sensory organs of the body via *contralateral* path-ways: Thus, the left hemisphere serves the right hand side of the body and receives auditory and tactile data relating to events on the right, whereas the right hemisphere similarly serves processes relating to the left hand side. Vision also has a left/right split, but into each half of the retinal image. A smaller number of *ipsilateral* pathways may adopt a crucial role in alleviating the effects of brain damage to one hemisphere, but seem to have other roles as yet little understood (Semmes, 1968).

The discovery that language functions tend to be localized in the left hemisphere stimulated a great deal of research aimed at estab-lishing the cortical representations of other kinds of cognitive skill. The surprising outcome of such studies was that only the left hemi-sphere appeared to be implicated in higher intellectual functions. Damage to the right hemisphere usually had purely physical conse-quences—paralysis and sensory deficits—or so it seemed. The left hemisphere was, consequently, referred to as the *major hemisphere*, while the right hemisphere was somewhat slightingly termed the *minor hemisphere*. Similarly, damage to the *corpus callosum* was found to have no discernible effects on cognition.[2] Here was a para-dox: anatomical evidence suggesting that the right hemisphere should be no less important than the left hemisphere, and clinical evidence implying that it was, at best, a redundant "back-up" for the major hemisphere. At the same time, a number of influential neuro-physiologists were claiming that cortical representation was essentially nonspecific, at least in lower animals.

The current interest in lateralization stems very largely from a se-ries of studies conducted in the 1960s. A Los Angeles surgeon, Philip Vogel, and his associate Joseph Bogen, developed a radical form of treatment for the cure of chronic epilepsy which involved complete severance of the corpus callosum (*cerebral commissurotomy*). Roger

---

[2]It has since become clear that partial callosal damage is insufficient to produce the deconnection syndrome. The posterior quarter of the *corpus callosum* is the critical portion.

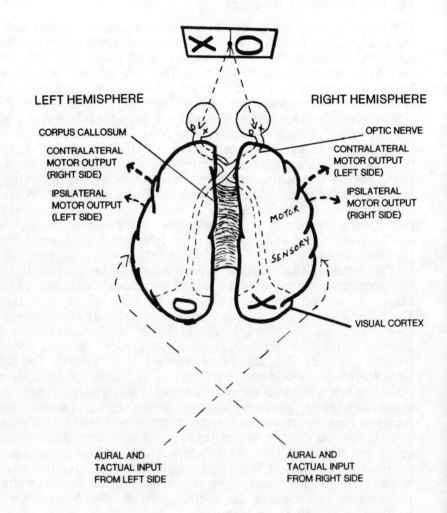

LEFT HEMISPHERE

RIGHT HEMISPHERE

CORPUS CALLOSUM

OPTIC NERVE

CONTRALATERAL
MOTOR OUTPUT
(RIGHT SIDE)

CONTRALATERAL
MOTOR OUTPUT
(LEFT SIDE)

IPSILATERAL
MOTOR OUTPUT
(LEFT SIDE)

IPSILATERAL
MOTOR OUTPUT
(RIGHT SIDE)

MOTOR

SENSORY

VISUAL CORTEX

AURAL AND
TACTUAL INPUT
FROM LEFT SIDE

AURAL AND
TACTUAL INPUT
FROM RIGHT SIDE

FIG. 6.2.   Lateral organization of the cerebral hemispheres.

Sperry, a psychologist at the California Institute of Technology who had studied the effects of cortical deconnection in monkeys, devised a number of novel techniques for assessing the cognitive effects of the operation. By projecting very brief stimuli into a subject's right visual field, input is restricted to the left hemisphere and vice versa. Placing objects in a subject's right hand (shielded from direct vision) similarly restricts tactual input to the left hemisphere. In the same way, a response made by the subject's right hand can be assumed to originate in his left hemisphere. Verbal responses, of course, imply left hemisphere output.

By carefully controlling the combination of input and output routes according to this rationale, Sperry therefore provided a potentially powerful way of investigating the lateral representation of different cognitive, perceptual, and behavioral functions. Sperry (1968) summarized the initial results of his research with commissurotomized patients as follows:

1. Apart from its generally beneficial effects on the epileptic condition of the patient, commissurotomy produces few obvious behavioral symptoms.

2. Presenting verbal material briefly to the right hemisphere shows that it possesses a low level of language comprehension. The subject can point to a picture of a named object with his left hand. At the same time, the left hemisphere may be insisting (verbally) that no stimulus was present.

3. Objects handled (out of sight) in the right hand may readily be identified verbally. The left hand cannot, of course, generate a verbal report, but it can select the same objects again from an array. If both hands are engaged in searching for different objects they work entirely independently.

4. In complex cognitive tasks the commissurotomized patient is less efficient than the normal subject, although the IQ is only slightly affected. Short-term memory, orientation, and tasks requiring extended periods of concentration, are adversely affected. "One gets the impression," remarks Sperry (1968, p. 727), "that their intellect is ... handicapped in ways that are probably not revealed in the ordinary tests."

5. In everyday life, and under less stringent testing conditions, the patients employ a variety of overt and covert interhemispheric transfer strategies: For example, and most obviously, the left hemisphere can communicate with the right hemisphere through speech, and the right hemisphere can cue the left hemisphere

gesturally.

6. Some tasks indicate a small ipsilateral motor control capacity remaining in some of the patients, although it is less efficient than the normal contralateral process,

7. The right hemisphere has capacities of intersensory transfer, concept membership, basic arithmetic, and basic word comprehension. In tests involving spatial relationships, the right hemisphere is superior to the left hemisphere. The right hemisphere has a strong emotional response (e.g., to surprise "pinups" inserted in a test sequence, or to unpleasant smells) and can trigger appropriate behavior which the left hemisphere may notice without knowing its cause.

In a further series of studies, Levy, Trevarthen, and Sperry (1972) employed a variant on their basic methodology to assess right hemisphere performance on nonverbal tasks. This time each hemisphere was flashed half of a different stimulus on each trial. Subjectively, each hemisphere perceived a whole stimulus, and neither was aware that its partner had seen something different! The patients were required to point to the stimulus presented (with left or right hand) or to give a vocal response. Four types of stimuli were presented: photos of faces, antler-like patterns, drawings of objects, or geometrical patterns. On all four tasks, manual responses were controlled by the right hemisphere, even when the right hand was doing the pointing (via ipsilateral channels). When vocal responses were required, the left hemisphere showed a small advantage. However, the left hemisphere performance was slower, less efficient, and more analytical than that of the right hemisphere. This difference in quality of performance emerged strongly when the subjects were asked to learn the names of the people in the photos. Only three names had to be remembered ("Bob," "Paul," and "Dick"), but the patients found this a demanding task. They could only link the names with the faces by verbal association (e.g., "Dick has glasses"), presumably because the left hemisphere could not draw on the superior visual recognition skills of the right hemisphere.

Such studies have been criticized on a number of grounds: First, because the epileptic condition of the subjects may have altered their cortical processing pattern prior to their operation; second because complex relearning strategies may be operating; and third, because information about the patients' preoperative cognitive skills is generally lacking. Nevertheless, these experiments do point to gross differences in the cognitive styles of the two hemispheres and have stimulated a number of research studies using subjects who do not suffer from any obvious neurological or physical impairment.

The difficulties associated with lateralization studies using subjects who are not brain-injured are considerable, because little can be done to prevent the rapid transference of information across the corpus callosum. Several techniques have been developed: (a) brief visual presentations in one or both of the visual fields, as employed by Sperry, but with more complex tasks, and with accuracy or latency measures recorded; (b) "knocking out" one hemisphere by an injection of anesthetic, and measuring the performance of the other; (c) dichotic listening methods (it being assumed that the right ear inputs primarily to the left hemisphere and vice versa); (d) tactile inputs to right or left hand; (e) electrically recording activity in the two hemispheres; and (f) observing blood flow or neural activity in the two hemispheres by means of a radioactive tracer or some kind of scanning system. Of these, methods (a), visual hemifield presentations, and (c), dichotic listening, have been commonly employed; method (f), bloodflow observation, is perhaps the most valuable method but has only recently been developed; (e), electrical recording, has rarely been used; and (b), anesthetic injection, is potentially risky and its use has been largely discontinued. All can be criticized conceptually and methodologically (see, e.g., Cohen, 1975; White, 1972).

There is no way of reviewing all the data accumulated by these methods in a few pages, but some general conclusions can be drawn. First, the left hemisphere consistently outperforms the right hemisphere in tests which can be described as verbal, especially if a vocal response is required. Word and letter identification show a left hemisphere advantage; so does the identification of most (but not all) phonetic stimuli (Code, 1981). The right hemisphere does have a limited capacity to comprehend words, but its nature and extent is uncertain. Therefore, the suggestions that (a) right hemisphere verbal processing is semantically based and may underlie the deficient language forms of dyslexics (and, perhaps, deaf people), and (b) that the right hemisphere is specialized to deal with concrete, easy to visualize concepts, are interesting, but they have as yet little experimental support (Lambert, 1982a, 1982b; Lambert & Beaumont, 1982).

Second, the right hemisphere appears to be specialized to deal with classes of stimuli that tend to be described rather loosely as nonverbal: the perception of faces, drawings, and geometrical shapes; the counting of dots; detection of line orientation; and so on. Clinical evidence tends to confirm this pattern (Bogen, 1969; Bogen & Bogen, 1969; McFie, 1972; White, 1972), implicating the right hemisphere strongly in processes such as orientation in space, musical skills (including singing), art, mathematical calculation (the left hemisphere has a limited capacity for simple arithmetic), and dreaming.

At this stage we should stress the uncertainty associated with some of these findings. We have already mentioned a few problems relating to the "split-brain" studies; these and others qualify the results of the examination of brain-damaged patients, especially when the precise location and extent of the damage is uncertain. Geschwind (1965) has noticed that many right hemisphere-damaged patients rationalize or simply lie to cover up the effects of their injury. Indeed, experimental studies, especially those using the divided visual field technique, raise a whole series of difficulties. Results can vary considerably as a function of incidental factors, such as whether stimuli are presented unilaterally or bilaterally, the angular distance of stimuli from the fixation point, the exposure time (which ideally should be set individually for each subject by trial and error), the number of trials, the subject's reading habits, the use of different strategies to solve the problem, and so on. Mode of response is also a critical variable; a vocal response biases the results toward the left hemisphere (Levy, Trevarthen, & Sperry, 1972). Finally, even if these problems are controlled, many of the measures of laterality used in such studies are themselves of dubious statistical validity (Cohen, 1975; Stone, 1980a, 1980b; White, 1972). Nevertheless, and despite these reservations, the consensus is impressive: Left and right cortical hemispheres do show regular functional differences under a variety of experimental and clinical conditions.

How can we characterize, and perhaps explain, the nature of this fundamental left hemisphere-right hemisphere difference? Until the 1960s, the prevailing view was that the left hemisphere was the dominant hemisphere, which mediated all of the vital intellectual functions, including language (by implication, the most important). The right hemisphere was considered relatively unimportant, even though much evidence linking right hemisphere damage with deficits in certain cognitive skills was readily available. Indeed, writers such as Wigan had proposed, as early as 1844, that the hemispheres constitute two almost independent brains. Bogen (1969) remarks:

> The likely explanation of the eclipse of the two-brain view was the emergence of the concept of cerebral dominance. The social disabilities of the dysphasic (especially in a society which emphasizes "rational" thought) were so much more obvious than the defects of the right-brain-injured person that when dysphasia was accepted as a left hemisphere symptom, the right hemisphere was soon forgotten. (p. 153)

Even Sperry (1968), whose work did so much to overturn the traditional conception, had asked, regarding the right hemisphere, "is it just an agnostic automaton that is carried along in a reflex or trancelike state?" (p. 730).

Defining the nature of nonverbal processes in the right hemisphere has proven to be a difficult task, and many dichotomies have been proposed to express the left hemisphere-right hemisphere distinction in a relatively concise form of words. The simplest, *verbal-nonverbal*, has the merits of linking neurology with the results of intelligence testing, which emphasize the basic division between verbal-educational and spatial-mechanical factors (Butcher, 1968; McFie, 1972). However, "nonverbal" seems vague and to imply the primacy of verbal processes. Others include *expression-perception*; *linguistic-visual/kinesthetic*; *eduction of relations-eduction of correlates*; and *logical/analytic-synthetic/perceptual* (Bogen, 1969). Bogen's own classification is *propositional* (emphasizing the verbal-logical nature of left hemisphere processing) versus *appositional* (implying "a capacity for apposing or comparing of perceptions, schemas, engrams, etc.").

Why should the human brain be characterized by such a complete (or near complete) division of labor? Semmes (1968) suggests that left hemisphere and right hemisphere capacities are rooted in two different and neuroanatomically incompatible modes of organization. The left hemisphere is *focally* organized, which makes it more vulnerable to the effects of local injuries, and more efficient at processing similar elements, than the right hemisphere. The right hemisphere is *diffusely* organized and so more efficient at integrating unlike units, hence its superior spatial skills. However, evidence for microscopic and biochemical left hemisphere-right hemisphere differences is, at present, somewhat uncertain (see, e.g., Beaton, 1982; Gruzelier, Eves, & Connolly, 1981; Wilsher, Atkins, & Mansfield, 1982). Alternatively, Dimond and Beaumont (1972) argue that having dual systems of processing confers an advantage on the human being; it permits the sharing of cognitive load. Bogen and Bogen (1969) also suggest that the existence of two independent streams of thought facilitates problem solving, and Ornstein (1972) emphasizes the intuitive, holistic nature of right hemisphere activity, which contrasts with the slow, laborious sequential procedures used by the left hemisphere, even when both hemispheres are working on the same problem (Zaidel & Sperry, 1973). In fact, some of the phenomena observed in the split-brain patients exaggerate and give expression to a situation that is normally hidden, perhaps by inhibitory cross-callosal influences (Gruzelier, Eves, & Connolly, 1981).[3] Such speculations mark a radical change in the way researchers are thinking about lateralization: The right hemisphere now tends to be seen as the seat of the human creative element, and the left hemisphere as a mechanistic, analytic computer-like system (Levy-Agresti & Sperry, 1968), which by virtue of its role as verbal mediator has gained almost an unfair advantage over the right hemisphere. No doubt this view too is grossly oversimplified and will have to be modified as more findings become available. Meanwhile, many writers such as Maxwell (1984) urge caution in the interpretation of lateralization data, and others (such as Cohen, 1975) are inclined to regard them with suspicion.

Lateralization and Deafness

Prelingual deafness provides a unique way to explore the complex linguistic, cognitive, and neurophysiological issues raised by the phenomenon of lateralization. The LRCS model implies that the acquisition of natural language is mediated primarily through the infant's analysis of incoming speech signals, using innate mechanisms in the language areas of the left hemisphere (in a majority of the population). If this view is substantially correct, we would expect early hearing impairment to disrupt the working of the genetic program for language acquisition. We would also question whether any intervention in another modality (lipreading or signing) could adequately substitute for a speech specific aural input. As we saw in chapter 4, oral language deficiency does indeed constitute the major cognitive effect of early deafness. However, the disruption is not complete: Even profoundly deaf children can acquire the rudiments of oral language, albeit over a grossly extended time scale. Moreover, deafness does not inhibit the acquisition of signing; that is, a language based on a visual rather than an auditory modality.

What do these facts tell us about the operation of the LRCS when deprived of its regular acoustic input? And is it possible to test hypotheses about the neuroanatomical representations of the language forms developed under these circumstances? Some obvious possibilities are:

---

[3]Zaidel and Sperry (1973) give the example of the left hemisphere deliberately, it would seem, talking through and obstructing the performance of the right hemisphere on the progressive matrices test, even though its own performance on the test was markedly inferior. This tendency surely did not result from commissurotomy but exemplifies a rather hostile left hemisphere attitude toward right hemisphere activities!

1. LRCS is specific to speech, and is usually and strongly localized in the left cortical hemisphere. In this case the natural language abilities of deaf children and adults must stem entirely from their capacity for exploiting residual aural capacity, and would be left hemisphere localized as usual. This model says nothing, however, about the representation of sign language; and it is inconsistent with the findings of research into ASL, which suggests that language systems can evolve in another medium.

2. LRCS is not specific to speech and is strongly left hemisphere localized. This model would predict both oral/aural and sign language are based in the left hemisphere.

3. LRCS is not specific to speech and only oral language is left hemisphere lateralized; sign language, because it operates in a spatial modality, and in a holistic, simultaneous mode of processing, would be right hemisphere lateralized. This hypothesis weakens the identification of LRCS with the left hemisphere (which in any case is not complete, even among the normally hearing population).

4. LRCS is not lateralized and not specific to speech. This is the weakest form of the genetic programming model, because we could identify LRCS with some more general cognitive structure (such as "communication" or "symbol manipulation"). Such a situation might predict a limited degree of lateralization for oral language, and little or, perhaps, no lateralization for signing.

At this stage, any attempt to state these hypotheses in detail would be premature: They are essentially the kinds of theory which evidence from lateralization studies could support, evidence we now examine in more detail.

Probably the first systematic attempt to examine lateralization in deaf subjects was made by Phippard (1974), who employed the visual hemifield technique. The stimuli, letters, finger spelled letters, line orientations, and faces, were presented unilaterally to deaf orally educated adolescents, other deaf adolescents educated using total communication, and two hearing control groups. The results indicated that (a) the total communication students showed no evidence of lateralization on any task; (b) the oral students showed a right hemisphere advantage for printed letters (whereas the hearing controls showed, of course, a left hemisphere advantage); and (3) the oral students showed a right hemisphere advantage for line orientation, but no lateral asymmetry for face recognition.

Lubert (1975), employing the same method, tested deaf and hearing groups for lateralization on pictures of ASL signs, finger spelling, and dot patterns. Both deaf and hearing subjects showed a right hemisphere advantage in processing ASL signs; dots and finger spelling produced no significant lateralization. Again using visual presentation, McKeever, Hoemann, Flovian, and Van Deventer (1976) employed both unilateral and bilateral stimuli. Deaf female students, and hearing female subjects with knowledge of ASL, were presented with printed words and letters, finger spelled letters, and ASL signs. The results were complicated: Hearing subjects showed a left hemisphere advantage for printed words and letters and a right hemisphere advantage for signed stimuli; deaf subjects showed a left hemisphere advantage for printed words when presentation was unilateral, but not when bilateral, and also a small right hemisphere advantage for signs. In contrast, Manning, Goble, Markman, and LaBreche (1977) found that the deaf subjects in their study showed a strong left hemisphere advantage on bilaterally presented words, whereas Wilson (1977) found no lateralization effects at all for printed or signed stimuli presented unilaterally.

Kelly and Tomlinson-Keasey (1977) reported one of the few visual hemifield studies to employ a reaction time (RT) measure of processing. Deaf and hearing children served as subjects; the stimuli were abstract and concrete words and pictures presented unilaterally for true/false judgments. The deaf group showed faster processing for right hemisphere presentation for all stimuli. In a second study, Kelly and Tomlinson-Keasey (1978) showed that hearing children processed stimuli faster when they were presented to the left hemisphere. Deaf children performed somewhat faster than hearing overall.

Neville and Bellugi (1978), using unilateral and bilateral presentation, found that deaf subjects showed a left hemisphere advantage for both ASL signs and dot localization. Poizner and Lane (1979), also using an RT metric and unilateral presentation, found similar patterns of data for deaf and hearing groups: All subjects showed a slight right hemisphere advantage for signs and an extremely small left hemisphere advantage for words. Reasoning that static drawings of signs do not fully encapsulate the dynamics of ASL, Poizner, Battison, and Lane (1979) attempted to introduce movement into some of their materials. The subjects were 15 deaf ASL users of deaf parents, and 8 hearing persons not familiar with manual communication. They were presented (unilaterally) with printed common three-letter words, static pictures of ASL signs, and moving pictures of ASL signs (three cinefilm frames presented rapidly in sequence). Hearing and deaf both showed left hemisphere advantage for words and right hemisphere advantage for static signs, but moving signs generated no significant lateralization effects. Moreover, the authors noted the presence of wide individual differences.

Boshoven, McNeil, and Harvey (1982) compared the performance of two hearing groups (one comprising ASL interpreters) and one deaf group on unilateral and bilateral presentation of four sets of stimuli: four-letter words, ASL static signs, and drawings (all relating to the same six objects), and dot patterns. The results were, again, highly complex. All groups showed a significant right hemisphere advantage for words and a slight right hemisphere superiority in dot counting. The hearing groups showed a left hemisphere advantage for signs; the deaf showed no lateralization. For drawings, the hearing subjects showed left hemisphere advantage, the deaf a right hemisphere advantage. Overall, the hearing groups showed a small left hemisphere advantage on bilateral tasks, whereas the deaf group showed a strong right hemisphere advantage. For unilateral presentation, the interpreters showed a slight left hemisphere advantage; both naive hearing subjects and the deaf showed small right hemisphere advantages. The study also noted that the deaf subjects performed more poorly overall, as assessed by mean presentation times, and concluded that "the exact mechanisms for these findings remain unexplained" (p. 525).

The most recent visual presentation experiment, that of Muendel-Atherstone and Rodda (1982), utilized an even more complex design. Four subject groups (two hearing and two deaf) and six types of stimuli (letters, words, finger spelling, ASL signs, signed idioms, and road signs) were employed. The hearing performed better than the deaf respondents in all stimulus classes, and all subjects showed a left hemisphere advantage for signed idioms and road signs and a nonsignificant right hemisphere advantage for signs and finger spelled letters. No lateralization effects were found within deaf and hearing groups, although the trends for both were similar. Factor analyses of the data revealed two major factors, comprising signed and unsigned stimuli, indicating that these two classes of material are psychologically distinct.

Vargha-Khadem (1982) reported an experiment employing tactual presentation of abstract three-letter words and nonsense shapes. The words were presented one letter at a time, paired with letters from concrete words, and subjects responded by pointing to multiple-choice test cards. Overall, hearing subjects scored better than the deaf, and a slight left hemisphere superiority was noted. However, the performance of the deaf subjects was relatively poorer when working with words presented to the right hemisphere.

It is difficult to summarize the results of these experiments, many of which contradict each other completely, or run counter to data gathered in studies using hearing subjects. Only one conclusion can be drawn (without much confidence): So far no evidence has emerged of a dramatic difference of cerebral organization between hearing and deaf subjects. A clear majority of the experiments so far reported show that deaf subjects perform better with verbal materials (mostly single words) presented to the left hemisphere and static sign drawings presented to the right hemisphere. The results for hearing subjects follow the same pattern. However, several studies find no evidence of lateralization, and one or two (e.g., Boshoven, McNeil, & Harvey, 1982) have generated data conflicting with the consensus.

Why are these results so inconsistent? Probably because all of the studies reviewed have serious defects, such as: (a) failure to control incidental variables known to influence performance; (b) insensitive response measures; (c) inadequate stimulus ensembles (e.g., three-quarters of Boshoven, McNeil, and Harvey's stimuli related to only six basic concepts); (d) small subject groups; (e) failure to introduce subject variables into the design (such as the use of speech or visual coding to process language); (f) use of statistically unreliable indices of laterality; (g) inappropriate methods of statistical analysis (few of the studies report tests of normality, or employ the "quasi F-ratio" test demanded by the basic design); and (h) insufficiently thought-out hypotheses. When we add to these the difficulties characterizing all such lateralization experiments, and the problems associated with the testing of deaf subjects, variability in results ceases to be surprising.

Clinical evidence of the effects of brain damage in deaf sign language users is available for a limited number of cases, and presents a far less ambiguous picture. Reviewing 11 such cases reported in the literature, Kimura (1981) found that of 9 right-handed patients exhibiting signing disorders, all had left hemisphere damage. Of the 2 lefthanders, 1 had left hemisphere damage, and 1 right hemisphere damage. These data do not, in themselves, enable us to distinguish between a genuine language disorder (aphasia) and a more generalized motor deficit (apraxia) of the kind that typically accompanies left hemisphere malfunction. However, in 6 out of 7 cases for which this information was available, Kimura noted the presence of difficulties in the comprehension of signs; and in 10 out of 11 cases, writing deficits. But out of 7 cases, there were no reports of reading disorders.

More recent studies by Bellugi and her associates at the Salk Institute have further clarified the clinical picture (Bellugi, Poizner, & Klima, 1983; Bellugi, Poizner & Zurif, 1982; Klima, Bellugi, & Poizner, 1983; Klima, Poizner & Bellugi, 1984; Poizner, Kaplan, Bellugi, & Padden, 1984). Four brain-damaged deaf ASL users were located, and profiles of their residual linguistic and cognitive abilities compiled using a large battery of tests. Three of the subjects with damage to the left hemisphere all presented various degrees and types of disruption in their ASL skills. One (G.D.) lost all syntactical production skills, and had great difficulty even in forming isolated ASL signs, a syndrome equivalent to Broca's aphasia in hearing patients. Another retained fluent signing (K.L.), but made many lexical errors. The third (P.D.) also signed fluently, but made many syntactical errors, such as the use of inappropriate or invalid inflections, a pattern akin to Wernicke's aphasia. The single right hemisphere-damaged subject (B.I.) retained her ASL skills, but showed severe deficits in visual-spatial abilities.

Bellugi and her research team regard these findings as entirely congruent with the effects of cortical damage in hearing patients, where various aphasic syndromes are produced by lesions in specific areas of the left hemisphere. It seems that the responsibility for processing lexical and grammatical aspects of ASL is distributed between those areas of the cortex known to be specialized for the equivalent spoken language functions. Even though ASL operates in a visual-spatial framework, its linguistic base appears to be rooted in the standard left hemisphere neural structures. Two reservations should be noted at this point, however. First, clinical evidence is notoriously hard to evaluate, especially when based on only four cases. Second, none of the four exhibited dramatic deficits in ASL comprehension commensurate with, in three cases, the impairment of sign production associated with left hemisphere injury; or, in the remaining case, the visual-spatial deficits resulting from right hemisphere damage. It may be merely a matter of chance that in these patients little damage was suffered by the neural centers responsible for comprehension; if so, these data leave open the issue of sign reception.

Taking the experimental and clinical evidence as a whole, it is still difficult to make confident statements about the neural representation of spoken and sign language in hearing-impaired persons. The perception of verbal and *static* sign stimuli seem to be mediated via the left and the right hemisphere respectively, and this is true both for deaf and hearing subjects. The production of signing and writing are both clearly localized in the left hemisphere, and the similarity of ASL aphasias to natural language aphasias implies a similar pattern of cortical specialization. More evidence is required; but we would suggest that the most plausible working hypothesis is that *no significant differences exist between deaf and hearing persons with regard to the neural mechanisms underlying signed and spoken language systems.* If this is indeed the case, Chomsky's notion of the genetically preprogrammed LRCS, capable of extracting the basic abstract structure of any language from a sufficiently large corpus of linguistic materials, receives strong support. But this finding also raises a profound problem. If, as Bellugi, Poizner, and Zurif (1982, p. 271) eloquently remark, "human languages have been forged in auditory-vocal channels throughout evolution," we have to ask how it is that the LRCS adapts so readily to accommodate linguistic data in the visual-gestural channel. The LRCS is obviously a highly specialized device, and it is a general evolutionary principle that the more specialized an organ, the harder it is to adapt it to novel situations. But, deprived of an acoustic input, the LRCS does not atrophy; instead it seizes on available visual-gestural information and proceeds to reconstruct the grammar of ASL with apparent ease (see chapters 3 and 8). This is really a most remarkable finding; and we try to explain it in the next section.

Questions About the Origins of Language

We have now reviewed evidence for the existence of innate brain mechanisms specialized for the processing of language. Human beings appear to possess such mechanisms; nonhumans do not, and the limited ability of chimpanzees such as Washoe to learn sign language seems to reflect the workings of a more generalized cognitive structure. But when and how did the human brain acquire the LRCS? What evolutionary processes contributed to its formation? Some of the efforts to find answers to such questions are of considerable interest, although equivocal. It is especially fascinating to find that sign language may have played a crucial role in the intellectual ancestry of man.

An Outline of Human Evolution

The fossil record has identified several distinct stages in the evolution of man. The early prehuman forms can be described and dated with some precision, but their relationship with each other and with modern man is a matter for debate. We list the major stages of development so far identified; for more detailed discussion see Leakey (1981) and Pfeiffer (1969).

Dryopithecus, the earliest ancestor of man, was an apelike tree-dweller who lived more than 14 million years ago. *Ramapithecus*, and associated animals who lived between 14 and 8 million years ago, had a more varied diet and habitat. From 8 to 4 million years ago, a gap in the fossil record obscures one of the crucial phases of evolution: the change to upright walking. Bipedalism seems to have been established around 4 million years ago: various forms of *Australopithecus* lived from around 3.5 to 2 million years back, and may have been the first types of hominid to use tools. *Homo habilis*, who lived around 2 million years ago, employed stone and bone tools, and exhibited a dramatically increased brain capacity, from the 400 cc typical of Australopithecus to some 800 cc. *Homo erectus*, who lived between 1.5 million and 300,000 years ago, developed a more sophisticated technology (the Acheulean) comprising standardized hand axes and cleavers. During this period, brain capacity showed a slow increase from 900 cc to 1,100 cc, and the cultural achievements of Homo erectus exhibited a corresponding gain: The key events were the discovery of fire (around 500,000 years ago), the construction of crude dwellings, the start of organized hunting, the appearance of ritual behavior, and, around 300,000 years ago, the first evidence of an emerging art form: an ox rib carved with a double arc motif.

Between 300,000 and 100,000 years ago various forms of *Homo sapiens*, the species that includes modern man, made their appearance: Swanscombe man, Steinheim man, and others. *Neanderthal* man, dating from about 100,000 years ago, was the most advanced. These hominids usually possessed a brain only slightly smaller than that of present day man, but the Neanderthals possessed a brain somewhat larger. The Neanderthals developed a more complex technology than the earlier species, the Mousterian, comprising some 60 distinct tools. As we discuss in the next section, Neanderthal culture provides evidence of ritual burials, the manufacture of religious objects, and diversification. But the relationship between the various prehuman strains and modern man is unclear. Leakey (1981) has summarized current knowledge as follows:

> The point in question is the origin of modern humans, *Homo sapiens sapiens*. Three things can be said with some confidence. Firstly, from somewhere in excess of one-and-a-half million years ago to around 300,000 years ago *Homo erectus* existed throughout the Old World as a relatively stable species, and, as far as is possible to guess, was the rootstock from which modern humans eventually evolved. Secondly, the first fossil remains that are unquestionably fully modern man, *Homo sapiens sapiens*, appear in the fossil record at about 40,000 years ago. Thirdly, before this time and back to just over 100,000 years ago, there are specimens that are certainly *Homo sapiens* but with some primitive features ... In the case of Europe, did the Neandertals evolve from *Homo erectus* and then give issue to *Homo sapiens sapiens*? Or did Neandertal Man arise from *Homo erectus* only to become an evolutionary dead end, while modern humans evolved directly from *Homo erectus* independently of the Neandertals? (p. 145).

Early Forms of Language

Of course, we have no direct evidence concerning the origin and structure of language during the millions of years of prehistory. But we do have indirect evidence of the evolution of intellect during this period, and we can make informed guesses about the mental capacity required to undertake certain activities in which our hominid ancestors were known to be engaged.

The most obvious and enduring traces of hominid behavior available to investigators are, of course, the stone tools and weapons which they constructed. The earliest artifacts, dating from 2.5 million years ago, are crude and functional. Tools from the Acheulean period, a million years later, show increased formalization and symmetry, but from this time until 200,000 years ago there were no observable improvements in design. Indeed, some of the later examples of the Acheulean technology seem crude in relation to the earliest forms. As we have already noted, about 100,000 years ago a dramatic change occurred. The Neanderthals developed and refined a new technique for deriving a wide range of tools from a prepared "core": About 60 different items—knives, axes, scrapers, arrow and spear tips—have been identified. In the same period, equally striking cultural developments took place: stylistic divisions in tool making, ritualistic behavior, burials, philanthropic behavior (evidenced by the survival of severely handicapped individuals), and aesthetic appreciation (the use of flowers for decorative and ritual purposes). Lyall Watson (1979) and others see this change as accompanied by the appearance of an advanced form of language.

The first appearance of modern man marks a yet more dramatic series of changes (Silverberg, 1970). Tools of bone and stone were made in great variety: Harpoons, needles, awls, and hide burnishers have been clearly identified. Around 30,000 years ago, artistic creativity appeared: the carving of small statuettes and cave painting. As a measure of cognitive advancement, the paintings of early modern man, as exemplified in the famous caves at Lascaux in France, are a revelation. Their portrayal of animals such as bulls, bison, stags, and horses—difficult subjects for the most experienced modern artists— testifies to a high level of technical proficiency. Considering that the artists worked from memory in poorly lit and often uncomfortable positions their accomplishments are all the more remarkable. One curious feature of the paintings is that humans are rarely portrayed, and, when they are, they are pictured very crudely—often in matchstick-man form—in contrast to the sophisticated handling of animal subjects. Whether this indicates a superstitious reluctance to represent men realistically (for example, for fear of capturing their souls), or inability to perceive people with objectivity, it is impossible to say.

Does cave art tell us anything directly about language? Incidental to the animal paintings in many of the caves so far discovered are various complex geometrical figures. Although carvings from an earlier period bear traces of simple designs—arcs, crosses, and chevrons—it is hard to determine whether these constitute anything more than decoration. But at Lascaux, and elsewhere, the designs are more complicated and are clearly symbolic. (Inevitably, some scholars have read sexual symbolism into the designs!) These are, in fact, the first unequivocal evidence for a capacity for symbolic representation and non-iconic form of communication on the part of early man.

We can also deduce something of the cognitive level of prehistoric men by considering their way of life. Group hunting, which began at least half a million years ago, must have demanded a variety of skills: organization, involving a certain degree of planning and communication; tracking; execution (Leakey points to the fact that only humans are capable of accurate throwing); and distribution of the kill. A few hunter-gatherer cultures have survived until recent times, and examining their hunting behavior emphasizes the very high level of perceptual and motor skills our ancestors must have possessed (Pfeiffer, 1969). Tracking, for example, requires not only well developed perceptual abilities, but the mental capacity for (a) persevering with a lengthy (and perhaps frustratingly unsuccessful) pursuit; (b) keeping in mind the object of the task, despite distractions; and (c) making complex deductions from small (and often near-invisible) visual cues. Pearce (1971) describes a test of the tracking abilities of an Australian aborigine. A man was sent on foot over a varied terrain comprising sand desert, marsh, and rock desert. A year later his route was traced, without apparent difficulty, by the aborigine tracker. Similarly impressive stories are told of the American Indians. What these skills point to is a fundamental property of language, known as *displacement*—the ability to separate the meaningful elements of a stimulus from its immediate physical and emotional impact. This is a performance based on a qualitatively different biological mechanism from that employed by a tracker dog, say, which is merely responding to an immediate (chemical) stimulus. The dog is detecting scent; the man is reading meaning from his visual environment. This capacity for extracting meaning from diverse stimuli undoubtedly lies at the root of our conceptual and linguistic accomplishments.

But how precisely did natural language evolve from such beginnings? Most modern primates are equipped with a very elementary vocal apparatus, which is used in a limited number of situations (for example, fear and aggression). The traditional view—and certainly the oldest—was that a small number of vocalizations were paired with certain socially agreed meanings, and that this led eventually to the birth of language. Around 50 B.C., Diodoros of Sicily described the socialization of the first men:

> Gathered together in this way by reason of their fear, they gradually came to recognize their mutual characteristics. And though the sounds which they made were at first unintelligible and indistinct, yet gradually they came to give articulation to their speech, and by agreeing with one another on symbols for each thing which presented itself to them, made known among themselves the significance which was to be attached to each term. (Toulmin & Goodfield, 1965, chap. 2).[4]

In common with many later accounts, this analysis is less than explicit about the mechanisms underlying the creation of language. And, at best, such models explain only the formulation of single words: Nothing is said about the evolution of syntax, which Chomsky and others would, of course, regard as the defining feature of natural language.

The Evolution of Language

Gordon Hewes (1971, 1973, 1974, 1976) has reviewed the major theories of language evolution and presented a model of his own that we discuss in some detail. He identifies the following major approaches: (a) interjection as a source of speech sounds; (b) imitative or onomatopoeic generation of sounds; (c) sounds imitative of objects being struck or worked; (d) sounds made while working (work-chant); (e) sounds made by the mouth imitating manual movements; (f) babbling sounds made by infants; (g) instinctivist, holding that language appeared because a critical stage of evolution had been reached; (h) the conventionalist theory, that language was agreed on as a social contract; (i) social contact; (j) divine intervention (to which today we should perhaps add alien intervention); (k) chance mutation; and Hewes' own theory (l) *that gestural communication preceded speech.* A further theory, presented

---

[4]This is not the only archaic discussion of evolution to have a strangely "modern" flavor. Anaximander of Miletos (611-545BC) claimed that life first appeared in swamps and marshy places and slowly migrated onto dry land. Ibn el-Arabi (1164-1240), known in the West as "Doctor Maximus," asserted that "thinking man" was 40,000 years old, a figure consistent with the best modern estimates. The Christian church, of course, succeeding in suppressing such notions until the 19th century, despite the fact that as a pictorial allegory, the first chapters of Genesis are a surprisingly accurate account of evolution.

by Pfeiffer (1969), suggests (m) that language was invented by hominid children during play.

Leaving aside the obvious inadequacies of the majority of these theories as models of the origins of syntax, we can see that they rely largely on identifying a single (often unlikely) process, and omit consideration of associated cognitive and neurological factors. Hypotheses (a)-(d), the imitative theories, possess a certain plausibility; (e) oral representation of manual movements, does not seem particularly convincing; (f) the infant-babbling theory is difficult to accept—in fact, babbling is essentially a stage in the acquisition of language by individuals already possessing LRCS and it can hardly be invoked as an explanation of the origins of language; the instinctivist view (g) offers a genuinely original viewpoint, but raises fundamental questions about the evolutionary process (Hoyle & Wickramasinghe, 1981; Koestler, 1978; Teilhard de Chardin, 1959); the two social theories, (h) and (i), provide details of part of the motivating pattern underlying language creation, but say little about mechanisms; and (j) intervention theories should be regarded strictly as a last resort, as perhaps should the convenient "chance mutation" (k). Given what we know about the rigid social hierarchies in hunter/gatherer groups, it seems unlikely that hominid adults would learn from or adopt a children's game as a system of communication (m). However, hypothesis (l) is of special interest because it proposes a well defined sequence of cognitive stages, and gives a prominent place to gestural communication in language evolution. It is also associated with writers such as Sir Richard Paget (1935, co-creator of the Paget-Gorman sign language) and Stokoe, but is best known through the work of Hewes himself. Armstrong (1983) has reviewed and criticized the theory and proposed a modified version in which speech and gesture coexisted and evolved together.

The problem confronting "speech" models of language creation is that there exists a wide gulf between the psychological and physiological capacities of present-day primates (and, presumably, of the early hominids) and those possessed by language-proficient modern man. The organs underlying speech production at a purely phonetic level are immensely complex, to say nothing of the sophistication of the neural machinery comprising the LRCS. It is difficult to envisage the gradual transition from (a) a situation in which a small hominid grouping may be using one or two calls with acquired meanings, to (b) the organized social use of a grammatically sophisticated communication system. The gestural model, in effect, attempts to fill this gulf by proposing an intermediate stage of language evolution in which a relatively small increase in manual dexterity could form the basis of a gestural grammar, which could in turn stimulate and direct a parallel development in the auditory modality.

Hewes argues that the motor skills associated with tool making and use, and those related to language, constitute a "fundamental capacity to acquire and utilize complex patterned sequences" which he identifies with Chomsky's deep structure (Hewes, 1973; also see Lashley, 1951). He also points out that neurological evidence supports the idea of a close relationship between motor and language skills. Indeed, with the increasing sophistication of stone age technology, Hewes suggests, came a corresponding increase in visuo-motor skills. The availability of such skill, as exemplified in fine control over hand and arm movements, made it a more likely candidate for an emerging communication channel than the limited vocal behavior of the hominids. Evolution generally proceeds by elaborating structures already available, rather than by creating wholly new mechanisms. Therefore, the conceptual problems associated with the transition from manual movements, through gesture to a genuine sign language, are considerably fewer than those associated with a model based only on speech. Once the neural structures capable of handling the grammar of sign were established, the final transition to a speech-based system became a more realistic enterprise. At this stage, the disadvantages of signing—its conflict with other manual activities, high energy expenditure, and its failure to work in the dark or behind obstacles—would have resulted in an evolutionary pressure promoting the development of spoken language.

The theory is plausible, then, and has clear formal advantages over the speech-only approach. It is supported by several lines of evidence. First, modern apes appear to be incapable of learning speech, but do succeed in acquiring a primitive form of signing. The point is not whether the behavior of Washoe and others constitutes language in its fullest sense—it would be surprising if it did—but that manual gesture is *easier* for the primates than vocalizing (for a recent attempt to teach speech to an orangutan, see Laidler, 1980). The problem does not lie at a purely physical level: Apes lack the neural equipment necessary for speech control, but they do possess basic manual skills. The vocal apparatus of the apes is coupled with the emotion and motivation centers of the brain, and Lancaster (1968) comments:

> [Primate communication] systems are not steps toward language, and have much more in common with the communication of other mammals than with human language ... these systems have little relationship with human language, but much with the ways human beings express emotion through gesture, facial expression, and tone of voice. (Klima & Bellugi, 1973, p. 96)

What Hewes is emphasizing is that the development of sensorimotor skills associated with the hunter-gatherer lifestyle of the hominids favors communication, at least initially, in a kinesthetic-visual modality. Displacement would be a feature of these skills, but not of early vocal calls, which would be tied closely to the immediate environment. Gesture would also adapt readily to the hunting context, where a method for communicating silently at a distance would have clear advantages.

The second line of evidence for the theory is found in the examination of Neanderthal remains by Lieberman and Crelin (1971) which suggests that Neanderthal man would have been unable to speak. As Armstrong (1983) notes, this evidence is open to other interpretations; and the relationship of the Neanderthals with modern man is also in question. Nevertheless, it still offers suggestive support.

Third, the human hand is a relatively ancient feature, and so was available for communication purposes early on in our evolution: Examination of tools suggests that hominids, along with the other characteristics referred to earlier, first became capable of the "precision grip" which differentiates human from primate behavior around 100,000 years ago. It is interesting to note that Holloway (1974), in studying casts of hominid brains derived from fossil skulls, has found evidence that the basic structure of the human brain is also evolutionarily ancient: Both hand and brain structure may date back 2 or even 3 million years. Moreover, he has detected signs of cerebral asymmetry in many of the casts.

Fourth, gestural communication offers means of iconic representation not available in the speech modality. Not only would manual signals be easier to produce, but their meanings would be more transparent. Armstrong suggests that this is Hewes' strongest single point, because it overcomes the problems already noted concerning the random pairings of sound and stimulus and permits a greater degree of displacement. A hominid trying to tell his fellows about some new animal in the vicinity would probably find it far easier to employ a gestural pantomime than to employ a limited oral vocabulary.

Armstrong's theory differs from Hewes' in asserting that signing and spoken language may have evolved simultaneously. But whether signing preceded speech, or merely accompanied it, it seems clear that it was the visual-gestural modality that provided the driving force in language evolution. Beside the points just considered, this general approach makes sense in the light of observations such as:

1. The survival, until recent times, of sign languages in the repertoire of many residual hunter-gatherer societies; and the use of

ritualized gesture in more advanced cultures.

2. The pervasiveness of gesture in all modern cultures and its close association with oral language, which testifies to the close neural linkages between speech and manual movement (Kimura, 1973). Kimura remarks that such data "raise the suspicion that the left hemisphere may be especially well adapted, not for symbolic function per se, but for the execution of some classes of motor acts, to which symbolic meaning can be attached" (p. 49).

3. The naturalness of gesture, which is supported by the formal studies of ASL and its use by deaf people, and also by the common experience of falling back on gesture and pantomime in situations in which a common language is absent (e.g., in helping a tourist). "Falling back on" implies a feeling that in some fashion signed communication draws on atavistic tendencies.

4. Perhaps one of the most extraordinary findings of recent years is the discovery that *deaf infants are capable of formulating an elementary form of sign language spontaneously* (Goldin-Meadow & Feldman, 1975, 1977; Kuschel, 1973; Mohay, 1982). The children in these studies do not, it seems, copy their mothers' informal gestures: Mostly they invent their own novel iconic symbols and incorporate them in multisign discourse (although Mohay, observing two subjects, found no evidence for sign invention in her data[5]). This research, if confirmed, provides powerful evidence for the existence of an innate communication mechanism capable of creating, as well as assimilating, a sign language system.

5. The probability that sign language is mediated by the same neurophysiological mechanisms used to process natural language.

The general thrust of such arguments is that the structural characteristics of sign language directed and refined the evolution of human language capabilities. If so, and if research on sign systems other than ASL confirmed the existence of a strong synthetic tendency on the part of manual communication, this would tie in very neatly with the observation that spoken languages tend to lose their synthetic characteristics as society becomes more advanced

---

[5]The observations cited were made in oral environments, and it can be assumed that spontaneous gesturing of this type would be rigidly excluded from formal instruction in oral schools for the deaf and by itinerant teachers visiting the children's homes. We have evidence that early diagnosis of hearing impairment is correlated with later poor emotional adjustment, implying that the suppression of such communication systems could have lasting consequences (see chapter 7, p. 317).

(Armstrong & Katz, 1981). But it must be admitted that all this is more guesswork than theory building. There are many possible alternative models of the process of linguistic evolution and, for the most part, no direct ways of testing them. For example, sign language and speech may have developed simultaneously for different purposes, sign language for use during hunting, and spoken language for socializing. With the advent of the agricultural revolution (10,000 years ago), signing would have diminished in importance. Another possibility is that written language, first in evidence around 6,000 years ago, took over the ecological niche previously occupied by sign language.

Synthetic and Analytical Language Evolution

Recently Armstrong and Katz (1981) have presented a major new linguistic theory that draws together cognitive, social, evolutionary, and neurological variables. It is a measure of the extent to which manual communication systems have assumed critical importance in psycholinguistics that Armstrong and Katz chose to publish their article in the journal *Sign Language Studies*. Their basic premise is that left and right cortical hemispheres are specialized for different types of linguistic functioning. The left hemisphere is implicated in complex syntactical processing, denotational semantic representation (i.e., conceptual relationships of a formal nature: class membership, possession of attributes, and similar characteristics), and elaborated coding. The right hemisphere, they suggest, possesses a capacity for connotational meaning (such as informal associations between ideas, and emotional properties of words) and restricted coding. Armstrong and Katz reject the views prevailing among many linguists that only the left hemisphere processes qualify as "language" and claim that processes of metaphor, poetry, myth, and so on, are equally important, and are mediated by the right hemisphere (Fig. 6.3).

The most radical aspect of Armstrong and Katz's model is their assertion that the right hemisphere is more strongly implicated in the processing of synthetic language types than analytical. If this is the case, then the drift toward the analytic form that characterizes advanced technological cultures corresponds with an increased dependence on left hemisphere activities. By correlating measurements of societal complexity with an index of left hemisphere processing, color differentiation, the authors claimed to have confirmed this model.

The weakest link in this line of reasoning is the ambiguity of evidence supporting the nature and extent of right hemisphere language processes (Lambert, 1982a, 1982b). The impasse might be resolved by referring more generally to "conceptual" or "cognitive" right hemisphere activities; in fact, Armstrong and Katz oppose any clear

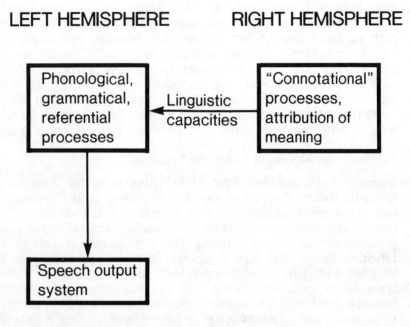

FIG. 6.3.   The language model of Armstrong and Katz (1981).

distinction between language and other aspects of cognition (Rodda, 1976, develops a similar argument in the context of communication disorders). In fact, there can be little dispute that the dominant western culture has had, until very recently, a strong left hemisphere bias and a reliance on analytic languages (especially English). But correlational evidence is notoriously difficult to interpret, and it could be argued that a relationship (if proven) between cultural complexity and the classification of colors tells us little about language synthesis or its lateralization. Indeed, it has long been recognized that advanced cultures employ more color terms than are used by less sophisticated communities; and Woodworth (1910) long ago gave a plausible explanation of this relationship without invoking complex linguistic or physiological mechanisms. Perhaps measures of a society's right hemisphere proficiency—art, poetry, literature, philosophy—might be more telling.[6] Another approach might involve correlating indices of language synthesis (such as that of Greenberg, 1960) with cultural changes through history.

Irrespective of its strengths and defects, the theory of Armstrong and Katz (1981) does represent an ambitious attempt to draw together a wide range of linguistic and psychological data into a unified whole. Such an approach has been notably lacking in previous formulations. It could form the basis for an extended model of language evolution, incorporating the gestural model of language genesis very easily, and strengthening from a different perspective the ethnic view of American Sign Language. Interestingly, our arguments have turned full circle, and the sign languages of deaf people become an evolutionary characteristic of us all, deaf and hearing alike. We have to ask—if man needed sign language to develop spoken language, why do we continue to question its utility and importance for deaf students and adults?

Summary

Studies of deafness and sign language are making contributions to psycholinguistics and psychology in two key areas. First, experiments investigating the patterns of hemispheric lateralization have so far shown no clear indications of a difference between deaf and hearing subjects. However, almost all the experiments to date have been open to methodological criticism, so conclusions as to the neurological consequences of hearing impairment, or the cortical representation of sign languages, would be premature. Second, analyses of the evolution of language cast doubt on the traditional view that speech developed independently in early man. Indirect evidence and argument suggest that a form of sign language developed as a by-product of increasing hominid sensorimotor skills, serving as a foundation for the subsequent (or parallel) evolution of spoken language. Armstrong and Katz (1981) have proposed a radical new theory that could serve as a framework for the integration of these data.

---

[6]Another objection to the theory is that it is easy to cite counterexamples, often dramatic, to the general relationship. China, for example, has the most analytic language known, yet has been active historically in the artistic and creative fields, besides being the home of Taoism and Zen. Ancient Greek was intensely synthetic but Greece is regarded as the birthplace of rationalism.

Further Reading

As yet there are few good nontechnical surveys of the areas covered in this chapter. For an introduction to the basic facts of neurology, Dean Wooldridge's (1963) *The Machinery of the Brain*, although dated, is a particularly lucid production. A good instructional text is by Richard Restak (1984), simply entitled *The Brain* and based on the Public Broadcasting System (PBS) series of the same title. For a general discussion on the problems of theorizing about brain functions, see Keith Oatley's (1978) *Perceptions and Representations*. Recent important books on the general study and theory of hemispheric processing are by Sally Springer and George Deutsch (1981) on *Left Brain, Right Brain* and M.P. Bryden (1982) on *Laterality: Functional Assymetry in the Intact Brain*. Richard Leakey's (1981) review of human evolution, *The Making of Mankind*, includes a chapter on the origins of language. A thorough review of the issues of linguistic evolution, with special reference to the Washoe study, is given by Eugene Linden (1975) in *Apes, Men, and Language*. Some of the wider issues associated with evolutionary biology are discussed in Lyall Watson's (1979) *Lifetide*, which summarizes novel material on the transmission of observationally learned skills among primates, including the enigmatic "Hundredth Monkey Phenomenon." Lighter reading, but still interesting and informative, is Keith Laidler's (1980) account of his attempts to teach speech sounds to a young orangutan, *The Talking Ape*.

7

SOCIAL AND EMOTIONAL DEVELOPMENT
AND THE PROBLEM OF COUNSELING

Prelingual profound deafness not only affects oral language and internal cognitive coding mechanisms, but presents an unusual and unique perspective on psychological and social development in both children and adults. As we have already seen, prelingually deaf individuals usually have normal nonverbal intelligence (Vernon, 1968), have the capacity to handle problems in symbolic logic (Furth, 1966), and develop elaborated conceptual models of their social environment (Gordon, 1977). Nevertheless, their vocational and educational achievements are poor, and the majority fail to acquire speech and lipreading skills sufficient to enable them to interact easily with hearing persons using this method of communication (Lewis, 1968; Mindel & Vernon, 1971). Their average level of competence in English rarely exceeds that of hearing 9-year-olds (Denmark et al., 1979; DiFrancesca, 1972; Myklebust, 1964; Rodda, 1970) only a very small minority gain entry to university; and the adult deaf population is characteristically employed in unskilled and manual work (Schein & Delk, 1974).

Hearing impairment also seems to exercise a significant effect on the development of personality. Deaf and hard of hearing respondents are prone to produce abnormal Minnesota Multiphasic Personality Inventory (MMPI) profiles and measures of social maturity that diminish through adolescence (Myklebust, 1964). They are said to exhibit lack of sensitivity for others, overdependency, unsociability, impatience, and to react to frustration with anger or overt aggression (Basilier, 1964; Remvig, 1969). Attempts have also been made to link acquired deafness with an alleged propensity to schizophrenic disorder (Cooper, 1976; Kay, Cooper, Garside, & Roth,

1976), but the evidence on this question is unclear and not supported by general clinical observation.

The problem was illustrated succinctly at the Association of Canadian Educators of the Hearing Impaired Conference in 1979. Jerome D. Schein presented a paper entitled "Educating Hearing Impaired Children to Become Emotionally Well Adjusted Adults" and, as he pointed out, the title seemed absurd. Who could believe that schools were not already doing so (Schein, 1980)? In fact, the prevalance rates for behavioral disturbances in deaf students vary, ranging from 1 in 3 to 1 in 10 students (Annual Survey, 1971; Meadow & Schlesinger, 1971), and (even if we use the more conservative estimate) on average, every second class of deaf children will contain at least one student whose educational program is seriously impaired by problems of emotional adjustment. Such problems are not to be confused with severe psychiatric illnesses: The prevalence rates for such illnesses are probably the same in both the hearing and the deaf populations (Montgomery, 1979). The problems in the classroom are mainly problems of behavioral adjustment. They are reactions to stress adopted by students whose social and language skills are inadequate to deal with the demands placed on them by the wider environment. In this chapter, we explore these issues and their relationship with language and cognition in more detail. We also discuss the aims and methods used when seeking to alleviate such problems by counseling deaf children and their families.

Causes of Social Maladjustment

A significant early paper by Sharoff (1959-1960) predated much of the pioneering work on psychiatric disorders in deafness started by F.J. Kallman in New York State Psychiatric Hospital in the late 1950s. The author reported several case studies, and his insightful summary is worth quoting in full. It neatly presents the arguments of the author, it is an interesting contrast between early academic writing style and that used in present day journals, and it shows that the changing of attitudes is a slow process:

> This paper does not criticize the great work that is being done to promote the meaningful growth and education of the deaf child and helping him to achieve as much oral facility as possible. It is presented in the hope that hand in hand with this, there will be a more tolerant attitude to the deaf child's need for language through signs, until such time as language through oral speech may replace it. It is felt that one may enhance the other, rather than being antithetical to each other. Some of the negative

aspects of the present attitude have been presented with the hope that
the questions raised here will arouse further interest in this matter and
stimulate others to study this problem. (p. 446)

We do not know if Kallman was influenced by Sharoff, but
Sharoff's place of residence, New York City, and his familiarity with
the work of Edna Simon Levine, another pioneer in this field,
suggests that he might have had a significant impact on Kallman's
early studies. The question is not of great practical importance, but
it might explain why Kallman, a geneticist, developed a sudden and
major interest in deafness (the argument that it resulted from his
interest in the genetic aspects of deafness has always seemed to us to
be rather weak).

Tracing causal relationships in behavioral disturbance is as complicated now as it was in the 1950s. To what extent can we define
the specific roles of potentially significant variables such as hearing
impairment per se, poor oral ability, retarded English language competence, a general reduction in auditory stimulation, lack of specific
important early intellectual and social experiences, the emotional response of parents, and so on? Some early investigators, notably
Pintner (Pintner, 1929; Pintner & Reamer, 1920), argued that deafness itself was the vital factor, but recent research has placed greater
emphasis on the secondary effects of hearing loss, rather than on its
primary consequences.

As we have already seen in this context, the primary consequences
of deafness appear to be an inability to exploit articulatory stimulus
characteristics in short-term cognitive encoding, and a tendency to
organize stimuli spatially rather than sequentially (chapter 4). There
is also evidence of atypical patterns of cortical functioning: Deaf
persons may not develop the left hemisphere dominance for verbal
materials usual for hearing people (chapter 6). All these effects will
clearly influence the way in which deaf children process language and
their verbal and nonverbal communication with others; and the importance of the interaction between the cognitive and the affective
domain is emphasized by Watts (1979). He quotes early studies by
Getz (1953) and Murphy (1957), showing that maladjusted deaf
children perform less satisfactorily on perceptual processing tasks. He
also draws attention to the fact that:

> The probability of normal affective maturation in deaf children may well
> be threatened by a breakdown of communication between mother and
> child. Parents have social and psychological needs of their own that must
> be met through communication. The lack of reaction or the bizarre re-
> sponse they receive from their child may change their behavior toward
> him/her, resulting in the withdrawal of verbal stimulation and affection.
> (Watts, 1979, p. 495)

Echoing Watts, a consensus has now emerged identifying a lack of appropriate cognitive, linguistic and social experiences as the most important secondary effect of deafness (Denmark et al., 1979; Stein, Mindel, & Jabaley, 1981). Unfortunately, for social and historical reasons (see chapter 2), discussion of these problems has frequently polarized around the question of which method of communication to use with deaf students, rather than on how to avoid these secondary effects. Proponents of oral methods of educating deaf students argue that the major aim of schools and programs for deaf students should be to equip the student to interact, at a certain minimal level, with hearing society; that spoken language is the essential route to this goal; and that the only way of attaining adequate spoken language is to restrict communication with the deaf child to the channels of speech, lipreading and amplified sound. Oralists reject the use of any system of sign language on the grounds that such systems interfere with the acquisition of oral skills and may encourage the formation of a deaf subculture. Unfortunately, in doing so they fail to identify the social values that are the basic premise on which their methodology is founded. Few people, including supporters of total communication, ask the unthinkable question—Does it really matter if the deaf student/adult cannot speak? It does, but are the reasons social or educational, and are they so important as to override all other factors?

In contrast, other teachers of deaf students, especially in the United States, and most applied psychologists and researchers have supported the use of total communication in schools and programs for deaf students. As we have already seen, such techniques allow the teacher to use a variety of combinations of oral and manual techniques with the aim of maximizing the amount of information available for visual or auditory processing. In general, the advocates of total methods of communication do not reject the aims of the oral tradition, but argue that placing too much emphasis on speech and lipreading restricts the cognitive and social development of the child and is also less likely to achieve the desired outcome. They also argue that limiting the child to oral communication also precludes parent-child communication in the early preverbal stages of development—vital if linguistic, social, and emotional development is to follow a normal pattern.

To resolve the questions referred to in the previous paragraph, a series of studies have compared the characteristics of children who used only oral communication throughout the larger portions of their early life with children who used total or manual communication in the same circumstances (see Mindel & Vernon, 1971; Vernon, 1969, for useful early summaries). In a classic paper, Meadow (1967) examined the achievement and personality development of two groups of deaf children: one group comprising children born to hearing parents, and brought up using oral methods; the other consisting of the deaf children of deaf parents, who had been exposed to the use of sign language from an early age. She found that in terms of achievement, reading skill, rated intellectual ability, facility in written language, and for every measure of social adjustment employed, the children of deaf parents proved superior. A study by Greenberg (1980), to be described in more detail later, showed that the deaf children of hearing parents using total communication also gained higher adjustment and achievement scores than those using oral communication. A similar study by Brasel and Quigley (1975) restricted the analysis to linguistic ability, but their findings were essentially the same—on almost all measures a "Manual English" group proved the most able, an "Average Oral" group least able. Finally, data reproduced in Table 7.1 (from Stokoe & Battison, 1981, p. 184) show that families in which both parents are deaf are significantly less likely to have an emotionally or behaviorally disturbed deaf child, a finding that is again attributed to the use of total communication, although Corson (1973) has shown that acceptance of deafness by deaf parents is also an important part of this process (cf. Carver, 1984, 1985).

Meadow's early study precipitated a number of others, most of which used slightly different paradigms. An interesting perspective is found in a study by Goss (1970). He used Bale's Interaction Process Analysis to explore the interactive language used between mothers and their hearing-impaired children. The mothers used oral language, and were found "less likely to use verbal praise and more likely to show verbal antagonism" (p. 96) than mothers of hearing children. An obvious conclusion is that in later life, these children will either withdraw or develop more aggressive responses, particularly because they probably rarely understood why their behavior generated negative reactions. Such a conclusion is also supported at a more practical level by studies such as that of Denmark (1966), Denmark and Eldridge (1969), Denmark and Warren (1972) and Denmark et al. (1979). These authors have explored the behavior problems of deaf adolescents and adults in a psychiatric setting and elsewhere, and their findings are replicated by Basilier in Norway (Basilier, 1964), by Norden in Sweden (Norden, 1981), by Kallman, Rainer, and Altshuler in the United States (see, for example, Rainer & Altshuler, 1967), and by Vernon in the United States (see Grinker et al., 1969). Many of the patients described in these studies were found to be suffering from behavior and adjustment disorders associated with a pattern of parental rejection and lack of communication. In such

TABLE 7.1

Reported Emotional/Behavioral (EB) Problems Occurring in the
Absence of Other Handicapping Conditions, for Deaf Students as
Related to Deafness of Parents (School Year 1969-1970)*

| Category of Deaf Children | Number of Parents Becoming Deaf Before Child Reaches Age 6 | | Total |
	0 or 1	2	
EB	1,237 (9.2%)	36 (5.0%)	1,273
Normal	12,223 (90.8%)	682 (95.0%)	12,905
Total	13,460	718	14,178

Chi square = 14.04, $p<.005$

*Data from the Office of Demographic Studies, Gallaudet College, Washington, DC

Table reproduced from W.C. Stokoe and R.M. Battison, 1981, p. 184, published by Grune & Stratton, Inc.

cases, the parents had been given inadequate counseling and guidance by the specialists with whom they had been in contact; in particular, they had been advised to communicate to their children using only speech and had not been informed of the value of manual methods. It was hypothesized, in the light of both research evidence and clinical experience, that (a) inappropriate counseling, (b) the inability to communicate in any language resulting from reliance on oral methods of teaching, and (c) parental feelings of guilt and frustration would result in a greater incidence of behavioral maladjustment, as well as inferior performance in scholastic and social settings. The data overwhelmingly supported these hypotheses, and although in some instances alternative explanations are also possible, it seems to us that those postulated by the authors are the most logically defensible.

Family Counseling and Guidance

The family has been described as a community in itself—a small group of people related to each other in the most intimate way. This community, particularly the nuclear family, is for the child the first and perhaps the most important agent of education and, indeed, it has a major influence on all aspects of the child's development.

Standards of acceptable and unacceptable codes of behavior are first learned within the family. The development of these values is of fundamental importance for the formation of adult character. The child perceives and appraises them in the most demanding situations and in direct face-to-face relationships with people who matter supremely. Any breakdown, for whatever reason, can affect the child's personality development in a damaging way and result in alienation from the family and society at large. On the other hand, a warm, mutually loving relationship between parent and child will tend to encourage the child to adopt the parents' norms and values, particularly if there is effective communication and a strong feeling of identification within the family.

Parental Reaction to a Handicapped Child

During pregnancy, parents experience many emotions. They are often anxious as to whether their child will be "normal." Nevertheless, they consider and plan for the roles they will adopt as the parents of a normal child.

When a child who is obviously not normal because of physical disability is born, the initial responses are those of anxiety and depression. The expected child, in some senses, is lost. They are now the parents of a child with a "defect," and feelings of guilt, anger, helplessness, disbelief, embarrassment, and shame are not uncommon. Natural feelings of pride are difficult to express. The parents, and often the whole family, will require help during this period, and successful progress will depend on acceptance of the child. After the first emotional shock, the question of the meaning of the handicap for parents and child becomes of crucial importance. Indeed, the parents will have little or no knowledge of its full implications. Later other problems will arise, and the extra work involved may leave parents physically and mentally fatigued. Overinvolvement of one of the parents with the child may also be the cause of feelings of rejection, damaging relationships between husband and wife or between parents and other children.

The situation following the birth of a deaf child is somewhat different from that of the child whose handicap is obvious at birth.

Because deafness is not usually detected at birth, the parents believe they have a "normal" child. Later, when deafness is finally diagnosed, many parents experience relief because someone has eventually put a name to their child's problem. Indeed, most parents suspect deafness long before it is "officially" confirmed, and insensitivity to their feelings often results in late diagnosis of hearing loss. Haas and Crowley (1982) found that in 80% of cases, deafness was first suspected by parents, relatives, and friends; only in 7% of cases was a doctor the first to detect it. However, diagnosis brings other problems. The parents are now the parents of a handicapped child, and they experience the feelings and emotions of parents of other handicapped children. At the same time they have to cope with the suddenly changed image of their child and with atavistic fears about deafness. The reactions, life cycle changes, attitudes, and values resulting from this diagnosis are described concisely and clearly by Robert Harris (1982), and a moving personal account is given by George Harris (1983):

> I felt such an intense isolation. I thought that no one, not even Rainelle, [his wife] could help. Doctors, audiologists, teachers, friends, and even my wife could not be trusted to understand. The burden, the responsibility was mine, and I was resentful. Ever so gradually, the process of sharing my feelings with others began to help me feel less alone.... It was irrational, I know, but I even resented Rainelle for the stress I felt during the encounter with the school district in Kansas City. I was angry because Rainelle couldn't accept the fact that schools were going to be imperfect. With work, school, and Jennifer, I felt drained, parched like a reservoir during a drought. I felt my soul becoming hardened and cracked like sunbaked mud. (pp. 127-128)

Counseling for Parents

Much of so-called counseling of the parents during the period when they are "grieving" the loss of their normal baby consists of giving advice, and such advice frequently, indeed often exclusively, focuses on directive advice to use oral methods of communicating with deaf children (see Denmark et al., 1979). As Luterman (1984) emphasizes, the most important aspect of counseling at this stage is to focus on the parents' affective feelings. If these are not resolved, most of the advice, good or bad, will probably be ignored or even forgotten. Unfortunately, the literature of deafness refers loosely to counseling and guidance as if they were synonymous. They are not, and it is important to distinguish them from each other, and from the advisory functions that are part of the responsibility of all professionals. The distinction is again made clearly by Denmark (see

Denmark et al., 1979, p. 57):

> *Counseling.* Counseling is a process whereby the person counseled is helped, gradually, to understand what the problem (in this case, the presence of a deaf child) means—for the child himself, for the family, and for others. It is simultaneously the art and skill of listening to people, and allowing them to express themselves in order that they might see their problems more clearly. In this area, workers who practice counseling must have a thorough knowledge of human growth and behavior as well as of the dynamics of interpersonal interaction and family dynamics.
>
> *Guidance.* Guidance differs from counseling in that the person receiving the guidance is given a number of options and through discussion comes to decide on certain modes of action. It also requires a knowledge of both statutary and voluntary helping services. Counseling and guidance are, in practice, inseparable, for in the course of counseling questions arise which require discussion. Counseling and guidance should be undertaken by professionals trained in counseling, but also with experience of all aspects of the handicap—including the psychosocial implications.
>
> *Advice.* Guidance is also confused with the giving of advice which is a more directive form of help. The giving of advice does not proffer a choice of options—indeed, in the field of deafness it is often more than directive, it is dogmatic. (p. 57)

It will be noticed that the view of counseling expressed in the definition just given focuses on the development of resources within the self. It is educational and developmental rather than psychotherapeutic, and develops the inner resources of the individual, parents, or family. It does not treat them as social casualties in need of therapy. Cumming (1982a) takes this analysis further. She explores the behaviors and feelings with which parents have to deal, and an analysis based on her conclusions is reproduced here:

	BEHAVIOR	ASSOCIATED FEELINGS	
	PROTEST (weeping, hostility, denial, somatic symptoms)	pain, anger, confusion, anxiety	
INPUT Loss reactions	DESPAIR (searching, restlessness, disorganization)	grief, depression, anguish	OUTPUT Acceptance
	DETACHMENT (automatic behavior, withdrawal)	apathy, isolation, resignation	

That parents need help in dealing with these feelings is extensively documented. Cumming reports the surveys of Fellendorf and Harrow (1970), Greenberg (1980), and Williams and Darbyshire (1982). To these we can add those of Denmark et al. (1979) and Freeman,

Malkin, and Hastings (1975). Denmark et al. (p. 76) concluded: "One of the most significant findings of this study has been the lack of psychological and social work support received by the families." The reason for this situation was rather tragic, particularly when it is realized that these families had been in contact with health, educational, and social services for many years. When they were asked why they did not receive help, "the most frequent response was that they had never realized that such support was available or they had never been approached. Very few parents felt that such help was not necessary, and clearly in the light of the problems described, it would almost certainly have been beneficial."

As we noted earlier, and as Cumming (1982), echoing Luterman (1979), points out, parent counseling in the field of deafness has, unfortunately, frequently become synonymous with *parent manipulation*. The term is a strong one, but it is justifiable, and the main offenders have been the proponents of the oral method. But they are not the only ones, and Cumming discusses an article by Dee (1981) as an example of counseling directed toward giving parents arguments supporting total communication. She rightly suggests that exclusively supporting total communication as "the method" is as undesirable as exclusively supporting oral communication. Indeed, a contrast can be made between the presentation of Freeman, Carbin, and Boese (1981) and that of Nolan and Tucker (1981) in a book called *The Hearing Impaired Child and His Family*. Despite advocating parental choice, Nolan and Tucker managed to write a 238-page text about the counseling of parents of deaf children that never once refers to sign language. Although supporting the use of total communication, Freeman, Boese, and Carbin, in contrast, make it clear that final choices of method have to to be made within the family setting and must take into account all relevant factors.

A Structure for Mental Health Problems

A recent study by Rodda, Denmark, and Grove (1981) may supply useful ways of providing a structure for the problem of the interaction of language and mental health problems in a deaf population. The study factor analyzed data on 93 hearing-impaired adolescents living in various communities in the North of England. It does not apply pre-existing theories concerning the causes of maladjustment in deaf students or adults; rather, it presents descriptive profiles of such maladjustment. The respondents and the data base are those used in the study by Denmark and Rodda and their colleagues, which has been referred to a number of times already (Denmark et al., 1979). The respondents came from a strongly oral background.

The data used in the study were subjected to factor analysis, a technique for identifying which clusters of variables intercorrelate with each other to form a single psychological dimension. The variables, identified by abbreviated names, comprised:

1. *Analogies*:   The analogies subtest of the Snijders-Oomen Test of Nonverbal Intelligence (Snijders& Snijders-Oomen, 1970). The mean score of the respondents on this measure (8.53) was within the normal range.

2. *Number*:   The Four Rules Test of Numerical Ability, devised by Montgomery (1967) for use with deaf students to assess their understanding of basic arithmetical functions.

3. *Maze*:   The Gibson Spiral Maze Test (Gibson, 1965): An objective measure of "impulsivity," which is reputed to be characteristic of deaf students.

4. *Comprehension* and

5. *Vocabulary*:   The Comprehension and Vocabulary subtests of the Gates-McGinitie Reading Test (Saville & Blinkhorn, 1973), Forms A and C combined. Using age-equivalent norms, the respondents had mean scores of 8.6 years for Comprehension and 9.4 years for Vocabulary.

6. *Communication*:   A measure of receptive communication skill provided by the Whittingham Test of Communication (WTC), a pictorial multiple-choice test comprising two equivalent forms, each of 24 items. Respondents were tested using both forms, one with a parent, the other with a social worker for the deaf. The aim was to compare the relative level of communication between parents and their deaf adolescents and skilled total communicators and the same adolescents. The mean scores under the two conditions were: Parents—16.55, Social Workers—18.13, a significant difference ($p<0.001$), and the correlation between the two sets of scores was 0.54 ($p<0.001$). For the factor analysis both were combined to create an overall measure of communicative ability.

7. *Social Class*:   The social class of the family, as defined by the United Kingdom Registrar-General's classification (Office of Population Census and Surveys, 1970).

8. *Family Size*:   Number of children in the family.

9. *Family Position*:   Ordinal position of the respondent within the

family.

10. *Diagnosis Time*:   Time elapsed between the parental observation
of the onset of deafness and formal diagnosis, classified arbitrarily as short (<6 months), medium (6 months, 12 months, or 18
months), or long (>2 years).

11. *Oral Skill*:   The parental rating of the respondent's speech and
lipreading ability on a 5-point scale, low ratings indicating
superior skill.

12. *Attends Club*:   Frequency with which the respondent attended a
Club or Institute for the Deaf (3-point scale).

13. *Number of Jobs*:   The number of jobs held by the respondent
after leaving school.

14. *Method of Communication used by the respondent at school.*

15. *Method of Communication used by the respondent with friends.*

16. *Method of Communication now preferred by the respondent*:
Variables 14, 15, and 16 are each classified as Oral or Combined.

17. *Sex*:   Sex of the respondent.

18. *Attitude to Sign Language*:   The parents' attitude toward the use
of sign language, classified positive or negative.

19. *Friends*:   A rating of the tendency for the respondents to have
deaf or hearing friends (5-point scale).

20. *Day or Residential School*:   Whether the respondent attended a
day or a residential school.

21. *Deaf Siblings*:   Whether or not the respondent had deaf siblings.

22. *Frustration.*

23. *Egocentricity.*

24. *Unsociability*, and

25. *Impatience*:   Four subscales of the Behaviour Rating Scale
(BRS), a 20-item instrument devised for the study (Denmark et
al., 1979). The BRS is designed to provide a quickly administered
measure of maladjustment in deaf students, as manifested in
parental assessments of responses to frustration, egocentricity,
unsociable tendencies, and impatience. Mean subscale scores range
from 1 to 5; *the impatience scale contains only one item.* High
scores are indicative of greater behavioral disorder.

26. *Hearing Scale*:   A rating of functional hearing assessed by the Schein Hearing Scale (Schein, Gentille, & Hasse, 1970), or prorated to this scale using putative audiometric equivalents.[1]

Table 7.2 shows the overall data from the factor analysis. The cutoff point of 0.2 for the factor loadings is arbitrary and somewhat lower than usual (0.4), but it gives rise to meaningful interpretation of the data and is justified on these grounds, as well as by the fact that the study is empirically descriptive rather than experimental in nature (see Hicks & Spurgeon, 1982, for a good description of the use of factor analysis in this way).

Factor 1: Aptitude and Achievement

The first factor accounted for one third of the variance, and was characterized by heavy loadings on the tests for Analogies, Number, Maze Completion, Vocabulary, Comprehension, Communication, and on Social Class and Family Size. It is clear that the loadings on the psychometric tests reflect a factor of general cognitive ability and also, perhaps, the concepts and methods of construction common to the rationale of all psychological tests. The loadings on social class and size of family are congruent with results obtained by studies employing hearing subjects (see, for example, Wedge & Prosser, 1973). The deaf child of a large family of lower socioeconomic status is likely to be deprived of the kind of intense intellectual stimulation that his or her condition demands, and the effect may be magnified by the tendency of conventional tests of aptitude to discriminate against such children. The pattern of the lower loadings suggests that girls are superior to boys (a finding in line with the observed differences in terms of verbal fluency, Norden, 1975); that greater oral ability is associated with general aptitude; and that a higher level of measured performance is correlated with greater ability to cope with frustration.

Of special theoretical interest is the high loading on this factor associated with receptive communication skill, a finding that supports the work of Montgomery (1968) and White and Stevenson (1975). Figure 7.1 presents the mean scores on Analogies, Vocabulary, Comprehension, and Oral Skill as a function of communicative

---

[1]Prior to analysis we considered this metric superior to the Better Ear Average audiometric loss, as recent audiograms were not available for the majority of respondents. The scale provides an estimate of functional hearing, taking into account the beneficial effects of wearing hearing aids. In fact, some of the evidence suggested that audiometric data are probably more reliable, at least in the context of hearing loss in adolescents.

TABLE 7.2

Major Loadings Generated by Factor Analysis Using Alpha
Factoring Techniques and Varimax Rotation

FACTOR:	1.	2.	3.	4.	5.	6.
VARIABLE*						
Analogies	0.44	−0.22	−0.22	0.45		
Number	0.61		−0.25		−0.23	
Maze	−0.42			0.25		
Vocabulary	0.83			−0.27		
Comprehension	0.75		−0.32	−0.22	−0.20	
Communication	0.57	−0.31				
Social Class	−0.48					
Family Size	−0.44					0.27
Family Position						0.65
Diagnosis Time		−0.29				−0.31
Oral Skill	−0.28		−0.25	0.23	0.38	
Attends Club			0.21			
Number of Jobs			1.00			
M.C.—School					0.31	0.32
M.C.—Friends					0.33	
M.C.—Preferred				0.61	0.34	
Sex	0.28	0.36		−0.37	0.22	−0.27
Attitude to S.L.				−0.37		
Friends				−0.38		
Day-Residential				0.22	0.36	
Deaf Siblings			0.22			−0.40
Frustration	−0.20	0.68				
Egocentricity		0.75				
Unsociability		0.70				
Impatience		0.60				
Hearing Scale					−0.59	
% OF VARIANCE:	32.5	19.0	17.0	13.2	8.9	8.4

*Loadings of 0.20 and above are shown. M.C. is Method of Communication (oral or total) and S.L. is Sign Language.

competence (with associated correlations and significance levels). As might be expected, the strongest linear relationship is with Comprehension; the association with Oral Skill is not so powerful. The latter result is slightly surprising, considering that the majority of the respondents used and relied on lipreading, and that the part of the Communication score obtained through the parent reflected dominantly oral modes of communication. The somewhat lower correlations with Vocabulary and Analogies imply that communication cannot readily be reduced to simple verbal and intellectual components, and in this regard it is interesting to note that the relationship between Comprehension and Vocabulary is markedly curvilinear. The shape of the curve suggests that subjects scoring high on the Vocabulary scale achieve very rapid gains in comprehension, and there are hints of a similar pattern for communication (Fig. 7.1c). Figure 7.1e shows Communication scores as a function of family size. Being a member of a large family slightly but significantly degrades the communicative competence of the deaf child.

Factor 2: Behavior

Early hearing impairment affects not only sensory and linguistic processes but also the development of self-concept and general emotional development. While the deaf child does possess other sensory systems that can physically compensate for the loss of auditory stimuli, the extent to which it is possible to reallocate cognitive capacity to another sensory system remains an open question (see chapter 5). In later years the handicap is also intensified by failure to acquire societal language, and apart from the obvious cognitive consequences of this secondary form of impairment, the deaf child is also deprived of the opportunity of verbally mediating social and interpersonal behavior. This phenomenon makes the development of an adequate self-image even harder. It is not surprising, therefore, that deaf persons are reported as having negative self-images, that deaf children are more likely to have temper tantrums, or that older adolescents and adults are more likely to respond aggressively in socially stressful situations.

The importance of the mechanisms identified in the previous paragraph are confirmed by the emergence of the second factor. It loads heavily on the four highly intercorrelated subscales of the Behavior Rating Scale (BRS), probably establishing that the maladjustment pattern constitutes a common syndrome. Further confirmation is found in the fact that this factor is not highly loaded on any other variables, and that only one BRS variable receives even a minimal loading on any other factor (Frustration in Factor 1). As we see

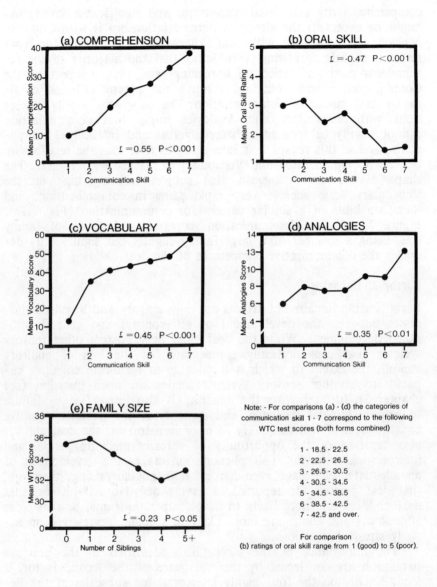

FIG. 7.1.   Correlates of communication skill.

from Table 7.2, the subscale that most characterizes the global BRS syndrome is Egocentricity: High scorers on this scale are described by their parents as "untruthful," "inconsiderate of others' feelings," "unwilling to share," "unhelpful," and "unreceptive to advice." It seems that social isolation, resulting from the use of an inappropriate method of communication, is probably the major causative factor in the development of this syndrome.

If we examine the pattern of the lower loadings, some puzzling effects are revealed. Communication, which we consider to be of paramount importance, gains only a small loading, and Oral Skill carries no significant loading, on the Behavior factor. This result might have occurred for two reasons. Firstly, by combining scores from the two communication conditions, we have introduced two separate components—a measure of receptive skill under optimum conditions (messages transmitted largely by total communication methods) and a measure reflecting the ability of the subjects to communicate with their parents. The respondents used in the factor analysis were not exposed to total communication early in life; therefore, it is possible that only oral communication with parents predicts degree of adjustment when the respondents are older. It may also be possible that the ability of the subjects to communicate with their parents is a better predictor of adjustment than is their ability to communicate under more favorable conditions using total communication techniques. If so, this result would not be surprising in the light of the earlier discussion in this chapter of the role of the family in providing empathy and support for the deaf child.

The most paradoxical result is reflected in the loading on the time taken to diagnose the impairment. Contrary to expectation, this does not seem to point to a permanently disabling effect of a lengthy period of parental distress and uncertainty. We find instead that children for whom diagnosis was delayed tend to be the better adjusted. Table 7.3 shows that of the three variables involved—age of onset, age at diagnosis, and time taken for diagnosis—the third is the best predictor of later poor adjustment. An analysis of variance of the logarithmically transformed BRS scores based on a 2 x 2 data classification (Early vs. Late diagnosis, and Short vs. Long delay of diagnosis) confirms that the effect of delay is highly significant: $F(1,88) = 7.34$, $p < 0.01$. The mean BRS score for the Short delay respondents is 50.13; the mean score of the Long delay group is 41.71. Age at diagnosis has no significant effect: $F(1,88) = 1.40$, n.s. There is no interaction between the two variables: $F(1,88) = 0.004$, n.s.

We can suggest two possible explanations for these surprising data. One is that more severely impaired children tend to be both more poorly adjusted and to be diagnosed more promptly. However,

TABLE 7.3

Degree of Adjustment as a Function of Age of Onset of Deafness,
Age of Diagnosis, and Time for Diagnosis

BRS Score	Age of onset		Age at diagnosis		Time for diagnosis		Total N
	under 14 mo	over 14 mo	under 22 mo	over 22 mo	under 6 mo	over 6 mo	
Over 44	25	18	30	13	29	14	43
44 and under	24	25	21	28	17	32	49
% poorly adjusted[a]	51	42	59	32	63	30	
X^2 (1)	0.448		5.668		8.558		
P level	n.s.		0.025		0.005		

[a] "poor adjustment" defined as a BRS score over 44.

a contingency analysis using audiometric measures and adjusted
hearing scale data fails to support this hypothesis ($X^2[1]=0.52$, n.s.).
Shocking though it may seem, a second possible explanation is that
deaf children are, at least in this context, negatively affected by
specialist intervention. Interview data describing the lack of support
and the lack of good counseling given to parents by official agencies,
at the time of diagnosis and subsequently, are not inconsistent with
this explanation. Recent evidence concerning the spontaneous development of manual communication between the deaf baby and his or
her parents suggests a possible causative mechanism: The suppression
of such communication in the interests of developing oral communication skills might permanently retard the child's socialization
(Goldin-Meadow & Feldman, 1977).

We regard these puzzling and disturbing findings as indicative of
some of the damage done by a rigid adherence to oral communication in early childhood and later. We can contrast these findings with
a major study of the deaf child in the hearing family using total
communication (Greenberg, 1980). Greenberg looked at 28 families
with deaf children (aged 3.5 to 5.5 years) and hearing parents—14

who used total communication and 14 who used oral communication. Adequate controls were introduced into the selection of the sample. The Alpern-Boll Developmental Profile (Alpern & Boll, 1972), the Hereford Parent Attitude Survey (Hereford, 1963), the Problem Areas Checklist (Tavormina, Boll, Dunn, Luscomb, & Taylor, 1975), and a nationally developed interview schedule were used to compare the two groups (oral and total communicators). Each group was subdivided into low-competence and high-competence children. The families had all received early intervention and parent counseling, so this study presents an effective test of the efficacy of counseling when it focuses on providing realistic options for the parents and on developing coping skills within the family setting.

Overall, developmental delays were recorded by Greenberg only in the area of communication, and the development of social skills seemed to be facilitated by the use of total communication. Indeed, interesting data showed that the higher level oral communicators were not as socially mature as those with less well developed oral skills—again, like our data, suggesting that a drive for oral proficiency is only achieved at some cost in other areas. The same mothers were also focused on the longer term goal of mainstreaming and "normalizing" their child, and Greenberg comments that they "appeared to be more interested in their child's possible future achievements than in their considerable present accomplishments" (p. 1069). The findings of both studies neatly confirm those of Meadow and Trybus (1979) who concluded from a review of the existing literature that the social development of the deaf child was facilitated by: (a) a lack of parental overprotectiveness, (b) the development of realistic expectations for the child; and (c) the development of effective parent-child communication.

Factor 3: Job Stability

The primary measure of occupational performance included in the analysis was job stability—the number of jobs held after leaving school. The most surprising finding concerning this variable is its "purity." The number of jobs is associated with no other factor, and other loadings on this factor were all small. There was a slight association with lower intelligence and verbal skills, poor numerical ability, absence of deaf siblings, and membership of deaf clubs—all of which would reasonably affect stability of employment. More puzzling was the low loading on oral skill (better oral ability is only slightly correlated with job stability), but this may reflect disillusionment or lack of opportunities when the oral student moves into competitive situations after leaving school.

Factor 4: Educational Background and Method of Communication

The fourth factor comprises a cluster of variables which seems to associate with the educational history of the respondents, their preferred method of communication, and their membership in the deaf subculture. The heaviest loading is on the presently preferred method of communication (a positive weighting implies a preference for total communication methods) but this, of course, is strongly influenced by the family and the attitudes of staff at the schools previously attended by the respondents. The interrelationships between oral ability, placement, parental attitude, and cognitive ability are exceedingly complex, and the picture becomes increasingly confused when we look more closely at the pattern of preferences for different methods of communication. Of 76 subjects for whom complete data are available, a majority (51) claim a current preference for oral methods. Only 25 admit a preference for total communication methods. However, observation by testers of the method of communication employed by the respondents during test administration indicates that a further 25 respondents who said they would prefer to use oral techniques in fact used total communication.

Parents' reports of their children's preferred methods of communication were frequently inconsistent with both the respondents' stated preferences and actual usage. Parental attitude to the use of signing ranged from strongly favorable to strongly unfavorable, but it should be noted that only 9 respondents had parents who learned any specific signs, and in only 2 cases did the parents learn sign language in the critical preschool period.

It seems that deaf children in the United Kingdom, at least prior to 1975, internalized the prevailing view of teachers, family, and society at large. They came to believe in the desirability of oral communication techniques and, more significantly, the undesirability of total communication. In conversation, adult deaf people confirm this finding. They frequently refer with sadness, anger, or both sadness and anger to the shame they felt in school about their language (sign language), their joy in subsequently discovering its beauty, and to their difficulty in using English because at school they were constantly corrected but provided with no real understanding of why their own English was wrong.

This unhappy and confused situation has obvious effects on overall psychological development and the formation of adequate self-esteem. The play "Sign Me Alice" (Eastman, 1974) makes the point in a very dramatic way. The play is about a hypothetical "Sign English" (called USE). We noted in chapter 2 that it bears a remarkable similarity to Shaw's "Pygmalion," but it is a commentary on the deaf student's experience. Alice, like Eliza, begins by being ashamed of her language and therefore, by definition, her culture, and herself. Toward the end of the play the following dialogue takes place:

DR. ZENO: Damn. That is where you were.

ALICE: Wait. Let me explain. We talked about Sign. I began see difference between Sign and English. I think I can do both. In my heart, Sign real mine. Use English to others. Yes, I sign English to you. But I feel more comfortable with my Sign. Nothing can change me. I have-been attended to your lectures, read your notes, books, articles in magazines, watched your TV, I must admit I learned a lot. But there is one thing that bothers me. I beg you tell truth.

DR. ZENO: What truth? I have not told lies.

ALICE: I did-not say lies. I don't-know what exact but there something missing from your philosophy on U.S.E. You must realize that U.S.E. has nothing to do with Sign. U.S.E. itself that English. Sign is another language. Your idea of having Sign Language classes for deaf or hearing. I can't call that Sign. That is English class. Where is the real Sign class? Tell me.

Later she says, "*U.S.E. has nothing to do with being a lady. A lady can use Sign. You will have to go ahead without me.*" Perhaps the inconsistency of attitudes that faced Alice is unavoidable. If so, its harmful effects on deaf children and/or adolescents should be recognized.

After Preferred Method of Communication, the strongest loading of the factor concerned with educational background and method of communication is on Analogies. Subjects with higher nonverbal intelligence tend to use nonoral methods of communication (mean Analogies score for subjects preferring oral is 8.35; for subjects using manual methods, 9.36). Lower loadings show that the use of manual methods of communication also associates with positive parental attitudes to sign language, attendance at a residential school for the deaf, poorer verbal and oral skills, and a larger number of deaf friends. We cannot deduce cause and effect from this pattern, and the underlying relationships are probably interactive. Possibly the deaf child of relatively higher intelligence, who fails to make progress under oral instruction, may opt for the use of sign language and thus tend to associate more with other deaf students. Success in using manual methods may also result in more positive parental attitudes, which in turn reinforce and encourage the deaf child. The implication is clear. It is not only the child of lower innate ability who is cognitively and socially handicapped by a failure to communicate using sign language. There are significant numbers of higher functioning deaf students who have difficulties in accommodating to schools using only oral methods of instruction. Expressing it another way, total communication systems are not only suitable for low achieving deaf students (the so-called "oral failures"), they are of equal value to deaf students whose only difficulty is their inability to develop good speech and lipreading skills.

Finally, it is important to note that the negative loadings of this factor on Vocabulary and Comprehension cannot be taken to support the notion of a connection between use of sign language in early life and inferior performance in language. The early experience of almost all the respondents was exclusively oral, and there are biases associated with the subsequent selection of those students using total communication. The child who makes adequate progress in speech and lipreading (as defined within the oral school) is discouraged from learning sign language. Those who subsequently take up manual methods of communication are, therefore, likely to have a functionally lower level of language, and comparisons between the two groups are confounded. This point is often missed in studies citing correlations between the use of sign language and poor English scores on standardized tests. The extent to which such a bias dominates the test scores of deaf children may be gauged by citing Sir Alexander Ewing. We referred earlier (p. 74) to the evidence he gave to the Lewis Committee on the Education of Deaf Children in Great Britain and his statement that he "would regard combined methods [total communication] as a last resort for children failing to achieve *any score* in language" (Lewis, 1968, paragraph 181, italics added). Despite this, change to a total communication regime at ages as late as 13 years has been shown to lead to significant improvements in verbal fluency and abstraction (O'Sullivan, 1977), even though it is likely that the measures of verbal ability employed by O'Sullivan failed to tap higher level conceptual processes involved in linguistic and advanced cognitive development.

Factor 5: Hearing Status

This factor is characterized by a moderately heavy loading on the Hearing Scale, and it accounts for only 8.9% of the variance. It may seem somewhat strange that an apparently fundamental feature of deafness—degree of impairment—should have such slight predictive value. There are several reasons why this should be so. First, as is the case with the fourth factor, the key variable is restricted in range because of the stringent criteria adopted for the selection of respondents. According to audiometric definitions, the majority of our subjects are profoundly or severely deaf, and so possess relatively little useful residual hearing. Once the critical point has been passed—and it is probably largely a matter of individual differences exactly what this point is in terms of decibels of hearing loss—the student is functionally deaf and unable to make effective use of amplified acoustic input.

A second reason for the low predictive power of degree of hearing loss in these students is that, as will hopefully now be apparent, the idea of a simple and direct relationship between hearing, language, and communication is an oversimplification. The primary features of hearing impairment, as it relates to lack of auditory experience, are manifested in their effect on the relatively "low-level" cognitive processing of auditory input and short-term memory. The higher level processes of conceptualization and long-term coding in memory remain unimpaired (see chapter 4), and such systems can still be used effectively provided that efficient use is made of the visual modality. The best way of making use of visual input is, of course, a matter for debate, but as we have already indicated, speech and lipreading make extraordinary demands on the perceptual processing capacities of the deaf student. Therefore, for many deaf students, they are not the best way of exploiting vision as a method of communication.

In Table 7.4 we present correlations reflecting the relative predictive value of three alternative measures of hearing impairment. The audiometric BEA measure is related to Oral Skill and slightly associated with the BRS measure of adjustment. The "no aid" Hearing Scale metric is equally highly correlated with Oral Skill, and also, interestingly enough, slightly related to Communication. The functional Hearing Scale score, which assesses hearing ability with the use of hearing aids, is clearly the poorest predictor, and this finding is quite puzzling, unless: (a) in respect of these variables, deafness exercises a permanent effect at a very early age, before hearing aids are employed; or (b) parental judgments about the effectiveness of hearing aids are, again, colored by expectation rather than evidence. It may be noted that of 37 subjects for whom data are available for both aided and unaided scale scores, 24 were said to have reported a significant improvement in functional hearing when wearing their aid, 12 reported no improvement, and one reported a reduction.

It is uniformly agreed that hearing loss inhibits speech development. The effect of this factor is to generate a secondary cluster of variables that have associations with difficulty in developing speech skills. One facet of this problem seems to be the growing use of manual communication at school, with friends, and the adolescent's general preference for using this method. The need to communicate is a basic human attribute, and if speech skills are limited, other

TABLE 7.4

Correlations Between Oral Skill, Communication Skill, Adjustment,
and Alternative Measures of Hearing Loss

VARIABLE	BEA	HS-F	HS-NA
BEA	---	-0.26*	-0.51***
Oral Skill	0.31**	-0.22	-0.31**
Communication	-0.13	0.06	0.29*
BRS Total Score	0.27*	0.16	-0.21

(BEA is Better Ear average hearing loss in dB; HS-F is the functional hearing scale score; HS-NA is the hearing scale score in the "no aid" condition.)

$*p<0.05$

$**p<0.01$

$***p<0.001$

modalities will be used instead. Even orally trained teachers accept that, left to their own devices, profoundly deaf children will communicate using sign language. Unfortunately, if they are not allowed to communicate in sign language early in life, the devastating effects of deafness on oral language development will be compounded by problems of behavioral maladjustment and the development of poor self-esteem.

Factor 6: Family

The final factor identifies a cluster of variables that characterize the subject's family. The major variable is ordinal position, but the factor is also connected with the size of the family and with the presence of deaf siblings. It seems that later born deaf children in large families are more likely to have deaf brothers and sisters. They also are more likely to attend schools that use manual communication. The polarity of loadings on the other constituents of the factor also imply that the deaf child occupying an early ordinal position in the family will experience a longer delay of diagnosis than the later born child. Presumably this finding arises because younger and less experienced parents, in the first instance, find it more difficult to take an active role in locating and obtaining services. They may also be less conscious of slower rates of development or profiles of development that differ from those of the hearing child. Finally, as a result of their inexperience, they are more likely to let matters rest, at least for a while, when told that their child will "grow out of it" or that they are worrying needlessly. Taking into account the small but significant relationship between communication skill and family size (Fig. 7.1e) and the quite strong link between delay of diagnosis and behavioral adjustment, the implication seems to be that if you are going to be born deaf, it is better to be a first- or second-born child in a small family.

A Synopsis

Although we have focused in this section on our own research, we feel we have done so with good reason. Other studies have covered similar ground, but as far as we are aware, it is the only study that has used factor analysis or some similar technique to tease out some kind of structure for the interactive constellation of variables associated with the family, education, language, and cognition that affect the mental health of deaf students in their later adolescent and young adult years. Furthermore, some of the findings are, to our knowledge, original.

The first factor clearly represents general cognitive skill. In view of the moderate loading on analogies, we would hesitate to identify it as "intelligence," whether verbal or nonverbal. The highest loading is on vocabulary, which one might be tempted to take as a measure of the number of concepts available to the child, student, or adult and, hence, as a reflection of their cognitive richness. Communication, as assessed by the Whittingham Test of Communication, is clearly most strongly identified with this factor.

The independence of the second factor, behavior, lends support to the notion of the concept of surdophrenia, which we feel is a useful and viable concept provided it is not misinterpreted in terms of a direct relationship between deafness and schizophrenia (Basilier, 1964). Deaf individuals exhibiting surdophrenia have immature ego development and are unable to gain adequate feedback into the social effects of their behavior. Their emotional immaturity also makes it difficult for them to form effective social relationships. Two unexpected features of the factor are its relationship with delay of diagnosis and the relatively small association with communication. We have suggested some reasons why the measure employed to assess receptive skill fails to correlate substantially with the BRS scores; another possibility is that maladjustment is likely to be more highly associated with expressive communication problems. Deaf persons are usually more efficient at oral reception than expression, and it is possible that feelings of isolation and frustration stem primarily from failure to communicate one's own ideas to others. Further research is required to investigate this issue and also to determine the type of information that the deaf person can process most easily. The ability to deal with abstract or social information might be a more critical determinant of adjustment than, say, the ability to transmit factual or concrete messages.

The finding that the remaining factors of job stability, educational background, hearing status, and family are all essentially independent emphasizes the invalidity of the claim that a single educational methodology can by itself resolve the problems of the deaf child. There is certainly no support here for the assumption that improvement of oral skills by themselves can, by whatever technique, lead to corresponding gains in cognition, language, or behavior. On the other hand, it should be restated that the sample in this study is limited with regard to range of educational experience. The work of Moores (1976), Brasel and Quigley (1975), and others indicate that more significant gains in language, achievement, and adjustment may be made under total communication regimes, and we cannot—and must not—rule out the possibility that the more sophisticated use of sign language from a very early age might further improve the performance of deaf students. Certainly all the evidence to date indicates that the early use of manual communication facilitates not only the development of an internalized language base, but also social skills and general social and emotional stability.

Language, Personality, and Behavior

The interaction between language, personality, and behavior is still widely misunderstood in the psychology of deafness, a misunderstanding that reflects our current lack of an adequate conceptual basis for structuring our thinking about how deaf people function. Most deaf people are socially competent, but by being so they strike at the sociocultural core of a hearing self-identity—hearing means speech, speech means language, language means intelligence, intelligence means humanness (see chapter 2 for a fuller discussion of this problem and its historical context). The fallacy is obvious; speech does not mean language. However, we perhaps need to state the obvious when the literature on deafness leads one sometimes to reach nonsensical conclusions such as: Of all deaf people, only Danish deaf people exhibit the psychiatric illness of paranoia. Strange though it may seem, 1 in 5 of Danish admissions of deaf people to psychiatric care are for paranoia whereas, in a recent study, this diagnosis never occurred in the United States or the United Kingdom (Remvig, 1973). In contrast, deaf people in the United Kingdom and the United States are frequently schizophrenic (1 in 2 admissions), but being a Dane (and deaf) largely protects you from this disorder (1 in 10 admissions). Only in the "hodge podge" class of "behavioral disorders" do the three countries agree—interesting because the primary source of data for this particular diagnosis are teachers, social workers, psychologists, parents, and others. Do the data mean that the specialized knowledge of psychiatrists leads to professional inconsistencies and that the ignorance of teachers is bliss?

Another example of the problem making psychiatric and other diagnoses in clients suffering from deafness and other developmental disorders is cited by Stokoe and Battison (1981). They refer to a study quoted by Tinbergen (1974) in his Nobel Prize lecture. When 445 young children were diagnosed twice, the agreement on eight possible diagnostic categories was random.

> The first opinion held 16 of the children to be psychotic, the second so diagnosed 10 children, but not 1 child was called psychotic by two doctors. Even closer to our topic, 12 children were diagnosed as deaf in their first examination, 13 children in the second; but these were 25 *different* children. Not one child in the whole 445 was diagnosed as deaf by two specialists. (Stokoe & Battison, 1981, p. 180)

Not unreasonably, Stokoe concludes, "it seems reasonable to suppose that a new way of looking at deafness, language and mental health could do no harm" (p. 180).

Language has emotional components in its own right that are referred to as its *orectic* aspects. The origin of these aspects of language is unclear, but in the hearing person they seem to be intimately interconnected with auditory experiences (perhaps even beginning in the fetal stages through exposure to sounds such as the mother's heartbeat). In contrast, language also has a mediating aspect. In the mediating aspect, language becomes a vehicle for thinking and determines how we analyze the world at large. A good example is that the spoken or signed word *mother* is more than a symbol; it is a complex emotional response, in which words and feelings are interrelated with each other. However, the statement, "Your mother is wearing a blue dress" is fairly neutral emotionally and, therefore, in this statement, *mother* is a more cognitively based concept. We react to the second statement intellectually; to the first we react with varying degrees of emotional response. Both are important.

In fact, two more likely reasons for the consistency of teacher based ratings of the behavioral problems referred to earlier are: (a) that disruptive behavior is more observable than some of the more specialized psychodiagnostic categories; and (b) there is some evidence (Leblanc, 1983) that teacher ratings of behavior, reflected in concepts such as self-esteem, are heavily loaded on language assessments. In other words, deaf children with good language skills tend to be *perceived* by their teachers as having fewer personality problems (perhaps because those with poor linguistic abilities naturally exhibit signs of frustration during classroom interactions), despite the evidence of Table 7.2 that communication/cognition and behavioral adjustment constitute independent factors.

The latter finding is not surprising, and Fig. 7.2 illustrates how cognition and language might interact with each other and with emotional development. In this structure, language becomes a key variable in the development of social coping skills and emotional stability. It is very important to remember that when deaf students are linguistically deprived, they miss out on language, not only as a vehicle for thinking, but also in emotional development. They cannot think out problems, and they are also deprived of developmentally important social and emotional experiences.

Figure 7.3 attempts to show that different therapies input into the emotional/cognitive/language system of deaf (and for that matter hearing) people at different points. It is not a complete listing of all therapies, but it shows how, knowingly or unknowingly, the different therapies invoke different mechanisms for producing change. It may clarify some of the confusions about these therapies and show why sometimes they work and sometimes they do not. Nevertheless, therapies can only attempt to correct. Preventative techniques are better, and of particular significance in prevention is the input of parents and teachers using general strategies of child rearing and developing an appropriate educational milieu. In the absence of an appropriate environment, the teacher or counselor may require assistance from a number of other specialists or may have to direct remediation at the behavioral symptoms of underlying social, emotional, linguistic, and cognitive problems. Post hoc remediation of this type is always difficult and often unsuccessful, and because language forms so much of a key for both emotional development and therapy, it seems indefensible to deny the deaf child the right to communicate easily, naturally, and spontaneously with at least some of the significant people in his environment. We cannot teach everybody to use sign language; we can ensure that teachers use it with some reasonable fluency and that we provide opportunities for parents to try to develop fluency.

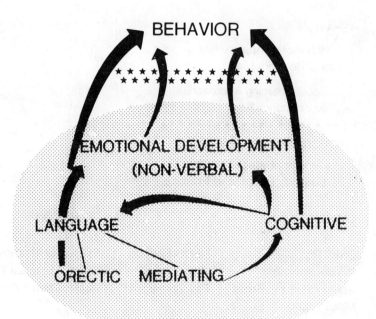

Total Input of Sensory /
Social Experiences

★ ★ ★   Interface Between Internal Self
and External Behavior

Interactive / Causal Relationships

FIG. 7.2.   Behavior and experience.
Source—Instructional Technology Centre, University of Alberta.

BEHAVIOR

Behaviorist Approaches
e.g. Behavior Mod.

Social Learning Approaches
e.g. Bandura

★ ★

EMOTIONAL DEVELOPMENT

General Strategies of Child
Rearing / Educational Practice

LANGUAGE   COGNITION
    ↓   ↓
ORECTIC   MEDIATING   Existential Therapy
Psychodynamic   "Short Term"   Rational Emotive Therapy
Approaches e.g. Freud   Psychotherapy   Reality Therapy*
Milieu Therapy
Encounter Groups
Client Centered Therapy*
Gestalt Therapy*

TOTAL ENVIRONMENT

Family Therapy
"Group Therapy"
Community Development
Approaches

* Also Language-Mediating

FIG. 7.3.   Types of therapy.
Source—Instructional Technology Centre, University of Alberta.

Behavior and Adjustment

Freeman and his colleagues conducted a major study of psychiatric aspects of sensory disorders in the Greater Vancouver area of British Columbia (see, for example, Freeman, 1977). They noted regarding 115 deaf children and adolescents: (a) that they were more likely to have been hospitalized in the first 2 years of life; (b) that the diagnosis of hearing impairment often was seriously delayed; (c) that parental concerns about hearing loss were frequently rejected by physicians; (d) that parent "shock" on hearing of the diagnosis was less frequent than suggested by Schlesinger and Meadow (1972); (e) that deaf students showed a constellation of behaviors that might be loosely described as aggressive/hyperactive; (f) that 1 in 5 of the respondents was rated as having a "persistent psychiatric disorder of moderate or severe degree"; and (g) that cerebral dysfunction was frequently present.

In the survey undertaken by Denmark et al. (1979) in the United Kingdom, the parents of hearing-impaired adolescents were asked as part of an interview to volunteer information about any aspects of their child's behavior that had given them cause for concern and which were, in their opinion, a direct result of his deafness. Table 7.5 shows an extremely high incidence of problems that parents thought were associated with deafness at all periods in their children's lives. There is little overall difference between the prevalence of problems in the profoundly deaf and partially hearing (hard of hearing) respondents. However, hard of hearing children seem to present slightly fewer problems than their profoundly deaf counterparts until they reach school leaving age. In both groups there seems to be a general reduction of problems during the school years, with an increase once school has finished. The data also seem to show that during the school years there appear to have been fewer areas of concern reported by parents when the children were actually in school, than when at home. However, this particular finding most probably reflects the fact that because parents were not confronted with their management, they were simply not aware of many of the problems that arose in school.

As the report by Denmark et al. (1979) shows, descriptive studies of the personality characteristics of deaf adults have identified several areas in which the handicap of deafness has a major influence on the adjustment of the individual concerned. We have previously referred in this chapter and in chapter 2 to the views of Rainer and Altshuler and of Myklebust. Rainer and Altshuler (1967) stated that

TABLE 7.5a

Deafness Associated with Behavior Problems at Home
% Respondents with Problems

Age	Deaf ($N=43$)	Partially Hearing ($N=32$)
Preschool	91%	84%
Primary	72%	63%
Secondary	61%	56%
Post Secondary	70%	72%

TABLE 7.5b

Deafness Associated with Behavior Problems at School
% Respondents with Problems

	Deaf ($N=43$)	Partially Hearing ($N=32$)
Primary School	37%	31%
Secondary School	37%	47%

many deaf persons are egocentric, rigid, impulsive, and lacking in insight and the ability to judge the effect of their behavior on other people. Myklebust (1964) suggested that they are on the whole aloof, disengaged, disassociated, and isolated with respect to other people. Remvig (1973), in a comprehensive review of the deaf person in literature, found these descriptions echoed with considerable frequency: "emotionally immature, authority bound, limited in social sensibility and insight, and impulsive" (p. 301).

Following up on these ideas, Table 7.6 shows the behavior characteristics associated with deafness as described by the parents of the respondents in the Denmark et al. study. For the main part they closely mirror characteristics identified in previous research. Temper and aggression arising from their handicap were referred to by the largest number of parents as characteristic of their children. Many parents also described their children as those who in adolescence were easily led by "bad company," which, on occasion, could result in delinquent activities. The survey also revealed a considerable number of parents who felt their children were withdrawn and, for profoundly deaf students, the number of individuals described in this way noticeably increased as they grew older.

Relationship Between Communication and Behavior

We can focus more closely on these problems by looking at data from the Behaviour Rating Scale devised for use in the survey by Denmark and his colleagues (Denmark et al., 1979; see p. 312). To put these findings into perspective, data from the main items of the scale were compared with results obtained from a United Kingdom study of a nationally representative British sample of 11,086 hearing adolescents, which used a scale of behavioral problems also completed by mothers (Fogelman, 1976). Table 7.7 shows that on the five matched items used in both studies, the sample of profoundly deaf adolescents were consistently reported by their mothers to have a higher incidence of behavior problems than the hearing adolescents. Using these data and drawing on clinical experience, we propose in the next section to explore the nature and types of these problems in more detail.

Classification of Behavior Problems

In 1974, Rodda first published a clinical assessment of the kinds of behavior problems that confronted him in working working with deaf adolescent clients. This classification forms the basis of the following discussion, but we refine and develop it because doing so may throw

TABLE 7.6a
Main Behavioral Anomalies Reported By Parents (Preschool Years)

	% Deaf (N=43)	% Partially Hearing (N=32)
"Frustration"	40	31
Temper	65	63
Aggression	21	25
Eating/Toiletry	33	28
Withdrawal	16	19

TABLE 7.6b
Main Behavioral Anomalies Reported By Parents (Postschool)

	% Deaf (N=43)	% Partially Hearing (N=32)
Withdrawal	23	9
"Bad Company"	16	16
Temper	9	13
Problems at Work	7	9

TABLE 7.7

Comparison of Deaf and Hearing Students on Specified Traits

	% Hearing (N=11,608)	% Deaf (N=43)
Fighting/Quarrelling	2	33
Irritable	11	9
Destroys Property	1	16
Often Lies	1	7
"Solitary"	14	14

some light on the changing patterns of etiology associated with maladjustment in deaf students and adults. The revised classification is shown in Fig. 7.4 (see Rodda, 1985). In the subsequent discussion, the capital letters refer to this figure.

There are three areas where little change has taken place in the last decade. There may be higher prevalence rates of multihandicapped deaf students (A), but even if not, our awareness of these problems has increased. In particular, we now realize that learning disability is commonly associated with certain exogenous causes of deafness. However, the classification of Multihandicapped Deaf People (I) includes not only learning disabilities that probably themselves have a base in language processing (Berry, 1980), but conditions such as apraxia and dispraxia (see van Uden, 1983). The Institutional Syndrome still exists (E), although we certainly are more aware of this problem and the need to prevent it. Finally, despite Cooper's work in the United Kingdom (see pp. 301 to 302), there is still little evidence that deafness of early onset generates depressive reactions (G). Indeed, the data reported in the earlier sections suggest that withdrawal is no more frequent in students with severe early impairments than it is in hearing students. Depressive reactions may, however, be a common reaction to deafness of later onset.

The concepts of Primitive Personality and Inappropriate Impulse Control (C and D) can be refined as a result of clinical observation and reporting over the last decade. As we have already suggested,

A. Delayed or Retarded Physical or Cognitive Impairments

B. Family or Environmentally Based Problems
    i) Family Problems / Poor Child Rearing
    ii) "Chip on the Shoulder" Syndrome
    iii) "Mainstream Failures"
    iv) Reflected Prejudice
    v) Parental Possessiveness
    vi) Second Language Failures

C / D. Primitive Personality / Inappropriate Control
    i) Surdophrenia
    ii) Other Affective Disorders

E. Institutional Syndrome

F. Drug Problems
    Substance Abuse

G. Depressive Reactions

H. Psychosexual Adjustment and Marital Problems

I. Multihandicapped Deaf People

FIG. 7.4.   Classification of behavioral problems of deaf persons.

and provided it is not misunderstood or overused, the concept of surdophrenia (see p. 325) developed by Basilier (1964) is a useful one, and it does describe the characteristics of deaf individuals having these kinds of difficulties. Fortunately, because it results from a poverty of linguistic and social experiences, it is much easier to remediate than schizophrenia (with which it is often confused) and other severe psychiatric disorders. However, deaf people are not immune from what we might paradoxically call normal psychopathological mechanisms. Therefore, in refining this classification it has been divided into Surdophrenia and the Other Affective Disorders, such as the denial of affect that is carried to extremes in sociopathic behavior.

As should be obvious from previous discussion in this chapter, one of the major changes in the last decade has been our greater understanding and awareness of Family or Environmentally Based Problems (B). However, it is important to note the distinctions we referred to between counseling, guidance, and advice. Our understanding of the needs of families has increased greatly in the last 20 years or so and, indeed, this classification has generated a separate category focused specifically on psychosexual adjustment and marital problems. No longer are deaf people regarded as eunuchs, a status we would probably ascribe to them on the basis of the literature prior to 1970. In fact, there has been a generally increased awareness of psychological problems, including an appreciation of the needs of homosexual deaf people. Changes such as these are part of a general trend, and we are beginning to realize that being deaf does not classify an individual into a homogenous subgroup. Rather, it is an additional variable that determines reactions and behavior. Sometimes the reactions and the behavior are specific to deafness. Other times, they are general reactions characteristic of the population at large.

In refining the category of Family/Environmentally Based Problems, it is worth mentioning a number of specific difficulties that have been identified in recent years. One particular problem is deaf people with what we might call a "chip on the shoulder" syndrome. Discrimination against deaf people meant that in the past most deaf people were "have nots." An increasing number of "haves" in the deaf population make it more likely that some deaf people become very resentful of their handicap and use it as a coping mechanism in itself. They feel, "If I was hearing, I wouldn't have any problems." Conversely, greater opportunities for deaf children and students have led to greater parental possessiveness. This is distinctly different from parental overprotection, although the latter can form part of the syndrome. In parental overpossessiveness, the parent becomes overconcerned that teachers, deaf people, and others are taking over their child. They feel a loss of control over their own lives, and blame deaf people or deaf and hearing professionals for their perceived loss of control. That social conditions may have changed or that their children might be growing up are not seen as logical alternatives.

It is also worth mentioning two other educationally based problems. Second language failures always existed, but in the last decade we have begun to recognize and understand the problem (see chapter 5). Such students are highly successful in their use of ASL or another sign language but fail to learn English. As a result they become educational failures, and a cycle of failure begins to repeat itself. Perhaps of even greater significance are Mainstream Failures. These students often emerge in mid- or late-adolescence by presenting major adjustment problems in the mainstream setting. Their problems result from the fact that they have not successfully mainstreamed and have failed to develop adequate self-esteem and social support networks. They are very lonely, and what might begin as attention seeking behavior or an agressive response to frustration, becomes an ingrained pattern. Often when such students are placed in a more empathetic environment, their problems disappear.

In Fig. 7.5 we try to show how teachers and schools can begin to facilitate better social adjustment in those deaf students who need help in this area, always remembering that they are a minority. The first line of defense for the counselor has to be through the classroom teacher, and it is the failure of this defense which generates later problems for which the counselor's special skills are required. The data from Schlesinger and Meadow (1972) in Table 7.8 are revealing—as understanding and acceptance of deafness increases, so does the self-image of the deaf student. Therefore, teachers and other professionals working with hearing-impaired people need to be particularly conscious of "burnout" (see Lewis, 1983).

Once we are sure that the attitudes of the teachers are sound, there are three main areas where they could be one of the primary leaders in the multidisciplinary team that should form the focus of all our remediation with deaf or, indeed, with hearing individuals. Teachers can program their classrooms to help prevent or overcome developmental delay in both cognitive and language skills and in emotional development. Teachers can also be very effective in ensuring that schools do not become institutions, and we include in this concept all kinds of schools, classes, and programs. A mainstream program can be just as institutionalized as a residential school—it depends on the staff and how the program is organized. Finally, teachers have a special role to play in the remediation of

	SOURCE	TREATMENT
A. Delayed Development	Teacher / Child Care Worker	Child Rearing / Education
B. Family / Environment	Therapist / Social Worker / Community Development Worker	Therapy / Environmental Modifications
C / D. Personality Disorders	Psychiatrist / Psychologist	Drugs / Therapy
E. Institutional Syndrome	Educational Administrator Teacher / Child Care Worker	Milieu and Attitudes
F. Substance Abuse	Therapist / Social Worker	Therapy / Retraining
G. Depressive Reactions	Psychiatrist / Psychologist	Drugs / Therapy
H. Psychosexual Adjustment	Therapist	Therapy
I. Multi-handicapped	Teacher / Child Care Worker / Psychologist	Education / Training

FIG. 7.5.   Treatment systems / sources.

340   7. The Problem of Counseling

TABLE 7.8
% Students with Good Self-Image

	Family Climate		
	Positive	Neutral	Negative
Residential/Deaf Parents	75%	67%	43%
Residential/Hearing Parents	47%	58%	37%
Day/Hearing Parents	69%	40%	27%

Reproduced from H.S. Schlesinger and K.P. Meadow, *Sound and sign: Childhood deafness and mental health*, p. 137. Copyright 1972, reproduced by permission of University of California Press, Berkeley, CA.

multihandicapped students, particularly, but not only, those with a learning disability.

The Counselor's Part in the Multidisciplinary Team

Deaf children are very heterogenous. They differ not only as regards their personality, intelligence, and family background, but also in respect of their handicap. As we noted in chapter 1, hearing impairment can be of varying degrees, from total deafness in both ears, to minimal impairment in one ear. Therefore, it is obvious that the potential for speech and language development must also vary from child to child. Children with useful residual hearing, children deafened after speech and language have been acquired, and exceptional prelingually deaf children may achieve good oral language competence. In contrast, most prelingually deaf children with no useful residual hearing will have great difficulty in acquiring such language.

When early profound deafness is complicated by an intellectual handicap, the affected child is likely to be not only nonspeaking, but nonverbal. For this reason, the counselor of parents of deaf children must be specially trained. He or she ought to have had necessary training in counseling and a thorough knowledge of the psychosocial aspect of all types of deafness. Indeed, one of the greatest barriers preventing parents of hearing-impaired children from fulfilling their roles as parents will be their inability to communicate easily and effectively with their child, and to relate to their special needs and problems. Unless they are able to cope on their own, or unless the counsellor helps them to cope, the outcome may be disappointment in, rejection of, and long-term failure to adjust to their child.

Family counseling and guidance should help the family to understand and accept their child. It should begin in early childhood, and should enable parents to come to a realistic understanding of the implications of their child's handicaps—for the child, for themselves, and for the rest of the family. In the case of parents of deaf children, counseling and guidance are usually necessary not only from the time that the handicap is diagnosed, but throughout infancy and childhood, often through adolescence and even into adult life. Once these things are achieved, the question of language competence can be addressed and the issues of communication method resolved without recourse to the emotional blackmail of parents by well meaning but misguided individuals favoring different methods of communication. The issue is not, "How does the child communicate?" It is "Does the child communicate?"

Summary

The purpose of this penultimate chapter has been to set the specifics of language, oral and sign, into the larger context of the emotional development and social maturity of the deaf child, adolescent, and adult. The large majority of deaf students grow up to lead stable lives and make their contribution to society in the same way as those who hear. Some do not, and probably more deaf than hearing students become casualties of the stress and pressures that are placed on us in modern society. We also explored the causes of social maladjustment and looked at the structure that emerges from a number of interactive variables. One of the conclusions was that poor counseling about the use of oral communication with young deaf children creates some major problems in the family setting. We also concluded that emotional instability and/or maladjustment sometimes result from the lack of a language with which to structure our thinking. Remarkably, most deaf students overcome this difficulty because the underlying cognitive mechanisms are unimpaired, but a suitable environment, supportive of the use of sign language for those children for whom it is appropriate and providing adequate role models, might make it easier for them and their parents.

Further Reading

The book *Psychology of Deafness* by Helmer Myklebust is still a classic even though it was published in 1964. Combined with Edna Levine's (1981) *Ecology of Early Deafness*, it will provide a comprehensive overview of the topic of this chapter. For impact, little can compare with Eugene Mindel and McCay Vernon's *They Grow in Silence*. Published in 1971, it is widely cited and has attracted considerable attention. Hard to obtain, but of major importance, are six volumes of papers published by Gallaudet College as part of the *Social Aspects of Deafness* conference in the summer of 1982. *Deafness and Society* by Jeffrey and Anedith Nash (1981) is an excellent discussion of the sociology of deafness, and Lazlo Stein, Eugene Mindel, and Theresa Jabaley (1981) have one of the few very recent specific books on this topic, *Deafness and Mental Health*.

8

CURRENT TRENDS AND FINAL CONCLUSIONS

Perhaps more than any other topic, the study of language, cognition, and deafness has shown major shifts in theory and practice over the last 50 years. When Pintner first published his historically important studies in 1916, the world was in the throes of the "war to end wars" and the depression of the 1930s loomed mistily on the horizon (see Pintner & Reamer, 1916). The prevailing professional view of deaf children was that they were "defective" and, although educable, they would have to be rehabilitated to take their place in life—a place that would by definition be more limited than that of a hearing person. Seventy or so years later, we are more likely to view the deaf person as an individual and to try to distinguish those effects that result from an inability to hear from the social, educational, and cultural deprivation that results from our attitudes toward deaf people and other minority groups. Although we cannot yet say that deaf people have social justice and equality with hearing people, we can say that in the last 20 years there have been major changes in our attitudes. We are now more likely to perceive deaf people as candidates for employment in senior positions, to offer them better educational opportunities, and to accept their right to self-government and self-organization within their own culture.

It is hard to say where we will be 70 years from now, or even where we will be when we enter the 21st century. The rapidity of medical, technological, and social advances means that we may find the inability to hear no longer a serious handicap in the year 2050. Alternatively, if man continues to pollute the environment with noise, we may find that hearing impairments are so common that they are regarded as normal (see Rodda, 1967). Be that as it may, in

343

this final chapter, we try to address some of the trends that we see developing in the current research in interactive studies of cognition, language, and deafness. We do not try to survey the whole field of deafness—only those trends that are immediately germane to our topic. Our final remarks return to the educational theme that remains central to discussions of sign language.

Deafness and Short-Term Memory

An interesting paper by Crittendon (1974) looked closely at the question of different coding processes and memory for signs. In two different experiments, signs were presented to adult hearing students of sign language, and a recall task required them to write the English word equivalent for each sign. They made a large number of cherologically based errors, suggesting that coding systems are as much a function of language experience as of hearing ability. Furthermore, because these were adult hearing subjects with no previous exposure to sign language, it seems that later language learning experience can affect the coding systems utilized in short-term memory, not just language learning experiences in the early years. Hamilton (1984) makes an insightful comment when he says, "The question for future research may not be, 'How do all people encode linguistic information in STM?' but rather, 'Who codes how, under what conditions?'" (p. 143). In fact, there is considerable evidence that hearing-impaired people can use both phonological and cheremically based coding systems, and that the absence of hearing does not completely preclude acquiring a code with some phonological characteristics (chapters 4 and 5). Therefore, placing deaf and hearing people into different categories may achieve little, and certainly tell us little about how to best provide educational and social experiences that will increase the language abilities of deaf students. In particular, we need to know the respective importance of early and later language experience, and to relate research on this topic to the more general questions of bilingual processing (see, for example, Paivio & Begg, 1981, chap. 13).

In addressing the question raised in the previous paragraph, it is interesting to note that adults surpass children in all aspects of language learning except phonology, and there is little evidence that there is a critical or optimal period in early life for second language learning. Lambert and Tucker (1972) argue persuasively that for hearing children second language learning should be by immersion, although they also point out that ethnic minorities will benefit by a dual exposure to two languages in school until they have consolidated their competence in their native language. Finally, it is important to emphasize that all the available evidence suggests motivation is a primary factor in language learning. If so, the weakness of much oral language instruction for deaf students results at least as much from its destruction of the motivation to communicate as from its use of a phonologically based code with children who cannot hear.

Despite evidence confirming the importance of motivation and the lack of a critical period for second language learning, we cannot entirely discount the importance of all early language experience for deaf students, and we certainly cannot equate the value of a phonological code with that of a cherological code. For deaf students, the phonological code can only be obtained through lipreading or through reading; the former is extremely difficult, and the latter cannot be learned until the child has developed some language structure. Indeed, a number of studies have shown that when deaf students and adults read, they recode the phonologically based print information into cherological codes (for example, Treiman & Hirsh-Pasek, 1983). Therefore, when printed ASL translations of English passages are used (Hoemann, 1975), deaf subjects are equally fluent in reading time and recall of material from the ASL material. Furthermore, when Morariu and Bruning (1984) used this technique, they found deaf high school students recalled more propositions in ASL syntax than in English syntax, and syntax was the most important aspect of language context. They suggested, and we agree:

> ASL triggers the application of familiar rules of a visual language system that are more effective in enhancing comprehension and recall than the predominant visual language of instruction (signed English). The roots of ASL are more likely to be established early in life for a child who derives meaning primarily through movement variations and other visual stimulation rather than through auditory input. (p. 161)

The processing of ASL syntax seems to be a characteristic of a visual-spatial perceptual system, not simply a characteristic of early language learning experiences. If so, the views of those people (primarily deaf) who support the use of ASL rather than some form of manually coded English are vindicated. ASL will provide them with motivating experiences and a tool with which to explore the world at large in ways that are impossible with either *oral language or sign language using English language codes*. Therefore, English language may be better learned through ASL, and speech and lipreading taught as separate skills from early life.

It may be that the importance of speech and lipreading lies not in their usefulness as tools for language learning but, quite simply, in their usefulness in communicating with a unilingual hearing world. If so, the confusion between language competence and communication competence has tended to so narrow our focus that we have usually failed to consider the similarities that exist between linguistically and culturally deprived hearing people and deaf people. We slavishly adopt a deficit model, and prevent ourselves from understanding that many of the problems of deaf children stem from their limited environmental experiences. In this context, Keane (1984) uses Feuerstein's "Mediated Learning Theory" to draw an insightful comparison between the culturally deprived and the deaf populations. For Feuerstein, an important part of learning and development in childhood is the intervention of an adult who "orientates and organizes the phenomenological world of the child" (Keane, 1984, p. 210). Deafness precludes parents from taking this role (see chapter 7) as effectively as they might and, as a result, the phenomenological world is distorted. There is no way of avoiding this problem, but its effects can be mitigated, and they need not be significant or long term.

Reading English and Context

We have already discussed in considerable detail the work of Conrad (1979). It is worth noting his conclusion that the effect of phonemic encoding was of greater significance than the degree of hearing loss, and the effects of hearing loss were mediated through the degree to which it allowed or prevented the child from using an "inner speech" code. The result is not surprising; as we saw in chapter 1 many variables interact with audiometrically established hearing loss. Deafness of later onset is generally less traumatic; deafness coupled with other neurological processing difficulties has a much greater effect.

Nolen and Wilbur (1984) took this point further and related it to the need for contextual cueing if deaf readers are to achieve optimum performance. They support the contentions that we made (pp. 255 to 257), and quote a significant study by McGill-Franzen and Gormley (1980) showing "that deaf readers can use context to obtain meaning from a shortened form of passive sentences when those sentences are presented in familiar stories" (Nolen & Wilbur, 1984, p. 389). Their own research indicated that familiarity with the plot of the story did not account for the effect found by McGill-Franzen and Gormley, even when the students were unfamiliar with the plot or were poor readers. They seemed to use the context of the whole sentence to facilitate reading. This, of course, ties in with the studies reviewed in chapter 4, showing reading to be the best receptive mode despite the poor syntactical skills of deaf readers.

An interesting comment on the effectiveness, or rather the ineffectiveness, of teaching practices used with deaf students emerged from additional data collected by Nolen and Wilbur. The overall results showed the anticipated finding that deaf children had difficulties with the passive voice, and that this construction was immune from contextual cueing. However, and correctly, these authors were concerned that the passive voice is taught early, systematically, and consistently by teachers of the deaf—after all, it is well known that deaf children have difficulties in dealing with it. They point out that as a result, "deaf students may employ a comprehension strategy when first learning about the passive voice, such as 'look for the word *by* and reverse the nouns'" (p. 400). Their data supported the contention that teaching sentence structure in the absence of context is counterproductive—deaf students, like hearing students, require contextual support when learning new structures, which means that language learning should result from a systematic exposure to naturally occurring language and connected discourse. Instead of seeing reading as a deficiency in deaf students, we would do well to heed the advice of Nolen and Wilbur: "To concentrate on isolated sentences in the classroom, rather than to use meaningful context, ignores a potentially powerful educational tool for teaching English to hearing-impaired students" (p. 402). It is a challenge to the educator to produce for the deaf written materials that employ relatively simple syntax to communicate complex semantic information.

British Sign Language Grammar

So far we have only made limited reference to British Sign Language (BSL) used in the United Kingdom, although cross-cultural studies of languages are a vital research tool. They establish universal features that enable us to distinguish biological or neurophysiological mechanisms from the effects of experience, context, and culture on language development. Unfortunately, psychologists and linguists in the United Kingdom have only recently begun to investigate the visual-gestural language of the British deaf community, and only limited cross-cultural comparisons are possible. In fact, prior to the mid-1970s, no systematic studies of BSL were reported, and like their American counterparts, British linguists generally dismissed any suggestions that sign language was, or could be, a language. The philologist Frederick Wood (1941) remarked:

> I am, of course, aware that we speak of "sign language," "deaf and dumb language," etc., and that many authorities consider that the earliest language was not spoken but rather a matter of gesture ... but in applying the term *language* to these methods of communication we are really using it metaphorically; and in any case they all lie outside the sphere of linguistic study (p. 2, f.n.).

However, the work on American Sign Language (ASL) in the United States by Bellugi and her associates (see chapter 3) has resulted in steadily increasing interest in BSL as a language. There are now two major centers of sign language research in the United Kingdom, at Bristol University and in Edinburgh, as well as a number of independent researchers such as Margaret Deuchar, who played a significant role in bringing BSL to the attention of British linguists.

Perhaps because of its suppression by an obsessively oral educational tradition, BSL has proven to be an extremely variable system. There are wide regional and social differences, both lexical and syntactic. Fourteen deaf informants studied by Deuchar (1981) exhibited no less than 10 different ways of signing the numbers SIX to TEN. Moreover, many deaf people in the United Kingdom employ a form of BSL strongly influenced by English word order, and their tendency to use Manual English may increase when addressing hearing researchers. Finally, some hearing-impaired BSL users, embittered by their experiences in schools for the deaf, are suspicious of the motives of linguists, and tend to be uncooperative. For these reasons, considerable caution is required in interpreting research findings about BSL. The following brief survey describes some of the major lines of enquiry established by present day investigators.

Notation

The coding system for BSL proposed by Kyle, Woll, and Carter (1979) is based on the Stokoe notation applied to ASL that has been widely adopted by researchers in the United Kingdom (see p. 128). The system defines 17 basic locations (tab, or PA), 18 handshapes, and 25 types of movement. In addition, a further parameter of *orientation* (ORI) of palm and fingers, each with 8 basic primes, appears to play a major role in the formation of BSL signs. Discourse in BSL is recorded using a "musical score" technique: Each feature is coded on a separate segment of lined paper. The seven levels of analysis suggested are: background information or context; discourse features, including modulation; nonmanual features; a gloss (word for sign notation); lexical coding; speech; and English translation. Used in conjunction with video recording equipment, such a framework provides a potentially effective means of analyzing both spontaneous and elicited sign discourse. But of course, ultimately, the responsibility for identifying significant characteristics of sign language rests with human observers. More recently, a further parameter, *secondary location* (points of contact between the hands), has been identified (Carter & Woll, 1981).

Syntax

The linguist Deuchar (1979) provided the first account of the overall characteristics of BSL, based on a 9-month period of observation at a club for the deaf. In terms of the traditional word classes applied to English and other Indo-European languages, she concluded that: (a) BSL has no articles (*a, the*); (b) BSL possesses a pronoun case system different from that of English—distinguishing, for example, between *you* (singular) and *you* (plural), but not between *I* (subject) and *me* (object); (c) BSL has a system of verb modulation incorporating features such as subject-object relationships; (d) BSL has no copula (the verb *to be*, which plays a general purpose role in cementing together the elements of English utterances); (e) BSL specifies tense by auxiliaries such as WILL or adverbials; (f) in BSL, negation may be signalled by the sign NOT or a sign glossed as NOTHING, or by simultaneous headshaking. NOT appears to be used in formal situations in preference to other forms (Deuchar, 1981).

Four areas of BSL syntax have received special attention from British researchers: the ordering of signs, temporal coding, verb modulation, and noun phrase modification.

Sign Order.   In considering claims that there is something fundamental about the subject-verb-object sequence of lexical units found in many spoken languages, and the implication that if signed languages do not employ a consistent ordering of these elements they must therefore be linguistically defective, we need to recall that these word classes were bequeathed to us by Greek and Roman grammarians (chapter 3). Many modern linguists have proposed alternative classification systems more suitable for dealing with a wider range of language types. In studying item order in samples of spontaneous BSL discourse, Deuchar (1983) found that combinations of Verb (V) and two Noun Phrases (NP) were very rare. Overt subjects were scarcely used, and there was no consistent Object-Verb or Verb-Object order among examples of V + NP utterances. In addition, other combinations included NP + Intransitive Verb (such as FATHER FALL, *Father fell*); NP + NP and NP + Adjective, structures different from English because of the absence of a copula (e.g., FARE THERE BACK TEN p, *The fare there and back is ten pence*); and, more problematical, Adverb + NP. Deuchar observed that although "word class" order varies apparently unsystematically in BSL, almost all the utterances conform to a *topic-comment* sequence, where the first segment introduces a topic, and the second—signalled by a nod of the head—comments on it. Often the BSL signer's right hand indicates the topic, and the left the comment. And Deuchar makes the interesting observation that this basic sequence may also characterize *informal* spoken language ("That door—we ought to see to that"), and that tighter constraints on item order characterize only more formal utterances.

Temporal Coding.   Linguists (with some disagreements) define two kinds of time-related syntax: tense (locating an event in time) and aspect (describing its internal temporal features). Brennan (1983) has described the tense and aspect systems of BSL in detail. The tense system is especially complex, having four different locations ("time lines") and a variety of manual and nonmanual adjuncts. Time Line A, above the right shoulder (corresponding to one major time line in ASL), is the location for signs such as YESTERDAY, TOMORROW, WILL, PAST, LONG AGO, and RECENTLY. Used as an auxiliary, PAST usually precedes the subject. Nonmanual modifiers pin down the times thus indicated more precisely. Line B, in front of the left arm, is used for attributes such as calendar units, and concepts of succession and duration. Some signs (e.g., NEXT WEEK) can be articulated on lines A or B. Line C (horizontally across the midriff) denotes continuity and duration (e.g., CONTINUE). Line D (vertically down the right side of the signer) suggests gradual change. The sign YEAR occurs in neutral space and is modulated to give YEARLY, TWO YEARS AGO, and the like. Age has a special location, the nose, used in constructions such as HOW OLD, and signs made here may be moved to line D to incorporate changes with age. In BSL discourse, tense specification is common, and some BSL users employ a spatial marking method of "placing" a specific time in the signing space for purposes of anaphoric reference, using the sign THEN. BSL also possesses a few past tense forms; sometimes compounds of a sign plus FINISH, sometimes a wholly different sign. As in ASL, aspect is largely transmitted through verb modulation, although (especially in Scottish BSL), FINISH often suggests what in English would be termed the perfective aspect. Modulations in BSL include reduplication, movement length and quality, speed, and freezing. Iterative aspect (e.g., WEEK AFTER WEEK) involves slow reduplication with an end hold; habitual aspect involves rapid, short reduplication. Other modulations match those of ASL (see chapter 3) except for the lack of a clear durational-continuative distinction; and again, nonmanual signs play a role in BSL modulation.

Verb Modulation. Brennan's (1981) anaysis of verb morphology in BSL places it firmly, like ASL, in the incorporating class of languages (McDonald, 1983). Many syntactic elements are incorporated into a verb-like root. Thus the message translated as *He walked toward the two people* incorporates both subject and object in a single process (Fig. 8.1), and could, of course, be further manipulated to incorporate variants such as *He frequently walked toward the two people*, etc.

As in spoken languages such as Latin, BSL signs in a phrase must fit together correctly morphologically; thus, if a subject is signed, it must agree with the subject incorporated in the action. Subject incorporation, as in the previous example, is accomplished by means of classifiers (pronoun-like signs), an upright finger for PERSON, all fingers extended for PEOPLE, and so on. Negative incorporation, when not accomplished by auxiliaries, comprises an opening hand movement (Deuchar, 1981), and appears to be restricted to a small set of verbs.

Noun-Phrase Modification. Incorporation can also be used to modify noun phrases (Carter, 1981b; Carter & Woll, 1981). Like ASL, BSL possesses a variety of means for specifying size, shape, and number. Thus, in the phrase LONG-HAIR, the length of hair can be shown by the final position of the hands. A second method, simultaneous modification, has the noun phrase head signed on one hand and the modifier on the other. Both incorporated and simultaneous modification may occur in some signs; generally physical constraints determine the selection of each. A third method, suspended modification, "holds" the noun phrase on the right hand while the left provides additional information. Finally, sequential combinations of elements may modify noun-phrase structures, often in conjunction with repetition of signs. Asked to judge the grammaticality of permutations of the BSL signs BIG, BLACK, and CAR, one informant rejected BIG BLACK CAR as "not BSL" and commented that BIG CAR BLACK would be improved as BIG CAR CAR BLACK. Other sequences seemed equally acceptable, except that informants indicated that the final adjective had special emphasis (Carter, 1981b).

Semantics

Woll (1983) has discussed aspects of the semantics of BSL signs. As with ASL, some sign parameters consistently map onto certain well defined semantic domains. Signs that connote emotion are made on the chest, whereas signs invoking cognition are made near the

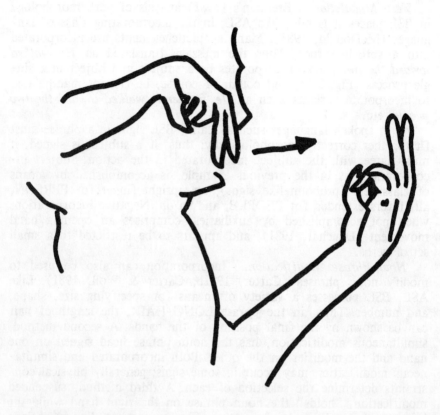

The right hand signs the (iconically transparent) action, while the left incorporates the number "two" in the classifier PERSON.

FIG. 8.1.   "He walked towards the two people" in British Sign Language.

Source—Brennan, 1981, p. 125. Reprinted from *Perspectives on British Sign Language and deafness* by permission of Croom Helm, Ltd., Publishers, Provident House, Burrell Row, Beckenham, England.

forehead. Similarly, A handshapes tend (in 56% of cases) to mean something good (CLEVER, APPROVE), while the I handshape connotes badness (WICKED, REJECT) in some 83% of instances. And, again following the example of ASL, signs falling in a specific semantic region tend to adopt the appropriate parameter value over historical time.

Another special case of sign structure (not purely semantic) is that of loan signs and initialization derived from finger spelling. PAPER, for example, incorporates a finger spelled "p." GOLD comprises both a "g" initial and a movement associated with brightness. Hence signs may originate in iconic, lexical, or semantic features.

BSL and ASL

As yet, BSL has not been subjected to as intensive a program of research as that associated with the Salk Institute's long-term study of ASL that we discussed in some detail in chapter 3. Nevertheless, sufficient data have been gathered to make possible a broad comparison between the two languages. In brief, we would suggest that:

1. Like ASL, BSL is an incorporating language, compressing a mass of information into a spatially and temporally complex matrix of formational features. Brennan (1981) cites a vivid example of multiple incorporation in BSL: a sentence equivalent to the phrase, "I used to sit and stare at the teacher without understanding a thing," expressed in a simultaneous set of manual and nonmanual features. Knowing the context of the utterance, all of this information can be recovered from a single frame of film; the danger, remarks Brennan, is that "an observer expecting the types of patterning found in spoken language will note only the activity of the dominant hand, and gloss the whole utterance as LOOK" (Brennan, 1981, p. 123). Like ASL, BSL exploits spatial processes to the full, using similar mechanisms: modulation of basic signs, a limited set of formational elements, spatial deictic processes, and size/shape specification.

2. Differences exist between ASL and BSL in terms of basic parameters and inflections, as one would expect. Certain other differences have emerged: BSL appears to possess a less restricted signing space than ASL and seems not to follow the symmetry constraint postulated for ASL (Carter & Woll, 1981, and p. 131). BSL also seems to rely more strongly on nonmanual signs than ASL: "when deaf people are deep in conversation ... their gaze is focused on the face, not the hands" (Carter, 1981a,

p. 3). BSL also seems to be less restrictive regarding feature combination, and more tolerant of mimetic extensions to formal signing. It is hard to tell, as yet, whether (a) BSL is less highly evolved than ASL—perhaps because of its enforced isolation; or (b) cultural factors may explain the differences. (For example, because the British are traditionally less facially expressive than many Americans, they may have a correspondingly greater free capacity for facial coding.)

3. Due to the problems outlined previously, BSL is harder to study than ASL. Within BSL, the boundaries of sign and gesture, syntax and morphology, and linguistic versus paralinguistic elements are difficult to define. Perhaps this tells us something about the inadequacy, if not the arbitrariness, of the traditional linguistic categories, and confirms the views of proponents of case grammars that semantic and functional features of language may be more fundamental (or "universal") than syntactical. So far, the scarcity of native BSL users with an understanding of the needs of linguists studying them has proven a stumbling block. This point is neatly made by an accidental observation described by Carter and Woll (1981) and by Carter (1981b). An informant who was about to sign a BSL narrative for the video camera first told the story to another informant, unaware that the camera was still running. Dramatic differences between the two recordings emerged despite the informant's professed understanding of the need to sign in a completely natural manner (Table 8.1). If nothing else, this illustrates the axiom that when people *know* they are being observed their behavior ceases to be normal, and closely parallels the experiences of Bellugi (p. 139).

Unfortunately, recent cuts in United Kingdom research funding have placed severe constraints on the current program of research into BSL. The situation is unfortunate, because the comparison of BSL and ASL has already proven to be a fruitful method of adding to our knowledge of linguistic universals and psycholinguistic processing. We hope the financial barriers to further research will soon be removed. In the meantime, one good sign is that increasing numbers of deaf researchers are becoming involved in linguistics and psycholinguistics with the intention of investigating the structure of BSL themselves. If this process comes to fruition, we can anticipate many new and insightful discoveries in the years to come.

TABLE 8.1

BSL Accounts of an Incident

A. First recording (to another deaf signer)

LIP MOVEMENT	Ernest	come	-	Gordon	
SIGN GLOSS		.e. COME-TO-MY-HOUSE INDEX .g. 2-COME			

LIP MOVEMENT			
SIGN GLOSS	COME-TO-MY-HOUSE COME TO-MY-HOUSE		
NONMANUAL	-	-	puzzled face

LIP MOVEMENT	said	go	with	-	cricket
SIGN GLOSS	INDEX GO WITH GO CRICKET				

("Ernest came to my house, then Gordon arrived. They both came, one after the other. Why? They wanted us to go with them to a cricket match.")

B. Second recording (for the camera)

LIP MOVEMENT		last	Sunday	-	brothers	came
SIGN GLOSS	BEFORE SUNDAY MY 2 BROTHERS COME					

LIP MOVEMENT	my house told my husband about cricket
SIGN GLOSS	MY HOUSE TELL MY HUSBAND ABOUT CRICKET

LIP MOVEMENT	for deaf
SIGN GLOSS	f.r. DEAF

The two glosses fail to express differences in the formation of the signs. In B. COME-TO-MY-HOUSE, the movement component of COME is combined with the handshape for HOUSE, and the sign finishes close to the body in the location for MY; similarly 2-COME is an example of number incorporation. Lower case letters such as .e. are finger spelled.

Adapted from M. Carter (1981b), Noun phrase modification in British Sign Language, *Research on deafness and British Sign Language*, published by School of Education Research Unit, University of Bristol.

Polar Features of Sign Language

Montgomery, Miller, Mitchell, Jordan, and Montgomery (1983) have recently developed a new technique for comparing movement characteristics of different sign languages. By regarding the mouth as the origin of a system of polar coordinates, the position of each hand can be accurately plotted at various stages during discourse (Fig. 8.2). These authors asked three groups of subjects, using American Sign Language (ASL), British Sign Language (BSL), and British Signed English (BSE), to translate into total communication four types of English text. In analyzing the results, samples of hand locations were taken every 10 seconds from video recordings, thus providing a global impression of each sign language. In the analysis, no account was taken of hand shape or modulation, nor of other linguistic features.

The mean dimensions of the polar triangles asociated with each subject group are shown in Fig. 8.3. Significant differences emerged in the variables ML (the distance between the mouth and the left hand that was longer for ASL), RL (the distance between the right and left hands, for which ASL>BSL>BSE), symmetry, and total transmission time (BSE slowest and ASL fastest). It was also noted that BSE relied more heavily on the use of finger spelling than did ASL or BSL.

Also shown in Fig. 8.3 are the percentages of crossovers of right hand into the left side of the signing space and vice versa. ASL shows a small number of crossovers with no right-left differences; both BSL and BSE exhibit many crossovers of the right hand to left side. Montgomery and his colleagues argue that this largely reflects the use of the two-handed finger spelling system, wherein alphabetical stimuli are presented to the observer's right visual field for input to the left hemisphere (see chapter 6). A further factor in determining hand location is visual acuity: If the receiver is focusing on the total communicator's mouth, signs made near the periphery of the signing space will be seen relatively less distinctly. The study found that in all three signing systems, the signer's right (active) hand was more likely to be closer to the mouth than his left hand. However, occlusions of the lips occurred rarely. Total communication may, therefore, be seen as a carefully controlled balance between the need to present signs sufficiently close to the mouth to be readily perceived and the need to avoid occluding lip movements (perhaps as a result of the influence of teachers at school, but also, perhaps, as a result of the need to provide the maximum information possible for the decoding process). Clearly, further studies of the distribution of attention to oral and manual components of totally transmitted

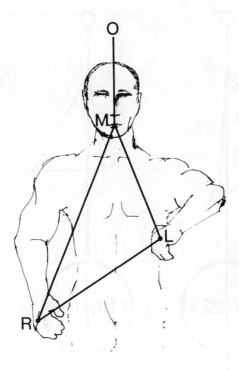

By regarding the mouth as the fixed point in a system of polar co-ordinates, the location of each hand can be precisely fixed by measuring the angles OML and OMR and the distances ML and MR.

M = Mouth
R = Right Hand
L = Left Hand
MRL = the "polar triangle."

FIG. 8.2.   Polar coding of sign language.

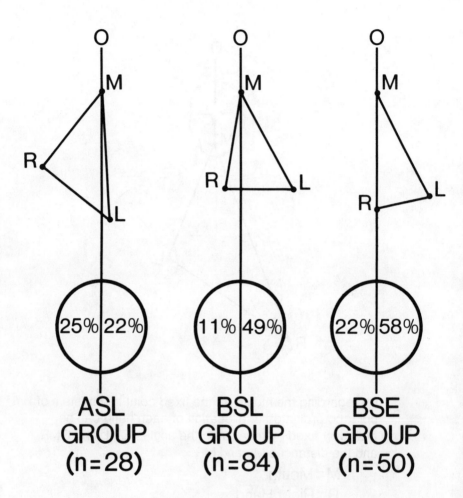

FIG. 8.3.   Mean dimensions of polar triangles for ASL, BSL, and BSE and frequencies of lateral crossovers.

Source—G.W.G. Montgomery, J. Miller, G. Mitchell, I.K. Jordan, and J. Montgomery (1983), Open communication or catastrophe? A model for educational communication, in J.G. Kyle and B. Woll (Eds.), *Language in Sign*. London: Croom Helm.

messages will resolve some of the theoretical problems we discussed in chapter 4.

Nonmanual Features of Sign Language

Another aspect of sign language that is beginning to receive increased attention is its systematic employment of facial expressions and head movements. At first sight the rapid and exaggerated grimaces, smiles, and squints that accompany manual discourse seem to have a purely emotional function. But it is now clear that in ASL, and probably most other sign languages, facial signals constitute part of the formal grammar of the system (Baker-Shenk, 1983; Johnson, 1984; Tweney, Liddell, & Bellugi, 1977)

In ASL, Baker-Shenk (1983) has identified approximately 20 nonmanual modifiers (equivalent to adjectives and adverbs) that operate in parallel with the sign modified. Thus pursed lips and squinting eyes signify the quality of *thinness*. Nonmanual cues also signal syntactical processes such as sentence topic, questioning, and embedding.

In BSL, as in ASL, nonmanual components play a vital role in the production of *multichannel signs*, which are more complex than simple signs and which cannot be mapped onto single English words. Lawson (1983) has listed many regular nonmanual features of BSL, including *head movements* (nodding, turning, shaking, or tilting in various directions); *facial expressions, eyes* (staring, ogling, closing, etc.); *eyebrows* (raising, knitting); *cheek movements* (puffing out, sucking in); *mouth patterns* (open, closed, pursed, teeth showing, smiling, protruding tongue, and many others). Lawson has also listed nonfacial features such as *shoulders* (shrugging, hunching, tilting), *chest* (sighing or heaving), and *body movements* (twisting and tilting in various directions). Some of the features just described perform specific grammatical roles such as *negative incorporation, time relations* (transmitting subtleties such as *not so long, suddenly*, and *unexpectedly*), and *cognitive meaning* (signs related to cognitive functioning). A specific example in the latter category is the multichannel sign that can be glossed as I-COMPLETELY-FORGOT-ALL-ABOUT-IT or as MY-MIND-WENT-BLANK. This comprises a closing hand movement and the sucking in of the signer's cheeks combined with blowing out through pursed lips (the "oo" mouth pattern). The sucking in of the cheeks signifies *not so long*; the "oo" sign means, in this context, shock.

The large contribution made by lip and cheek movements to manual communication raises an important question about the operation of total communication systems. Clearly it is impossible to combine both oral lip movements and lip movements constituting part of the sign language being employed. Thus total communication may imply the use of a degraded or inadequate sign language component. Vogt-Svendsen (1983), a Norwegian teacher of the deaf, has reported that such interchannel interference creates real problems in an educational context. In Norway, a system of Signed Norwegian (similar in structure to the various methods of manual English) was produced to replace Norwegian Sign Language (NSL) in the classroom. The experiment has failed, Vogt-Svendsen reports, because only a few deaf pupils can understand Signed Norwegian; these then act as interpreters to the rest:

> For example, a teacher may describe the expression "in olden days" as meaning that there were no cars, no television and so on. After some time, sometimes hours or days, at least one pupil grasps the meaning. This pupil then turns around and facing the rest of the class he/she translates the expression from Signed Norwegian to NSL in a matter of seconds. (p. 87)

That this problem may not be limited to BSL and NSL is indicated by reports of formal lip movements as morphological features in Swedish Sign Language (Bergman, 1983). It remains to be seen whether a satisfactory way can be found of combining sign and oral language channels without doing violence to those aspects of sign language grammar that make obligatory use of labial movements. In the meantime, some supporters of manual methods have been led to reject total communication altogether. It is ironic that both committed oralists and manualists wish to maintain the "purity" of their respective methodologies, despite the evidence (reviewed in chapter 4) that total communication does have significant advantages over both, and the implication that total communication users can overcome interchannel interference problems.

Acquisition of Sign Language

Recent years have seen increased interest in the deaf child's acquisition of oral and sign language. Two studies in this area are worth considering in some detail.

Pre-Speech

We have discussed in chapter 6 some of the arguments concerning the nature of the language acquisition process. On one side, Chomsky and others have argued for the automatic, preprogrammed mechanisms of acquisition associated with the left cortical hemisphere. On the other, Bruner, Wells, and others have asserted that language is acquired in a complex social and cognitive interplay between the child and his or her environment. Examination of early exchanges between hearing infants and their mothers has pinpointed the emergence of communicative behavior as manifested in eye contact, gesture, and turn-taking; the terms *protoconversation* and *pre-speech* have been coined to capture the essential quality of this phase of development.

Terry Nienhuys and Jennifer Tikotin of the University of Melbourne have investigated the role of pre-speech in the development of deaf children and their hearing mothers. In an interesting paper (Nienhuys & Tikotin, 1983), they contend that such studies both provide a way of assessing the role of vocalization in pre-speech and test the assumption, often made by educators of deaf students, that nonverbal aspects of mother-child interaction remain unimpaired when the infant is suffering prelingual hearing loss. Nienhuys and Tikotin examined video recordings of two mother-child dyads; in one case the child was deaf, in the other the child was normally hearing. The behavior of the subjects was classified into several basic classes of Monadic Phases.

Although dramatic individual differences are known to exist between hearing infants in terms of their pre-speech behavior, some of the results of this study do seem to indicate possibly fruitful lines of further research. The deaf infant spent some 98.5% of his time in monadic phases with a neutral or negative emotional connotation, whereas the hearing child divided his time equally between neutral-to-negative and positive emotional phases. Similarly, the mother of the deaf child spent over half her time in emotionally neutral behavioral phases, and only 14.6% of time in play, the most positive and intimate form of interaction, whereas the mother of the hearing child spent some 54.8% of the time in play. Nienhuys and Tikotin note that their findings could be an artifact of individual differences or age differences (the deaf child was somewhat older during the sampling period). However, if they are not artifactual, they could reflect the need of deaf children to allocate more time to scanning their environment (as against interacting socially), and also the mother's greater need to monitor her infant's behavior. Alternatively, they could reflect an emotional response on the part of the mother who has still not come to terms with her child's impairment. In either case, the findings, if replicated on a larger sample, call into question the claim that the pre-speech communication of deaf infants and their mothers is essentially normal in character. Indeed, even without research to increase our understanding of these processes, there is already strong evidence that early verbal interaction between deaf children and their hearing parents differs in many ways from the norm. Goss (1970) has shown that the mothers of deaf children are more likely to show tension, disagreement, or antagonism, more likely to use abnormal speech patterns, and less likely to ask for opinions or show solidarity than the mothers of the hearing. Such data cannot be encouraging for the proponents of purely oral methods of instruction.

Hearing Children's Acquisition of ASL

A more robust study of the acquisition of ASL by the children of deaf parents has been reported by Bonvillian, Orlansky, and Novack (1983), who have attempted to identify cognitive skills essential for language acquisition. In the children of hearing parents, a level of cognitive achievement equivalent to Piaget's final sensorimotor stage (object representation) is said to be a prerequisite for the acquisition of natural language. Rapid growth of vocabulary typically cannot occur until the child is capable of mentally representing objects in its environment. Intuitively, this makes a certain sense: How can you learn names when you have not yet grasped the idea of external objects to which the names are attached? But what happens when the child is required to learn signs rather than words? Does the same rule apply?

The subjects in the study reported by Bonvillian, Orlansky, and Novack were 11 children, aged 1-2 years, from nine families with deaf parents. All but one of the infants had normal hearing, and were exposed to ASL as a first language. Parental records and direct observation over a 16-month period were the major sources of data on the subject's acquisition of signs. The Uzgiris-Hunt tests of development were used to assess cognitive skills.

Despite wide individual variations, certain trends in sign acquisition were evident. For children of hearing parents, the first word is typically produced at 11-14 months; the subjects in this experiment produced their first sign around 8.5 months. Vocabulary size generally reaches 10 words at 15.1 months; for signs, the corresponding age was found to be 13.2 months. Normal children begin to combine words at 18-21 months; again, the children of deaf parents began to combine signs at a mean age of 17 months. In other words, for both vocabulary and elementary syntax, ASL is acquired somewhat faster than English. Interestingly, no significant relationship between early vocabulary size and age of onset of sign combination was observed.

In all respects except vocal imitation, the children acquired basic sensorimotor skills at a normal rate. However, there was wide variation within and between scores on the separate scales of the Uzgiris-Hunt test. Despite this finding, it was obvious that many aspects of sign acquisition were *not* dependent on completion of the sensorimotor phase. Half of the subjects still had not mastered "object permanence" when they produced their first sign combination. This finding tends to reinforce the Chomskian notion of a distinct mental structure, the LRCS (see chapter 6), which functions independently of other cognitive mechanisms.

Bonvillian, Orlansky, and Novack (1983) draw four major conclusions from their data. First, it is clear that signs are easier to produce than words, both mechanically and because parents can exert more direct guidance over the child's behavior. Second, the data support observations that the motor system develops neurologically faster than the speech system. Third, iconicity was not found to be a significant factor in sign acquisition. And fourth, previous findings concerning the relationship between language acquisition and cognitive development may be an artifact of relying on production measures of speech. Because comprehension of language precedes production, it may (or may not) be related to different underlying skills.

Returning to the theme of chapter 6, this study also provides circumstantial support for the gestural theory of language evolution. If deaf children, deprived of a major sensory channel, succeed in acquiring sign language at an early age, it is easy to assert that this does no more than reflect the capacity of the human cognitive system to overcome potentially devastating handicaps. But if hearing children, lacking such a powerful incentive, succeed in acquiring ASL easily—and more rapidly than oral language itself is acquired under normal circumstances—this argues very strongly that sign language is itself natural, possibly even more natural, from an evolutionary perspective, than speech.

Screening for Oral Skills

It is evident from the discussion presented in previous chapters that one of the ways in which the educational controversy might be resolved would be to identify, at a very early age, which deaf children are likely to adapt successfully to the various methods of communication. In particular, it would be helpful to detect the (relatively small) percentage of children capable of developing good oral skills. We suggested in chapter 4 that lipreading ability may be largely determined by heredity, implying that efforts to train children who lack the necessary cognitive mechanisms in lipreading are likely to go unrewarded. Unfortunately, many of the psychological tests that correlate substantially with oral skill can only be applied to older respondents. If there is a critical period for first language learning, it may be ended within as little as 3 years of birth (Maxwell, 1984). The need for early screening is clear.

Recently, evidence has been presented that may point to a solution of this dilemma. The evidence comes from two studies that examined the electroencephalic brain responses of normally hearing subjects to brief flashes of light. By repeating the process many times, it is possible to summate the electrical potentials occurring in a subject's brain to produce the Averaged Visual Evoked Response (AVER) associated with the stimulus. Typical AVERs take the form of a brief series of increasingly negative waves followed by a large positive peak appearing around 200 milliseconds after the flash. Shepherd, DeLavergne, Frueh, and Clobridge (1977) measured the latency of the negative wave just preceding the positive peak in AVERs recorded from right and left sides of the heads of 20 normal subjects. They then administered a short filmed test of lipreading comprising 31 sentences; in line with the findings reported by Conrad (1977) and Arnold and Walter (1979), the scores of these entirely untrained subjects averaged around 39%. Correlations were then computed separately between the AVERs recorded from right and left hemispheres and the subjects' lipreading scores based on either words or sentences correct. All the correlations (r) were about 0.90, indicating that good lipreading performance was strongly related to speed of AVER.

In a replication and extension of the Shepherd experiment, Samar and Sims (1983) employed a computer program to break the AVER into its constituent waveforms. Eleven different wave components of the overall (centroid) AVER were identified. However, only three components correlated with lipreading scores: Factor 5, characterized by a very early positive peak 16 milliseconds after the flash, gave a correlation of $r=0.60$; Factor 3, a late positive peak, $r=0.45$; and Factor 10, a positive peak, $r=0.38$. Combined together, these three factors could predict some 71% of the variance in individual lipreading scores. Factor 5 proved to be unrelated to the latency measure used by Shepherd; Factors 3 and 10 together predicted the Shepherd statistic, but proved, in this study, not to correlate so highly with lipreading skill.

The conclusions to be drawn from these data are qualified by the need to replicate them on a younger deaf sample. But if this is successfully achieved, it may be possible to develop a simple screening test that can be applied to deaf infants with the aim of telling us which are able to benefit from lipreading training at an early age.

The theoretical payoff would also be considerable. It would be con-firmed that lipreading ability is governed by genetic rather than by environmental factors. It would also be confirmed that, as we argued in chapter 4, peripheral rather than central mechanisms play the major role in determining oral skill: Intuitively, a very rapid neural response of the kind exemplified by Samar and Sims' Factor 5 would appear to be a vital prerequisite for detecting and utilizing transient lip movement stimuli. The fact that no differences have been ob-served between AVERs from the right and left hemispheres also lends weight to this interpretation, because it indicates that central (linguistic) mechanisms are not involved at this early stage. In any case, the latencies under study (all under 400 milliseconds) preclude the operation of semantic retrieval mechanisms (which typically gen-erate much slower responses).

The Educational Controversy Continues

In recent years, the question of which sign language to use in the education of deaf children has become almost as big an issue as the oral versus manual controversy that dominated the education of deaf students in previous decades. A useful study by Gustason (1981) looks at this problem in some detail in five special schools. It con-cludes that some younger deaf children exposed to total communica-tion are achieving higher levels of achievement in English language, but it is too early to say if this is merely an acceleration of their performance, or if it is an enduring and continuing increase. The article also concludes that the question of which is the best sign sys-tem to use in a classroom or with parents is essentially unresolved.

> The present study raises far more questions than it answers. Much of the data came from school records or parental self-reporting and was thus uncontrolled. While schools included in this study stated they used Signing Exact English, the consistency of this use among teachers varied a great deal from school to school. In addition, the length of time this mode of communication had been the school policy varied widely. No attempt was made to assess the signing skills of parents or teachers, or to consider the other possibly influential factors such as the school's language curriculum, parent socioeconomic status, and the like. While no conclusions can be drawn concerning Signing English use per se, it is interesting to note that of those parents responding at all five schools, 56% reported both parents signing at home and an additional 27.3% one parent signing. (Gustason, 1981, p. 20)

A note of discord to the general finding that the use of sign lan-guage improves developmental skills and academic achievement is found in a number of review papers published at regular intervals over the years. One of the better ones is by Owrid (1972), one of the more recent ones by Nix (1983). The Nix paper is important. It echoes a number of more specific studies, and a general theme that continues to pervade some of the literature on deafness. In summary, Nix (1983) states:

> The results are not offered to suggest that auditory/oral communication is a panacea for the complex problems surrounding the disability of deafness but they do cast considerable doubt on the efficacy of simultaneous communication. If the auditory/oral students were receiving "partial" information and the sim-com students were receiving "total" information, the results would be the inverse of the actual findings. (p. 181)

To support this contention, Nix cites applied studies that he claims show that deaf students educated using an auditory/oral approach do significantly better academically than those educated using total communication (which is misleadingly referred to as "sim-com," i.e., simultaneous communication). Because the paper reflects a position held by a number of influential educators, it is worthwhile considering why and how they have managed to reach conclusions that are not justified by the bulk of the available evidence.

Sampling and Selection

In discussing the results of research on total communication, questions are rarely asked about the samples of students used in the different studies. Nix refers to this problem, but then fails to consider the selective processes that operate in any educational system. He discusses studies that partial out variables; that is, attempt to remove effects that are interactive with the skill under investigation. Unfortunately, while the easy-to-measure variables that are usually included in studies of this type, such as hearing loss, do systematically effect academic achievements and language competence, they are not the only ones to do so. Generally, although not always, children are placed in total communication programs when they are already regarded as failures. The reasons for their failure are rarely analyzed in detail, and even if they are, they are so multifaceted that drawing comparisons between classroom performance in different types of programs is very difficult. Researchers assume that all children attending programs for the hearing-impaired are deaf or hard of hearing, that all are similar in other auditory processing characteristics, and that only the variables they identify have a significant effect on academic performance. Of course, skilled researchers also realize that these assumptions are invalid and that we can only look closely at a limited number of variables, but this does not always prevent others from drawing erroneous conclusions.

It is not the research itself, but the interpretation of the research that frequently neglects to consider the major influences that educational policy will have on educational placement and educational achievement. As yet, we have insufficient knowledge to be able to remove the influence of these policies and to be able to make completely satisfactory empirical pronouncements about the effects of oral language or sign language on educational performance. But we do have suggestive evidence that derogatory attitudes toward an ethnic minority will destroy motivation and seriously impair educational performance. We also have a great deal of positive evidence to support the contention that using sign language is advantageous for deaf children. Therefore, arguments covering the multivariate nature of educational achievements and the effects of sampling error are important for the refinement and improvement of our research techniques. They are not a valid reason for rejecting the shifts in educational policy that have started to take place in recent years.

Fallacious Assumptions About Theory

We referred in chapters 2 and 3 to the divergent views of linguists about the relationship between American Sign Language and English. Some see it as a continuum with Pidgin Sign English existing as a variant on this continuum; others see iconic characteristics as common to both spoken and visual languages; still others see the two languages as distinctly different and not forming any kind of continuum. Despite this controversy, many supporters of oral communication implicitly assume that aural English language is a standard model against which visual languages are to be judged. Therefore, Nix quotes Baker (1979, p. 20) on "simultaneous communication" as saying: "they [teachers] were still speaking much faster than they were signing and deleting some important information from the signed portion." Like most detractors of the use of sign language, Nix fails to consider that the important information is deleted from the signed portion of the message only because of the constraints introduced by the introduction of spoken language, not because of some fundamental defect in the method of communication itself. We referred elsewhere (chapter 7) to the work of Greenberg with families of deaf children and to his suggestions that ease and fluency of communication might be more important on some occasions than exposure to the language form of spoken English. We refer also to the need to consider teaching English as a second language (chapter 5).[1] These perspectives may or may not be the right ones, but along with many others, they often are ignored in a discussion of the education of deaf students. There is a presupposition in the arguments of those who rigidly advocate oral communication. It is that language can only be learned through oral communication systems and that an inability to use such a system is by definition a language deficiency. If this presupposition is invalid, then the rest of the arguments become equally invalid.

Evidence for the Proposition

Arguments for the rigid use of only oral communication in the education of deaf children are rarely based on positive empirical evidence. Papers are presented that either describe what is done, or present some highly selected case studies or, with varying degrees of proficiency, present critical appraisals of the research showing that the use of sign language with deaf children has beneficial outcomes. Indeed, it is notoriously difficult for empirical researchers to gain access to oral programs to document the abilities and clinical characteristics of the students attending them. When they do, the results are often surprising. For example, Rodda (1970) writing of two selective schools for deaf students in Great Britain, found that students attending the schools "were significantly more likely to be adventitiously deaf (37% as opposed to 28% for all special school children) and to have a significantly lower hearing loss (77.8 dB average loss as opposed to 89.8 dB for all special school children)" (p. 84). If this is the situation in two schools that are able to selectively bias their intake, it suggests that, despite claims to the contrary, empirical studies might show other successful oral institutions are similarly biased to include more children with lower degrees of hearing impairment, children who are less likely to have other marginal handicapping conditions, and children who come from a supportive home environment. Greater oral success with such children does not justify depriving them, or other students, of the use of sign language. More importantly, it certainly does not justify assuming that all deaf children can be orally successful.[2]

---

[1]Interestingly, the paper that Nix quotes by Baker is from a whole symposium devoted to the topic of bilingual education of deaf children.

[2]As we saw in chapter 4, and in the section on AVERs, "oral success" may depend on a number of innately determined cognitive factors. We are not, of course, claiming that all orally successful students have significant levels of residual hearing, but that it is vital to ensure that comparisons are not confounded with the degree of hearing loss.

Of course, most of the studies supporting the use of total communication with deaf students at school and deaf children at home have varying degrees of methodological inadequacies. Some are so biased in their arguments and conclusions that they must be rejected entirely. The methodological inadequacies are hardly surprising, for no single piece of research is conclusive in itself, and the ability to replicate a finding or a conclusion is a cardinal attribute of scientific methods. It is the total bulk of the evidence that strongly supports the use of sign language with deaf children and that rejects entirely the notion of a rigid commitment to oral education. Linguists, psychologists, educators, sociologists, and other specialists have looked at the question in very different ways, and, for many different reasons, have rejected the tenets of rigid oralism. We fail to see how the uncommitted observer could fail to do otherwise; and if oral language warrants the status it has been given in the past, we fail to understand why overwhelming evidence to support this proposition has not been forthcoming.

In contrast to the conclusions reached by the neo-oralists, it is possible that manual English codes are more important as a supplementary aid to lipreading, rather than as replacements for sign language. Coupled with finger spelling, they may permit deaf students to access and benefit from written English that is widely available through books and, increasingly, through television and films. As Evans (1981) points out, finger spelling may have a "special role as a lexical tool for learning technical terms and names, and for reinforcing the orthographic pattern of new words" (p. 160). Evans also points out that finger spelling is a useful way of representing English function words in a manual code and that in English, signs and finger spelling have "complementary roles, signing for conveying content words, and finger spelling for conveying function words, together representing the syntax of English" (p. 160).

Cornett (1967) would argue that cued speech already provides an excellent method of facilitating and developing oral communication and resolving the problems raised by Evans. The problem seems to focus not so much on the objective as on the particular coding system used to achieve this objective. The choice is considerable, and can include Signed English (Bornstein, Hamilton, Saulnier, & Roy, 1975), SEE 1 (Anthony & Associates, 1971), SEE 2 (Gustason, Pfetzing, & Zawolkow, 1972), LOVE (Wampler, 1971), Paget-Gorman (Craig, 1976; Paget & Gorman, 1968), Signed Exact English (see Lawson, 1981), as well as a number of less formalized systems. Our own view of the best system is one that most closely approximates the natural signs of ASL (or another endogenous sign language). A greater degree of isomorphism between the natural sign language and the coded English system will allow students more opportunities for transfer and will not result in the confusion that often arises when a number of different sign systems are in use. Moreover, it simplifies the problem of lexical storage, and although we have no evidence for this statement, we believe it is highly probable that some of the more divergent systems of signed English require young deaf students to try to develop three lexicons (assuming that they are being taught English by speech and lipreading as well as by a signed English system).

Ethnicity and Paternalism

In chapters 1 and 5 we commented on the emerging awareness of the ethnicity of deafness. The concept maintains a sense of identity and belongingness within a group, and we would be unwise to try to suppress the values associated with it, at least until we are assured that equality of opportunity is available for deaf students. Indeed, Lawson (1981) sounds a similar note of warning. She says, "if bilingual education is promoted solely by hearing people, it will probably fail" because:

> No social change (and bilingual education is a social change), should be attempted without adequate knowledge of all the possible social ramifications involved. Sociolinguistic studies of the local deaf communities are absolutely necessary, and these studies must include the consideration of the attitudes of deaf people, deaf parents and deaf schoolchildren toward the local and/or standard language varieties used; toward diglossia; and identification of the local sign varieties in use.

> Since research into BSL has begun so recently, we can look forward to exciting developments. It is to be hoped that these developments will promote the full and active participation of all deaf people in both the British deaf community and in British society as a whole. (Lawson, 1981, p. 177)

With the illogic that often characterizes desirable motives and actions, it is possible that the enthusiasm with which the concept of bilingualism and deafness has been seized by hearing people working with deaf students reflects a continuing paternalism rather than liberalized acceptance of deaf people in their own right. Certainly it is hard for hearing people to be willing to work with deaf people as equals (and, sometimes, as hard for deaf people to avoid looking to hearing people to take over a leadership role).

It is interesting that in a survey in Great Britain of all types of disability, Mildred Blaxter (1976) commented that the officials of various voluntary organizations working with disabled people felt "uneasy about their welfare functions" (p. 218), *except in organizations serving blind and deaf people.* We discussed earlier the attitudes of teachers and other professionals (chapter 2). These attitudes form a direct threat to the acceptance of the ethnic nature of deafness, and are still in many ways responsible for the veneration of the English language in educational systems for deaf students and for adults in other settings. Carver and Rodda (1978) commented thus:

> In discussing social attitudes toward the handicapped, we must not allow society to become the scapegoat for our own individual problems.... We have to get away from the motives of self-satisfaction which stress *helping* those less fortunate than ourselves.... As a doctor undertaking an operation, a teacher teaching the child in basic academic skills, a rehabilitation counselor or social worker attempting to provide occupational skills or opportunities, or as a neighbor guiding a blind person across the road, we have to see our work as a privilege that the disabled person confers on us rather than as something that reflects our own humanity toward our fellow man. It is easy to be "kind" to someone whose power to resist patronage is small. A true democracy has no room for patronage: it depends on respect by all for the essential humanity in every other member. (p. 114)

The needs of the organization often dominate institutional practices, and organizations become self-perpetuating. When this happens, there is extreme pressure to conform to the norm, and individual or minority group differences are perceived as threatening the stability of the organization. Blaxter's (1976) insightful comments are worth repeating in full:

> In general, and excepting the societies for the blind and the deaf, the officials of voluntary organizations seemed uneasy about their welfare functions. Many placed great emphasis on delicacy in money matters, which may have been appreciated by their members, but might also be felt to reinforce the "charity" image of voluntary organizations.... Only a very few organizations (for instance, the Multiple Sclerosis Society) offered total supportive services defined by their perception of the individual family's needs rather than by the society's own categories of "the things the organization does." In any case, any attempt at a precise definition of the difficult concept of "social needs," which could be universally applied to "the disabled," would have been resisted by the potential clients. They were happy to admit that they might be disabled in some particular area of life—might need transport or a job, or an income—but they rarely saw themselves as socially disabled. (p. 218)

Unfortunately, by denying the ethnicity of deafness we have delayed the search for an adequate solution:

The distinction between the social entity of the deaf and the deaf aggregate, for example, is not my invention. It was merely discovered in the course of a probe for *what is*. But in my opinion the distinction is very important because it tends to clarify existing obscurities about who we are. And a clear picture of *who-we-are* is fundamental to valid hypotheses about the whys and wherefores of our language, our norms and values. (Schowe, 1979, p. 145)

And for those who still feel that the hearing world has an intrinsic superiority over the deaf world, perhaps the words of Fred Schreiber will form a salutory reminder:

Obviously, this is an irreverent question and ought to be treated with the contempt it deserves. But if one takes the question in the same context in which the claims for the hearing world are made, it is not as idiotic as it seems. The world as we know it is dominated by people who hear. And one can see merely by looking at the headlines in the papers that it is in a hell of a mess. There is hardly a thing to indicate that hearing people are doing a great job in managing the world we live in. In fact, there is a great deal in the papers that leads one to think that one might, if he had a choice, do better than to choose this world. It is safe to say that all the wars in the world were started by people who hear: 99 and 11/100ths of all the crimes are committed by people who hear; and the same is true of all the vehicular homicides. Truly, there is little to support the desirability of living in the world of the hearing.

If I have not provided sufficient indictments of hearing people, let me add the crowning touch—all the silly TV commercials are also written by people who hear! (Schein, 1983, p. 59)

Postscript

American Sign Language, the dominant language of North American deaf people, to some extent represents a threat to both hearing and deaf native English language users. However, its rejection in schools and elsewhere is also an example of the organizational convenience that is so often a major criterion in policy decisions. It is understandably difficult for us to accept multiculturalism in an ethnically dominant English language society, even though research data clearly confirm second language learning of English is a better approach for many deaf students (chapter 5). Once ASL is elevated to the status of a first language, the special skills and knowledge of the English language possessed by hearing people become much less important than the special skills in ASL or an equivalent language possessed by many deaf people. Indeed, we establish a requirement that people who choose to work with deaf people either acquire skills in ASL or obtain the services of an interpreter. Such a requirement changes the status relationship between hearing and deaf people, and makes communication as much a responsibility of the hearing as of the deaf person. Attitudes are changing, but most of us are still unwilling to make the switch. Therefore, we continue to suppress ASL as the chosen language of deaf people.

Educational policies concerning the use of ASL or a manual English code will not be properly resolved until we reconceptualize our attitudes toward deafness. The historical roots of the definition of deafness are found in a medical/audiological condition, the inability to hear. It was classified a major defect not because of its implications for life and health, but because we prize the ability to speak as that characteristic that separates man from lower life forms (Linden, 1975). Consequently, it is possible Chomsky contributed as much to philosophy as to linguistics. By enunciating the concept of a deep structure of language and a species-specific Language-Responsible Cognitive Structure, he allowed a separation of speech and language as well as competence and performance. Once this separation was made, it became possible to see deaf students and adults as linguistically proficient, albeit linguistically different. They were no longer defective; or if they were it was only in the inability to speak.

The massive social changes which have occurred for deaf people since the early 1960s are the result of many influences, not only changing views of linguistics and psycholinguistics. But these changing views were important and interacted with the social changes—they provided the intellectual climate for both theoretical researchers, such as Stokoe and Furth, and social activists, such as Fred Schreiber and Jerry Schein, to impact on our views of deafness and our views of deaf people. They enabled us to perceive signs as a language, to prove that they are a language, and to enhance the dignity of deaf people. If the next 2 decades are as productive, we may be able to cast off the residue of antiquated attitudes and elevate sign language to an equality of status with spoken language. Is it possible that after more than 2,000 years, we will heed the instructions of Socrates and use the language of signs? If we do not, we will not destroy ASL, we will merely continue to suppress it. Gil Eastman (1979), describing another of his plays, "Hands" expresses it graphically, and it is fitting we leave the last word to a deaf person:

> There was a definite rhythm in our signs made up of a series of visual beats that made music without sound. This rhythmic signing appears to be a natural form for deaf people. This form has been acted out mischievously in school dormitories, heartily shared among deaf families, privately used as entertainment at deaf parties; and secretly used among ourselves; it has long been suppressed and unrecognized by the general public and most educators of the deaf. This form, a definite part of our

culture, has passed from hand to hand, generation to generation, through storytelling. It is the traditional deaf folk sign and it is still popular in deaf society. It will never die because it is an integral part of us, and it is our way and representative of our culture. (p. 127)

For us, the arguments for the use of ASL or an equivalent language in programs and classrooms for deaf children and students are partly based on entirely practical considerations: Sign language is the best way of communicating with a deaf child. However, they are also derived from more fundamental considerations. American Sign Language seems to be the best way for deaf people to process information through language, and accepting American Sign Language or its equivalent in other countries opens up the whole culture of deafness to deaf children and students; indeed, to all of us. If, in this book, we have opened up that culture in some small way, we will be more than satisfied. We will feel highly privileged.

Summary

We have tried to open a few windows and close a few doors. We have reviewed some of the more recent trends in sign language research, with particular reference to the educational controversy that continues to dominate discussions of manual methods of communication. As a result, we think that there is sufficient research evidence to justify the conclusion that American Sign Language is a language and that it should be used more widely in schools than at present. We also believe that knowledge of the culture of deafness is a vital part of being a deaf person—knowledge that is often denied to them at present. We hope books of this type will not be required 100 years from now but, somehow, we feel they will. Much of the controversy in the education of deaf children stems from dedication, and we believe dedicated hearing and deaf people will continue to want to work with deaf children and will continue to believe fervently in what they are doing. We are not cynical about the situation—merely accepting of the fact that the field of deafness in many ways represents the best and the worst of human nature—intense and dedicated professionalism, coupled with a tendency to ignore the obvious when it does not conform to our point of view. Deaf people have realized this for many years, and now hearing people are beginning to do so. Perhaps without realizing it, we are in the middle of a revolution in educational practice. If so, time will tell.

Further Reading

Current research is reported in major journals such as *American Annals of the Deaf* and *Sign Language Studies*. Additionally, the journal of the Association of Canadian Educators of the Hearing Impaired, *The ACEHI Journal/ La Revue ACEDA*, makes a uniquely Canadian contribution to this topic, and the journals of the Royal National Institute for the Deaf, the British Deaf Association, and the British Association of Teachers of the Deaf provide a United Kingdom perspective. Bencie Woll, James Kyle, and Margaret Deuchar (1981) edit an interesting summary of most of the recent British research into sign language, *Perspectives on British Sign Language and Deafness*. A valuable collection of recent papers presented at the Second International Conference on Sign Language Research, held at Bristol, 1981, has been published by Jim Kyle and Bencie Woll (1983) under the title *Language in Sign*, a book that was an invaluable source in writing this chapter. Other recent books of interest include those of Thomas and James Spradley (1978), *Deaf Like Me*, and *Can't Your Child Hear?* by Roger Freeman, Clifton Carbin, and Robert Boese (1981). Finally, *Deaf Heritage—A Narrative History of Deaf America* by Jack Gannon (1981) covers the whole range of deaf culture from 1812 to 1980.

References

Aarsleff, H. (1983). *The study of language in England: 1780-1860*. London: Athelone Press.

A.G. Bell Association. (1970, March). Alexander Graham Bell and the Volta Bureau. *Volta Review*, 148-159.

Alpern, G.D., & Boll, T.J. (1972). *The developmental profile*. Indianapolis: Psychological Developmental Publications.

Altom, M., & Weil, J. (1977). Young children's use of temporal and spatial order information in short-term memory. *Journal of Experimental Child Psychology, 24*, 147-163.

Altshuler, K. (1962). Psychiatric considerations in the adult deaf. *American Annals of the Deaf, 107*, 560-561.

Altshuler, K. (1963). Sexual patterns and family relationships. In J. Rainer, K. Altshuler, & F. Kallman (Eds.), *Family and mental health problems of a deaf population* (pp. 92-112). New York: New York State Psychiatric Institution.

Annett, M. (1973). Laterality of childhood hemiplegia and the growth of speech and intelligence. *Cortex, 14*, 4-29.

Annual Survey of Hearing Impaired Children and Youth. (1971). *Additional handicapping conditions*. Washington, DC: Gallaudet College.

Anon. (1852). Indian Language of signs. *American Annals of the Deaf and Dumb, 4*, 157-172.

Anthony, D.A., & Associates (Eds.). (1971). *Seeing Essential English*. Anaheim, CA: Education Services Division, Anaheim Union High School.

Armstrong, D.F. (1983). Iconicity, arbitrariness, and duality of patterning in signed and spoken language: Perspectives on language evolution. *Sign Language Studies, 38*, 51-83.

Armstrong, D.F., & Katz, S.H. (1981). Brain laterality in signed and spoken language: A synthetic theory of language use. *Sign Language Studies, 33*, 319-349.

Arnold, P. (1978a). The deaf child's written English: Can we measure its quality? *Teacher of the Deaf, 6*, 196-200.

Arnold, P. (1978b). Mental rotation by deaf and hearing children. *Perceptual and Motor Skills, 47*, 977-978.

Arnold, P. (1979). The memory of deaf children. *Journal of the British Association of Teachers of the Deaf, 4*, 102-106.

Arnold, P. (1983). Does pure oralism cause atrophy of the hearing-impaired child's brain? *Volta Review, 85*, 229-234.

Arnold, P., & Walter, G. (1979). Communication and reasoning skills of deaf and hearing signers. *Perceptual and Motor Skills, 49*, 192-194.

Arooshian, L., & Bryan, J. (1979). The effects of early auditory deprivation on temporal perceptions: A comparison of hearing and hearing impaired children on temporal pattern matching tasks. *Journal of Speech and Hearing Research, 22*, 731-746.

Baker-Shenk, C. (1983). *A microanalysis of the nonmanual components of questions in American Sign Language.* Unpublished doctoral dissertation, University of California.

Baker, C. (1979). How does "sim-com" fit into a bilingual approach to education? In F. Caccamise & D. Hicks (Eds.), *American Sign Language in a bilingual context.* Proceedings of Second National Symposium on Sign Language Research and Teaching, Coronado, CA, 13-26.

Baker, C., & Cokely, D. (1980). *American Sign Language: A student text.* Silver Springs, MA: T.J. Publishers.

Bartlett, F.C. (1932). *Remembering.* Cambridge: Cambridge University Press.

Basilier, T. (1964). Surdophrenia. *Acta Psychiatrica Scandinavica Supplementum, 40*, 362-374.

Bates, E. (1976). *Language and context: The acquisition of pragmatics.* New York: Academic Press.

Battison, R.M. (1974). Phonological deletion in American Sign Language. *Sign Language Studies, 5*, 1-19.

Bazin, G. (1962). *A concise history of art: Part one.* London: Thames & Hudson.

Beaton, A.A. (1982). *Can neurophysiology explain hemisphere differences?* Unpublished manuscript, University College of Swansea.

Beck, K., Beck, C., & Gironella, O. (1977). Rehearsal and recall strategies of deaf and hearing individuals. *American Annals of the Deaf, 122*, 544-552.

Bellugi, U. (1980). Clues from the structural similarity of signed and spoken language. In U. Bellugi & M. Studdert-Kennedy (Eds.), *Signed and spoken language: Biological constraints on linguistic form* (pp. 115-140). Weinheim: Verlag Chemie.

Bellugi, U., & Klima, E.S. (1979). Language: Perspectives from another modality. *Brain and Mind (CIBA Foundation Symposium 69).* Amsterdam: Excerpta Medica.

Bellugi, U., & Klima, E.S. (1982a). From gesture to sign: Deixis in a visual-gestural language. In R.J. Jarvella & W. Klein (Eds.), *Speech, place and action: Studies in deixis and related topics* (pp. 297-314). New York: Wiley.

Bellugi, U., & Klima, E.S. (1982b). The acquisition of three morphological systems in American Sign Language. *Papers and Reports on Child Language Development, 21*, 1-35. Stanford, CA: Stanford University.

Bellugi, U., Klima, E., & Siple, P. (1975). Remembering in signs. *Cognition, 3*, 93-125.

Bellugi, U., Poizner, H., & Klima, E.S. (1983). Brain organization for language: Clues from sign aphasia. *Human Neurobiology, 2*, 155-170.

Bellugi, U., Poizner, H., & Zurif, E.B. (1982). Prospects for the study of aphasia in a visual-gestural language. In M.A. Arbib, D. Caplan, & J.C. Marshall (Eds.), *Neural models of language processes* (pp. 271-297). New York: Academic Press.

Belmont, J.M., & Karchmer, M.A. (1978). Deaf people's memory: There are problems testing special populations. In M.M. Gruneberg, P.E. Morris, & R.N. Sykes (Eds.), *Practical aspects of memory* (pp. 581-588). London: Academic Press.

Belmont, J.M., Karchmer, M.A., & Pilkonis, P.A. (1976). Instructed rehearsal strategies' influence on deaf memory processing. *Journal of Speech and Hearing Research, 19*, 36-47.

Bender, R.E. (1981). *The conquest of deafness*. Cleveland OH: Case Western Reserve University.

Berger, K.W., & Popelka, G.R. (1971). Extra-facial gestures in relation to speechreading. *Journal of Communication Disorders, 3*, 302-308.

Bergman, B. (1983). Verbs and adjectives: Morphological processes in Swedish Sign Language. In J. Kyle & B. Woll (Eds.), *Language in sign* (pp. 3-9). London: Croom Helm.

Bernstein, B. (1972). Social class, language and socialization. In P. Giglioli (Ed.), *Language and social context* (pp. 157-178). London: Penguin.

Bernstein, B., & Henderson, D. (1969). Social class differences in the relevance of language to socialization. *Sociology, 3*, 1-20.

Berry, M. (1980). *Teaching linguistically handicapped children*. Englewood Cliffs, NJ: Prentice Hall.

Besner, D., & Davelaar, E. (1982). Basic processes in reading: Two phonological codes. *Canadian Journal of Psychology, 36*, 701-711.

Bever, T.G. (1973). The influences of speech performance on linguistic structures. In G.B.F. D'Arcais (Ed.), *Advances in psycholinguistics*. Amsterdam: New Holland Press.

Blackwell, P.M., Engen, E., Fischgrund, J.W., & Zaracadoolas, C. (1978). *Sentences and other systems: A language and learning curriculum for hearing impaired children*. Washington, DC: A.G. Bell Association.

Blair, F.X. (1957). A study of the visual memory of deaf and hearing children. *American Annals of the Deaf, 102*, 254-263.

Blank, M., & Bridger, W.H. (1966). Conceptual cross-modal transfer in deaf and hearing children. *Child Development, 37*, 29-38.

Blaxter, M. (1976). *The meaning of disability*. London: Heinemann.

Bloom, L. (1970). *Language development: Form and function in emerging grammar*. Cambridge, MA: Massachusetts Institute of Technology Press.

Bloom, L., & Lahey, M. (1978). *Language development and language disorders*. New York: Wiley.

Bloomfield, L. (1933). *Language*. New York: Holt, Rinehart & Winston.

Blumberg, C. (1973). A school for the deaf facilitates integration. In W.H. Northcott (Ed.), *The hearing impaired child in a regular classroom* (pp. 169-176). Washington, DC: A.G. Bell Association.

Boatner, M. (1959). The Gallaudet papers. *Library of Congress Journal of Current Acquisitions, 17,* 1-12.

Bockmiller, P.R., & Coley, J.D. (1981, February). A survey of methods, materials and teacher preparation among teachers of reading to the hearing impaired. *The Reading Teacher, 34,* 526-529.

Bode, L. (1974). Communication of agent, object, and indirect object in signed and spoken languages. *Perceptual and Motor Skills, 39,* 1151-1158.

Bogen, J.E. (1969). The other side of the brain. II—An appositional mind. *Bulletin of the Los Angeles Neurological Societies, 34,* 135-162.

Bogen, J.E., & Bogen, G.M. (1969). The other side of the brain. III—The corpus callosum and creativity. *Bulletin of the Los Angeles Neurological Societies, 35,* 191-220.

Bolton, B. (1971). A factor analytic study of communication skills and nonverbal abilities of deaf rehabilitation clients. *Multivariate Behavioral Research, 6,* 485-501.

Bonvillian, J.D., Charrow, V.R., & Nelson, K.E. (1973). Psycholinguistic and educational implications of deafness. *Human Development, 16,* 321-345.

Bonvillian, J.C., Orlansky, M.D., & Novack, L.L. (1983). Early sign language acquisition and its relation to cognitive and motor development. In J. Kyle & B. Woll (Eds.), *Language in sign* (pp. 116-125). London: Croom Helm.

Boothroyd, A. (1982). *Hearing impairments in young children.* New York: Prentice Hall.

Bornstein, H., Hamilton, L.B., Saulnier, K.L., & Roy, H.L. (1975). *The Signed English dictionary for preschool and elementary levels.* Washington, DC: Gallaudet College Press.

Boshoven, M.M., McNeil, M.R., & Harvey, L.O. (1982). Hemispheric specialization for the processing of linguisitic and nonlinguistic stimuli in congenitally deaf and hearing adults: A review and contribution. *Audiology, 21,* 509-530.

Brannigan, C., & Humphries, D. (1969, May). I see what you mean. *New Scientist,* 406-408.

Brasel, K.E., & Quigley, S.P. (1975). *The influence of early language and communication environments on the development of language in deaf children.* Urbana, IL: University of Illinois, Institute for Research on Exceptional Children.

Brennan, M. (1975). Can deaf children acquire language? *American Annals of the Deaf, 120,* 463-479.

Brennan, M. (1981). Grammatical processes in British Sign Language. In B. Woll, J. Kyle, & M. Deuchar (Eds.), *Perspectives on British Sign Language and deafness* (pp. 120-135). London: Croom Helm.

Brennan, M. (1983). Marking time in British Sign Language. In J. Kyle & B. Woll (Eds.), *Language in sign* (pp. 10-13). London: Croom Helm.

Brennan, M., & Hayhurst, A.B. (1978). The Renaissance of British Sign Language. In C. Baker & R. Battison (Eds.), *Sign Language and the deaf community: Essays in honor of William C. Stokoe* (pp. 233-344). Silver Springs: National Association of the Deaf.

Breslaw, P.I., Griffiths, A.J., Wood, D.J., & Howarth, C.I. (1981). The referential communication skills of deaf children from different educational environments. *Journal of Child Psychology, 22*, 269-282.

Brill, R.G. (1970). *Total communication as a basis of educating prelingually deaf children*. Paper presented at the Communication Symposium, Frederick, MD: Maryland School for the Deaf.

Brill, R.G. (1971). *Administrative and professional developments in the education of the deaf*. Washington, DC: Gallaudet College Press.

Brill, R.G. (1978). *Mainstreaming the prelingually deaf child*. Washington, DC: Gallaudet College Press.

Brill, R.G., & Fahey, J.A. (1971). A combination that works in a preschool program for deaf children. *Hearing and Speech News, 4*, 17-19.

Broadbent, D.E. (1965). Applications of information theory and decision theory to human perception and reaction. In N. Wiener & J.P. Schade (Eds.), *Progress in brain research: Vol. 17, Cybernetics of the nervous system* (pp. 309-320). Amsterdam: Elsevier.

Bronowski, J.S., & Bellugi, U. (1970). Language, name, and concept. *Science, 168*, 666-673.

Brooks, P.H. (1978). Some speculations concerning deafness and learning to read. In L. Lieben (Ed.), *Deaf children: Developmental perspectives* (pp. 87-101). New York, New York: Academic Press.

Brown, R. (1958). *Words and things*. Glencoe, IL: Free Press.

Brown, R. (1973). *A first language: The early stages*. Cambridge, MA: Harvard University Press.

Brown, R. (1977). Introduction to symposium on language input and acquisition. In C.E. Snow & C.A. Ferguson (Eds.), *Talking to children* (pp. 1-27). Cambridge, MA: Cambridge University Press.

Brown, R.N., Black, A.H., & Horowitz, A.E. (1955). Phonetic symbolism in four languages. *Journal of Abnormal and Social Psychology, 50*, 388-393.

Bruner, J. (1975). The ontogenesis of speech acts. *Journal of Child Language, 2*, 1-19.

Bryden, M.P. (1982). *Laterality: Functional assymetry in the intact brain*. New York: Academic Press.

Bunch, G. (1977). Mainstreaming and the hearing impaired child: Decision making. *B.C. Journal of Special Education, 1*, 11-17.

Burns, T. (1964). Non-verbal communication. *Discovery, XXV*(10), 30-35.

Butcher, H.J. (1968). *Human intelligence: Its nature and assessment.* London: Methuen.

Calvert, D., & Silverman, R. (1975). *Speech and deafness.* Washington, DC: A.G. Bell Association.

Carbin, C. (1983). Historical and personal perspectives on deafness. *The ACEHI Journal, 9*(2), 130-138.

Carey, P., & Blake, J. (1974). Visual short-term memory in the hearing and the deaf. *Canadian Journal of Psychology, 28,* 1-14.

Carter, M. (1981a). Some issues involved in attempting a linguistic analysis of BSL. *Research on deafness and British Sign Language I.* School of Education Research Unit, University of Bristol.

Carter, M. (1981b). Noun phrase modification in British Sign Language. *Research on deafness and British Sign Language II.* School of Education Research Unit, University of Bristol.

Carter, M., & Woll, B. (1981). Describing British Sign Language. *Research on deafness and British Sign Language.* School of Education Research Unit, University of Bristol.

Carver, R.J. (1984). *Environmental factors in linguistic and cognitive development of deaf children.* Unpublished research report, Department of Educational Psychology, University of Alberta, Edmonton.

Carver, R.J. (1985). *Thinking, language, and the deaf student: A self-analysis.* Unpublished manuscript, Department of Educational Psychology, University of Alberta.

Carver, V., & Rodda, M. (1978). *Disability and the environment.* London: Paul Elek.

Ceram, C.W. (1952). *Gods, graves, and scholars.* London: Gollancz.

Chafe, W.L. (1970). *Meaning and the structure of language.* Chicago: University of Chicago Press.

Charrow, V. (1976). A psycholinguistic analysis of 'deaf English.' *Sign Language Studies, 1,* 139-150.

Charrow, V., & Fletcher, J.D. (1974). English as a second language of deaf children. *Developmental Psychology, 10,* 463-470.

Chess, S., Korn, S.J., & Fernandez, P.B. (1971). *Psychiatric disorders of children with congenital rubella.* New York: Brunner-Mazel.

Chomsky, N. (1957). *Syntactic structures.* The Hague: Mouton.

Chomsky, N. (1959). Review of B.F. Skinner's *Verbal behavior. Language, 35,* 26-58.

Chomsky, N. (1965). *Aspects of the theory of syntax.* Cambridge, MA: Massachusetts Institute of Technology Press.

Chomsky, N., & Walker, E. (1978). The linguistic and psycholinguistic background. In E. Walker (Ed.), *Explorations in the biology of language* (pp. 15-26). Montgomery, VT: Bradford Books.

Christensen, K. (1981). *Conceptually signed English*. Unpublished manuscript, San Diego State University, CA.

Clarke, J.L. (1973). Verbal and nonverbal learning disabilities. In M.R. Burkowsky (Ed.), *Orientation to language and learning disorders* (pp. 54-100). St. Louis, MO: Warren H. Green.

Code, C. (1981). Dichotic listening with the communicatively impaired: Results from trials of a short British-English dichotic word test. *Journal of Phonetics, 9*, 375-383.

Cohen, G. (1975). Cerebral apartheid: A fanciful notion. *New Behaviour, 2*, 458-461.

Coleman, J.S., Campbell, E.Q., Hobson, C.J., McPartland, J., Mood, A.M., Weinfield, F.D., & York, R.L. (1966). *Equality of educational opportunity*. Washington, DC: U.S. Government Printing Office.

Collins-Ahlgren, M. (1975). Language development of two deaf children. *American Annals of the Deaf, 120*, 524-539.

Collins, J.L. (1969). Communication between deaf children of preschool age and their mothers. *Dissertation Abstracts International* (60-A) 2245.

Coltheart, M. (1980). Mysteries of reading in brain defects. *Rehabilitation, Great Britain, 1*, 32-35.

Connor, L.E. (Ed.). (1971). *Speech for the deaf child: Knowledge and use*. Washington, DC: A.G. Bell Association.

Connor, L.E. (1976). New directions in infant programs for the deaf. *Volta Review, 78*, 8-15.

Conrad, R. (1964). Acoustic confusions in immediate memory. *British Journal of Psychology, 55*, 75-83.

Conrad, R. (1970a). Short-term memory processes in the deaf. *British Journal of Psychology, 61*, 179-195.

Conrad, R. (1970b). Profound deafness as a psycholinguistic problem. In G. Fant (Ed.), *Speech communication ability and profound deafness*. Washington, DC: A.G. Bell Association.

Conrad, R. (1971). The effect of vocalizing on comprehension in the profoundly deaf. *British Journal of Psychology, 62*, 147-150.

Conrad, R. (1972). Short-term memory in the deaf: A test for speech coding. *British Journal of Psychology, 63*, 173-180.

Conrad, R. (1973a). Some correlates of speech coding in the short-term memory of the deaf. *British Journal of Speech and Hearing Research, 16*, 374-384.

Conrad, R. (1973b) Internal speech in the profoundly deaf child. *The Teacher of the Deaf, 71*, 384-389.

Conrad, R. (1977). Lip-reading by deaf and hearing children. *British Journal of Educational Psychology, 47*, 60-65.

Conrad, R. (1979). *The deaf school child*. London: Harper & Row.

Conrad, R., & Rush, M.L. (1965). On the nature of short-term memory encoding by the deaf. *Journal of Speech and Hearing Disorders, 30,* 336-343.

Coombs, A.W., & Snygg, D. (1959). *Individual behavior: A perceptual approach to behavior.* New York: Harper & Row.

Cooper, A.F. (1976). Deafness and psychiatric illness. *British Journal of Psychiatry, 129,* 216-226.

Cooper, R.L., & Rosenstein, J. (1966). Language acquisition of deaf children. *Volta Review, 68,* 58-67.

Cornett, R.O. (1967). Cued speech. *American Annals of the Deaf, 112,* 3-13.

Cornish, E.R. (1971). Pragmatic aspects of negation in sentence evaluation and completion tasks. *British Journal of Psychology, 62,* 505-511.

Corson, H. (1973). *Comparing deaf children of oral deaf parents and deaf parents using manual communication with deaf children of hearing parents on academic, social and communicative functioning.* Unpublished doctoral dissertation, University of Cincinnati.

Costello, E. (1972). *Appraising certain linguistic structures in the receptive sign language competence of deaf children.* Unpublished doctoral dissertation, Syracuse University, Syracuse, NY.

Craig, E. (1970). A supplement to the spoken word: The Paget-Gorman Sign System. In P. Henderson (Ed.), *Methods of communication currently used in the education of deaf children* (pp. 50-53). London: Royal National Institute for the Deaf.

Craig, W., & Collins, J. (1970). Analysis of communicative interaction in classes for deaf children. *American Annals of the Deaf, 115,* 79-85.

Crittendon, J.B. (1974). Categorization of cheremic errors in sign language reception. *Sign Language Studies, 5,* 66-71.

Crystal, D. (1971). *Linguistics.* Harmondsworth: Pelican.

Crystal, D., Fletcher, P., & Garman, M. (1976). *The grammatical analysis of language disability.* Guildford, England: Billing & Sons.

Cumming, C.E. (1982a). *Counseling with parents of hearing impaired children.* Unpublished manuscript, University of Alberta, Edmonton.

Cumming, C.E. (1982b). The role of sign in the academic environment. *The ACEHI Journal, 8,* 149-153.

Cumming, C.E., & Rodda, M. (1985). The effects of auditory deprivation on successive processing. *Canadian Journal of Behavioral Science, 17,* 232-245.

Cumming, C.E., Grove, C., & Rodda, M. (1985). A note on reading comprehension in hearing impaired adolescents. *Journal of the British Association of Teachers of the Deaf, 9,* 57-60.

Dale, D.M.C. (1974). *Language development in deaf and partially hearing children.* Springfield, IL: Charles C. Thomas.

Daraul, A. (1961). *Secret societies.* London: Muller.

Darbyshire, J.O., & Reeves, V.R. (1969-70). The use of adaptations of some of Piaget's tests with groups of children with normal and impaired hearing. *British Journal of Disorders of Communication. 4-5*, 197-202.

Darwin, C. (1877). Biographical sketch of an infant mind. *Mind, ii*, 285-294.

Das, J. (1983). Memory for spatial and temporal order in deaf children. *American Annals of the Deaf, 128*, 894-899.

Davey, B., LaSasso, C., Macready, G., & Swaiko, N. (1982, March). *Comparability of deaf and hearing subjects' performance on selected reading comprehension tasks.* Paper presented at the Annual Meeting of American Educational Research Association, New York.

Davis, A.C. (1983). Hearing disorders in the population: First phase findings of the MRC National Study of Hearing. In M.E. Lutman & M.P. Haggard (Eds.), *Hearing science and hearing disorders* (pp.35-60). London: Academic Press.

Day, P. (1982). The expression of communicative intention: Deaf children and hearing mothers. In H. Hoeman & R. Wilbur (Eds.), *Interpersonal communication and deaf people.* Washington, DC: Gallaudet College.

Deacon, J.J. (1974). *Joey* (originally *Tongue tied*). London: National Society for Mentally Handicapped Children.

de l'Epée, L'Abbé, C.M. (1784). *La veritable manière d'instruire les sourds et muets.* Paris: Chez Nyon l'Aîré.

Dearman, N., & Plisko, V. (1981). *The condition of education.* Washington, DC: Center for Education Statistics.

Dee, A. (1981). Meeting the needs of the hearing parents of deaf infants: A comprehensive parent education program. *Language, Speech and Hearing Services in the Schools, 12*, 13-18.

Deland, F. (1931). *The story of lipreading.* Washington, DC: Volta Bureau.

Denmark, J.C. (1966). Mental illness and early profound deafness. *British Journal of Medical Psychology, 39*, 117-123.

Denmark, J.C. (1976). Methods of communication in the education of deaf children. In P. Henderson (Ed.), *Methods of communication currently used in the education of deaf children* (pp. 73-79). London: Royal National Institute for the Deaf.

Denmark, J.C., & Eldridge, R.W. (1969, August 2). Psychiatric services for the deaf. *Lancet*, 259-262.

Denmark, J.C., Rodda, M., Abel, R.A., Skelton, U., Eldridge, R.W., Warren, F., & Gordon, A. (1979). *A word in deaf ears.* London: Royal National Institute for the Deaf.

Denmark, J.C., & Warren, F. (1972). A psychiatric unit for the deaf. *British Journal of Psychiatry, 120*, 423-428.

Deno, E. (1968). Educational aspects of minimal brain dysfunction in children. *Proceedings of Sixth Delaware Conference on the Handicapped Child* (pp. 41-65). Wilmington, DE: A.I. duPont.

Denton, D.M. (1972). A rationale for total communication. In T.J. O'Rourke (Ed.), *Psycholinguistics and total communication: The state of the art*(pp. 53-61). Washington, DC: American Annals of the Deaf.

Deuchar, M. (1979). The grammar of British Sign Language. *British Deaf News*, June, Supplement.

Deuchar, M. (1981). Variation in British Sign Language. In B. Woll, J. Kyle, & M. Deuchar (Eds.), *Perspectives on British Sign Language and deafness* (pp. 109-119). London: Croom Helm.

Deuchar, M. (1983). Is BSL an SVO language? In J. Kyle & B. Woll (Eds.), *Language in sign* (pp. 69-76). London: Croom Helm.

Dimond, S., & Beaumont, G. (1972). Processing in perceptual integration between and within the cerebral hemispheres. *British Journal of Psychology, 63*, 509-514.

DiFrancesca, S. (1972). *Academic achievement test results of a national testing program for hearing impaired students (Series D, No. 9)*. Washington, DC: Office of Demographic Studies, Gallaudet College.

Dodd, D.H., & White, R.M. (1980). *Cognition: Mental structures and processes*. New York: Allyn & Bacon.

Donaldson, M. (1978). *Children's minds*. London: Fontana.

Donoghue, R. (1968). The deaf personality: A study in contexts. *Journal of Rehabilitation of the Deaf, 2*, 35-51.

Dore, J. (1977). Children's illocutionary acts. In R. Freedle (Ed.), *Discourse: Production and comprehension* (pp. 227-244). Norwood, NJ: Ablex.

Eastman, G.C. (1974). *Sign me Alice: A play in sign language*. Washington, DC: Gallaudet College Press.

Eastman, G.C. (1979). Sign language translation for the theatre. In I. Ahlgren & B. Bergman, (Eds.), *Collected papers: First international symposium on sign language research* (pp. 121-128). Stockholm: Swedish Association of the Deaf.

Edmondson, W. (1983). A story chain: Sign language communication skills in children and adults. In J. Kyle & B. Woll (Eds.), *Language in sign* (pp. 225-237). London: Croom Helm.

Edwards, V.K. (1979). *The West Indian language issue in British schools*. London: Routledge & Kegan Paul.

Engelmann, S. (1970). How to construct effective language programs for the poverty child. In F. Williams (Ed.), *Language and poverty* (pp. 102-122). Chicago: Markham.

Erber, N.P. (1972). Auditory, visual, and auditory-visual recognition of consonants by children with normal and impaired hearing. *Journal of Speech and Hearing Research, 15*, 407-412.

Erber, N.P. (1974). Effects of angle, distance, and illumination on visual reception of speech by profoundly deaf children. *Journal of Speech and Hearing Research, 17*, 99-112.

Erber, N.P. (1975). Auditory-visual perception of speech. *Journal of Speech and Hearing Disorders, 40*, 481-492.

Erber, N.P. (1979). Auditory-visual perception of speech with reduced optical clarity. *Journal of Speech and Hearing Research, 22*, 212-223.

Erting, C. (1978). Language policy and deaf ethnicity in the United States. *Sign Language Studies, 19*, 139-152.

Evans, L. (1964). *Psychological factors related to the lipreading achievement of deaf children.* Unpublished master's thesis, University of Liverpool.

Evans, L. (1978). *Visual communication in the deaf: Lipreading, fingerspelling and signing.* Unpublished doctoral dissertation, University of Newcastle-on-Tyne.

Evans, L. (1981). Psycholinguistic perspectives on visual communication. In B. Woll, J. Kyle, & M. Deuchar (Eds.), *Perspectives on British Sign Language and deafness* (pp. 150-161). London: Croom Helm.

Evans, L. (1982). *Total communication: Structure and strategy.* Washington, DC: Gallaudet College Press.

Ewing, A.W.G., & Ewing, E.C. (1964). *Teaching deaf children to talk.* Manchester: University Press.

Ewing, I.R., & Ewing, A.W.G. (1961). *New opportunities for deaf children.* Manchester: University Press.

Ewoldt, C. (1981). A psycholinguistic description of selected deaf children reading in sign language. *Reading Research Quarterly, 17*, 58-87.

Fant, L.J. (1974-1975). Ameslan. *Gallaudet Today, 5*(2), 1-3.

Farwell, R. (1976). Speech reading: A research review. *American Annals of the Deaf, 121*, 19-30.

Feldman, H. (1975). *The development of a lexicon by deaf children of hearing parents or "There's more to language than meets the ear."* Unpublished doctoral dissertation, University of Pennsylvania College Park, PA.

Fellendorf, G., & Harrow, I. (1970). Parent counseling, 1961-68. *Volta Review, 72*, 51-59.

Feuerstein, R. (1979). *The dynamic assessment of retarded performers.* Baltimore: University Park Press.

Fillmore, C.J. (1968). The case for case. In E. Bach & R.T. Harms (Eds.), *Universals in language* (pp. 1-88). New York: Holt, Rinehart & Winston.

Fischer, S. (1972). Some properties of ASL. In U. Bellugi & S. Fischer (Eds.), A comparison of sign language and spoken language (Appendix). *Cognition, 1*, 173-200.

Fitts, P.M., & Posner, M.I. (1967). *Human performance.* Belmont, CA: Brooks/Cole.

Fogelman, K. (1976). *Britain's sixteen year olds: Preliminary findings from the third follow up of the National Child Development Study.* London: National Children's Bureau.

Font, J.F., & Ladner, E.S. (1979). *Silent knights of the chess board*. Berkeley, CA: West Coast Print Centre.

Freeman, R.D. (1977). Psychiatric aspects of sensory disorders and intervention. In P.J. Graham, (Ed.), *Epidemiological approaches in child psychology* (pp. 275-304). New York: Academic Press.

Freeman, R.D., Carbin, C.F., & Boese, R.J. (1981). *Can't your child hear? A guide for those who care about deaf children*. Baltimore: University Park Press.

Freeman, R.D., Malkin, S., & Hastings, J.O. (1975). Psychosocial problems of deaf children and their families: A comparative study. *American Annals of the Deaf, 121*, 391-405.

French, S.L. (1971). The acquisition of speech. In E.L. Connor (Ed.), *Speech for the deaf child: Knowledge and use* (pp. 207-220). Washington, DC: A.G. Bell Association.

Friedman, L. (1977). Formational properties and American Sign Language. In L. Friedman (Ed.), *On the other hand* (pp. 13-56). New York: Academic Press.

Frostig, M., Lefever, D.W., & Whittlesey, J.R.B. (1964). *The Marianne Frostig Development Test of Visual Perception*. Palo Alto, CA: Consulting Psychology Press.

Fry, D.B. (1968). The development of the phonological system in the normal and the deaf child. In F. Smith & G.A. Miller (Eds.), *The genesis of language: A psycholinguistic approach* (pp. 187-206). Cambridge, MA: MIT Press.

Fudge, E.C. (1970). Phonology. In J. Lyons (Ed.), *New horizons in linguistics* (pp. 76-95). Harmondsworth: Pelican.

Fulcanelli. (1971). *Le mystère des cathédrals*. London: Neville Spearman.

Furth, H.G. (1961). Influence of language on the development of concept formation in deaf children. *Journal of Abnormal and Social Psychology, 63*, 386-389.

Furth, H.G. (1963). Conceptual discovery and control on a pictorial part-whole task as a function of age, intelligence, and language. *Journal of Educational Psychology, 54*, 191-196.

Furth, H.G. (1964). Research with the deaf: Implications for language and cognition. *Psychological Bulletin, 62*, 145-164.

Furth, H.G. (1966). *Thinking without language: Psychological implications of deafness*. New York: Free Press.

Furth, H.G. (1973). *Deafness and learning: A psychosocial approach*. Belmont, CA: Wadsworth.

Gannon, J.R. (1981). *Deaf heritage: A narrative history of deaf America*. Silver Springs, MD: National Association of the Deaf.

Gardner, B.T., & Gardner, R.A. (1969). Two-way communication with an infant chimpanzee. In A. Schrier & F. Stollnitz (Eds.), *Behavior of non-human primates, III* (pp. 117-184). New York: Academic Press.

Garretson, M.D. (1981). The deaf child and the unwritten curriculum. *Directions*, *2*, 9-12.

Garrison, W.M., Tesch, S., & DeCara, F. (1978). Assessment of self concept levels amongst post-secondary deaf adolescents. *American Annals of the Deaf, 123*, 968-975.

Genesee, F. (1976). The role of intelligence in second language learning. *Language Learning, 26*, 267-280.

Geschwind, N. (1965). Disconnexion syndromes in animals and men. *Brain, 88*, 237-294, 585-644.

Geschwind, N. (1973). The brain and language. In G.A. Miller (Ed.), *Communication language, and meaning* (pp. 61-72). New York: Basic Books.

Getz, S. (1953). *Environment and the deaf child*. Springfield, IL: Charles C. Thomas.

Gibson, H.B. (1965). *Manual of the Gibson spiral maze*. London: University of London Press.

Gniadzowsky, P.A. (1977). *Counselor preferences of the hard of hearing*. Unpublished master's thesis, University of Alberta.

Goffman, E. (1963). *Stigma: Management of a spoiled identity*. Englewood Cliffs, NJ: Prentice Hall.

Goldin-Meadow, S., & Feldman, H. (1975). The creation of a communication system: A study of deaf children of hearing parents. *Sign Language Studies. 8*, 225-234.

Gordon, A. (1977). Thinking with restricted language: A personal construct investigation of pre-lingually profoundly deaf adolescents. *British Journal of Psychology, 68*, 253-256.

Gormley, K.A., & Geoffrion, L. (1981). Another view of using language experience to teach reading to deaf and hearing impaired children. *The Reading Teacher, 34*, 519-524.

Goss, R.N. (1970). Language used by mothers of deaf children and mothers of hearing children. *American Annals of the Deaf, 115*, 93-96.

Graves, R. (1961). *The white goddess*. London: Faber & Faber.

Greenberg, J. (1960). A quantitative approach to the morphological typology of language. *International Journal of American Linguistics, 26*, 178-194.

Greenberg, M.T. (1980). Hearing families with deaf children: Stress and functioning as related to communication method. *American Annals of the Deaf, 9*, 1063-1071.

Greenberg, M.T., & Marvin, R.S. (1979). Attachment patterns in profoundly deaf school children. *Merrill-Palmer Quarterly, 25*, 265-279.

Greene, J. (1972). *Psycholinguistics: Chomsky and psychology*. Harmondsworth: Penguin.

Greene, J. (1975). *Thinking and language*. London: Methuen.

Gregory, S. (1976). *The deaf child and his family*. New York: Halsted Press.

Grinker R.R., Vernon, M., Mindel, E., Rothstein, D.A., Easton, H., Koh, S.D., & Collums, L. (1969). *Psychiatric diagnosis, therapy and research on the psychotic deaf*. Washington, DC: U.S. Department of Health, Education and Welfare. (SRS-RSA-192-1971)

Groce, N. (1982). Beyond institutions: History of some American deaf; An example from Martha's Vineyard. In P. Higgins & J. Nash (Eds.), *Deaf community and the deaf population*. Washington: Gallaudet College.

Groen, G.J., & Parkman, J.M. (1972). A chronometric analysis of simple addition. *Psychological Review, 79*, 329-343.

Grove, C., O'Sullivan, F.D., & Rodda, M. (1979). Communication and language in severely deaf adolescents. *British Journal of Psychology, 70*, 531-540.

Grove, C., & O'Sullivan, F.D. (1976). *Theoretical background and proposals for the Test of Communication Skills of deaf adolescents*. London: Department of Health and Social Security. (J2/R198/65)

Grove, C., & Rodda, M. (1984). Receptive communication skills of hearing impaired students: A comparison of four methods of communication. *American Annals of the Deaf, 129*, 378-385.

Gruzelier, J., Eves, F., & Connolly, J. (1981). Reciprocal hemispheric influences on response habituation in the electrodermal system. *Physiological Psychology, 9*, 313-317.

Gunzberg, H.C., & Gunzberg, A.L. (1973). *Mental handicap and the physical environment*. London: Balliere Tindall.

Gustason, G. (1981). Does signing exact English work? *Teaching English to the Deaf, 7*, 16-20.

Gustason, G., Pfetzing, D., & Zawolkow, E. (1972). *Signing exact English*. Rossmor, CA: Modern Signs Press.

Haas, W.H., & Crowley, D.J. (1982). Professional information dissemination to parents of preschool hearing-impaired children. *Volta Review, 84*, 17-23.

Haggard, M., Gatehouse, S., & Davis, A. (1981). The high prevalence of hearing disorders and its implications for services in the United Kingdom *British Journal of Audiology, 15*, 241-251.

Halliday, M.A.K. (1970). Language structure and language function. In J. Lyons (Ed.), *New horizons in linguistics* (pp. 140-165). Harmondsworth: Pelican.

Halliday, M.A.K. (1979). One child's protolanguage. In M. Bullowa (Ed.), *Before speech* (pp. 171-190). Cambridge: Cambridge University Press.

Hamilton, H. (1984). Linguistic encoding in short-term memory. In D.S. Martin (Ed.), *International Symposium on Cognition, Education and Deafness* (pp. 129-140). Washington, DC: Gallaudet College.

Hanson, V.L. (1982). Short-term recall by deaf signers of American Sign Language: Implications of encoding strategy for order recall. *Journal of Experimental Psychology: Learning, Memory and Cognition, 8*, 572-583.

Hanson, V.L., & Bellugi, U. (1980). *Memory for ASL sentences.* San Diego, CA: Salk Institute for Biological Studies.

Hanson, V.L., & Bellugi, U. (1982). On the role of sign order and morphological structure in memory for American Sign Language sentences. *Journal of Verbal Learning and Verbal Behavior, 21,* 621-633.

Hardyck, C., Tzeng, O., & Wang, W. (1978). Cerebral lateralization of function and bilingual decision process: Is thinking lateralized? *Brain and Language, 5,* 56-71.

Harris, A.E. (1978). The development of the deaf individual and the deaf community. In L. Lieben (Ed.), *Deaf children: Developmental perspectives* (pp. 217-233). New York: Academic Press.

Harris, G.A. (1983). *Broken ears, wounded hearts.* Washington, DC: Gallaudet College Press.

Harris, R.I. (1982). Early childhood deafness as a stress producing family experience: A theoretical perspective. In C. Erting & R. Meisegieier (Eds.), *Deaf children and the socialization process* (pp. 155-232). Washington, DC: Gallaudet College.

Harvey, M.A. (1982). The influence and utilization of an interpreter for deaf persons in family therapy. *American Annals of the Deaf, 127,* 821-827.

Heider, F.K., & Heider, G.M. (1940). A comparison of sentence structure of deaf and hearing children. *Psychological Monographs, 52,* 42-103.

Heider, F.K., & Heider, G.M. (1941). Studies in the psychology of the deaf. *Psychological Monographs, VIII.* Evanston, IL: American Psychological Association.

Henderson, H.G. (1959). *An introduction to Haiku.* Garden City, NY: Doubleday Anchor Books.

Hereford, C.F. (1963). *Changing parental attitudes through group discussion.* Austin: University of Texas Press.

Hermelin, B. (1972). Locating events in space and time: Experiments with autistic, blind, and deaf children. *Journal of Autism and Childhood Schizophrenia, 2,* 288-298.

Hermelin, B., & O'Connor, N. (1973). Ordering in recognition memory after ambiguous initial or recognition displays. *Canadian Journal of Psychology, 27,* 191-199.

Hermelin, B., & O'Connor, N. (1975). The recall of digits by normal, deaf and autistic children. *British Journal of Psychology, 66,* 203-209

Herriot, P. (1969). The comprehension of active and passive sentences as a function of pragmatic expectations. *Journal of Verbal Learning and Verbal Behavior, 8,* 166-169.

Herriot, P. (1970). *An introduction to the psychology of language.* London: Methuen.

Hewes, G.W. (1971, April). *An explicit formulation of the relationship between tool-using, tool-making, and the emergence of language.* Paper presented at the Annual Meeting of the American Anthropological Association.

Hewes, G.W. (1973). Primate communication and the gestural origin of language. *Current Anthropology, 14,* 5-24.

Hewes, G.W. (1974). Language in early hominids. In R. Wescott, G.W. Hewes, & W. Stokoe (Eds.), *Language origins* (pp. 1-34). Silver Springs, MD: Linstok Press.

Hewes, G.W. (1976). The current status of the gestural theory of language origin. In S. Harnad, H. Steklis, & J. Lancaster (Eds.), *Origins and evolution of language and speech* (pp. 482-504). New York: Academy of Sciences.

Hicks, C., & Spurgeon, P. (1982). Two factor analytic studies of dyslexic sub-types. *British Journal of Educational Psychology, 52,* 289-300.

Higgins, P.C. (1980). *Outsiders in a hearing world.* Beverly Hills, CA: Sage.

Hill, A.C. (1911). On "methods" of teaching the deaf. *Volta Review, 13,* 152-153.

Hitch, A., Arnold, P., & Phillips, L. (1983). Counting processes in deaf children's arithmetic. *British Journal of Psychology, 74,* 429-437.

Hodgson, K.W. (1984). *The deaf and their problems.* New York: Philosophical Library.

Hoemann, H.W. (1972). The development of communication skills in deaf and hearing children. *Child Development, 43,* 990-1003.

Hoemann, H.W. (1975). *American Sign Language.* Silver Springs, MD: National Association of the Deaf.

Hoemann, H.W., & Tweney, R.D. (1973). Is the sign language of the deaf an adequate communicative channel? *Proceedings of the American Psychological Association,* 801-802.

Hoffmeister, R.J. (1982). Acquisition of signed languages by deaf children. In H. Hoeman & R. Wilbur (Eds.), *Interpersonal communication and deaf people.* Washington, DC: Gallaudet College.

Hollingshead, A.B., & Redlich, F.C. (1958). *Social class and mental illness: A community study.* New York: Wiley.

Holloway, R.L. (1974). The casts of fossil hominid brains. *Scientific American, 231,* 106-114.

Hough, J. (1983). *Louder than words.* Cambridge: Great Ouse Press.

Houvet, E. (1968). *The cathedral: Chartres.* Chartres: Helio-Lorraine.

Howarth, S.P., Wood, D.J., Griffiths, A.J., & Howarth, C.I. (1981). A comparative study of the reading lessons of deaf and hearing primary school children. *British Journal of Educational Psychology, 51,* 156-162.

Hoyle, F., & Wickramasinghe, C. (1981). *Evolution from space.* London: Dent.

Ives, L. (1976). A screening survey of 2060 hearing impaired children. *British Deaf News, 10,* Supplement 1.

Ivimey, G.P. (1976). The written syntax of an English deaf child: An exploration in method. *British Journal of Disorders of Communication, 11,* 102-120.

Ivimey, G.P. (1977a). The perception of speech: An information-processing approach. 1—The acoustic nature of spoken utterances. *Teacher of the Deaf, 1,* 40-48.

Ivimey, G.P. (1977b). The perception of speech: An information-processing approach. 2—Perceptual and cognitive processes. *Teacher of the Deaf, 1,* 64-73.

Ivimey, G.P. (1977c). The perception of speech: An information-processing approach 3—Lipreading and the deaf. *Teacher of the Deaf, 1,*90-100.

Ivimey, G.P. (1981). The production and perception by profoundly deaf children of syntactic time cues in English. *British Journal of Educational Psychology, 51,* 58-65.

Jacobs, L. (1982). *A deaf adult speaks out* (2nd ed.). Washington, DC: Gallaudet College Press.

Jakobson, R., & Halle, M. (1956). *Fundamentals of language.* The Hague: Monton.

Jensema, C. (1975). A statistical investigation of the 16PF, Form E as applied to hearing impaired college students. *Journal of Rehabilitation of the Deaf,* 8, 14-18.

Johansson, G. (1973). Visual perception of biological motion and a model for its analysis. *Perception and Psychophysics, 14,* 201-211.

John, J.E.J., & Howarth J.N. (1965). The effect of time distortions on the intelligibility of deaf children's speech. *Language and Speech, 8,* 127-134.

Johnson, D.D. (1976). Communication characteristics of a young deaf adult population: Techniques for evaluating their communication skills. *American Annals of the Deaf, 121,* 409-424.

Johnson, R.C. (1984). The nonmanual dimensions of sign language. *Gallaudet Research Institute Newsletter,* Spring pp. 3-4.

Jordan, I.K. (1974, April). *A referential communication study of linguistically adult deaf signers.* Paper presented at the 1st Annual Sign Language Conference, Gallaudet College, Washington, DC.

Jordan, I.K. (1983). Referential communication among Scottish deaf pupils. In J. Kyle & B. Woll (Eds.), *Language in sign* (pp. 238-247). London: Croom Helm.

Jorm, A.F. (1983). Specific reading retardation and working memory: A review. *British Journal of Psychology, 74,* 311-342.

Kahn, D. (1968). *The codebreakers.* London: Weidenfeld & Nicolson.

Kannapell, B. (1974). Bilingualism: New directions for the education of the deaf. *Deaf American, 26,* 9-15.

Kannapell, B. (1979). A preliminary report on developing bilingual materials to teach deaf students. In I. Ahlgren & B. Bergman (Eds.), *Collected papers: First international symposium on Sign Language research* (pp. 189-206). Stockholm: Swedish Association of the Deaf.

Kannapell, B. (1980). Personal awareness. In C. Baker & R. Battison (Eds.), *Sign language and the deaf community: Essays in Honour of William J. Stokoe* (pp. 105-116). Silver Springs, MD: National Association of the Deaf.

Kantor, R. (1982). *Communicative interaction in American Sign Language between mothers and their deaf children: A psycholinguistic analysis.* Unpublished doctoral dissertation, Boston University.

Karchmer, M.A., & Trybus, R.J. (1981). Who are the deaf children in mainstream programs? *Directions, 2,* 13-17.

Kates, S.L. (1972). *Language development in deaf and hearing adolescents.* Northampton: Clarke School for the Deaf.

Kaufman, M., Gottlieb, J., Agard, J.A., & Kukic, M.B. (1975). Mainstreaming: Towards an explanation of the construct. In G.A. Meyen, G.A. Vergasson, & R.J. Whelan (Eds.), *Alternatives for teaching exceptional children* (pp. 35-54). Denver: Love Publishing.

Kay, D.W.K., Cooper, A.F., Garside, R.F., & Roth, M. (1976). The differentiation of paranoid from affective psychoses by patients' premorbid characteristics. *British Journal of Psychiatry, 129,* 207-215.

Kean, M.L. (1978). The linguistic interpretation of aphasic syndromes. In E. Walker (Ed.), *Explorations in the biology of language* (pp. 67-138). Montgomery, VT: Bradford Books.

Keane, K.J. (1984). Application of Feuerstein's Mediated Learning Construct to deaf persons. In D.S. Martin (Ed.), *International Symposium on Cognition, Education and Deafness* (pp. 207-220). Washington, DC: Gallaudet College.

Kegl, J. (1976). *Pronominalization in American Sign Language.* Unpublished manuscript, Massachusetts Institute of Technology.

Kegl, J., & Wilbur, R. (1976, April). When does structure stop and style begin? Syntax, morphology, and phonology vs. stylistic variation in American Sign Language. In S. Mufwene, C. Walker, & S. Steven (Eds.) Papers *Twelfth Regional Meeting, Chicago Linguistic Society.* Chicago: University Press.

Kelly, E.L. (1967). *Assessment of human characteristics.* Belmont, CA: Brooks/Cole.

Kelly, R.R., & Tomlinson-Keasey, C. (1977). Hemispheric laterality of deaf children for processing words and pictures visually presented to the hemifields. *American Annals of the Deaf, 122,* 523-533.

Kelly, R.R., & Tomlinson-Keasey, C. (1978, April). *A comparison of deaf and hearing children's hemispheric lateralization for processing visually-presented words and pictures.* Paper presented at the Meeting of the American Educational Research Association, Toronto.

Kempley, S.T., & Morton, J. (1982). The effects of priming with regularly and irregularly related words in auditory word recognition. *British Journal of Psychology* , *73*, 441-454.

Kensicki, C. (1980). T.E.D. interview. *Teaching English to the Deaf*, *6*, 20-22.

Kimura, D. (1973). Manual activity during speaking: I. Right-handers. *Neuropsychologia, 11*, 45-50.

Kimura, D. (1981). Neural mechanisms in manual signing. *Sign Language Studies*, *33*, 291-312.

Kinchen-Smith, F. (1948). *Teach yourself Latin*. London: English Universities Press.

Kirby, J. (1980). Individual differences and cognitive processes: Instructional applications and methodological difficulties. In J. Kirby & J. Biggs (Eds.), *Cognition, development and instruction* (pp. 119-143). New York: Academic Press.

Klima, E.S., & Bellugi, U. (1973). Teaching apes to communicate. In G.A. Miller (Ed.), *Communication, language, and meaning* (pp. 95-106). New York: Basic Books.

Klima, E.S., & Bellugi, U. (1979). *The signs of language*. Cambridge, MA: Harvard University Press.

Klima, E.S., Bellugi, U., & Poizner, H. (1983). *Sign language and brain organization*. Unpublished manuscript, Salk Institute, San Diego, CA.

Klima, E.S., Poizner, H., & Bellugi, U. (1984). *What the hands reveal about the brain: Evidence from American Sign Language*. Unpublished manuscript, Salk Institute, San Diego, CA.

Koestler, A. (1978). *Janus: A summing up*. London: Hutchinson.

Koh, S.D., Vernon, M., & Bailey, W. (1971). Free-recall learning of word lists by prelingual deaf subjects. *Journal of Verbal Learning and Verbal Behavior, 10*, 542-547.

Kohl, H.R. (1966). *Language and education of the deaf*. New York: Center for Urban Education.

Kretschmer, R.R., & Kretschmer, L.W. (1978). *Language development and intervention in the hearing impaired*. Baltimore, MD: University Park Press.

Kuschel, R. (1973). The silent inventor: Creation of a sign language by the only deaf mute on a Polynesian island. *Sign Language Studies, 3*, 1-27.

Kyle, J.G. (1983). Looking for meaning in sign language sentences. In J.G. Kyle & B. Woll (Eds.), *Language in sign* (pp. 184-194). London: Croom Helm.

Kyle, J.G., & Woll, B. (Eds.). (1983). *Language in sign: An international perspective*. London: Croom Helm.

Kyle, J.G., Woll, B., & Carter, M. (1979). *Coding British Sign Language*. School of Education Research Unit, University of Bristol.

Labov, K. (1970). The logic of nonstandard English. In F. Williams (Ed.), *Language and poverty* (pp. 153-189). Chicago: Markham.

Labov, K. (1976). Systematically misleading data from test questions. *Urban Review, 9*, 146-169.

Ladd, P., & Edwards, V.K. (1982). British Sign Language and West Indian Creole. *Sign Language Studies, 35*, 101-126.

Laidler, K. (1980). *The talking ape*. London: Collins.

Lambert, A.J. (1982a). Right hemisphere language ability. 1 - Clinical evidence. *Current Psychological Reviews, 2*, 77-94.

Lambert, A.J. (1982b). Right hemisphere language ability. 2 - Evidence from normal subjects. *Current Psychological Reviews, 2*, 139-152.

Lambert, A.J., & Beaumont, J.G. (1982). On Kelley & Orton's dichotic perception of word pairs with mixed image values. *Neuropsychologia. 20*(2), 209-210.

Lambert, W.E., & Tucker, G.R. (1972). *Bilingual education of children*. Rowley, MA: Newbury House.

Lancaster, J.B. (1968). Primate communication systems and the emergence of human language. In P.C. Jay (Ed.), *Primates: Studies in adaptation and variability* (pp. 439-457). New York: Holt, Rinehart & Winston.

Lane, H. (Ed.). (1984). *Deaf experience: Classics in language and education.* Cambridge, MA: Harvard University Press.

Lane, H., Boyes-Braem, P., & Bellugi, U. (1976). Preliminaries to a distinctive feature analysis of handshapes in American Sign Language. *Cognitive Psychology, 8*, 263-289.

Large, D.W. (1980). Special problems for the deaf under the Education for All Handicapped Children Act of 1975. *Washington University Law Quarterly, 58*, 213-275.

Lashley, K.S. (1951). The problem of serial order in behavior. In L.P. Jeffress (Ed.), *Cerebral mechanisms in behavior: The Hixon symposium* (pp. 112-136). New York: Wiley.

Laver, J. (1970). The production of speech. In J. Lyons (Ed.), *New horizons in linguistics* (pp. 53-75). Harmondsworth: Pelican.

Lawson, L. (1978). The nature of deafness. In G. Montgomery (Ed.), *Deafness, personality and mental health* (pp. 3-5). Edinburgh: Scottish Workshop Publications.

Lawson, L. (1981). The role of sign in the structure of the deaf community. In B. Woll, J. Kyle, & M. Deuchard (Eds.), *Perspectives on British Sign Language and deafness* (pp. 166-177). London: Croom Helm.

Lawson, L. (1983). Multi-channel signs. In J. Kyle & B. Woll (Eds.), *Language in sign* (pp. 97-105). London: Croom Helm.

Leakey, R.E. (1981). *The making of mankind*. New York: E.P. Dutton.

Leblanc, G.A. (1983). *An investigation of self-esteem and communication modes of hearing impaired students*. Unpublished master's thesis, University of Alberta.

Lee, L. (1974). *Developmental sentence analysis*. Evanston, IL: Northwestern University Press.

Lenneberg, E.H. (1964). A biological perspective of language. In E.H. Lenneberg (Ed.), *New directions in the study of language* (pp. 65-88). Cambridge, MA: Massachusetts Institute of Technology Press.

Lenneberg, E.H. (1966). The natural history of language. In F. Smith & G.A. Miller (Eds.), *The genesis of language* (pp. 219-252). Cambridge, MA: MIT Press.

Lenneberg, E.H. (1967). *Biological foundations of language*. New York: Wiley.

Lenneberg, E.H. (1973). Biological aspects of language. In G.A. Miller (Ed.), *Communication, language, and meaning* (pp. 49-60). New York: Basic Books.

Levine, E.S. (1948). *An investigation of the personality of normal and deaf adolescent girls*. Unpublished doctoral dissertation, New York University.

Levine, E.S. (1981). *The ecology of early deafness: Guides to fashioning environments and psychological assessments*. New York: Columbia University Press.

Levy-Agresti, J., & Sperry, R.W. (1968). Differential perceptual capacities in major and minor hemispheres. *Proceedings of the National Academy of Science, 61*, 1151.

Levy, J., Trevarthen, C., & Sperry, R.W. (1972). Perception of bilateral chimeric figures following hemispheric deconnexion. *Brain, 95*, 61-78.

Lewis, J. (1983). Burnout: An issue amongst teachers. *The ACEHI Journal, 9*, 115-123.

Lewis, M.M. (Chairman). (1968). *Department of Education and Science: The education of deaf children: The possible place of finger spelling and signing*. London: Her Majesty's Stationery Office.

Liddell, S.K. (1978). Nonmanual signs and relative clauses in American sign language. In P. Siple (Ed.), *Understanding language through sign language research* (pp. 59-90). New York: Academic Press.

Lieberman, P., & Crelin, D.S. (1971). On the speech of Neanderthal man. *Linguistic Inquiry, 11*, 203-222.

Linden, E. (1975). *Apes, men, and language*. New York: E.P. Dutton.

Lindfors, J.W. (1980). *Children's language and learning*. Englewood Cliffs, NJ: Prentice Hall.

Ling, D. (1976). *Speech and the hearing impaired child: Theory and practice*. Washington, DC: A.G. Bell Association.

Ling, D. (1984). *Early intervention for hearing impaired children: Total communication options*. Washington, DC: A.G. Bell Association.

Ling, D., & Ling, A.H. (1978). *Aural rehabilitation*. Washington, DC: A.G. Bell Association.

Locke, J.L., & Locke, V.L. (1971). Deaf children's phonetic, visual, and dactylic coding in a grapheme recall task. *Journal of Experimental Psychology, 89*, 142-146.

Lowell, E.L. (1957-1958). *John Tracy Clinic Research Papers, III, V, VI, & VII.* Los Angeles: John Tracy Clinic.

Lowell, E.L. (1976). *Methods of communication currently used in the education of deaf children.* London: Royal National Institute for the Deaf.

Lubert, B.J. (1975). *The relation of brain asymmetry to visual processing of sign language alphabetic and visuo-spatial material in deaf and hearing subjects.* Unpublished master's thesis, University of Western Ontario.

Luetke-Stahlman, B. (1982). A philosophy for assessing the language proficiency of hearing impaired students to promote English literacy. *American Annals of the Deaf, 127*, 844-850.

Luetke-Stahlman, B. (1983). Adapting bilingual instructional models for hearing impaired classrooms. *American Annals of the Deaf, 128*, 873-877.

Luetke-Stahlman, B., & Weiner, F. (1982). Assessing language and/or system preferences of Spanish-deaf preschoolers. *American Annals of the Deaf, 127*, 789-796.

Luria, A.R. (1959). The directive function of speech in development and dissolution, Part I. *Word, 15*, 341-352.

Luria, A.R. (1982). *Language and cognition.* New York: Wiley.

Luterman, D. (1979). *Counseling parents of hearing impaired children.* Boston: Little, Brown.

Luterman, D. (1984). *Counseling the communicatively disordered and their families.* Boston, MA: Little, Brown.

Lutman, M.E., & Haggard, M.P. (1983). *Hearing science and hearing disorders.* Toronto: Academic Press.

Lyon, D.J., & Lyon, M.F. (1981-1982). The importance of early detection. *The ACEHI Journal, 8*, 15-37.

Lyons, J. (1970). Generative syntax. In J. Lyons (Ed.), *New horizons in linguistics* (pp. 115-119). Harmondsworth: Pelican.

MacDougall, J. (1979). Development of visual processing and short-term memory in deaf and hearing children. *American Annals of the Deaf, 124*, 16-22.

Maeder, J. (1980, April). *Effects of inserted postquestions on the reading comprehension of hearing impaired students.* Paper presented at the Annual Meeting of the American Educational Research Association, Boston.

Manning, A.A., Goble, W., Markman, R., & LaBreche, T. (1977). Lateral cerebral differences in the deaf in response to linguistic and nonlinguistic stimuli. *Brain and Language, 4*, 309-321.

Markides, A. (1983). *The speech of hearing impaired children.* Manchester: University Press.

Martin, C. (1981). *The skill of lip-reading.* London: BBC Publications.

Martin, D. (1986). *Cognition, education and deafness: Directions for research and instruction*. Washington, DC: Gallaudet College Press.

Martin, F. (1986). *Introduction to audiology* (3rd ed.). Englewood Cliffs, NJ: Prentice Hall.

Matthei, E.H., & Roeper, T. (1983). *Understanding and producing speech*. London: Fontana.

Maxwell, D.L. (1984). The neurology of learning and language disabilities: Developmental considerations. In G.P. Wallach & K.G. Butler (Eds.), *Language learning disabilities in school-age children* (p. 35-59). Baltimore: Williams & Wilkins.

Mayberry, R., Fischer, S., & Hatfield, N. (1983). Sentence repetition in American Sign Language. In J. Kyle & B. Woll (Eds.), *Language in sign* (pp. 206-214). London: Croom Helm.

McCall, E.A. (1965). *A generative grammar of sign*. Unpublished master's thesis, University of Iowa.

McDaniel, E.D. (1980). Visual memory in the deaf. *American Annals of the Deaf, 125*, 559-563.

McDonald, B. (1983). Levels of analysis in sign language research. In J. Kyle & B. Woll, (Eds.), *Language in sign* (pp. 32-40). London: Croom Helm.

McFie, J. (1972). Factors of the brain. *Bulletin of the British Psychological Society, 25*,11-14.

McGill-Franzen, A., & Gormley, K. (1980). The influence of context on deaf readers' understanding of passive sentences. *American Annals of the Deaf, 125*, 62-69.

McGinnis, M.A. (1963). *Aphasic children: Identification and education by the association method*. Washington, DC: A.G. Bell Association.

McGurk, M., & MacDonald, J. (1976). Hearing lips and seeing voices. *Nature, 264*, 746-748.

McIntire, M. (1974). *A modified model for the description of language acquisition in a deaf child*. Unpublished master's thesis, California State University, Northridge, CA.

McKeever, W.F., Hoemann, H.W., Flovian,, V.A., & Van Deventer, A.D. (1976). Evidence of minimal cerebral asymmetries for the processing of English words and American Sign Language stimuli in the congenitally deaf. *Neuropsychologia, 14*, 413-423.

McLaughlin, J.R. (1980). *The self concept of hearing impaired pupils in different educational settings in British Columbia: A preliminary investigation*. Unpublished master's thesis, University of British Columbia.

McNeill, D. (1966). The creation of language. *Discovery, 27*(7), 34-38.

Meadow, K.P. (1967). *The effect of early manual communication and self image on the deaf child's environment*. Unpublished doctoral dissertation, University of California, Berkeley.

Meadow, K.P. (1980). *Deafness and child development*. Berkeley: University of California Press.

Meadow, K.P., Greenberg, M.T., Erting, C., & Carmichael, H. (1981). Interactions of deaf mothers and deaf preschool children: Comparisons with three other groups of deaf and hearing dyads. *American Annals of the Deaf, 126,* 454-468.

Meadow, K.P., & Schlesinger, H.S. (1971). The prevalence of behavioral problems in a population of deaf school children. *American Annals of the Deaf, 116,* 346-348.

Meadow, K.P., & Trybus, R.J. (1979). Behavioral and emotional problems of deaf children: An overview. In L. Bradford & W. Hardy (Eds.), *Hearing and hearing impairment* (pp. 395-403). New York: Grune & Stratton.

Meier, R. (1980). *Acquisition of inflections in American Sign Language. Working paper*. La Jolla, CA: Salk Institute of Biological Studies.

Menyuk, P. (1969). *Sentences children use*. Cambridge, MA: Massachusetts Institute of Technology Press.

Miller, E.J., & Gwynne, G.V. (1973). *A life apart*. London: Tavistock Publications.

Miller, G.A. (1965). Some preliminaries to psycholinguistics. *American Psychologist, 20,* 15-20.

Miller, G.A. (Ed.). (1967a). *The psychology of communication*. New York: Basic Books.

Miller, G.A. (Ed.). (1967b). Project Grammarama. *The psychology of communication*. New York: Basic Books.

Miller, G.A. (Ed.). (1973). *Communication, language, and meaning*. New York: Basic Books.

Miller, G.A., Galanter, E., & Pribram, K.H. (1960). *Plans and the structure of behavior*. New York: Holt, Rinehart, & Winston.

Miller, G.A., & Isard, S. (1963). Some perceptual consequences of linguistic rules. *Journal of Verbal Learning and Verbal Behavior, 2,* 217-228.

Miller, G.A., & Licklider, J.C.R. (1950). The intelligibility of interrupted speech. *Journal of the Acoustical Society of America, 22,* 167-173.

Miller, G.A., & McKean, K.O. (1964). A chronometric study of some relations between sentences. *Quarterly Journal of Experimental Psychology, 16,* 297-308.

Milner, B., Branch, C., & Rasmussen, T. (1964). Observations on cerebral dominance. In A.V.S. De Reuck & M.O. O'Connor (Eds.), *Disorders of language: A CIBA Foundation symposium*. London: Churchill.

Mindel, E.D., & Vernon, M. (1971). *They grow in silence*. Silver Springs, MD: NAD.

Mohay, H. (1982). A preliminary description of the communication systems evolved by two deaf children in the absence of a sign language model. *Sign Language Studies, 34,* 73-90.

Montgomery, G.W.G. (1966). The relationship of oral skills to manual communication in profoundly deaf adolescents. *American Annals of the Deaf, 111,* 557-566.

Montgomery, G.W.G. (1967). *Vocational guidance for the deaf.* Edinburgh: Livingston.

Montgomery, G.W.G. (1968). A factorial study of communication and ability in deaf school leavers. *British Journal of Educational Psychology, 38,* 27-37.

Montgomery, G.W.G. (Ed.). (1979). *Deafness, personality and mental health.* Edinburgh: Scottish Area Workshop With the Deaf.

Montgomery, G.W.G., Miller, J., Mitchell, G., Jordan, I.K., & Montgomery, J. (1983). Open communication or catastrophe? A model for educational communication. In J.G. Kyle & B. Woll (Eds.), *Language in sign* (pp. 248-261). London: Croom Helm.

Montgomery, J., & Montgomery, G.W.G. (1981). Integration and the communication gap. In G.W.G. Montgomery (Ed.), *The integration and disintegration of the deaf in society* (pp. 71-87). Edinburgh: Scottish Workshop Publications.

Moog, J.S., & Kozak, V.J. (1982). *Teacher assessment of grammatical structures.* St. Louis, MO: Central Institute for the Deaf.

Moores, D.F. (1974). Nonvocal systems of verbal behavior. In R. Schiefelbusch & L. Lloyd (Eds.), *Language perspectives: Acquisition retardation and intervention* (pp. 377-417). Baltimore, MD: University Park Press.

Moores, D.F. (1976). A review of education of the deaf. In L. Mann & D. Sabatino (Eds.), *Third review of special education.* New York: Grune & Stratton.

Moores, D.F. (1978). *Educating the deaf: Psychology, principles and practices* (1st ed.). Boston: Houghton Mifflin.

Moores, D.F. (1982). *Educating the deaf: Psychology, principles and practices* (2nd ed.). Boston: Houghton Mifflin.

Moores, D.F., McIntyre, C.K., & Weiss, K.L. (1972). *Evaluation of programs for hearing impaired children.* Minneapolis: Research, Development and Demonstration Center in Education of Handicapped Children, Department of Health, Education and Welfare.

Morariu, J., & Bruning, R. (1984). A contextualist perspective of language processing by prelingually deaf students. In D. S. Martin (Ed.), *International Symposium on Cognition, Education and Deafness* (pp. 149-166). Washington, DC: Gallaudet College.

Morris, T. (1978). A comparison of the receptive oral language development of children educated in schools for the deaf in two English speaking countries. *Journal of British Association of Teachers of the Deaf, 2,* 58-60.

Muendel-Atherstone, B., & Rodda, M. (1982). *Differences in hemispheric processing of linguistic material presented visually to deaf and hearing adults*. Unpublished manuscript, University of Alberta.

Murphy, K.P. (1957). Tests of abilities and attainments. In A.W.G. Ewing (Ed.), *Educational guidance and the deaf child*. Manchester: University Press.

Murrell, G.A., & Morton, J. (1974). Word recognition and morphemic structure. *Journal of Experimental Psychology, 102*, 963-968.

Mussen, P.H., Conger, J.J., & Kagan, J. (1969). *Child development and personality*. New York: Harper & Row.

Myklebust, H.R. (1964). *The psychology of deafness*. New York: Grune & Stratton.

Nash, J.E., & Nash, A. (1981). *Deafness in society*. Toronto: Lexington Books.

Neisser, A. (1983). *The other side of silence: Sign language and the deaf community in America*. New York: Knopf.

Neisser, U. (1967). *Cognitive psychology*. New York: Appleton-Century Crofts.

Nelson, K. (1979/1980). *Children's language* (Vols. 1 & 2). New York: Gardner Press.

Nesfield, J.C. (1930). *Manual of English grammar and composition*. London: Macmillan.

Neville, N.J., & Bellugi, U. (1978). Patterns of cerebral specialization in congenitally deaf adults: A preliminary report. In P. Siple (Ed.), *Understanding language through sign language research* (pp. 239-260). New York: Academic Press.

Nicolaci-da-Costa, A., & Harris, M. (1983). Redundancy of syntactic information: An aid to young children's comprehension of sentential number. *British Journal of Psychology, 74*, 343-352.

Nienhuys, T.G., & Tikotin, J.A. (1983). Pre-speech communication in hearing and hearing-impaired children. *Journal of the British Association of Teachers of the Deaf, 7*, 182-194.

Nitchie, E.B. (1910). The spiritual side of lip-reading. *Volta Review, 12*, 547-548.

Nix, G.W. (1977). Mainstream placement question checklist. *Volta Review*. (Monograph).

Nix, G.W. (1983). How total is total communication? *Journal of the British Association of Teachers of the Deaf, 6*, 177-194.

Nolan, M.J., & Tucker, I.G. (1981). *The hearing impaired child and his family*. London: Souvenir Press.

Nolen, S.B., & Wilbur, R.B. (1984). Context and comprehension: Another look. In D.S. Martin (Ed.), *International Symposium on Cognition, Education and Deafness* (pp. 389-403). Washington, DC: Gallaudet College.

Norden, K. (1975). *Psychological studies of deaf adolescents*. Falk, Sweden: Department of Education and Psychological Research.

·Norden, K. (1981). Learning processes and personality development in deaf children. *American Annals of the Deaf, 126,* 404-410.

Northern, J.L., & Downs, M.P. (1978). *Hearing in children* (2nd ed.). Baltimore: Wilkins & Wilkins.

Oatley, K. (1978). *Perceptions and representations.* London: Methuen.

O'Connor, N., & Hermelin, B. (1971). Inter- and intra- modal transfer in children with modality specific and general handicaps. *British Journal of Social and Clinical Psychology, 10,* 346-354.

O'Connor, N., & Hermelin, B. (1972). Seeing and hearing and space and time. *Perception and Psychophysics, 11,* 46-48.

O'Connor, N., & Hermelin, B. (1973a). The spatial or temporal organization of short-term memory. *Quarterly Journal of Experimental Psychology, 25,* 335-343.

O'Connor, N., & Hermelin, B. (1973b). Short-term memory for the order of pictures and syllables by deaf and hearing children. *Neuropsychologia, 11,* 437-442.

O'Connor, N., & Hermelin, B. (1975). Modality-specific spatial coordinates. *Perception and Psychophysics, 17,* 213-216.

Office of Population Census and Surveys. (1970). *Registrar General: Classification of occupations.* London: Her Majesty's Stationery Office.

Ornstein, R. (1972). *The psychology of consciousness.* San Francisco, CA: W.H. Freeman.

Osgood, C.E. (1952). The nature and measurement of meaning. *Psychological Bulletin, 49,* 192-237.

O'Sullivan, F.D. (1977). *Written language of deaf adolescents: A comparative pilot study.* Unpublished master's thesis, University of Surrey, Guildford.

Owrid, H.L. (1971). Studies in manual communication with hearing impaired children. *Volta Review, 73,* 428-438.

Owrid, H.L. (1972). Education and communication. *Volta Review, 73,* 225-234.

Paget, R. (1935). *This English.* London: Kegan Paul, Trench, Tribner.

Paget, R., & Gorman, P. (1968). *A systematic sign language.* London: Royal National Institute for the Deaf.

Pahz, J.A., & Pahz, C.S. (1978). *Total communication.* Springfield, IL: Charles C. Thomas.

Paivio, A. (1971). *Imagery and verbal processes.* New York: Holt, Rinehart & Winston.

Paivio, A., & Begg, I. (1981). *Psychology of language.* Englewood Cliffs, NJ: Prentice Hall.

Palmer, F. (1971). *Grammar.* Harmondsworth: Pelican.

Parasnis, I., & Lylak, E. (1985, April). *Knowledge of modal auxiliary usage and deafness*. Paper presented at American Educational Research Association Annual Meeting, Chicago.

Parasnis, I., & Samar, V.J. (1982). Visual perception of verbal information by deaf people. In D. Sims, G. Walter & R. Whitehead (Eds.), *Deafness and communication: Assessment and training* (pp. 53-71). Baltimore: Williams & Wilkins.

Pearce, J.C. (1971). *The crack in the cosmic egg*. New York: Julian Press.

Pearson, D., & Johnson, D. (1978). *Teaching reading comprehension*. New York: Holt, Rinehart & Winston.

Pehrssen, R. (1978). *Semantic organization: An approach to teaching deaf children to process written language*. Unpublished doctoral dissertation, Hofstra University.

Perry, A.L. (1978). A lipreading curriculum for adults. *Volta Review, 80*, 86-92.

Pfeiffer, J.E. (1969). *The emergence of man*. New York: Harper & Row.

Phippard, D.E. (1974). *Hemifield differences in visual perception in deaf and hearing subjects*. Unpublished doctoral dissertation, McGill University.

Pintner, R. (1929). *The Pintner nonlanguage mental test*. New York: World Book.

Pintner, R., & Reamer, J.F. (1916). Learning tests with deaf children. *Psychological Monographs, 20*(4).

Pintner, R., & Reamer, J.F. (1920). A mental and educational survey of schools for the deaf. *American Annals of the Deaf, 65*, 451.

Pintner, R., Eisenson, J., & Stanton, M. (1941). *The psychology of the physically handicapped*. New York: F. S. Crofts.

Poizner, H., Battison, R., & Lane, H. (1979). Cerebral asymmetry for American Sign Language: The effects of moving stimuli. *Brain and Language, 7*, 351-362.

Poizner, H., Bellugi, U., & Lutes-Driscoll, V. (1981). Perception of American Sign Language in dynamic point-light displays. *Journal of Experimental Psychology: Human Perception and Performance 7*, 430-440.

Poizner, H., Bellugi, U., & Tweney, R.D. (1981). Processing of formational, semantic and iconic information in American Sign Language. *Journal of Experimental Psychology: Human Perception and Performance, 7*, 1146-1159.

Poizner, H., Kaplan, E., Bellugi, U., & Padden, C.A. (1984). Visual-spatial processing in deaf brain-damaged signers. *Brain and Cognition, 3*, 281-306.

Poizner, H., & Lane, H.L. (1979). Cerebral asymmetry in the perception of American Sign Language. *Brain and Language, 7*, 210-226.

Poizner, H., Newkirk, D., Bellugi, U., & Klima, E. (1981). Representation of inflected signs from American Sign Language in short-term memory. *Memory & Cognition, 9*, 121-131.

Postal, P.M. (1964). Underlying and superficial linguistic structure. *Harvard Educational Review, 34*, 246-266.

Potter, S. (1950). *Our language.* Harmondsworth: Pelican.

Potter, S. (1960). *Language in the modern world.* Harmondsworth: Pelican.

Power, D.J. (1973, March). Deaf children's acquisition of sentence voice and reversibility. *Proceedings of the Language Conference of the Australian College of Speech Therapists.*

Priesler, G. (1981). Modifications of communication by a small deaf girl. *American Annals of the Deaf, 126,* 411-416.

Prinz, P.M., & Prinz, E.A. (1979). Simultaneous acquisition of ASL and spoken English. *Sign Language Studies, 25,* 283-296.

Prinz, P.M., & Prinz, E.A. (1981). Acquisition of ASL and spoken English by a hearing child of a deaf mother and a hearing father: Phase II, early combinational patterns. *Sign Language Studies, 30,* 78-88.

Pritchard, D.G. (1963). *Education and the handicapped, 1760-1960.* London: Routledge & Kegan Paul.

Puthli, V. (1977). *Deaf children's memory for natural language under different stimulus conditions.* Unpublished master's thesis, University of Surrey.

Quigley, S.P. (1982). Reading achievement and special reading materials. In R. Kretschmer (Ed.), Reading and the hearing impaired individual. *Volta Review, 84,* 95-106.

Quigley, S.P., Babbini, B.E., & Marshall, W.J.A. (1969). *Educational and occupational status of young deaf adults in Illinois.* Urbana, IL: University of Illinois Institute for Research on Exceptional Children. (Final report: RSA RD-2922)

Quigley, S.P., Montanelli, D.S., & Wilbur, R.B. (1976). Some aspects of the verb system in the language of deaf students. *Journal of Speech and Hearing Research, 19,* 536-550.

Quigley, S.P., & Kretschmer, R.E. (1982). *The education of deaf children: Issues, theory and practice.* Baltimore, MD: University Park Press.

Quigley, S.P., & Paul, P.V. (1984). *Language and deafness.* San Diego, CA: College-Hill Press.

Quigley, S.P., Power, D.J., & Steinkamp, M.W. (1977). The language structure of deaf children. *Volta Review, 79,* 73-84.

Quigley, S.P., Smith, N.L., & Wilbur, R.B. (1974). Comprehension of relativized sentences by deaf students. *Journal of Speech and Hearing Research, 17,* 325-341.

Quigley, S.P., Steinkamp, M.W., Power, D.J., & Jones, B.W. (1978). *Test of syntactic ability.* Beaverton, OR: Dormac.

Quigley, S.P., Wilbur, R.B., & Montanelli, D.S. (1974). Question formation in the language of deaf students. *Journal of Speech and Hearing Research, 17,* 669-713.

Quigley, S.P., Wilbur, R.B., & Montanelli, D.S. (1976). Complement structures in the language of deaf students. *Journal of Speech and Hearing Research, 19*, 448-457.

Quillian, M.R. (1967). Word concepts: A theory and simulation of some basic semantic capabilities. *Behavioral Science, 12*, 410-430.

Quillian, M.R. (1969). The teachable language comprehender: A simulation program and theory of language. *Communications of the Association for Computing Machinery, 12*, 459-476.

Radford, J.K., & Burton, A. (1974). *Thinking: Its nature and development*. New York: Wiley.

Rainer, J.D., & Altshuler, K.Z. (1967). *Psychiatry and the deaf*. Washington, DC: U.S. Department of Health, Education and Welfare.

Reeves, J.K. (1976). The whole personality approach to oralism in the education of the deaf. In *Methods of communication currently used in the education of the deaf*. Papers of residential seminar held April 11-14, 1975 at Garnett College, Roehampton, London. Letchworth, Hertfordshire: Garden City Press.

Reitman, W.R. (1970). What does it take to remember? In D.A. Norman (Ed.), *Models of human memory*. New York: Academic Press.

Remvig, J. (1969). *Three clinical studies of deaf mutism and psychiatry*. Copenhagen: Munksgvard.

Remvig, J. (1973). Psychiatric services for the deaf in Denmark. *Proceedings of WFD International Congress: Israel*. Rome: World Federation of the Deaf.

Restak, R. (1984). *The brain*. New York: Bantam Books.

Reynolds, H.N. (1976). The development of reading ability in relation to deafness. *Proceedings of VIIth World Congress of the Deaf* (pp. 241-259). Washington, DC: National Association of the Deaf.

Reynolds, H.N. (1978). Perceptual effects of deafness. In R.D. Walk & H.L. Pick (Eds.), *Perception and experience*. New York: Plenum Press.

Risberg, A., & Agelfors, E. (1978). Information extraction and information processing in speechreading. *Quarterly progress and status report 2-3*. Stockholm: Speech Transmission Laboratory.

Robbins, N. (1976, April). Selecting sign systems for multi-handicapped students. *American Speech and Hearing Association Conference*, Houston.

Robinson, L. (1972). *Language and social behavior*. Harmondsworth: Penguin Books.

Rodda, M. (1967). *Noise and society*. Edinburgh: Oliver & Boyd.

Rodda, M. (1970). *The hearing impaired school leaver*. London: University of London Press.

Rodda, M. (1974). Behavioral disturbance in deaf clients. *Journal of Rehabilitation of the Deaf, 7*, 1-12.

Rodda, M. (1976). Language and specific language disorders in children. In R. Hinchcliffe & D. Harrison (Eds.), *Scientific foundations of otolaryngology* (pp. 609-622). London: William Heinemann Medical Books.

Rodda, M. (1977). Language and language disordered children. *Bulletin of British Psychology. 30*, 139-142.

Rodda, M. (1985). Behavioral disturbance in deaf adults: A clinical perspective. *Rehabilitation and Deafness, 18*, 1-6.

Rodda, M., & Carver, R. (1983). *Alberta survey of the hearing impaired.* Unpublished report, Edmonton: Alberta Advanced Education, Alberta Education, and Alberta Social Services and Community Health.

Rodda, M., Denmark, J.C., & Grove, C. (1983). *A factor analytical study of social, linguistic and cognitive skills in deaf adolescents.* Unpublished manuscript, University of Alberta.

Rodda, M., Ellis, R., & Chaddock, P. (1983). A brief history of education of deaf students in the Maritime provinces. *The ACEHI Journal, 9*, 188-208.

Rogden, M. (1979). Knowing what to say and wanting to say it: Some communicative and structural aspects of single-word responses to questions. *Journal of Child Language, 6*, 81-90.

Rogers, C. (1951). *Client centered therapy.* Boston: Houghton-Mifflin.

Romano, P., & Berlow, S. (1976). Vision requirements for lip reading. *American Annals of the Deaf, 119*, 383-386.

Rommetveit, R. (1974). *On message structure.* London: Wiley.

Rosch, E., Mervis, C.B., Gray, W., Johnson, D., & Boyes-Braem, P. (1976). Basic objects in natural categories. *Cognitive Psychology, 8*, 382-439.

Ross, M. (1976). Assessment of the hearing impaired prior to mainstreaming. In G. Nix (Ed.), *Mainstream education for hearing impaired children and youth* (pp. 101-108). New York: Grune & Stratton.

Ross, M. (1982). *Hard of hearing children in regular classrooms.* Englewood Cliffs, NJ: Prentice Hall.

Rothery, G.C. (1985). *Concise encyclopedia of heraldry.* London: Bracken Books.

Royal National Institute for the Deaf. (1976). *Methods of communication currently used in the education of deaf children.* London: RNID.

Rudner, M. (1968) Using standardized tests with the hearing impaired. *Volta Review, 80*, 31-40.

Rudy, J.P., & Nace, J.G. (1973). A transitional instrument for the selection of hearing impaired students for integration. In W. H. Northcott (Ed.), *The hearing impaired child in the regular classroom* (pp. 128-133). Washington, DC: A.G. Bell Association.

Russell, W.K., Quigley, S.P., & Power, D.J. (1976). *Linguistics and deaf children.* Washington, DC: A.G. Bell Association.

Sachs, J.D.S. (1967). Recognition memory for syntactic and semantic aspects of connected discourse. *Perception and Psychophysics, 2*, 437-442.

Saffran, E.M. (1982). Neuropsychological approaches to the study of language. *British Journal of Psychology, 73*, 317-337.

Samar, V.J., & Sims, D.G. (1983). Visual evoked-response correlates of speechreading performance in normal-hearing adults: A replication and factor analytic extension. *Journal of Speech and Hearing Research, 26*, 2-9.

Saussure, F., de. (1915). *Cours de linguistique générate*. Paris: Payot.

Savage, R.D., Evans, L., & Savage, J.F. (1981). *Psychology and communication in deaf children*. Toronto: Grune & Stratton.

Saville, P., & Blinkhorn, S. (1973). *The Gates-McGinitie Reading Test: British manual*. Slough: National Foundation for Educational Research.

Savin, H.B., & Perchonock, E. (1965). Grammatical structure and the immediate recall of English sentences. *Journal of Verbal Learning and Verbal Behavior, 4*, 348-353.

Schein, J.D. (1983). *A rose for tomorrow*. Silver Springs, MD: National Association of the Deaf.

Schein, J.D. (1980). Educating hearing impaired children to become emotionally well adjusted adults. *The ACEHI Journal, 7*, 3-9.

Schein, J.D. (1984). *Speaking the language of signs*. New York: Doubleday.

Schein, J.D., & Delk, M.T. (1974). *The deaf population of the United States*. Silver Springs, MD: National Association of the Deaf.

Schein, J.D., Gentille, A., & Hasse, K.W. (1970). *Development and evaluation of an expanded Hearing Loss Scale questionnaire*. Washington, DC: Health, Education and Welfare; Vital Health Statistics, Series 2, 37.

Schever, K.R., & Ellman, P. (Eds.). (1982). *Handbook of methods in nonverbal behavior research*. New York: Cambridge University Press.

Schlesinger, H.S. (1978). The effects of deafness on childhood development. In L. Liben (Ed.), *Deaf children: Developmental perspectives* (pp. 157-169). New York: Academic Press.

Schlesinger, I.M. (1971). The grammar of sign language and the problems of language universals. In J. Morton (Ed.), *Biological and social factors in psycholinguistics* (pp. 98-121). London: Logos Press.

Schlesinger, H.S., & Meadow, K.P. (1972). *Sound and sign: Childhood deafness and mental health*. Berkeley, CA: University of California Press.

Schmitt, P. (1968). *Deaf children's comprehension and production of sentence transformations and verb tenses*. Unpublished doctoral dissertation, University of Illinois.

Schowe, B.M. (1979). *Identity crisis in deafness*. Tempel, AZ: The Scholars Press.

Schroedel, J.G. (1976). *Variables related to the attainment of occupational status among deaf adults*. Unpublished doctoral dissertation, New York University.

Scouten, E.L. (1984). *Turning points in the education of deaf people*. Danville, IL: Interstate Printers & Publishers.

Semmes, J. (1968). Hemispheric specialization: A possible clue to mechanism. *Neuropsychologia, 6,* 11-26.

Shannon, C.E. (1948). *A mathematical theory of communication.* Bell Telephone System. Monograph B-1598.

Shannon, C.E., & Weaver, W. (1949). *The mathematical theory of communication.* Urbana, IL: University of Illinois Press.

Sharoff, R.L. (1959-1960). Enforced restrictions on communication: Its implications for the emotional and intellectual development of the deaf child. *American Journal of Psychiatry, 116,* 443-446.

Shepherd, D.C., DeLavergne, R.W., Freuh, F.X., & Clobridge, C. (1977). Visual-neural correlate of speechreading ability in normal-hearing adults. *Journals of Speech and Hearing Research, 20,* 752-765.

Silverberg, R. (1970). *The morning of mankind.* Kingswood, Surrey: World's Work.

Silverman-Dresner, T., & Guilfoyle, G.R. (1972). *Vocabulary norms for deaf children.* Washington, DC: A.G. Bell Association.

Sinha, C., & Walkerdine, V. (1974). *Spatial and temporal relations in the linguistic and cognitive development of young children.* Unpublished manuscript, Research Unit, School of Education, University of Bristol.

Sinha, C., & Walkerdine, V. (1975). *Functional and perceptual aspects of the acquisition of spatial relational terms.* Unpublished manuscript, Research Unit, School of Education, University of Bristol.

Siple, P. (Ed.). (1978). *Understanding language through sign language research.* New York: Academic Press.

Siple, P., Fischer, S., & Bellugi, U. (1977). Memory for nonsemantic attributes of American Sign Language signs and English words. *Journal of Verbal Learning and Verbal Behavior, 16,* 561-574.

Skinner, B.F. (1957). *Verbal behavior.* New York: Appleton-Century-Crofts.

Skinner, P.H., & Shelton, R.L. (1979). *Speech, language and hearing.* Don Mills, ON: Addison-Wesley.

Slobin, D. (1966). Grammatical transformations and sentence comprehension in childhood and adulthood. *Journal of Verbal Learning and Verbal Behavior, 5,* 219-227.

Sluckin, W. (1972). *Imprinting and early learning.* London: Routledge & Kegan Paul.

Sluckin, W., Herbert, M., & Sluckin, A. (1983). *Maternal bonding.* Oxford: Basil Blackwell.

Smith, J.L. (1897). Characteristic errors of pupils. *American Annals of the Deaf. 42,* 201-210.

Snijders, J.T., & Snijders-Oomen, M. (1970). *Snijders-Oomen nonverbal intelligence scale—Manual.* Slough, England: National Foundation for Educational Research.

Sobsey, R., & Bienick, B. (1983). A family approach to functional sign language. *Behavior Modification. 7*, 488-502.

Sperling, G. (1967). Successive approximations to a model for short-term memory. *Acta Psychologica, 27*, 723-733.

Sperling, G. (1978). Future prospects in language and communication for the congenitally deaf. In S. Lieben (Ed.), *Deaf children: Developmental perspectives* (pp. 103-114). New York: Academic Press.

Sperry, R.W. (1968). Hemisphere deconnection and unity in conscious awareness. *American Psychologist, 23*, 723-733.

Spradley, T.S., & Spradley, J.P. (1978). *Deaf like me.* New York: Random House.

Springer, S.P., & Deutsch, G. (1981). *Left brain, right brain.* San Francisco, CA: W.H. Freeman.

St. John Roosa, D.B. (1885). *A practical treatise on the diseases of the ear including a sketch of aural anatomy and physiology.* New York: Wood.

Stein, L.K., Mindel, E.D., & Jabaley, T. (1981). *Deafness and mental health.* New York: Grune & Stratton.

Steutenburgh, G. (1971). A psycholinguistic approach to study the language deficits in the language performance of deaf children. Unpublished doctoral dissertation. Syracuse University, NY.

Stokes, W., & Menyuk, P. (1975). *A proposal for the investigation and acquisition of ASL and signed English by deaf and hearing children.* Unpublished master's thesis, Boston University.

Stokoe, W.C. (1960). Sign language structure. *Studies in Linguistics. Occasional Paper 8.* Buffalo: University of Buffalo Press.

Stokoe, W.C. (1973). Comments on back translation. *Sign Language Studies, 1*, 73-76.

Stokoe, W.C. (1975). The use of sign in teaching English. *American Annals of the Deaf, 120*, 417-421.

Stokoe, W.C., & Battison, R.M. (1981). Sign language, mental health and satisfactory interaction. In L. M. Stein, E.D. Mindel, & T. Jabaley (Eds.) *Deafness and mental health* (pp. 179-194). New York: Grune & Stratton.

Stokoe, W.C., Casterline, D., & Croneberg, C. (1965). *A dictionary of American Sign Language.* Washington, DC: Gallaudet College Press.

Stone, M.A. (1980a). Measures of laterality and spurious correlation. *Neuropsychologia, 18*, 339-345.

Stone, M.A. (1980b). *A note on the use of measures of laterality in neuropsychological research.* Unpublished manuscript, School of Research, Preston Polytechnic.

Streng, A.H., Kretschmer, R.R., & Kretschmer, L.W. (1978). *Language, learning and deafness.* New York: Grune & Stratton.

Strevens, P.D. (1964). Varieties of English. *English Studies, 45*(1). Reprinted in P.D. Strevens, *Papers in language and language teaching*. London: Oxford University Press, 1965.

Supalla, T., & Newport, E. (1978). How many seats in a chair? The derivation of nouns and verbs in American Sign Language. In P. Siple (Ed.), *Understanding language through sign language research* (pp. 91-132). New York: Academic Press.

Sussman, A.E. (1966). Sociological theory and deafness: Problems and prospects. *American Speech and Hearing Association Journal, 8*, 303-307.

Tartter, V., & Fischer, S. (1983). Perceptual confusions in ASL under normal and reduced conditions. In J. Kyle & B. Woll (Eds.), *Language in sign* (pp. 215-224). London: Croom Helm.

Tavormina, J.B., Boll, T.J., Dunn, N.J., Luscomb, R.L., & Taylor, J.R. (1975, September). *Psychological effects of raising a physically handicapped child on parents*. Paper presented at the American Psychological Association Meetings, Chicago.

Taylor, I.G. (1964). *Neurological mechanisms of hearing and speech in children*. Manchester: University Press.

Teilhard de Chardin, P. (1959). *The phenomenon of man*. London: Collins.

Tervoort, B.T. (1968). You me downtown movie fun? *Lingua, 21*, 455-465.

Tervoort, B.T., & Verberk, A. (1967). *Analysis of communicative structure patterns in deaf children*. Groningen, Holland: Z.W.O. Onderzoek.

Thompson, H. (1927). An experimental study of the beginning reading of deaf mutes. *Columbia University Contributions to Education. Teachers College Series, No. 254*. New York: Teachers College, Columbia University.

Thorne, J.P. (1964). Grammars and machines. *Transactions of the Philological Society*, 30-45.

Tinbergen, N. (1974). Ethology and stress disease. *Science, 185*, 20-27.

Toulmin, S., & Goodfield, J. (1965). *The discovery of time*. London: Hutchinson.

Treiman, R., & Hirsh-Pasek, K. (1983). Silent readings: Insights from second generation deaf readers. *Cognitive Psychology, 15*, 39-65.

Treisman, A.M. (1965). Verbal responses and contextual constraints in language. *Journal of Verbal Learning and Verbal Behavior, 4*, 118-128.

Trudgill, P. (1974). *Sociolinguistics*. Harmondsworth: Pelican.

Trybus, R.J. (1973). Personality assessment of entering hearing impaired college students using 16PF, Form E. *Journal of Rehabilitation of the Deaf, 6*, 34-40.

Tweney, R.D., Heiman, G.W., & Hoemann, H.W. (1977). Psychological processing of sign language: Effects of visual disruption on sign intelligibility. *Journal of Experimental Psychology: General, 106*, 255-268.

Tweney, R.D., & Hoemann, H.W. (1973). Back translation: A method for the analysis of manual languages. *Sign Language Studies, 2*, 51-80.

Tweney, R.D., Hoemann, H.W., & Andrews, C.E. (1975). Semantic organization in deaf and hearing subjects. *Journal of Psycholinguistic Research, 4,* 61-73.

Tweney, R.D., Liddell, S.K., & Bellugi, U. (1977). *The perception of grammatical boundaries in sign language.* Unpublished manuscript, Bowling Green State University, Bowling Green, OH.

Tyack, D., & Gottsleben, R. (1974). *Language sampling analysis and training: A handbook for clinicians.* Palo Alta, CA: Consulting Psychologists Press.

van Uden, A. (1970). *A world of language for deaf children: Part 1, Basic principles.* Rotterdam, Holland: University of Rotterdam Press.

van Uden, A. (1977). *A world of language for deaf children.* Amsterdam, Holland: Swets Northholland.

van Uden, A. (1983). *Diagnostic testing of deaf children: The syndrome of dyspraxia.* Lewiston, NY: C. J. Hogrefe.

Vandenberg, D.M. (1971). *The written language of deaf children.* Wellington: New Zealand Council for Educational Research.

Vardy, J. (1980, December). *Methods for promoting attitude change toward disabled persons.* Unpublished manuscript, University of Alberta.

Vargha-Khadem, F. (1982). Hemispheric specialization for the processing of tactual stimuli in congenitally deaf and hearing children. *Cortex, 18,* 277-286.

Verney, A. (1976). Planning for a preferred future. In P. Henderson (Ed.), *Methods of communication currently used in the education of deaf children* (pp. 67-72). London: Royal National Institute for the Deaf.

Vernon, M. (1968). Fifty years of research on the intelligence of the deaf and hard of hearing: A survey of the literature and discussion of implications. *Journal of Rehabilitation of the Deaf, 1,* 1-11.

Vernon, M. (1969). Sociological and psychological factors associated with hearing loss. *Journal of Speech and Hearing Research, 12,* 541-563.

Vernon, M. (1970). *Myths about the education of deaf children.* Paper presented at the Communication Symposium, Frederick, MD: Maryland School for the Deaf.

Vernon, M., & Koh, S. (1970). Early manual communication and deaf children's achievement. *American Annals of the Deaf, 115,* 527-536.

Vernon, M., & Koh, S. (1974). Effects of oral preschool compared to early manual communication on education and communication in deaf children. *American Annals of the Deaf, 119,* 569-574.

Vogt-Svendsen, M. (1983). Lip movements in Norwegian Sign Language. In J. Kyle & B. Woll (Eds.), *Language in sign* (pp. 85-96). London: Croom Helm.

Volterra, V., & Taeschner, T. (1978). The acquisition and development of language by bilingual children. *Journal of Child Language, 5,* 311-326.

Von Eckardt Klein, B. (1978). What is the biology of language? In E. Walker (Ed.), *Explorations in the biology of language* (pp. 1-14). Montgomery, VT: Bradford Books.

Vorce, E. (1971). Speech curriculum. In L. E. Connor (Ed.), *Speech for the deaf child: Knowledge and use* (pp. 221-244). Washington, DC: A.G. Bell Association.

Vorih, L., & Rosier, P. (1978). Rock Point Community School: An example of a Navajo-English bilingual elementary school program. *TESOL Quarterly, 12*, 263-269.

Waite, H.E. (1967). 100 years of conquest of silence. *Volta Review, 69*. 118-126.

Walker, M., & Buckfield, P.M. (1983). The Makaton Vocabulary. *New Zealand Speech and Language Therapy Journal, 38*, 26-36.

Wallace, G. (1972). *Short term memory and coding strategies of the deaf.* Unpublished doctoral dissertation, McGill University.

Wallace, G., & Corballis, M.C. (1973). Short-term memory and coding strategies in the deaf. *Journal of Experimental Psychology, 99*, 318-348.

Wampler, D.W. (1971). *Linguistics of visual English.* Santa Rosa, CA: Early Childhood Education Department, Aurally Handicapped Prof., Santa Rosa Schools.

Watson, L. (1976). *Gifts of unknown things.* London: Hodder & Stoughton.

Watson, L. (1979). *Lifetide.* London: Hodder & Stoughton.

Watts, W.J. (1979). Deaf children and some emotional aspects of learning. *Volta Review, 81*, 491-500.

Webster, A., Wood, D.J., & Griffiths, A.J. (1981). *Reading retardation or linguistic deficit? (1) Interpreting reading test performances of hearing-impaired adolescents.* Deafness Research Group, University of Nottingham, England.

Wedell-Mannig, J., & Lumley, J. (1980). Child deafness and mother-child interaction. *Child Development, 51*, 766-774.

Wedge, P., & Prosser, H. (1973). *Born to fail?.* London: National Children's Bureau.

Welford, A.T. (1968). *Fundamentals of skill.* London: Methuen.

Wells, G. (1974). Learning to code experience through language. *Journal of Child Language, 1*, 243-269.

West, J.J., & Weber, J.L. (1974). A linguistic analysis of the morphemic and syntactic structures of a hard of hearing child. *Language and Speech, 17*, 68-69.

White, A.H., & Stevenson, V.M. (1975). The effects of total communication, manual communication, oral communication and reading on the learning of factual information in residential school deaf children. *American Annals of the Deaf, 120*, 48-57.

White, M.J. (1972). Hemispheric asymmetries in tachistoscopic information-processing. *British Journal of Psychology 63*, 497-508.

Whorf, B.L. (1940). Science and linguistics. *Technological Review, 42*, 229-231, 247-248.

Whorf, B.L. (1956). *Language, thought and reality.* Cambridge, MA: Massachusetts Institute of Technology Press.

Wilbur, R.B (1977). An explanation of deaf children's difficulty with certain syntactic structures of English. *Volta Review, 79,* 85-92.

Wilbur, R.B (1979). *American Sign Language and sign systems.* Baltimore, MD: University Park Press.

Wilbur, R.B (1982). Interpersonal communication and deafness. In H.W. Hoemann & R.B Wilbur (Eds.), *Interpersonal communication and deaf people.* Washington, DC: Gallaudet College.

Wilbur, R.B., & Jones, M.L. (1974). Some aspects of the bilingualism/bimodal acquisition of Sign and English by three hearing children of deaf parents. In R. Fox & A. Bruck (Eds.), *Proceedings of the Tenth Regional Meeting of the Chicago Linguistic Society,* Chicago, IL.

Wilbur, R.B., Montanelli, D.S., & Quigley, S.P. (1976). Pronominalization in the language of deaf students. *Journal of Speech and Hearing Research, 19,* 120-140.

Wilbur, R.B., Quigley, S.P., & Montanelli, D.S. (1975). Conjoined structures in the language of deaf students. *Journal of Speech and Hearing Research, 18,* 319-335.

Williams, D., & Darbyshire, J. (1982). The diagnosis of deafness: A study of family responses to needs. *Volta Review, 84,* 24-30.

Williams, F. (1970). Some preliminaries and prospects. In F. Williams (Ed.), *Language and poverty* (pp. 1-10). Chicago: Markham.

Williams, T.R. (1972). *Introduction to socialization: Human culture transmitted.* St. Louis, MO: C.V. Mosby Co.

Wilsher, C., Atkins, G., & Mansfield, P. (1982). *Effect of piracetam on dyslexics' reading ability.* Unpublished manuscript, University of Aston.

Wilson, B.A. (1975). *Dactylic coding in the prelingually deaf.* Unpublished B.A. thesis, University of Reading, England.

Wilson, B.A. (1977). *Lateralization of sign language.* Unpublished master's thesis, University of London.

Winslow, L. (1973). *Learning to see a language: Development of the language of signs.* Unpublished honor thesis, Harvard University, Cambridge, MA.

Witelson, S.F., & Pallie, W. (1973). Left hemisphere specialization for language in the newborn: Neuroanatomical evidence of asymmetry. *Brain, 96,* 641-646.

Wolfensberger, W. (1972). *Normalization: The principle of normalization in human services.* Toronto: National Institute on Mental Retardation.

Wolff, S. (1977). Cognition and communication patterns in classrooms for deaf students. *American Annals of the Deaf, 122,* 319-327.

Woll, B. (1983). The semantics of British Sign Language signs. In J. Kyle, & B. Woll (Eds.), *Language in sign* (pp. 41-55). London: Croom Helm.

Woll, B., Kyle, J., & Deuchar, M. (1981). *Perspectives on British Sign Language and deafness.* London: Croom Helm.

Wood, D.J. (1980). A developmental psychologist looks—with teachers—at the education of deaf children. *Educational Analysis, 2,* 61-83.

Wood, D.J. (1982). Linguistic experiences of the prelingually hearing impaired child. *Teacher of the Deaf, 6,* 86-93.

Wood, D.J. (1984). Aspects of the linguistic competence of deaf children. *British Journal of Audiology, 18,* 23-30.

Wood, D.J., Griffiths, A.J., & Webster, A. (1981). *Reading retardation or linguistic deficit? (II) Test-answering strategies in hearing and hearing-impaired school children.* Unpublished manuscript, Deafness Research Group, University of Nottingham.

Wood, D.J., Wood, H., Griffiths, A., & Howarth, I. (1986). *Teaching and talking with deaf children.* New York: Wiley.

Wood, D.J., Wood, H., & Howarth, S.P. (1983). Mathematical abilities of deaf school leavers. *British Journal of Developmental Psychology, 1,* 67-73.

Wood, F. (1941). *An outline history of the English language.* London: Macmillan.

Woodworth, R.S. (1910). The puzzle of color vocabularies. *Psychological Bulletin, 7,* 325-334.

Wooldridge, D.E. (1963). *The machinery of the brain.* New York: McGraw-Hill.

Wright, P. (1968). Sentence retention and transformation theory. *Quarterly Journal of Experimental Psychology, 20,* 265-272.

Yates, F.A. (1966). *The art of memory.* London: Routledge & Kegan Paul.

Yussen, S.R., & Santrock, J.W. (1978). *Child development: An introduction.* Dubuque, IA: William C. Brown.

Zaidel, D., & Sperry, R.W. (1973). Performance on the Raven's colored progressive matrices test by subjects with cerebral commissurotomy. *Cortex, 9,* 34-39.

Glossary of Some Additional Terms

Analysis of Variance   A statistical test of the effects of several variables and their interactions.

Audiometer   An instrument for testing the acuity of hearing.

Auditory Nerve   The nerve linking the cochlea to the higher centers of the brain.

Bel   The ratio of two measures of sound power expressed as a logarithm to the base 10. A *decibel (dB)* is one-tenth of a bel. Being a ratio, the bel has no dimensions, and in air the sound-pressure level in decibels is equal to $20 \log_{10} (p / p_0)$, where p is the sound-pressure level of a given sound and p_0 is an arbitrary sound-pressure level usually taken to be 0.0002 dynes/cm^2 or 1 dyne/cm^2.

Bilateral Presentation   The presentation of stimuli to both sides of a subject's visual field simultaneously.

Confusion Method   A way of determining the encoding method used by a subject to store information by assessing the degree of confusion induced by similar stimuli.

Conservation   In the theory of Piaget, the ability of the child to understand that certain physical properties of matter are conserved despite changes of shape or position, marking a significant stage of cognitive development.

Correlation Coefficient (r)   A mathematical expression of the strength of a relationship between two variables, ranging from +1 (perfect correlation) through 0 (no relationship evident) to –1 (perfect negative relationship).

Cortex   The evolutionarily most advanced outermost portion of the brain.

Decibel (dB)   See Bel.

Dyslexia   Language difficulty associated with problems in perceiving and ordering verbal elements.

External Ear   The pinna and the external auditory canal terminating in the ear drum.

Factor Analysis   A method of determining the factors underlying the correlations between a large number of variables; somewhat controversial but widely used in educational research.

Frequency   The number of times that a periodic quantity repeats itself in a unit interval of time, conventionally measured in hertz (Hz) or kilohertz (kHz).

Fundamental Frequency   The pure tone in a complex sound that has the same period as the periodic quantity which is that sound.

Harmonics   The integral multiples of the fundamental frequency of a complex tone. For example, if the fundamental frequency of a sound is 256c/s, the first harmonic is 2x256(512)c/s and so on.

Inner Ear   Consists primarily of the cochlea and its associated structures. It also includes the *semi-circular canals* that are concerned with balance.

Intensity   A measure of the amount of sound energy that flows through a unit area in a unit interval of time. It is usually measured by recording the pressure of the sound which is related to intensity in the following way: $I=p^2/dxv$ where I is the intensity of the sound, p is the pressure of the sound, d is the density of the medium, and v is the speed of sound.

Loudness   The psychological response made by an observer to the physical intensity and which enables sounds to be rated on a continuum or louder to softer.

Mainstreaming   An educational philosophy based on the proposition that all handicapped children should be taught together with normal children.

Masking   The process whereby the presence of one sound (the masking sound) raises the threshold of audibility for a given sound.

Middle Ear   Consists of three small bones (the malleus, the incus, and the stapes) which transmit vibrations from the tympanic membrane (the eardrum) to the oval window in the cochlea.

Ossicular Chain   See Middle Ear.

Pitch   The psychological response made by an observer to the physical frequency and which enables sounds to be rated on a continuum of higher or lower.

Pure Tone   A sound in which the sound pressure changes sinusoidally with the time.

Regression Function   The mathematical relationship between two variables, expressed as the best-fitting straight line function.

Sensory Deprivation   The cutting off or reduction of sensory input, in one or more modalities, to the human or animal organism.

Short-Term Memory (STM)   The mechanism presumed to underlie the retention of small amounts of information over short periods. In hearing subjects, STM is auditory in nature.

Significance Level   The probability that a set of experimental data can be explained as purely random variations. Low probabilities imply high levels of significance.

Sound Pressure   Pressure is defined as the action of a force on something resisting it. In the case of sound waves the force is due to the movement of molecules in the medium of transmission

Sperling Paradigm   Method for investigation very short-term visual traces using briefly presented two-dimensional displays.

Tachistoscope   Device for presenting subjects with very brief visual stimuli.

Timbre   The characteristic quality or distinctiveness which differentiates the perception of sounds with similar acoustic characteristics

Unilateral Presentation   Presentation of a stimulus to one side only of a subject's visual field.

Variance   A mathematical estimate of the variation within a given set of experimental data.

Name Index

426

Subject Index

432

434

Spatial bias, 250, 255
Spatial processes, 41, 205-206, 272
Speaker, effect of, 192
Specific deficit, 161, 189, 192, 195
Specific gesture, 260
Speech, 24-28, 108-109, 114, 199,
    201-202, 212-213, 258
    and coding, 199, 201-202, 212-213,
    258
    and deaf, 24-25
    production, 108-109, 114
    teaching, 26-28
Statement and performance, 233
Steinheim Man, 289
Structuralism, 108, 123, 154
Stuttering, 17, 20, 22, 49
Successive processing (see Sequential
    processes), 114
Surdophrenia, 325, 337
Swanscombe Man, 289
Swedish Sign Language, 240, 360
Symbolization disorders, 18
Symmetry constraint, 130, 134, 244
Syntactic competence, 119
Syntax, 103, 119-120, 122-123,
    125-126, 214
Synthetic languages, 103, 140, 152,
    281, 296-297, 299
Teacher-child interaction, 248
Teachers of the deaf, 79, 257, 304,
    320, 324, 327
Teaching, 26-28, 257-260, 266
    methods, 266
    of mathematics, 258
    of reading, 257-260
    of speech, 26-28
Telephone Devices for the Deaf
    (TDD), 13, 252
Temporal coding, 140-141, 144-145,
    350-351
Temporal mechanisms, 41
Tense, 41, 103, 126, 173-175, 179, 260,
    349-350
Test of Syntactic Abilities, 173-180,
    208, 210-211, 222-223
Tests, 30, 40, 88-89, 95, 161-163, 165,
    167, 173-180, 182-183, 201,
    213-215, 222-223, 241, 311-313,
    319, 362-363
    bias, 88-89
    communication and language, 30,
    40

early cognitive, 241, 362-363
IQ, 182-183
Piagetian, 182
speech coding, 201
strategies, 222-223
validity, 167
Theatrical signs, 46
Therapies, 28, 85, 309, 328
Thugs, 46
Timbre, 20
Tool-making, 289-290, 294-295
Transfer tasks, 181
Transformational-Generative
    Grammar, 119-120, 122-126, 154
    criticisms, 123-125
    modified for ASL, 154
Trilingualism, 262-263
TV captions, 13, 252
Verb, 41, 50, 88, 101, 103, 110-111,
    116, 120, 126-127, 134, 139-140,
    144-145, 149-150, 152, 174-175
    agreement in ASL, 149
    inflections in ASL, 144
    number in ASL, 144
    system, English, 174-175
Verbal reasoning, 214
Visible Speech Symbols, 64, 67
Visual, 203-204, 214, 278-279
    closure, 214
    memory, 203-204
    recognition, 278-279
    synthesis, 214
Vocabulary, 17, 23, 40, 88, 104-105,
    138, 163, 165, 214-215, 221, 234,
    236-237, 239, 244, 295, 311,
    313-315, 322, 325, 362
Voice disorders, 18
Volta Bureau, 65, 68
Volta Prize, 65
Volta Review, 82
Wernicke's Aphasia, 287
Wernicke's Area, 274
West Indians, 78-79, 265-266
Word association, 163
Writing and ASL, 251-252
Written materials of deaf, 167,
    172-173